Oct 2018

FIERCE ENIGMAS

FIERCE ENIGMAS

A HISTORY OF THE
UNITED STATES IN SOUTH ASIA

SRINATH RAGHAVAN

BASIC BOOKS
New York

Basic Books
Hachette Book Group
1290 Avenue of the Americas, New York, NY 10104
www.basicbooks.com

Printed in the United States of America

First Edition: October 2018

Published by Basic Books, an imprint of Perseus Books, LLC, a subsidiary of Hachette Book Group, Inc. The Basic Books name and logo is a trademark of the Hachette Book Group.

The Hachette Speakers Bureau provides a wide range of authors for speaking events. To find out more, go to www.hachettespeakersbureau.com or call (866) 376-6591.

The publisher is not responsible for websites (or their content) that are not owned by the publisher.

Library of Congress Control Number: 2018953976
ISBNs: 978-0-465-03019-4 (hardcover), 978-1-5416-9881-9 (ebook)

LSC-C

10 9 8 7 6 5 4 3 2 1

For Sir Lawrence Freedman

Passage to you, your shores, ye aged fierce enigmas!
Passage to you, to mastership of you, ye strangling problems!
You, strew'd with the wrecks of skeletons, that, living,
never reach'd you.
—Walt Whitman, "Passage to India"

CONTENTS

INTRODUCTION

A T AROUND SEVEN O'CLOCK on the morning of May 21, 2016, a middle-aged Pashtun man crossed the border from Iran to Pakistan. Although he was carrying a Pakistani passport bearing the name Muhammad Wali, he was detained at the border crossing for nearly two hours. When allowed through, he got into a white sedan and proceeded on the eight-hour drive to Quetta, capital of the Pakistani province of Balochistan. As the car approached the small town of Ahmad Wal, about two-thirds of the way to Quetta, Hellfire missiles from an American drone tore into it, incinerating the driver and passenger. The US Joint Special Operations Command had assassinated Mullah Akhtar Muhammad Mansur, the leader of the Taliban.

Two days later, President Barack Obama announced the killing in a press conference in Hanoi. The strike, he said, "removed the leader of

1

an organization that has continued to plot against and unleash attacks on American and Coalition forces, to wage war against the Afghan people, and align itself with extremist groups like al Qaeda." Stating that Mansur had rejected efforts by the Afghan government to engage him in talks, Obama expressed hope that the Taliban would "seize the opportunity…to pursue the only real path for ending this long conflict—joining the Afghan government in a reconciliation process that leads to lasting peace and stability." Obama added that the United States would continue to "work on shared objectives with Pakistan, where terrorists that threaten all our nations must be denied safe haven."[1]

The Obama administration hailed the assassination of Mansur for two reasons, primarily. First, it was part of a strategy to bring the Taliban to the negotiating table, a strategy that now seemed likely to succeed. Mansur himself had taken over as leader of the Taliban less than a year prior—after revelation that he had muzzled news of the April 2013 death of Taliban supreme commander Mullah Mohammad Omar. Mansur's killing, it was assumed, would throw the organization into disarray and embolden the moderates within the Taliban to enter into talks with the Afghan government.

Second, the strike would send a strong signal to Pakistan that it could no longer harbor Taliban leaders while pocketing American financial aid. Pakistan's policy of running with the hares and hunting with the hounds was well known to American policymakers. In Obama's first intelligence briefing in 2009, the director of central intelligence had wearily told him that the Pakistanis were "a living lie." American officials believed that Pakistan's mendacious stance stemmed not just from its desire to prop up the Taliban and ensure that Afghanistan remained its strategic backyard but also from its long-running rivalry with India over Kashmir and its fear of Indian influence in Afghanistan. Over the years Obama realized there were limits to how much Washington could cajole India into engaging with Pakistan even as the latter supported anti-Indian terrorist outfits. Instead, he came to rely heavily on a covert action program—human and technical intelligence,

Special Forces, and Predator drones—begun under his predecessor to target terrorist leaders inside Pakistan.[2]

The assassination of Mansur did not, however, deliver the desired outcomes. Days after the strike, the Taliban leadership council in Quetta chose Mawlawi Hibatullah Akhundzada, a religious scholar, as his successor. And they soon escalated attacks inside Afghanistan. By the time Obama left the White House in early 2017, more than 40 percent of Afghanistan's districts were under the Taliban's control or influence, or contested by them. With more than 11,000 civilians killed, 2016 was the most violent year in the country since 2009. The Afghan security forces too suffered heavy casualties that year, with over 6,700 dead and nearly 11,800 injured.[3]

As for the impact on Pakistan, it turned out that the United States might have grossly misjudged the dynamic between the Pakistanis and Mansur. Former associates of Mansur as well as knowledgeable Afghan officials subsequently disclosed that in the month prior to his assassination, the Taliban leader had been at loggerheads with the Pakistani Inter-Services Intelligence (ISI), the intelligence agency known for its far-reaching power and influence over the very top layers of the Pakistani government. Mansur had apparently resisted ISI orders to target infrastructure in Afghanistan, to promote a hardline Pakistani protégé, Sirajuddin Haqqani, as his deputy, and to advance Pakistan's particular interests in future negotiations with the Afghan government. During this period Mansur had conveyed to Taliban commanders under him that he was prepared to negotiate for peace. In a bid to loosen the ISI's grip on the Taliban, he was reportedly prepared to accord greater autonomy to his commanders in the field and was exploring the possibility of securing assistance from Iran to avoid relying so heavily on Pakistan. The ISI, in fact, may well have created the trail that led the Americans to Mansur.[4]

These details emerged over fourteen months after Mansur's assassination. By then, the war in Afghanistan had garnered the dubious distinction of being the longest war in American history: twice as long already as the Vietnam War. Despite a heavy commitment of troops and money, drones and Special Forces, the United States still found it difficult to distinguish who was on which side of this tangled conflict.

Barack Obama was not, of course, the first American president to grapple with the complexities of South Asia. Nor were George W. Bush or his immediate predecessors. In fact, the story of US covert action in the region goes all the way back to 1827, when Josiah Harlan raised the Stars and Stripes at the outskirts of the town of Ludhiana in the Punjab and recruited a ragtag militia to foment a rebellion in Afghanistan against its ruler, Dost Mohammed Khan.[5]

Born in 1799 to a family of Philadelphia Quakers, Harlan had come to Calcutta in 1822 as "supercargo"—the agent responsible for overseeing cargo and its sale—on a merchant vessel. A year later, he signed up to serve as a doctor in the British East India Company's army for the war on Burma. During a period of convalescence after being wounded in the field, Harlan chanced upon a recently published book on Afghanistan by the British official Mounstuart Elphinstone. Although the British nominated Elphinstone as their envoy to the court in Kabul, a regime change in which Dost Mohammed had deposed Afghan ruler Shah Shuja prevented him from taking up his appointment or living in the city. That did not prevent Elphinstone from concocting stories of Oriental splendor and strife, bejeweled princes and wild tribesmen.

The adventurer in Harlan was hooked and decided to redeem Shuja. He set off on a covert expedition into Afghanistan aimed at restoring Shuja to the throne of Kabul and securing for himself a little kingdom to rule. It did not quite work out as he had planned. After much intrigue and travail, Harlan actually ended up training an Afghan force for Dost Mohammed Khan. In the summer of 1838, Harlan himself led this force in a campaign against the khan of Kunduz. Thereafter, he claimed to have struck a bargain with a Hazara chieftain to become the ruler of that province as a reward for securing it from its traditional enemies. By this time, the first Anglo-Afghan war was underway, and a bitter Harlan had to depart Afghanistan. Back in the United States, he embarked on several failed business ventures, including one to import camels from Afghanistan.

Harlan's encounters with India and Afghanistan were a product of attempts by commercial and entrepreneurial classes in the young American republic to edge into the maritime commercial world dominated by the older European empires.[6] But they also prefigured the themes that would shape American engagement with South Asia over the following centuries: power and hierarchy, race and religion, ideology and empire. In his quest for wealth and power, Harlan may have relinquished some core tenets of his Quaker faith; yet it deeply informed his paternalistic belief that even the "barbarians" of Afghanistan could receive the benefits of "civilization." Harlan also took a dim view of British rule in the subcontinent and contrasted it unfavorably with Thomas Jefferson's vision of an imperial republic of yeomen farmers committed to the improvement of the land and securing their own liberties.[7]

Harlan's forays, and the significance thereof, later became the subject of a remarkable story by Rudyard Kipling, "The Man Who Would Be King." While Kipling never directly conceded the inspiration, he apparently picked up Harlan's story from a fellow Freemason in India. In Kipling's version, two adventurers, Daniel Dravot and Peachy Carnehan, set off to win the kingdom of Kafiristan in a remote corner of Afghanistan. They train a local militia, fashion a new religion, and manage to convince the tribe to proclaim Dravot king. When the illusion of power spun by the interlopers is broken, the local inhabitants turn on Dravot. Back in Lahore, Peachy meets the narrator and produces his friend's shriveled head from a bag: "You behold now the Emperor in his habit as he lived—the King of Kafiristan with his crown upon his head."

Published in England in 1888, the story was a parable of the temptations of empire. At the same time, though, Kipling was elsewhere calling on the Americans to take up the "white man's burden." Kipling's exhortations had a considerable impact on America's turn toward empire—even if many readers did not catch the nuances of his view of imperialism. More importantly, Kipling's writings provided the first, and often only, introduction to South Asia for most educated Americans and informed their attitudes for generations to come.

American involvement in South Asia was not a one-sided affair though. Even as Americans were drawn to the region for a variety of reasons, South Asians were pulled toward the United States—not least by the allure of American modernity and technological expertise. Thus, in 1910 Amir Habibullah Khan—son and heir of Amir Abdur Rahman, founder of the modern Afghan state—invited prominent American engineer A. C. Jewett to install a hydroelectric plant to power the nascent workshops and production facilities of Kabul as well as the royal palace. Jewett was a pioneer in electrical infrastructure, having built a number of electrical streetcars and power stations on the Pacific coast. He was also well known in the subcontinent. He had installed a power plant in the Kolar Gold Fields of the southern Indian princely state of Mysore as well as built the Jhelum power installation in the northern state of Kashmir. Indeed, soon after his stint in Kashmir, he received the commission from Habibullah Khan.

Jewett reached Kabul in May 1911. He was the first American to reside in that city since Harlan. Nothing in Jewett's storied career had prepared him for the assignment. No skilled laborers were available, so he had to train his own workforce. The equipment ordered by the amir from a British firm in Bombay took a long time to arrive. "None of the plant has reached Kabul yet," he wrote in November 1912, "but I hear there is some on the way. Inshallah [god willing], it will come some time." There were more delays with the onset of World War I and the resulting scarcity of motor transports. Eventually the power-generation equipment had to be carted across the Khyber Pass on elephants. And then there was the sheer geographic challenge of building a power plant in the mountains of Jabal-us-Siraj.

The work took six and a half years to complete. When the lights came on, it seemed almost magical. "You should have seen the natives," Jewett wrote home, "first wide-eyed and staring—then a broad grin on every face. Most of them had never even seen a kerosene lamp." While Jewett worked tirelessly to bring a slice of American modernity to South Asia, he shared his countrymen's racial and paternalistic condescension toward the region's inhabitants. "The average Afghan's mental development seems to have stopped at about the age of fourteen," he wrote, after spending years in the country. "The Afghans are a lot like very bad children." As for the people of Kabul in particular, they were "a lazy, lying, thieving, licentious lot. They are cowards too; the barbarians are better fighters and better men all round."[8]

Ambivalence continued to thread American engagement with the country long after Jewett left. But the broader context changed. In a prefatory note to Jewett's account of Afghanistan that she compiled from his letters and journals, his daughter Marjorie Jewett Bell wrote in June 1948, "The British Raj is gone and beyond the Khyber lies the friendly state of Pakistan. To the north, on the other hand, along a thousand-mile border in old Turkestan, are the Soviet Turkomen, Uzbek and Tajik—republics of a new and powerful Russia." As Afghanistan was "building a modern nation to maintain her position in Central Asia," she noted, there was "an influx of Americans—technical advisers, industrial engineers, contractors, and skilled workmen—to plan and promote these improvements, which are destined to bring about a revolution in the industry and living of the Afghans."

Bell underestimated the tensions between Afghanistan and Pakistan and overestimated the scale of American commitment to the country. Yet she was right in thinking not only of regional matters of but geopolitics. Even as she wrote, the American civil engineering and construction firm Morrison-Knudsen was embarking on an ambitious attempt to dam the Helmand River in southern Afghanistan to provide electricity and canal water to the valley's inhabitants. This enormous project would have significance far beyond its immediate environs.

Not until 1975 did the US Agency for International Development (USAID) install two 16.5-megawatt hydropower generators on the dam and provide the first burst of electricity to the cities of Lashkar Gah and Kandahar. Before a third turbine could be installed, there was a Communist-led coup in Kabul. In the ensuing years, the Helmand Valley became a site of major battles between the Soviet forces and the Islamist fighters backed by the United States. The region was also the cradle of the Taliban, deposed on the heels of the American invasion of Afghanistan in 2001.

Soon after, USAID returned to the Helmand dam. In 2003, it hired the Louis Berger Group, an American engineering firm, to repair the two old turbines and install a third. The project pulled 4,000 North Atlantic Treaty Organization soldiers away from their combat duties to secure a convoy carrying equipment. The organizers of the convoy, however, failed to include the seven hundred tons of cement needed to complete the repairs. In the event, Louis Berger relied on expensive helicopter flights to transport equipment and experts to rehabilitate the two older turbines. Plans for the third remained in abeyance. "What had once been a manifestation of America's initiative and generosity," writes Rajiv Chandrasekaran, "now stood as a monument to its incompetence."[9] In a bid to deflect the failure, American officials talked up the schools and clinics they were building. They also blamed the avarice, corruption, and unreliability of Afghan subcontractors.

THESE THUMBNAIL SKETCHES REVEAL the long and varied history of American involvement in South Asia. And this history continues to shape American policy in and engagement with the region today. Yet most accounts of the United States and South Asia tend to focus on shorter periods (especially the early Cold War), on limited subjects (especially high politics), or on relationships between the United States and individual countries in the region (especially India).[10]

While this body of scholarship has enriched our understanding of the United States in South Asia, we still lack a longer, broader account. Twenty-five years after the end of the Cold War, treating the history of American involvement in the region primarily as a subset of Washington's antagonism toward the former Soviet Union seems decidedly inadequate. We need to look behind and beyond the Cold War and place South Asia in the longer story of the United States' ascent to global dominance. Such an account would need to view US engagement with the region against the backdrop of key trends in American and global history since the late eighteenth century.

Such are the aims of this book, which narrates the United States' relations with South Asia from the founding of the republic to the present. My treatment is neither encyclopedic nor geographically comprehensive. I do not try to cover American relations with all countries of the region. In contemporary usage, "South Asia" refers to India, Pakistan, Bangladesh, Sri Lanka, Nepal, Bhutan, Afghanistan, and the Maldives. An older parlance collectively referred to the first five of these countries as the Indian subcontinent. Given the span of this book, I use the terms interchangeably, but I focus on India, Pakistan, and Afghanistan because these three countries were of greatest interest and concern to Americans over this long period.

I wish to suggest that the history of the United States in South Asia illuminates the particular histories of both regions. Historians of US foreign relations typically tend to treat South Asia as peripheral to the concerns of American policymakers. As the thinking goes, even at the zenith of American power, let alone in other periods, South Asia ranked lower in priority than, say, East Asia or the Middle East. This assumption is seriously misleading. In the first place, history has seldom played out in accordance with the intentions of even the most powerful policymakers and statesmen. To paraphrase Helmuth von

Moltke, no policy-planning document has survived contact with the vicissitudes of international politics. The periphery often ends up imposing itself on policymakers who would prefer to concern themselves with core challenges—a pattern that appears in the history of United States and South Asia perhaps most strikingly in the coincidence of the India-China war of 1962 with the Cuban Missile Crisis.

More problematic is the tacit assumption that studying engagement with the periphery is not particularly useful in understanding the course of American ascendancy—except to show, at various times, how the United States frittered away some portion of its material and moral resources. If we wish to understand the establishment and character of American hegemony, then we would be better off focusing on the interplay of coercion and consent in western Europe and East Asia. This book argues, by contrast, that an ostensibly peripheral region like South Asia actually tells us more, and something different, about American hegemony in the twentieth century.

This book also aims to provoke us to reconsider our assumptions about the historical interactions between South Asia and the world. Scholars of the early modern era have already encouraged us to look behind the colonial experience in order to understand "connected histories" of societies that have not been placed within a common historical framework.[11] Yet historians of modern South Asia remain resolutely focused on the encounter with the British Empire.[12] Temporally, too, they remain hesitant to look beyond the moment of decolonization in 1947. In consequence, the United States rarely features in the historiography of modern South Asia. I have tried to broaden our view by underscoring the significance of the United States in understanding the modern history of the subcontinent, especially but not exclusively in the twentieth century.

The narrative that follows is not one of smooth, sustained, and deepening American engagement with the Indian subcontinent over time but one marked by ruptures, retrenchment, and recalibration. Starting soon after the founding of the United States with attempts by

New England merchants to enter the India trade, I explore the early so-journs and exploits of American traders, missionaries, and travelers in South Asia up to the mid-nineteenth century. The subsequent decade marked a major break in US engagement with the subcontinent, owing to the great rebellion of 1857–1858 in India and the American Civil War. Over the next seven decades, both the United States and India engaged in seemingly autonomous projects that actually touched each other at important points: national regeneration after the Civil War paralleled the gradual development of nationalist ideas and political movements in India; the US acquisition of overseas empire spurred a renewed interest in India's colonial experience, while the onset of World War I drew both the United States and the Indian subcontinent into more global concerns.

From the late 1930s, as another major war loomed in Europe, the United States began to regard South Asia as a region of strategic impor-tance. Indeed, the Allies relied on the subcontinent's strategic location, vast reservoir of manpower, and potential industrial strength for the campaigns against the Axis powers in Southeast Asia, the Middle East, and North Africa. In turn, US political support in particular proved crucial at significant moments in the run-up to India's independence. Decolonization in South Asia came with partition and the creation of the new state of Pakistan. It also coincided with the onset of the Cold War. The conjunction of decolonization in South Asia and the Cold War created recurrent problems in the United States' engagement with the region over the following decades.

Some of these proved intractable and periodically neuralgic for American policymakers. Above all, they made the exercise of US he-gemony trickier than in regions like East Asia and western Europe, where internecine rivalries between non-Communist powers were pac-ified. In South Asia, India and Pakistan were locked in a bitter rivalry and fought three wars in as many decades, and Pakistan and Afghan-istan were at odds over territorial and ethnic claims and periodically embroiled in crises. What is more, both India and Afghanistan took a stance of nonalignment in the Cold War. And the American decision in 1954 to pull Pakistan into a military alliance at once complicated South Asian geopolitics and opened up the region to Soviet influence.

In the wake of the India-Pakistan war of 1971, the United States had to grapple with two further developments in the region that would eventually push aside the usual Cold War concerns. The first was the competitive pursuit of nuclear weapons by India (which tested its first in 1974) and Pakistan—a dynamic that threatened to tear a gaping hole in the nuclear nonproliferation regime constructed by the United States and to increase instability in the region. The second was the rise of Islamist politics in Pakistan and Afghanistan in the 1970s. Pakistan initially used the Islamists as a check on Afghan irredentist ambitions. Following the Soviet invasion of Afghanistan in 1979, the United States relied on the Islamist military dictator of Pakistan to support and provision the Islamist Afghan fighters in their jihad against the Red Army. The two developments were connected, too, for while encouraging Islamist militancy, the United States willingly turned a blind eye to Pakistan's covert pursuit of nuclear weapons.

The late 1970s were thus as important in the long history of US–South Asian relations as the mid-nineteenth century, the late 1930s, or the mid-1950s. The difference is that in the 1970s, we can see most clearly the origins of the present day. Although the collapse of the Soviet Union and the end of the Cold War made the exercise of US hegemony in South Asia easier than before, the combination of nuclear weapons and Islamist terrorism means that the problems facing American policymakers are perhaps graver than ever. At least two recent presidents—Bill Clinton and Barack Obama—have declared the subcontinent the "most dangerous place in the world."[13]

In the narrative that follows, I focus on three key dimensions of US engagement with the region. The first is power—economic, political, and military—and its expression and pursuit. The balance of importance among these facets of power has varied with time and shifting contexts and policies.

The search for profits first drew merchants of the young republic to the Indian subcontinent. As American capitalists subsequently turned their gaze to the continent-sized market at home, their interest in India declined. Nevertheless, the globalization of factor markets in the nineteenth century ended up linking the American and Indian economies in important ways. From the late 1930s, American economic and strategic interests in the subcontinent were intertwined. American policymakers saw decolonization as imperative to integrating South Asia into a liberal capitalist global order. But pursuit of markets and profits for American businesses was not the primary driver of this objective. Rather, they wanted to preserve capitalism globally in order to ensure that the United States was not forced down an autarkic path. Later, when India sought to pursue a model of state-led economic development and disregarded American calls for an open economy, the United States still aided its economic efforts in order to ensure that it did not move into closer orbit around Moscow. Similarly, so long as Pakistan has been willing to contribute militarily to advance American interests, the United has continued to funnel aid, ignoring the actual state or performance of its economy.

The second dimension is ideology. From the start, a religious belief in divine favor and a political faith in republican liberty have shaped American ideology.[14] From Thomas Jefferson's idea of an "empire of liberty" to the notion of "Manifest Destiny," from Woodrow Wilson's proclamation of American moral leadership to Barack Obama's avowal of the United States as the "indispensable nation," the notion of the United States' providential role in helping the spread of liberty has conditioned American engagement with the wider world.

Few recall, however, that India played an important role in these providential beliefs: the brutality of the British conquest of India provided the background against which the United States could expound the blessings of American expansionism in the nineteenth century. Wilson and Franklin Roosevelt would invoke a similar distinction between American "leadership" and old-world imperialism exemplified in places like India. The US-led attempt over the past fifteen years to turn Afghanistan into a passably democratic state shows that the ideology is not a mere fig leaf for naked American power. Likewise, successive American presidents (as well as Indian leaders) over the past two decades have extolled India's success as a liberal democracy and regarded its political system as a lynchpin of the United States' strategic partnership with India.

The third major dimension of US involvement in South Asia is culture, in particular religion, race, and notions of hierarchy. I am interested in two specific aspects of culture. The first is its role in providing a mode of perceiving and making sense of another society. The second is its function, especially in the form of popular culture, as a conveyer belt of values, norms, and meanings. This, of course, takes place in both directions in any cultural encounter. Religion was the first feature of South Asian culture that made an impression on early American travelers to India. Most of them were strongly repelled by the rituals and practices of the Hindus. By contrast, the monotheistic religion of the subcontinent's Muslims seemed more comprehensible and palatable. The Hindus' rigid social world also stood in stark relief against the egalitarian mores of the Muslims. These impressions hardened under the gaze of American missionaries who first came to the subcontinent in the early nineteenth century and sent their opinions home. Indeed, the contrast between Hindus and Muslims and stereotypes of each religion would shape US policymakers' views of India and Pakistan through to the 1970s. All along, some American intellectuals regarded the Hindu religion as the epitome of metaphysical thought and a refuge from the materialism and militarism of their own country. From Ram Mohun Roy and Swami Vivekananda down to Mohandas Gandhi and the New Age gurus in California, Indian figures who have tried to adapt Hinduism to the demands of modernity have attracted successive generations of Americans.

Ideas of racial superiority structured Americans' encounters with South Asia from the outset. By the mid-nineteenth century older ideas of racial difference took on a scientific cast, and a clear ordering placed Anglo-Saxons on top of the civilizational hierarchy. American paternalism was one result, and it persisted even after the Nazis had discredited overt racism in international politics. In the postwar period, the old hierarchical worldview acquired another "scientific" patina in American theories of modernization that ranked societies not explicitly on race but on a scale of "development." The persistence of older hierarchical notions was also evident in the paternalistic attitude of American policymakers, who often regarded South Asian leaders as immature, childlike, and in need of adult supervision.

Power, ideology, and culture—these provide the warp and weft of the story told in this book. Their interaction and transformation over time are crucial to explaining the course of US involvement in South Asia. Consider just one example: the growing political proximity between the United States and India over the past decade. It is commonplace to argue that India and the United States stood apart during the Cold War owing to the former's policy of nonalignment and that, with the end of the Cold War, India had no option but to seek a rapprochement with America. Some also argue that the two nations came closer owing to their common concerns about the rise of China.

These arguments are not sufficient to explain the recent shift in US policy toward India—a country about which it had entertained so many qualms in the past. Two other factors were in play. For one, India's recognition of American primacy in the world coincided with its willingness to liberalize its economy and embrace American-led globalization. This not only made India a more attractive partner, owing to its large market, but opened up a range of possibilities for the exercise of American hegemony—most prominently by exporting ideas of consumer culture that had been so important in cementing American hegemony in western Europe and East Asia. For another, from the 1990s on there was a dramatic shift in American cultural attitudes toward India owing to the extraordinary success of Indian immigrants to the United States. This remarkable change in long-held cultural attitudes was critical in that American policymakers and leaders now regard India in an entirely different light.

What follows, then, is a narrative that pays attention to high politics and the concerns of policymakers as well as perspectives from below—of traders and missionaries, economists and musicians, architects and agronomists. This is also a work of history shaped by contemporary concerns. As a historian, I have spent years reading about and researching American involvement in South Asia. Indeed, this book draws on multiple archives and thousands of declassified documents. Over the years, I have also been a regular commentator about and analyst of contemporary US policies in the region. In attempting to bring together these parallel endeavors, I am acutely conscious of my own opinions and attitudes about the recent past and the present. Yet, in writing this history, I have sought to view them as hurdles to overcome rather than biases to confirm. My main concern is to show how the past has shaped the present and help us make better sense of both.

1

FORTUNE, FANTASY, AND FAITH

As the *United States* sailed beneath the guns of Pondicherry on December 26, 1784, the crew looked out at the gathering crowd onshore. The ship's surgeon, Thomas Redman, noted in his journal that the vessel's red-and-white-striped flag with thirteen stars "caused much speculation to the inhabitants what country our flag belonged to." Not surprising perhaps, for "this was the first ship that ever hoisted American colours on the coast of Coromandel."[1] The *United States* was in fact the first US ship to visit India. The four-hundred-ton vessel manned by a crew of forty had departed from Philadelphia in March 1784—shortly after the first US ship, the *Empress of China*, left New York for Canton.

Packed with tobacco and ginseng, copper and iron, lead and twine, pitch and tar, staves and cordage, as well as a "considerable sum in dollars," the *United States* too had originally headed for China via Mauritius. But as Americans would repeatedly realize over the next two centuries, the passage to China often ran through the Indian subcontinent. On this occasion, the ship had called at Madeira and picked up a hundred pipes of the finest Madeira wine. Looking for the best market in which to offload it, the *United States* made for the southeastern coast of India. Captain Thomas Bell had chosen Pondicherry because it was a French enclave: he was unsure how the British would receive a US vessel at one of their ports so soon after the American War of Independence. The French commandant at the Pondicherry fort received them "with the greatest demonstrations of pleasure and satisfaction and mentioned that every indulgence and privilege should be shewn our ship that a French ship was entitled to."[2]

This was entirely in keeping with the United States and France's "perpetual" alliance of 1778. But, surprisingly to the Americans, the British retained effective possession of Pondicherry, not yet having restored the enclave to the French as agreed in the treaty of 1783 and complicating American access to the port there. Bell traveled overland by palanquin to Madras, where he met with the nawab of Arcot and some leading European merchants. Officials of the East India Company naturally kept their eyes peeled and ears cocked during this American foray into their colonial world. They picked up rumors that Bell had brought a letter from the US Congress to the nawab and that the latter's "answer was not unfavourable." The governor of Madras, Lord George Macartney, initially suspected that the Yankees sought "a settlement on the coast." Eventually he concluded that the *United States*'s voyage was exploratory and of little consequence. In any event, the ship did not engage in extensive trade and set sail from Pondicherry on February 13, 1785. By the time it dropped anchor in Philadelphia six months later, many of its crew had succumbed to scurvy. Yet the news of its safe passage marked the beginning of the Indo-American trade.[3]

Thomas Bell and his crew were not, of course, the first Americans to seek their fortunes in India. Well before American independence, the British Empire had soldered together America and the Indian subcontinent. Elihu Yale, a twenty-four-year-old from Connecticut, went to India in 1672 in the employ of the East India Company. Starting with a clerkship at £10 per year, he rapidly worked his way up to the prized governorship of Madras (1687–1692). Even after his retirement to the English countryside, he continued to partake of the lucrative diamond trade in India. Yale also contributed to the founding of an eponymous college, later to become Yale University, in New Haven, Connecticut. His endowment consisted of Indian textiles sold in Boston.[4] Yale's successor as governor of Madras was another Connecticut man: Nathan Higginson. Career circuits ran in the other direction too. William Duer went to India from Devonshire and served as aide-de-camp to Robert Clive. On returning home, he quit the army and went into the lumber business. This eventually took him to Saratoga, New York, where he built a profitable lumber mill. Duer ended up as an active participant in the independence movement, serving as delegate to the Continental Congress. He was also one of the earliest investors in trade with the East Indies.[5]

The British Empire had created structural links between America and India. As the East India Company bored deeper into the subcontinent, it began to export large quantities of Indian products, especially textiles and spices, to the American colonies. Indeed, by the mid-eighteenth century, people of all social backgrounds, not just colonial elites, used Indian cloth of all kinds, from coarse fabric to the finest muslin, for a variety of purposes. London, however, controlled this trade. The East India Company had a monopoly, and Americans could not directly procure from (or sell to) India.

Evolving imperial policy compounded New England merchants' resentment at being cut out of the eastern trade. In 1773 the British government passed the Tea Act, which did away with the export duties on tea for the East India Company, allowing it to sell its product in North America for less than any other company. In this way London hoped to help the company stabilize its finances, which were in a tailspin owing to the costly wars of conquest in the subcontinent. The British government also believed that the Americans would welcome the cheaper tea. Instead, New England elites took double offense. Not only had Parliament passed the act without consulting them, but the duties no longer levied on the East India Company would continue to apply to other traders. On December 16, 1773, in what came to be known as the Boston Tea Party, protestors attacked an East India Company tea consignment and upended it into the ocean. London responded by depriving Massachusetts of its right to self-government. Soon the American Revolution was underway.[6]

Even as Britain's grip on the American colonies loosened, its hold over India strengthened. The career of Major General Charles Cornwallis perhaps best illustrates the shifting fortunes of the two parts of the empire. In October 1781, Cornwallis famously surrendered his army to George Washington in Yorktown. Yet five years later, the British government appointed him governor-general of India and commander in chief of its army. Cornwallis acquitted himself better in these roles, defeating the East India Company's most dangerous adversary, Tipu Sultan of Mysore, in 1792. Ironically, Cornwallis was at the helm in Calcutta when the US India trade got off the ground.

THE WAR OF INDEPENDENCE left the American economy in tatters: markets had been disrupted, inflation became rampant, and debt piled up. No sooner had the war ended than the country experienced its first full-fledged depression. Britain's refusal after the conflict to conclude a commercial treaty enabling trade between the United States and all parts of the British Empire aggravated these problems. American ships could trade with the British Isles but not with British colonies. This situation dealt a huge blow particularly to northern shipowners who had relied on trade with the West Indies. Merchants in leading ports, who had profited rather handsomely from the Revolution, suddenly found themselves without suitable outlets for investment. Worse, the British again began wielding the whip in peacetime trade and flooded American markets with their goods. Their success owed much to the weakness of the US government under the Articles of Confederation and the US Congress's inability to agree on tariffs that would have precluded the dumping of British imports.[7]

Against this backdrop, northern shipowners and merchants—from Boston, Providence, and, above all, Salem—started looking further east. Following the *United States*'s initial foray, other ships began visiting the main Indian port of Calcutta, as well as other trading points along the coast. The early reports of profits—the *General Washington* yielded $3 for every $1 invested in a venture—drew in other merchants and consortia. By 1788, the most prominent player in the early East Indies trade, Elias Hasket Derby of Salem, had no fewer than nine of his largest ships plying the Indian Ocean. He had also acquired two smaller vessels exclusively for coastal trading in India. British officials estimated that Derby made whopping profits from trading in India— "as much as 700 per cent" at times.[8]

Given the prohibition against direct trade, however, not many American merchants were willing to risk sending ships to India. Americans knew little about the links between coastal and inland trade in India. They had yet to establish relationships with Indian merchants. Nor did they have any sense of the demands of the Indian market. The British, for their part, were ambivalent about American transgressions on trade. The growing presence of American ships and the potential threat to the British monopoly alarmed some British merchants. One warned the directors of East India Company that American vessels' venturing "amongst the quiet Gentoo [Hindu] natives of Indostan" was akin to "the Devil sowing the Tares amongst the Wheat."[9] But keen not to add another dispute to the already tangled Anglo-American relationship, London held that the size of the United States' trade with

India was small and ancillary to its trade with China. The East India Company also saw the Americans as a useful source of silver specie. Cornwallis thus instructed his officials, "Vessels belonging to the citizens of the United States of America, shall be admitted and hospitably received, in all sea ports and harbours of the British territories in the East Indies."[10] In 1788, US commerce was accorded "most favoured nation" treatment. By the time the US federal government was organized the following year, few hindrances to formal trade with India remained.

Nevertheless, the trade deck was still stacked against new entrants such as the Americans. Having no overseas colonies, the United States could not offer reciprocal port facilities and privileges to the established colonial powers. Whatever the formal position, local officials could arbitrarily close their ports to American ships or impose local levies and charges to the same effect. Without the ability to intervene in such situations, American shipping was subject to the caprice of colonial administrators. To redress this situation and protect its foreign trade, the federal government established a consular service in 1790. Soon leading New England merchants began demanding a consulate in India. Prominent investors in Massachusetts wrote to Senator George Cabot underlining the growing commerce with India and seeking immediate appointment of a consul. They recommended Benjamin Joy of Newburyport, who had lived many years in India as a private trader and speculator. On Cabot's urging, President George Washington nominated the thirty-seven-year-old Joy as "Consul of the United States at Calcutta and other ports and places on the coast of India and Asia." The appointment was confirmed in November 1792.[11]

Joy would reach Calcutta a year and a half later. In the meantime, he pondered the problems he would tackle as consul in India. "As American ships are frequently sold in India," he wrote to Secretary of State Thomas Jefferson, "there will of course be many sailors left in that country, and probably a number of them will get sick from the unhealthyness of it." The daily allowance Congress provided for sick men overseas was insufficient to meet their needs. Calcutta had an excellent hospital maintained by the East India Company to which "all white men that are sick are admitted on their paying after the rate of ten sicca rupees [Indian currency] per month." Joy wondered if as consul he could perhaps levy a fee on all American ships touching India— "according to her tonnage or number of hands"—to pay for the hospital care of sick sailors.[12]

Barely two months after Joy's confirmation, revolutionary France declared war on Britain and the Netherlands. The French Revolutionary and Napoleonic Wars were altogether more intense and incendiary than earlier European conflicts of the eighteenth century, though, like them, they spanned the globe and drew into the vortex the colonies of the belligerents. The war in Europe soon spread to the Americas, the Mediterranean, and the Indian subcontinent. The United States was determined to steer clear, however. The new nation was weak and vulnerable, with a population under 4 million, a standing army short of five hundred, and no navy. As primarily a producer of raw materials, it depended on access to European markets, goods, and capital. Consequently, when war broke out in February 1793, neutrality seemed the best option—never mind the older US alliance with France. American leaders believed that by not choosing a side they could maximize their freedom to maneuver. Further, they realized that war would at once increase the demand for American products and open up ports previously closed to American shipping. As Jefferson smugly put it, the "new world will fatten on the follies of the old."[13]

Although the United States' repudiation of its alliance treaty irked the French, the European powers preferred benevolent American neutrality. They deemed the United States too weak and fickle to serve as a useful ally. Retaining access to American foodstuffs and stores, shipping and ports would be more profitable. But each side in the burgeoning conflict sought to deny the same access to the other. So the United States was not all that insulated. No sooner had war erupted than Jefferson instructed Joy to exert his "utmost vigilance in protecting our vessels in the rights of neutrality, and in preventing the usurpation of our flag by vessels of other nations."[14]

Joy reached Calcutta in April 1794. Soon after, he informed the governor-general of his appointment and sought a meeting. "Sir John Shore," Joy reported, "did not see fit to have any official conversation on the business, but desired to see me unofficially." He told Joy that the East India Company government had received no information or instruction from Britain about the appointment of a US consul in India. Without some directive from London, Shore could not formally receive him. While Shore took up the matter with his home government, Joy could stay on in Calcutta as a "Commercial Agent, subject to the Civil and Criminal jurisdiction of the Country."[15]

Joy cooled his heels for six months before concluding that the East India Company had no desire to allow him to function as consul. For one thing, the "mixt government" in Calcutta would find it difficult to decide on the powers and protections a consul ought to have. He perceptively observed that while the members of "the Company possess much power...they are not Sovereigns." The East India Company enjoyed untrammeled power only to the extent that it did not clash with the policy of the British government in London or interfere with the jurisdiction of the supreme court established by the British parliament, "which is totally independent of the Government here."[16] While the governor-general might be well disposed, the treatment of American vessels and seafarers would invariably depend on the stance taken by the courts. Further, there was "a jealousy existing among British Merchants in this Country of the rising commerce of the Americans in this quarter of the world." In particular, plans were brewing to "thwart us in what they call the Country trade which is from port to port in India." By the end of year, Joy decided to quit, citing a bout of a disease he had earlier picked up in India and the possibility of war between America and Britain.[17] His main contribution during his abortive tenure in India was to secure the release of two American vessels—carrying sugar from Manila—seized by the British East India squadron and taken into port on suspicion of illegal trading with the enemy.

President Washington picked William J. Miller of Philadelphia as Joy's successor. As Miller had lived in Calcutta for the past decade as a partner in a well-known mercantile house, the thinking went, the British might more readily accept him as the American consul. The Senate confirmed Miller's nomination in February 1796 and forwarded his commission to Calcutta. But it drew a blank with the British. Jacob Lewis of Massachusetts, sent to Calcutta in 1802, had much the same luck. This time, the American minister in London took the matter up with the British foreign secretary. But Lord Hawkesbury flatly refused to entertain the application, citing the absence of a precedent: "As no foreign nation has a consul in Calcutta, His Majesty's government cannot sanction Mr. Lewis's appointment." In 1818, the United States tried yet again to no avail. Four decades would pass before another American consul appeared in Calcutta and was accepted by the British Indian government.[18]

BRITAIN'S RELUCTANCE TO SANCTION an American consul stemmed mainly from its desire not to dilute its hold over the Indian economy. Until 1813, the East India Company had monopoly trading rights. When its charter was renewed that year, the company was stripped of its monopoly. This opened up the field to private merchants, traders, and agency houses—primarily British and, to a much lesser extent, Indian. Yet during the first decade and a half of the French Revolutionary and Napoleonic Wars, the American footprint in the India trade increased rapidly. While reliable data are hard to come by for this period, we know that between 1795 and 1804 Indian imports from America rose from 840,000 to 4.5 million sikka rupees, while exports on American ships went from 1.95 million to 6.76 million sikka rupees. The total American trade with India for the ten years starting from 1795 exceeded the combined total for all of Europe by

25 percent. Indeed, in 1807 an East India Company official noted that the American trade surpassed "everything of the kind recorded in the Commercial History of British India....A trade which seven years ago did not exceed S.Rs. 6,718,992 or Sterling 839,784 had advanced in the year under Report the enormous sum of S.Rs. 20,020,432 or Stg 2,502,554, exceeding...the total amount of our Private Trade with Great Britain."

Interestingly, American trade with India overtook that with China during the war. Imports from India increased from $500,000 in 1796 to $3.4 million in 1804, while imports from China went up during the same period from $300,000 to $1.6 million.[19]

Americans flourished in the India trade during these years partly owing to a treaty concluded with Britain. In 1794, as Benjamin Joy had foreseen, the two countries teetered on the brink of war. The crisis centered on the United States' claims to neutrality rights for its ships as well as its quest for profits. As a disastrous war seemed imminent, President Washington sent Chief Justice John Jay on a special mission to London to negotiate a settlement. The resultant agreement was arguably the most controversial international treaty in the history of the United States. Although it had just one clause on trade with India, this too stirred passions on all sides.

On its face, Article XIII of the Jay Treaty seemed to circumscribe Indo-American commerce. While the article allowed US citizens to "freely carry on a trade" with India, it was "expressly agreed that the vessels of the United States shall not carry any of the articles exported by them...to any port or place, except to some port or place in America." What is more, the article specifically forbade American vessels from taking "any part of the coasting [coastal] trade" in the subcontinent. Jay assured Secretary of State Edmund Randolph that this article was "a manifestation and proof of goodwill towards us." The American merchants knew better. As Miller and his partner William Macarty wrote to Governor-General Shore, "The Americans enjoyed a free trade in India, in common with all other nations before the Treaty with Great

Britain took place; & we believe it is the first instance in any treaty where privileges have been diminished." Unsurprisingly, Congress censured Jay for trading away American rights in India, and New Englanders burnt him in effigy.[20]

In practice, however, the Jay Treaty did nothing to crimp the United States' India trade. If anything it provided a measure of legal protection for US commerce, allowing it to balloon during the war. US merchants were adept at making their way through legal and practical loopholes. Ships sailing from the United States stopped at European ports to pick up merchandise before proceeding to India. After all, the treaty did not explicitly state that American vessels had to sail directly to India. Similarly, American ships carrying cargo out of India touched ports in the Persian Gulf, the Mediterranean, or Europe before reaching home; the clause did not explicitly prohibit exports to "any part of Europe" or, for that matter, any other place.

In both contexts, British courts and the British government interpreted the clause liberally. When directors of the East India Company decried America's violation of the treaty, Henry Dundas—president of the company's Board of Control—insisted that they should not add more rigors into the text of the treaty and should be lenient in their "commercial principles." Some private British merchants who already resented the East India Company's monopoly found the growing US trade equally galling. But others saw things differently. Sir Francis Baring, founder of Baring Brothers and Company, argued in 1807 that Americans would "contribute to the general prosperity of India by the silver they bring in payment for the productive industry of the Empire, leaving full scope for the sale of British manufactures, for America has none of her own to send."[21] British merchants and officials often couched these arguments in the language of political economy—free trade versus mercantilism—and American trade with India contributed to these ideological battles.

American merchants also carried on with coastal trade in India. By taking care to weave a non-British port—Dutch Serampore, Danish

Tranquebar, and French Pondicherry, among others—into their itin-eraries, American vessels plied the coasts of India without much prob-lem, clearly with the connivance of British officials in India. Why were they willing to overlook American transgressions? Historians have ar-gued that the British were indulgent because "Americans were never thought of as foreigners."[22] But this projects back in time attitudes that developed in a later period. The real reasons were at once more prosaic and grubbier. To begin with, the British knew that, if curbed, American ships would just trade out of other European ports in India. More im-portantly, exports to Europe on American ships were a crucial means of repatriating the illegal wealth amassed by employees of the East India Company in India. Doing so through the ships plied by the East India Company carried obvious risks. Senior company officials in London knew of this money laundering but never confronted the problem head on.[23] The gravy train was evidently a long one.

Even as accusations in Britain over American perfidy rose to a cre-scendo, American trade with India began to decline. Napoleon Bona-parte fired the first salvo on American shipping. Following his victory over Austria, Prussia, and Russia, he sought to blockade Britain. In November 1806, he announced that any ship coming from or calling on Britain or its colonies would be denied entry into any port on the European continent. Although Napoleon had no naval resources with which to enforce this diktat, he goaded the British to respond with a decree of their own. London issued a series of Orders in Council an-nouncing a blockade of France and its allies, declaring "all trade with them and in their produce prohibited" and recalling all British seamen. These tit-for-tat measures had the cumulative effect of shrinking the space for neutral trade. Both the British and the French seized Amer-ican vessels with growing frequency. In June 1807, a British warship attacked the American frigate USS *Chesapeake*, which had taken on board a number of British deserters, and seized four men. The incident triggered outrage in the United States. Unable either to compromise or retaliate, President Thomas Jefferson took the moral high ground and urged Congress to impose an embargo on all foreign trade.[24]

The Embargo Act of 1807 reflected Jefferson's view of the United States as a self-sufficient agrarian economy of yeoman farmers. Not surprisingly, it had a devastating impact on merchants and shipowners engaged in foreign trade, especially trade with India. Henry Lee of Boston—a leader in the India trade—accurately predicted the consequences of the embargo: "Some very rich houses will be ruin'd....I cannot but hope that such a constrain'd situation of things will end either by a relaxation of Decrees on the part of France and England, or by a general peace—till one of these two events occur our trade will be in a dreadful state."[25] The embargo, however, had no effect on British or French policy. Indeed, it simultaneously strengthened Napoleon by depriving Britain of trade with America and, for the same reason, enraged Britain. Although the embargo was repealed in 1809, the climate of hostility and uncertainty persisted. By 1811, the bottom had been knocked out of Lee's business.

The Bengal government noted with a mix of sadness and sanctimony that the "American Embargo" had "entirely interdicted all commerce." American imports from India plunged from $4.2 million in 1807–1808 to $680,000 the following year. A brief spike in imports, once the embargo was lifted, to $3.3 million in 1809–1810 proved short-lived.[26] In November 1810, Napoleon made a crafty announcement that France would withdraw its decrees if Britain followed suit. President James Madison was so eager for peace that he promptly took Napoleon at his word and gave the British three months to revoke their orders. When London failed to comply, Madison imposed an embargo on trade with Britain. Assuming that conflict was inevitable but would be brief and inexpensive in blood and treasure, Madison sleepwalked into a war with Britain in June 1812.

The war dragged on for three years and dealt another huge blow to American trade with India. American imports plummeted from $1.15

million in 1812–1813 to just over $190,000 a year later. As the Bengal government observed, "With America our Intercourse has almost entirely failed." So outraged were British authorities in India that they prevented Americans from entering the country and kept a close watch on those already residing there. Among those stuck in India during the war was Henry Lee, who had moved to Calcutta a month before the declaration of war in a bid to revive his fortunes. A year into the war, he wrote to his cousin back home, "Should the war [continue] God only Knows what may be the consequences, you & all other commercial men largely in trade I suppose will be ruin'd." Lee pinned the blame entirely on the US federal government, adding that "the only good effect which can result will be the separation of States, & that is quite uncertain. I hope with all my heart it may happen."[27]

WHEN THE WAR IN EUROPE ended in the summer of 1815, the US India trade had slipped well below its former height. Soon it would become a dim and distant memory. Imports from India dropped from $4.5 million in 1816 to $1.15 million in 1824. The trend line ran further south thereafter. Apart from blockades, embargos, and war, American merchants and shipping had to contend with their British counterparts, who had dissolved the monopoly of the East India Company and enjoyed official patronage in Britain and India. More importantly, the Indian and American economies underwent far-reaching changes in the aftermath of the conflict. The manufacture of Indian textiles and handicrafts slumped dramatically owing to the rise of Lancashire and the treatment of India as a captive market, turning it from one of the largest exporters of textiles into an importer. As Britain began integrating India into its economy as a supplier of commodities, the latter had little to offer America.

Americans too shifted their gaze from overseas markets to those at home. The embargo and wartime restrictions ensured that Americans imported far fewer manufactured goods from Britain and that the price of such imports rose steeply. This led to a spurt in patents and encouraged increasing numbers of investors to shift their capital from overseas shipping to domestic manufacturing. As domestic trade rose, Americans began to realize the advantages of a continental marketplace. Soon demand heightened for roads, bridges, canals, and ferries—all aimed at reducing transaction costs and binding the republic together. Over the following three decades, the United States underwent a "communications revolution" marked by the introduction of steamboats, turnpikes, and railroads, newsprint and electric telegraphy. The domestic market also swelled with extraordinary growth both in population, reaching 33 million by 1860 owing to high fertility rates and immigration, and in territory, owing to the relentless expansion to the south and west and subjugation of native inhabitants. Tariffs were kept high to nurture infant industries. The seed drills and steel plows, mowers and reapers made in American industries enabled spectacular growth in agricultural production. The accompanying belief that "the home market for productions of the earth and manufactures is more important than all foreign ones" marked a revolutionary change from the outlook that originally fired the quest for trade with India.[28]

As the United States began to transition from farm to factory, the nature of imports from India changed. In the 1820s and 1830s, indigo replaced cotton textiles as the main import until chemical dyes in turn displaced it. The growth of shoe manufacturing in factories generated demand for goatskins and buffalo and cattle hides. Saltpeter (potassium nitrate) imported from Calcutta went into the production of gunpowder. In the 1840s, two new products became prominent on the lists of merchandise carried from India by American ships. Linseed provided oil used to manufacture paint and varnish. Jute—in the form of yarn, twine, cloth, and bags—was increasingly used for bulk packing and transport, not just of industrial goods but also of agricultural products such as cotton and corn. Between 1840 and 1855, the jute exported from Bengal rose tenfold in quantity and thirty times in price. And the United States was a major market. The cessation of trade between Britain and Russia during the 1854–1856 Crimean War enabled Indian linseed and jute to eat into the share of Russian exports to the United States.

Meanwhile, American exports to India were profoundly transformed as well. Textiles produced in the mills of New England—jeans, drill, and light and heavy twilled cotton—accounted for almost half the value of exports in 1854. Newer goods, like glassware and clocks, joined older staples, such as tobacco and naval stores.[29]

Trade with India had its share of exotica. The first Indian elephant, "Old Bet," arrived in the United States in 1795. Four decades later, demand arose in Philadelphia for elephants and other beasts. The sale of a tiger, a leopard, and even a rhinoceros turned a tidy profit for J. W. Rulon of Philadelphia and his partner in Calcutta, Thomas Richards.[30] Less exotic but much more profitable was the export of ice from America to India. The Indo-American ice trade, begun by Frederic Tudor of Boston in 1833 and continuing until 1880, was the outcome of a peculiar conjunction. On the one side was the insatiable demand for ice from the British to cope with the subcontinent's heat. Attempts to manufacture ice in India had proved unsatisfactory—not least because the process was highly labor-intensive and the product could not last through the year. On the other side was the availability of high-quality ice in the ponds of New England. Ecology alone could not do the trick. It had to be yoked with technology and entrepreneurship. Tudor experimented with a range of existing and new technologies before devising an effective and profitable method of insulating ice on ships and storing it in icehouses of his own design.[31]

American ice proved a great success with Anglo-Indians. The community chittered and quivered with excitement the day public sales commenced: "All business was suspended until noon....Everybody invited everybody to dinner, to taste of claret and beer cooled by the American importation." Urged by influential Britons in Calcutta, the East India Company not only exempted American ice from import regulations but also provided substantial incentives for the trade. By the 1860s, ice had almost ceased to be a luxury item. As one contemporary observed, "The arrival of our English mail is not more anxiously expected than that of an American Ice-ship when supplies run low!"[32] Over the following decade, the British mastered artificial refrigeration and ice manufacture. As so often in history, the impetus came from the requirements of the military: the need to cool the gun turrets and magazines of the Royal Navy's fleet. In 1878, the Bengal Ice Company was set up in Calcutta. Close on its heels came the Crystal Ice Company. Soon, it was curtains for the Indo-American ice trade.

All along, the balance of trade remained firmly tilted in favor of India. Despite diminishing commerce, the United States opened consulates in Calcutta and Bombay. Yet the allure of trade with India had dimmed. As Boston merchant J. D. Alden noted wistfully in his journal,

> *Though absent I recall thy charms*
> *And wish—as lovers when they part—*
> *I'd like the vine, a thousand arms*
> *to clasp thee, hold thee, to my heart*

Indo-American trade almost jolted to a halt in 1857 and 1858. In May 1857, Indian soldiers of the East India Company's Bengal Army mutinied in the cantonment of Meerut near Delhi, killing not just their officers but every British resident they could lay their hands on: "Kill the White Man" was their slogan. The next day a group of Indian soldiers entered the Red Fort in Delhi and asked the ageing Mughal emperor, Bahadur Shah Zafar, to assume titular leadership of their uprising. Meanwhile, Delhi, gripped by violence, soon slipped out of British control. In Meerut and Delhi, peasants, artisans, and the working poor joined soldiers in attacking the British. The mutiny turned into a massive revolt as it spread across northern India.[33] Recovering from the initial setbacks, the British retaliated with ferocity. In a series of brutal military and extrajudicial sweeps, they went after Indians of all stripes suspected of sympathizing with or supporting the rebels. The slaughter was deliberately indiscriminate and public. Eventually, the British prevailed in the escalating cycle of violence, though the basis of their rule in India had been unhinged.

The Indian revolt coincided with the Panic of 1857 in the United States, where nerves about financial markets led to bank runs, which in turn led to factory closures, railroad bankruptcies, a collapse in construction, a drop in crop prices, massive unemployment, and a sharp squeeze on imports. Against this backdrop, American merchants grew substantially more circumspect about India. As George Wendell wrote to his father in September 1857, "Business in India looks anything but good. I may go to China."[34]

Four years later, the United States descended into its own civil war. Arguably the first industrial war of the modern age, it killed 600,000 Americans in a population of about 40 million.[35] Historians have in recent years encouraged us to understand the 1857–1858 Indian rebellion and the American Civil War of 1861 to 1865 as part of a series of "interregional shocks" that divided the nineteenth century and had global ramifications.[36] Indeed, the US slide into civil war put paid to the prospects of trade with India. But the American Civil War also boosted Indian exports—albeit to other markets.

Over the previous five decades, the United States had emerged as the world's leading producer of the most important commodity: cotton. British textile manufacturers watched the spectacular output of American cotton plantations with periodic trepidation. For one thing, they worried that Americans would funnel increasing quantities of their cotton into their own mushrooming industries. For another, they wondered about the morality and practicality of banking on the system of slavery that underpinned the production of American cotton.[37]

From the mid-1830s, British manufacturers began to look at India as an alternative source of high-quality cotton. As one of them warned in 1844, "the safety of this country depends upon our obtaining an improved supply of Cotton from British India." Commercial bodies in textile manufacturing districts hectically lobbied the East India Company and the British government to promote cotton growing in India. Dozens of studies and surveys—including one in 1848 covering almost the entire subcontinent—looked into improving India's cotton productivity and quality. Cottonseeds, particularly of American origin, were introduced on the subcontinent, and the East India Company also helped set up experimental farms in western and southern India during the 1840s.[38]

Interestingly, cotton planters from the United States ran these farms. Several Americans offered their services. W. W. Wood of New Orleans, "born and bred on cotton plantations," wrote to the East India Company in June 1842 that he had been "entertaining the Idea for some time of going to India to cultivate the Cotton plant on my account but would much prefer [the company's] patronage and support." Wood and nine other planters traveled to Bombay with seeds, gins, and equipment from the United States. They spread out to various parts of the country and were provided land, a house, and a cotton press to grow exotic varieties from American seeds.[39]

This turn toward American cotton experts met with demurral from certain quarters of the Anglo-Indian community. In a bid to tamp down the Agri-Horticultural Society of India's enthusiasm for American expertise, British expert Henry Piddington wrote publicly to Governor-General Lord Auckland, pointing out that not all varieties of American cotton were equally suited to cultivation in all parts of India. Local soil, ecological, and climatic conditions ought to be taken into account before any planting took place. Piddington also suggested pairing American experts with teams of Britons and Indians who knew the local conditions: "They [Americans] must be as wholly unable, from want of knowledge of the language and experience, to lead and guide the speculation in a country of which they are so ignorant, as one of our Indigo assistants would be to manage a negro farm in Carolina and Virginia."[40] This view of American experts would echo down the decades and into the next century as well.

Initially, the going was good. The *Asiatic Journal* commended the "zeal and diligence" of American planters. But soon the farms ran into difficulties for a variety of reasons: rainfall patterns were not suitable for American farming practices, poor infrastructure impeded transportation, American techniques proved too capital-intensive. Above all, Indian peasants put up resistance. They opposed the use of "wastelands," where they traditionally grazed their cattle at no expense, for these farms. They also resisted the Americans' more coercive methods. An American farmer named Mercer "had his bungalow burnt down, and the estate and works, together with his whole property, destroyed, except the suit of clothes he had on him." Mercer himself concluded that "the experimental farms were only a useless expense to Government" and that Indian peasants were "able to cultivate better and much more economically." The first instance of American technical assistance for economic development in India, these cotton farms presaged the problems experienced by later American experts confronting the social realities of the subcontinent. The British, for their part, had to reconcile themselves to the inexorable American domination of the world cotton market. As an Anglo-Indian official concluded in 1848, "competition with America seems a hopeless task."[41]

The outbreak of the US Civil War rekindled their hopes. British merchants and manufacturers, publicists and statesmen, all convinced that India had to be the main source of cotton, worked assiduously throughout these years to increase and improve its production. They urged the new government of India (under the British Crown, which took over from the East India Company after the rebellion of 1857) to invest massively in infrastructure, amend the criminal code to make adulteration of cotton a crime, and enact new property laws to facilitate the market for land.[42] Even that leading organ of laissez-faire capitalism, *The Economist*, supported state involvement in Indian cotton production. It justified this doctrinal lapse on the grounds that "there appears to exist in many important parts of Indian society very peculiar difficulties, which to some extent impede and counteract the action of primary motives upon which political economy depends for its efficacy.... There is no greater anomaly in recommending an unusual policy for a State destitute of the ordinary economical capacities, than in recommending an unusual method of education for a child both blind and deaf."[43]

In the event, government intervention coupled with the soaring prices in European markets led to a considerable expansion of India's cotton economy. By 1862, cotton's output had grown by 50 percent, while its value had quadrupled. In 1860 India had accounted for just 16 percent of Britain's cotton imports and 1.1 percent of France's, but two years later it provided 75 percent of British and 80 percent of French imports. In 1863, ships laden with cotton left Bombay for New York.[44] The US Civil War resulted in a boom for Indian peasants and in the growth of western Indian cities and towns, especially the metropolis of Bombay. The inevitable postwar decline in India's commanding position in world cotton markets coincided with a wave of famines in western India, leading to the growth of a new militancy in towns and the countryside. In the meantime, Indian merchants who had raked in profits in the US Civil War years began to turn from commerce to industry. An Indian cotton textile industry emerged in the western cities of Bombay and Ahmedabad. These industrialists went on to bankroll the emerging class of Indian nationalists. At the end of the US Civil War, the Bombay Chamber of Commerce called the "emancipation of slaves a matter of paramount importance" for India's future. It could have hardly realized that the US Civil War had also helped set India on the road to its own freedom.[45]

COMMERCE WITH INDIA WAS also critical in enabling antebellum Americans to experience the subcontinent and form their first concrete impressions of the land and its peoples. The images garnered in these early encounters were by no means fixed or unchanging. Yet they left a genetic imprint on the United States' subsequent approach to South Asia. Much of what Americans learned about the subcontinent during those decades they picked up in the cities and towns along or near the coastline of India. Though hardly involved in that country's internal trade and little acquainted with the towns and countryside deeper inland, American traders and seamen did encounter more of the subcontinent than today's India.

The itinerary of Master Mariner Benjamin Carpenter, who sailed out of Boston on the *Ruby* in December 1789, was typical. After halts in Madeira and Mauritius, the ship made its first landfall in the Dutch port of Point de Galle in Ceylon. Galle, Carpenter noted, "is a small place of little commerce, however I think it an object for vessels bound to India to touch at." Thereafter the ship made for Madras, glancing en route at Trincomalee in Ceylon ("nothing more than a garrison"), Nagapattinam, and Cuddalore on the southern coast of India. From Madras, Carpenter took another ship to Calcutta and from there traveled upriver to the French town of Chandernagore. At the end of his trip, Carpenter recommended other voyages for American ships: Calcutta to Rangoon and Pegu in Burma via the Nicobar Islands; Calcutta to Bombay via Colombo in Ceylon, then Cape Comorin, Anjengo, and Cochin on the western Indian coast. American seafarers and traders frequented all these places and more.[46]

Though their backgrounds were far from uniform, American travelers noticed remarkably similar things about the subcontinent. Accustomed to largely homogenous and well-ordered American cities, they usually found their first encounter with an Indian town bewildering. Visiting Bombay in 1818, lawyer and merchant William August Rogers was astonished "to be placed instantaneously in a crowded city, its houses of a style totally different from any we have ever seen, streets thronging with every cast and kind from the pale European resident to the jet Black Kauffree/Caffie [African]…English, Americans, French and Portuguese, Armenians and Jews, Parsees, Gentoos and Mahommedans, each wearing the costume of his nation, displaying its peculiar manners."[47]

Another noticeable aspect of Indian cities was their racial segregation into "Black Towns" and "White Towns." On arriving in Madras in 1799, Salem merchant Dudley Pickman immediately noticed the layout of the city. Fort St. George, which housed most of the Europeans, was "a regular built town, containing several houses, many stores, shops etc. besides an English Church, the Government offices and accommodations for the troops. The buildings [are] of brick, generally lofty and spacious." Entry into this part of town was also strictly regulated: "No black is permitted to go into the Fort in a palanquin; they must walk in from the gates." By contrast, the Black Town where the "natives, with Armenians and Portuguese reside…is irregularly built. The streets are narrow and unpaved, many of them dirty…. The habitations of the poorest class of natives are made of mats…. Many have low one story houses, built of brick and plastered outside. The rich natives have large, handsome houses, with considerable gardens adjoining."[48]

Pickman observed the same when he visited Calcutta three years later: "The principal streets in which Europeans reside are wide and generally straight…. The streets more particularly inhabited by the natives are narrow, confined and crooked."[49] While most Americans noticed the racial grid imposed on Indian cities, none of them regarded as it as at all incongruous—not surprising in light of the racism licensed back home. All the same, it underscored the fact that Americans took their racial superiority over Indians as a given.

They were rather more troubled by the torrid weather of the subcontinent, especially the humidity in the coastal towns. As much as the British, Americans in India benefited from the ice trade. Nineteen-year-old Edwin Blood woke up with heat stroke after his first day in Calcutta during the summer of 1854. "Bring me a glass of water," he told his Indian servant. "Nag junta, sahib [I don't understand, sir]," came the reply. Blood paused and blurted out the only words in Hindustani that he had learned on the boat: "Bruf pawnee lao [bring ice water]!" The Indian returned in a twinkle with "a huge tumbler of water, in which was floating and clinking musically against the glass, a large piece of Wenham Ice"—from the eponymous lake in Boston.[50]

Not all features of the subcontinent could be attributed to nature. The poverty of the people stunned Americans, but it also filled them with repugnance. "There are many beggars in the streets," wrote Pick-man, adding for good measure, "Almost every native may be considered a beggar; varying their claim however, according to their situation, from begging for fanams [money], to the more delicate request for 'master's favor.'" "The streets of Bombay are filled with beggars," noted Rogers, "the most deplorable objects, victims of vice, or wretched survivors of some dreadful accidents or loathsome disease." A beggar in Calcutta's Old China Bazaar importuned Blood and refused to yield despite be-ing given a rupee. "Had he been a common man I should have knocked him down," wrote Blood, "but the loathsome object that he was I dared not touch him."[51]

Equally repellant were the social mores of the subcontinent. While Americans approved of the prevailing racial hierarchy, they looked askance at the egregious workings of the caste system. The Brahmins atop the system, noted Pickman, "will not touch any not of their own denomination, without immediately washing themselves entirely after it." The Brahmins held those deemed outside the caste system alto-gether "in such horror" that they forbade the latter from even making eye contact with them.[52] So the caste system provided another avenue for Americans to assert their superiority over Indians.

The same was true of gender and sexuality. Americans noted that Indians married when they were still children and that marriage among relations was widely prevalent. However they held that this "early per-fection of procreative powers, is but a hot house precocity which is repaid by premature old age." Indeed, in the years when people like themselves were "in the vigor of their prime, these [Indians] are already fast going in decay." What is more, such early marriage cramped the freedom of women, who, "after marriage, are scarcely seen except by their husbands, to please whom is their great object."[53] Yet Americans also viewed the exceptions to these practices as depraved. Visiting the southeastern coastal town of Calicut, Rogers observed, "A woman may marry a number of husbands, each has her by turns for about 10 days. When pregnant she names the father of child who supports it." The "dancing girls" were another category of women who did not fit the Indians' societal codes. These women, Pickman wrote, "were distinct from any other class, living by their own rules." Their moves, he added, "bear no resemblance to European dancing, but they aim principally at attitudes calculated 'to captivate the other sex.'" Rogers surmised that these women "have generally two or three men in company. All the guests give them money and they often get very large sums in a night."[54]

In their early commercial dealings, some Americans were smug about their moral superiority over Indians. Indian clerks and accountants, merchants and agents—functioning as interpreters, or *dubashes*, literally meaning "men of two languages"—struck them as deceitful.[55] The supercargo of the *General Washington* reported from Madras in 1787, "The whole life and study of the Indians is to cheat you." Writing in 1800, Pickman claimed, "Even among the richest and most respectable of the natives...very few are seen in whose honor and integrity great confidence can be placed, or possessing views sufficiently intensive to believe that honesty will bring its own reward and be always found the best policy." Not that he followed this high-minded advice. In order to avoid duties, he conceded, "invoices are generally made out at reduced prices, tho' those inward are sworn to."[56]

Others, however, understood the importance of Indian middlemen. "Pauls Vincaty is the best dubash in Madras," wrote Carpenter in 1790. "He has served me in two voyages and I have no reason to be dissatisfied with him. He will procure you a store and everything you are in want of. He will also supply you with cash to a considerable amount." By the time Pickman returned to India in 1803, he had gradually changed his initial impressions of his Indian counterparts. In Calcutta, Ramdulal Dey, who handled much of the New England business, was "very shrewd and capable, extremely avaricious and possesses great talents for business." It helped that Dey was very wealthy—"worth three to five million rupees." Others whom Pickman dealt with may not have been as rich, but he was "satisfied with the manner in which they managed the business I entrusted to them."[57]

The Americans' sense of racial, social, and cultural superiority sat uneasily with their deepening commercial and financial ties with Indian merchants. When Ramdulal Dey complained about delay in payment, Patrick Jackson of Newburyport wrote, "You have lost nothing by your acquaintance with [me]...You have not only got considerable business from us, but some more from our recommendations. I am certainly obliged by the confidence you shew in giving me so large a credit, but you know I could have...found others who could have done the same."[58]

Even as the US India trade dwindled after 1815, Indian merchants and agents began to come into their own. The abolition of the East India Company's monopoly in 1813 enabled the growth of British and, to a lesser extent, Indian mercantile agency houses. Parsee firms in Bombay began trading in a range of commodities. As early as 1818, Rogers was much impressed with Nusserwanjee Maneckjee Wadia as "a man who sustained a most estimable character. He did all the American business at Bombay....[The Parsees] are clever and honest." In 1834, Dwarkanath Tagore, the wealthiest Indian businessman of his time and Calcutta's leading public figure, set up Carr, Tagore & Company, the first "managing agency" in India. Both Tagore and Wadia were closely involved with the Indo-American ice trade.[59] The next generation of Calcutta merchants who dominated the American trade, Raj Kissen Mitter and Rajinder Dutt, were kinsman of Ramdulal Dey. As such, they inherited long-standing business ties with New England mercantile families. Educated in English, attuned to Western mores, and possessed of reformist inclinations, these men commanded higher cultural capital than their predecessors and managed to develop closer ties with their American counterparts. By that time, however, Indo-American trade had long passed its zenith.

AMERICAN PERCEPTIONS OF INDIA during these decades might seem similar to those of the British. After all, the British also sought to justify their dominion over India by emphasizing its essential difference along several axes: history, race, gender, and society.[60] But American dispositions toward the subcontinent drew on an altogether different ideological repertoire. Its keynotes were the providential belief, stemming from the initial Puritan settlement, in the United States as a sacred space blessed with divine favor, and the secular notion, fired by the War of Independence, of the new republic as a herald of liberty for all of humankind. This peculiar but powerful blend of exceptionalism and universalism rendered American nationalism fundamentally different from the European variant—a contrast cast into sharp relief by the weakness of the American state until the turn of the twentieth century.[61]

This combination of millenarian and republican concepts also allowed the Americans to regard their own unceasing continental expansion as entirely different from European empire building.[62] At the apogee of American expansionism in the 1840s, John O'Sullivan famously proclaimed "the right of our *manifest destiny* to overspread and to possess the whole continent which providence has given us for the development of the great experiment of liberty and federated self government." This powerful notion of manifest destiny rested on an explicit contrast drawn with the British approach of slaughter and conquest in the subcontinent. In India and Afghanistan, O'Sullivan wrote, the British had engaged in "constant aggression, without any shadow of excuse or apology." The American system, however, offered no "pretext or excuse for such wholesale oppression, robbery, and murder."[63]

This ideological prism shaped the field of vision of early American travelers to the subcontinent. During his visits to India between 1800 and 1804, Dudley Pickman noted the rapacity of the British: "The natives are…oppressed and defrauded. Their money is borrowed, without probability or expectation of repaying it." He had an interesting explanation for such behavior. The British came to India "to make an immediate fortune, to be spent at home." They did not consider the subcontinent "their abode for life, and the inheritance of their children."

Hence, they did not insist on "justice in their dealings, or take so much pains to make improvements [to the country]." The unspoken assumption was, of course, that the Anglo-Indians were not settlers like the Anglo-Americans and their descendants. During a visit to the coastal fort of Tranquebar, Pickman looked favorably on the Danish merchants "who usually end their days here." This, he claimed, "induces a much better treatment to the natives than they experience from the English, who consider themselves merely as 'birds of passage.'"[64]

The Anglo-American War of 1812 led to another eruption of anti-British feeling and boosted American nationalism. During his 1817–1818 sojourn, Republican lawyer and merchant William August Rogers was appalled by the consequences of British rule in India. His views fell squarely within the ideological matrix of the young republic. Rogers insisted he was no enemy of the British: "I revere their laws, their government and their religion. I boast my descent from a nation yet renowned for acts and arms and for patriotism unequalled by any nation but America." The British, however, were in thrall to the "demon of jealousy": "I have no doubt that the U.S.A. with their prosperity and growing greatness, struck terror into their [British] souls. In perspective they beheld their scepters broken, their thrones and palaces converted to the purposes of liberty and justice.... Yet that day is fast approaching when...man shall be left to exercise that freedom which nature intended should ever be identified with his existence."

Rogers's verdict on the British Empire in the Indian subcontinent was utterly damning. "In satisfying their thirst for conquest," he wrote, "they have in India passed the barriers of justice and humanity; have created wars and dictated peace; deposed their rightful sovereigns.... Their public officers have been tyrants, their individuals extortioners. They have overrun the peninsula of Hindoostan and extermination has been the order of the day." Interestingly, after a stay in Ceylon, he concluded, "In no one instance has their [British] rapacity been more strongly exhibited than on this island, within a few years."[65]

Supporters of slavery in the United States found such views handy when faced with the abolitionist criticism emerging from Britain in the 1830s and 1840s. Defenders routinely argued that British abuses in India were worse than American slavery and that Britain cynically supported abolition in America to advance its own interests. In *Abolitionism Unveiled*, published in 1856, Henry Field James wrote, "The East Indian Company has amassed immense wealth. The last statement I have seen places the annual income at ~29,000,000 sterling. Whence is this vast sum derived? From the groans, sweat, and tears of the toiling millions she holds there under absolute sway. It is wrought out of the bones and sinews of the 160,000,000 natives subject to her power.... The slaves of the United States—only three millions in number—have engrossed all her sympathy. She has none left for the millions oppressed in her East India possessions."[66]

British criticism of "filibustering"—attempts by freebooting Americans to snitch territory in the Caribbean Basin and Mexico—invoked similar arguments. Traveling through India in 1856, George Francis Train sneered at British hypocrisy: "Annexation in America is robbery; in India, friendship and protection." Indeed, the British regarded Lord Dalhousie's "political filibustering seizure of Oude [Awadh] a master stroke."[67]

That said, in the mid-1850s American travelers began to strike a more approbatory note about British rule in India. This, too, stemmed from ideological modulations back home. Destinarian expansionism and the escalating conflicts over slavery were increasingly couched in the pseudoscientific theories of race that had begun to grip the Western world at the time. An upshot of this was the production of an "internal" ranking of Caucasians that accorded the top spot to Anglo-Saxons. Although white Americans shared this position with the English, the former understood themselves to be the purer breed—having recovered their true Anglo-Saxon liberties in their revolution.[68] Nevertheless, they were now more forgiving of Anglo-Saxon rule in the subcontinent.

When Bayard Taylor landed in Bombay in 1853, he had gathered his impressions of British rule largely from the American press, which was "unsparing in its denunciations." At the end of his travels, he conceded that there were "wrongs and abuses that call for severe reprehension." In particular, he noted the oppressive system of land tenure and taxation. Besides, Taylor was "disgusted and indignant" at the "contemptuous manner in which the natives, even of the best and most intelligent classes, are almost invariably spoken of and treated." He had "heard the term 'niggers' applied to the whole race," including to Eurasians, "those of our Caucasian blood, where there is no instinct of race to excuse [the Brits'] unjust prejudice." And he wondered how the British could "tolerate this fact without a blush, yet condemn with pharisaic zeal, the social inequality of the negro and white races in America."

Yet Taylor was convinced that "in spite of oppression, in some instances of the most grinding character…the country has prospered under the English Government." The government had "done much for the education of the natives." British administration "secures to the native a more just and equitable administration of law than he could obtain from magistrates of his own race." Reprehensible social practices such as *sati*, or the immolation of a widow on her husband's funeral pyre, had been "totally suppressed." The "confederation of Thugs or Stranglers," practitioners of *thugee*—the alleged ritual strangling of travelers by highway bandits aimed at propitiating the Hindu goddess Kali—had been broken up. All in all, "order and security reign[ed] throughout the whole of India." In a telling instance of the range of positions that the ideological constellation of manifest destiny could accommodate, Taylor, who opposed slavery and held a benign view of racial hierarchy, insisted that the recent spate of British annexation of territory was "a fortunate thing for India"—"and who are *we*, that we should cast a stone against this sin?"[69]

Around the same time, Edwin Blood wrote in Calcutta, "Since the days of Warren Hastings the administration of India…has savored strongly of the drum stick and court martial, and conquest has been its end and object." But under the "paternal care" of Dalhousie "many and great internal improvements" were in the works. Above all, he was impressed with the introduction of railways: "The shrill neighing of the iron horse even now startles the tiger from his lair in the jungles of Bengal." Soon the iron ribbons would crisscross the country and "all classes in India be greatly benefited."[70]

Passing through the Bengal countryside a couple of years later, Train noted that the East India Company's tax system "grinds the life blood out of the poor ryot [peasant] at the rate of twelve dollars per annum, without rations, or house, or home (the lion's share of which finds its way into the Bengal treasury)—worse in some instances than the Legrees of 'Uncle Tom's Cabin,' that raised such a storm of virtuous indignation and false philanthropy at the Sutherland House [in England]." All told, he conceded, for "a conquered country, the East India Company may make as good masters as any other company or any other government."[71]

The 1857–1858 Indian rebellion shook such complacent assessments of the solidity of British rule. But the rebels' violence against "the whites" also forged closer bonds between Anglo-Indians and Americans in India. Visiting India the following year, Robert Minturn wrote, "During the recent disturbances in Bengal, the American residents in Calcutta formed themselves into a military body and offered their services to the Governor-General, which were most gratefully accepted." Minturn traveled up to Lucknow and Cawnpore, sites of some of the most gruesome incidents during the uprising. His account of the origins of the revolt was straight out of the British script. Equally in sync were his views on how to deal with the rebels: "The gallow and the cannon are a fit punishment for the coward and the traitor."[72] By the time he set sail from Bombay to Aden, Minturn was overwhelmed by "what I believe ought to be the feelings of every member of the Anglo-Saxon race, as he looks upon the progress of that mighty power which is spreading our laws, our liberty, our civilization, and our religion into the furthest bound of the habitable world." Minturn was consciously repeating the words of Bayard Taylor. Americans traveling to the subcontinent later in the century would echo these sentiments.

MORE THAN THE LURE of fortune pulled Americans to the subcontinent. Faith was as important in drawing them to the region and shaping their attitudes toward it. Over fifty years before independence, the influential Boston Puritan minister and thinker Cotton Mather had written *India Christiana*, a tract purporting to show the best ways of converting the Indians of the East as well as those of America.[73] Well before the first American Protestant missionaries stepped into the subcontinent, American seafarers and traders had remarked the strange religious practices of its inhabitants.

Visiting Americans tended to notice the religious diversity of the subcontinent. "All religions are tolerated here," wrote Dudley Pickman. "Some of the natives have been converted to the Roman Catholic, some are Mahometans [Muslims], but the great body are gentoos or Hindoos, the original religion of the country." Initially, Americans invariably focused on Hindus' idolatry and polytheism. Pickman noted on his first voyage that "scarce a day passed" when one did not find Hindus "carrying through the streets, images, highly decorated, which they called their gods." These processions were invariably "accompanied by music, and large concourses of people, and great respect and obeisance was paid, some even prostrating to their faces in the dust." Not surprisingly, he thought all this "very rude." Pickman was also stunned to see "a fanatic who professed to have devoted himself entirely to god... dancing etc. before the image, and applying fire to different parts of his body, apparently without effect."[74]

More appalling was the ritual mortification undertaken by the lower castes during religious ceremonies. "Some cut two gashes in each side of their bodies, about two inches long....Others pass a rattan or iron bar...through their tongues." These practices, Pickman recorded, were "voluntary because not imposed and because...no compulsion can ever be used"; thus they were intrinsic to the Hindu faith. William Rogers similarly observed, "The Gentoos on their festivals carry their idols in triumph in a wagon, to the wheels of which are affixed crooked iron hooks, on these they throw themselves and are crushed to pieces."[75]

The most revolting images of the Hindus, however, came from the practices of *sati* and *thugee*.[76] David Humphreys's 1790 play *The Widow of Malabar* was a close adaptation of Antoine-Marin Lemierre's *La veuve du Malabar*—a farrago of fact and misinformation. The play, portraying the burning of a Hindu widow, was staged in New York, Boston, and Philadelphia by the turn of the century.[77] And growing up in the Mississippi Valley in the 1840s, Mark Twain heard "vague tales and rumors of a sect called Thugs...who waylaid travelers in lonely places and killed them for the contentment of a god whom they worshipped."[78] But few Americans had seen these practices up close. Among those who actually witnessed a *sati* was Benjamin Crownin-shield, a New England merchant who later became secretary of the navy under President James Madison. In 1789 two Irish friends took him to see the "barbarous operation." Crowninshield left a detailed ac-count of that "most horrid sight" but was remarkably detached in his assessment: "Whether it is right or wrong, I leave it for other people to determine. There is this in it, it appeared very solemn to me. I did not think it was in the power of a human person to meet death in such a manner."[79]

Crowninshield was perhaps exceptional in his reaction to this gruesome practice. Americans who came later to the subcontinent were altogether more judgmental. At the other end of the spectrum from Crowninshield stood William Rogers, who observed in 1818 that the Hindu religion was "the most disgusting and at the same time the most degrading to the human mind that can be imagined. It united everything frivolous and horrible, childish and cruel, with the most disgusting lewdness and superstitious bigotry." The Hindus were "a low, cheating, brutal race, but a short remove from the brute creatures." Yet he hoped that soon "the example of Christians...will induce these deluded and degraded people to embrace the Doctrine, which insures the pleasures of this life and the immortal honors of the next....By exhibiting the superiority of our advantages, by instilling the gentleness, the principles of Christian morality...by using such means the Christian world may soon boast of an addition of millions."[80]

By contrast, Rogers found the Muslims not just "very clever" but "zealous...you will see them on the esplanade at sunset performing their religious prostrations and praying very earnestly." Blood noticed that during the holy month of Ramadan, Muslim workers punctiliously offered their prayers—never mind the "serious interruption of business." Their orderly prayers were a sharp contrast to the cacophony of Hindu rituals: "Like well trained soldiers they stand shoulder to shoulder fixed and immovable: but it is only for a minute; now with a simultaneous movement every head is bowed." As an Abrahamic religion, Islam was easier to comprehend. While the Muslims did not regard Jesus as a messiah, they saw him "as a very great man, endowed with supernatural powers and of vast capacity of mind as regards knowledge of the mankind."[81] The attractive aspects of Islam and the Muslims when compared to the Hindus and their religion would travel down the century and beyond.

Rogers's take on the Hindu religion and his call for proselytization in India reflected important developments back home. Although the new republic had separated its churches from the state, it retained the sense of divine election that had fired the Puritan settlements in colonial America. The Great Awakening of the mid-eighteenth century that had led to the establishment of new Protestant churches— Baptist, Methodist, Presbyterian—continued to pervade and influence all aspects of public life. By 1810, the United States was in the throes of a Second Great Awakening, seeking a return to fundamentals and the prospect of imminent redemption. As Samuel J. Mills, the student at Williams College who led this revival, put it, "We must not rest satisfied till we have made our influence extend to the remotest corner of this ruined world."[82] The American Board of Commissioners for

Foreign Missions was established that year. Consisting of clergymen from various denominations, as well as businessmen, lawyers, physicians, and educators, the board aimed to set up missionary stations in the American Southwest, India, China, Africa, and the Middle East.[83] It was not the last time a movement spearheaded by American students would impinge on the history of South Asia.

Two years later, in 1812, the first American missionaries, Adoniram Judson and Samuel Newell, arrived with their wives in Calcutta. They were denied entry and ordered to sail back to America, for the East India Company prohibited missionary activity. Eventually they managed to find sanctuary with the Baptists in the Dutch enclave of Serampore. The three Americans who followed in their wake—Samuel Nott, Gordon Hall, and Luther Rice—were similarly forbidden from pursuing their activities in British India. But the following year, the British government changed the charter of the East India Company, and the new Charter Act of 1813 allowed missionaries of all faiths to work in the country. Over the next decade the number of American missionaries grew slowly but steadily. And the 1830s saw a significant spurt of missionaries from America. A century after Judson and Newell were stranded outside Calcutta, there were 1,800 American missionaries in India.

Unlike traders, who were largely confined to the coastal cities and towns, missionaries fanned out to work in practically every corner of the subcontinent. Already by 1815, Americans were preaching in Bombay and nearby parts of western India. In the 1830s, Presbyterian missions and stations were set up in the Punjab (Ludhiana, Jalandhar, and Ambala in today's India; Lahore, Rawalpindi, Peshawar, Sialkot, and Gujranwala in today's Pakistan) and the North-Western Provinces (Uttar Pradesh in India). Reverends Judson and Rice founded the Baptist mission in Burma as early as July 1813. Two decades later, a Baptist mission was set up in the eastern Indian province of Assam—largely because it afforded a suitable entry point into western China and Tibet. In the event, the Baptist mission in northeastern India harvested many more souls than any other mission in the subcontinent. Its influence, especially in the hills of Assam, shaped the politics of the region in the twentieth century and beyond. By 1840, Baptist missions were also at work in the Telugu-speaking parts of the Madras Presidency in southern India. In the following decade, American Methodist missionaries began working in North India. Soon, more unorthodox groups, such as the Unitarians and the Friends, came along.

To work in various parts of the subcontinent, Americans had to pick up the local languages and dialects. They sought not only to preach the gospel in Indian languages but also to translate the Bible into them. Consequently, missionaries did much to foster the linguistic standardization of these languages. They were often the first to compile dictionaries. More importantly, they set up printing presses in various Indian languages, as well as English, and so contributed to the emerging print culture in several parts of India. American missionaries, for instance, launched the highly popular *Anglo-Marathi Dynanodaya* (*The Rise of Knowledge*), which became the most widely read newspaper in western India in the 1850s and 1860s. The emerging lower-caste critique of the Hindu caste system, especially in the hugely influential work of Jotirao Phule, also shaped such circulation of missionary ideology.[84]

Soon missionary schools began to dot the landscape of the subcontinent. Students, including girls, flocked to them, attracted by the promise of an education in English. In many places, the insistent demand for such education by the lower castes spurred missionaries into action. In the Madras Presidency, the American missions worked primarily in the settlements inhabited by the "pariahs" or "untouchables." Apart from proselytization, the American missionaries played an important role in helping these communities in their dealings with the colonial state, especially on matters pertaining to land rights.[85] The early missionaries also undertook some medical work, notably in caring for people suffering from leprosy. Medical work, however, expanded considerably in the decades after 1850 and became something of a model for organized social work in colonial India.[86]

American missionaries were much less successful in their core mission of converting the heathen Hindus. From the outset, their countrymen in India doubted they would accomplish much. Henry Lee wrote to his wife that the pioneers Nott and Hall "appeared ... to be mad": "All of them seemed ignorant of the world, and extremely ill-informed of the country and the inhabitants which they had come to convert. I pitied them most sincerely." Even Rogers, who advocated proselytization in India, found Newell and his associates in Bombay disappointing: "They never have yet made a convert nor will they by the means now used."[87]

Part of the problem was that Nott and friends were voicing in public the sentiments about the Hindu religion that Rogers confided in the privacy of his journal. From the outset they latched onto the uncongenial aspects of the Hindus' faith. In one of her earliest letters home from India, Newell's wife wrote about the "idolatory and wretchedness of the Asiatics," whom she called a "savage people." A few days later she wrote of "how wretched, how ignorant they are, and how greatly they need the gospel."[88]

In a tract published in 1817, Nott claimed that Hindu gods were "like men in their passions and feelings, and the places where they dwell are filled with folly, disorder and contention." John Lowrie, who preached in North India, similarly held that "the gods and goddesses are exemplars of every vice and crime."[89] In 1819 Bishop Reginald Heber penned his famous lines in the Episcopal Church hymnal about the call that had come from "Greenland's icy mountains, from India's coral strand" to "deliver their land from error's chain." The second verse went

What though the spicy breezes
Blow soft o'er Ceylon's isle;
Though every prospect pleases,
And only man is vile:
In vain with lavish kindness
The gifts of God are strown;

The heathen in his blindness
Bows down to wood and stone.

These lines would be repeated in countless Protestant churches in India and America.

As Edwin Blood observed in his journal, the missionaries obliviously condemned Hindu practices while holding fast to strange beliefs of their own: "That anybody could go to Heaven...[if they] kept all the fasts, abstained from meat and ate fish Fridays and pancakes at Shrovetide, and did many other things...would appear equally ridiculous to the Hindoos, as do many of their religious observances to us."[90] Such arguments cut no ice with the missionaries, but by mid-century the failure of their endeavor to convert the Hindus in appreciable numbers was evident. After a survey of missionary stations in North India, Bayard Taylor summarily pronounced, "I have not yet witnessed any results which satisfy me that the vast expenditure of money, talent and life in missionary enterprises, has been adequately repaid."[91]

Visiting Bombay in 1850, Horace Putnam was not surprised that American missionaries had failed to make much headway. They had apparently taken to the easy life: "Many times I have met them when coming into the city in most costly carriages...or carried in 'Pallanquins' upon the shoulders of four natives. They live out of the city abought [*sic*] three miles in beautiful country seats which would be quite palaces at home."[92] This portrayal of American missionaries, many of whom worked in hardly congenial circumstances, may have been unfair. Nevertheless, Putnam rightly pointed out the Americans' desire to set themselves apart from the very people whose souls they had come to save.

By the mid-nineteenth century, the literati in the United States had access to a rather different image of Indian religion. The pioneering efforts of the British "orientalists" had opened up the body of literature and philosophy in Sanskrit. But the main stimulus of interest in Indian thought came from Bengali intellectual and social reformer Raja Ram

Mohan Roy. A man of extraordinary learning in Sanskrit, Persian, and European traditions, Roy held that "cows were of different colours, but their milk was all the same; so with religions."[93] Apart from his progressive social views, Roy stood for reformation of the Hindu religion by stripping away superstitions, dispensing with idolatry, abolishing *sati*, and returning to the universalist philosophy of the Vedanta. Roy's interpretation of Christianity and his attempts to reconcile it with Hinduism, especially in his 1820 book *The Precepts of Jesus*, evoked much interest in the United States. American Protestants were delighted that a native Indian was apparently endorsing their views on everything that was wrong with his religion and seemed to see the light of Christianity. This was a reductive reading of Roy's thought. Nevertheless, sects like the Unitarians commenced a long and remarkable engagement with Roy and his followers.[94]

The following decades saw a surge in the professional study of India in the United States. Isaac Nordheimer began teaching Sanskrit at the City University of New York in 1836. Five years later, Edward Elbridge Salisbury was appointed professor of Sanskrit and Arabic at Yale. Chairs and manuscript collections in Indology were established at several major universities. Perhaps the most distinguished Indologist of this period was William Dwight Whitney, whose studies of the Vedas were a notable combination of learning, insight, and sympathy. The founding of the American Oriental Society in Boston in 1842 gave further impetus to the study of Indian languages and religions. This emerging body of scholarship not only kindled interest in India among a small sliver of American intellectuals but also established tenacious myths in thinking about the country—especially by way of contrast with the West. Whitney insisted, for instance, that "historic sense has always been conspicuously wanting" in India. Building on G. W. F. Hegel, he added that while the Hindu is "great in constructing systems of absolute truth ... he despises a record of facts; he has a scheme of astronomical cycles reaching back almost into infinity, and can tell precisely how many days ago the creation of the universe was completed; but he cannot give the real, prosaic date of any event, civil or literary, back of our Middle Ages."[95]

All this provided the backdrop to the emergence of the group of writers and intellectuals known as the transcendentalists. Ralph Waldo Emerson's curiosity about India owed much to the Boston of his youth, dominated by the East India trade and its adventurous merchants. Emerson had sampled the new orientalist literature on India as early as 1818. By the time he delivered his famous *Representative Men* lectures in 1845 and 1846, he had immersed himself deeply in the main Hindu religious texts: the Vedas, the Upanishad, the Bhagavad Gita, and the Vishnu Purana. While Emerson had a deep interest in Indian metaphysics—ideas about the immortal soul and illusion of the phenomenal world, for instance—he tended to see the idealism and spiritualism of India as a corrective to American materialism and Protestant dogmatism. This, too, proved a persistent mode of American engagement with Indian philosophy.[96]

Henry David Thoreau encountered the Hindu tradition in the late 1830s. Thereafter he systematically made his way through the most accessible texts. Thoreau considered the Hindu scriptures to be on an altogether loftier plane than those of Christianity: "The reader is nowhere raised into and sustained in a higher, purer, or rarer region of thought than in Bhagavat-Geeta." "One wise sentence" of the Vedas, he enthusiastically noted, "is worth the state of Massachusetts many times over." Thoreau often couched his critique of American commercialism and materialism in a contrast with Indian spiritualism. In *Walden* he observed that men are so caught up with the external, tangible world that "its finer fruits cannot be plucked by them": "Certainly there is a life of the mind above the wants of the body and independent of it." Even America's material ties with India reminded him of the latter's idealism. Watching ice cutters at work in Walden Pond, Thoreau wrote, "Thus it appears that the sweltering inhabitants of Charleston and New Orleans, of Madras and Bombay and Calcutta, drink at my well. In the morning I bathe my intellect in the stupendous and cosmogonal philosophy of the Bhagvat Geeta.... The pure Walden water is mingled with the sacred water of the Ganges."[97]

Not many of Thoreau's contemporaries would have made such a lofty connection with the subcontinent. India, to many Americans, remained a country of inscrutable inhabitants and strange superstitions. Popular representation of India in the United States reinforced the fantastic images brought back by sailors and merchants, missionaries and travelers. The first elephant brought by Jacob Crowninshield from India in 1795 became something of a celebrity. The public was invited to see "the greatest natural curiosity ever presented to the curious" at the Columbian Museum of Boston for "one quarter of a dollar—children nine pence." The curious were duly warned, "The Elephant having destroyed many papers of consequence, it is recommended to visitors not to come with such papers."[98] Americans returning from India brought back with them artifacts, paintings, sketches, and etchings depicting a range of such curiosities: camels and jugglers, pole climbers and naked saints. Long after India ceased to be land of fortune, it remained a realm of fantasy.

2

UNDER AMERICAN EYES

O N A SUNNY MORNING in January 1896, the visiting American, decked out in a white suit and straw hat, took a stroll on the outskirts of Bombay. On seeing a row of Indian washer men sweating it out, he asked his guide, "Are they breaking those stones with clothes?" Samuel Langhorne Clemens had kept his sense of humor despite having practically been forced to travel to India. A failed venture with a typesetting machine and the bankruptcy of his publishing firm had left Mark Twain ensnared in a web of debt: of over $100,000. To shake this off, the fifty-year-old writer had embarked on a yearlong lecture tour covering a hundred cities in Australia and New Zealand, South Africa and the British Isles, Ceylon and India.

In Bombay, Twain debuted at the Novelty Theatre before an overflowing Indian audience worshipping "at the shrine of the world's great humourist." Twain spoke of, among other things, the 352 different kinds of sins, allowing "industrious persons [to] commit them all in one year and be inoculated against all future sins." He told stories, some apocryphal, about George Washington and other great Americans and read a chapter from *Tom Sawyer*. Twain lunched with the governor in his official residence and met leading Indian businessman Jamsetji Tata over dinner.[1]

Like many well-informed Americans of his generation, Twain had thought of India as a land of fantasy: "an imaginary land...a fairy land, a dreamland, a land made out of poetry and moonlight for the Arabian Nights to do their gorgeous miracles in."[2] Ahead of his trip, he had written jocularly to Rudyard Kipling, "I shall come riding my ayah with his tusks adorned with silver bells and ribbons and escorted by a troop of native howdahs richly clad and mounted upon a herd of wild buffalos; and you must be on hand with a few bottles of ghee, for I shall be thirsty."[3] After visiting over sixteen cities and towns over two months, Twain concluded that India was the most interesting country on the planet. But his view of it was a tad more realistic: "This is indeed India—the land of dreams and romance, of fabulous wealth and fabulous poverty, of splendor and rags, of palaces and hovels, of tigers and elephants, the cobra and the jungle...the one land that *all* men desire to see, and having seen once, by even a glimpse, would not give that glimpse for the shows of the all the rest of the globe combined."[4]

Twain was a curious and sympathetic traveler. The people, he wrote, were "pleasant and accommodating": "They are kindly people.... The face and bearing that indicate a surly spirit and a bad heart seemed rare among Indians." The sight of a European manager needlessly striking an Indian servant in his hotel reminded him of his childhood in the American South and the stain of slavery on his own country. The "thatched group of native houses" along the Hoogli River took him back to "the negro quarters, familiar to me from nearly forty years ago—and so for six hours this has been the sugar coast of the Mississippi."[5] Even Indian religion and spirituality, of which he had had no high opinion,

Twain encountered with an open mind. On the massive Hindu religious festival in Allahabad, he wrote, "It is wonderful, the power of a faith like that." Meeting an Indian saint in Benares, Twain gave him an autographed copy of *Adventures of Huckleberry Finn* and noted his admiration for men who "went into the solitudes to live in a hut and study the sacred writings and meditate on virtue and holiness and seek to attain them." Twain had heard of the storied bandit tradition of *thugee*, or ritual strangling, as a boy in America and wrote at inordinate length about it in his account of his passage through India. Nevertheless, he also observed, "We white people are merely modified Thugs; Thugs fretting under the restraints of a not very thick skin of civilization."[6]

All the same, a sense of civilizational hierarchy shaped Mark Twain's views of India. Although "the cradle of human race, birth place of human speech" and so forth, it had no notion of "progress," "repeating and repeating and repeating, century after century, age after age, the barren meaningless process." India had been the "first civilization" and never advanced past that point. If this thinking was redolent of Britain's ideological justification for the conquest of India, Twain more explicitly endorsed the political rationale of the Raj: "Where there are eighty nations and several hundred governments, fighting and quarrelling must be the common business of life; unity of purpose and policy are impossible." The beneficence of British rule flowed logically from these premises. "When one considers what India was under her Hindoo and Mohammedan rulers, and what she is now; when he remembers the miseries of her millions then and protections and humanities which they enjoy now, he must concede that the most fortunate thing that has ever befallen that empire was the establishment of British supremacy here."[7]

Twain had set out on his transcontinental journey to India at a crucial moment in the history of the United States and of the world. The Cuban people had risen in revolt against their Spanish overlords, and the United States had sided with the rebels and sent the USS *Maine* steaming toward Havana. Soon after Twain's sojourn in

India, Theodore Roosevelt's troops would charge up San Juan Hill in Cuba, and Admiral George Dewey's fleet would make for Manila Bay in the Philippines. Sharpening imperial thrusts by the older European powers—not least Britain, soon to be embroiled in a war with Dutch settlers in South Africa—accompanied the United States' first steps toward acquiring an overseas empire. In the wake of the bloody colonization of the Philippines, Twain emerged as a prominent critic of American imperialism. In a furious polemic, "To the Person Sitting in Darkness," he asked, "Shall we go on conferring our Civilization upon the peoples that sit in darkness, or shall we give those poor things a rest?...Would it not be prudent to get our Civilization-tools together and see how much stock is left on hand...so that we may intelligently decide whether to continue the business."[8] Then again, Twain's anti-imperialism rested on the same bedrock assumptions of civilizational hierarchy that helped him justify British rule in India.

Mark Twain's encounter with India is interesting because it encapsulates the wider currents of change washing through the United States. Between the Civil War and World War I, Americans yearned for regeneration. The Civil War itself was recast in the popular imagination as a sacrifice that would pave the way for national renewal. Following Reconstruction, reconciliation between the white elites of the North and South was effected by presenting the war as an expression of the Anglo-Saxon martial ethic. This set the stage for the subsequent disenfranchisement of the blacks in the South, the codification of segregation through Jim Crow laws, and the sharpening of white racial antagonism. Notions of Anglo-Saxon racial supremacy—euphemistically referred to as "Civilization"—were yoked to the older providential sense of manifest destiny and were crucial in justifying the turn-of-the-century imperial ventures abroad. The Progressive reformers who opposed this trinity of militarism, racism, and imperialism nevertheless bought into some of its foundational premises.[9]

The idea of an Anglo-Saxon civilization was in many ways central to the imagination of both sides in this quest for national regeneration.

A shared sense of destiny could only arise between the British and the Americans after rapprochement between their two states and the abatement of anti-British sentiment in American nationalism. This began to take shape after the Civil War, but it took years before Anglo-Saxonism displaced traditional American distrust and resentment of the British. As late as 1895, the standoff between Britain and America over Venezuela triggered a virulent burst of Anglophobia in the United States. Nevertheless, as the United States entered the imperial age, consanguinity rather than hostility became the leitmotif in their relationship.[10]

This shared discourse of civilization organized various parts of the world in a racial hierarchy, insisted that the white races—and within them, the Anglo-Saxons—were superior, and held that progress depended on the transmission of civilizational values from the higher to the lower civilizations.[11] The disagreements between the imperialists and anti-imperialists turned primarily on the appropriate means of this spread of civilizational norms. In the context of these preoccupations, India came increasingly under American eyes. American perceptions of India—especially as recorded by travelers, explorers, and missionaries—drew on and reinforced prevailing assumptions about the evolutionary scale of human achievement and progress. In the cracked mirror of India, Americans saw themselves. To Americans of diverse persuasions, India became a peg on which to hang their own hopes and fears.[12]

THIS WAS EVIDENT WELL before the scramble for empire at the end of the nineteenth century. Just a year before his death in 1872, William Henry Seward, US secretary of state from 1861 to 1869, visited India as part of his global travels. Seward had been a leading advocate of American continental expansion from the late 1840s. Like many opponents of slavery in the Whig Party, he believed that the innate superiority of the Anglo-Saxons was incontestable and that African

Americans were unfit for republican citizenship. Seward was ahead of his contemporaries, however, in articulating a vision of an American "empire of liberty" based on overseas commercial expansion—even before the Civil War had settled matters at home.[13]

Not surprisingly, India served as a foil for Seward's ideas of an Anglo-Saxon imperial mission. Seward found that India had "a very imperfect and unsatisfactory civilization.... The native population could never achieve a better one if left to themselves. Their whole hope of a higher civilization depends on the instruction and aid of the Western nations...chiefly on the guidance and aid of Great Britain." The Hindus, he conceded, were "not intellectually inferior to the Western nations." They had ancient languages and literature, ethics and crafts, mathematics and hydraulics. But they had "never known how to constitute a civil government." They had "never even written a history of themselves." Worse, they were trapped in a vicious system of caste and gender hierarchy.

Under British tutelage India was steadily, if gradually, improving. But the Raj's task was enormous. Bringing civilization to India "required nothing less than the destruction of caste, the restoration of woman, and the conversion of the natives." If Britain were to pull out of India, "the country must inevitably relapse into the wretched condition in which it was found by the Europeans." Seward not only painted the objectives and benefits of British rule in glowing terms but also presented extenuating circumstances for the visibly slow progress. Whereas earlier American travelers had criticized the British for refusing to settle in India, Seward insisted that the country could not be colonized by settlement like the Americas and Australia: "Climate forbids this." Nevertheless, he did not foresee any serious challenge to British rule in India. If Britain proved incapable of bearing this historical burden, he insisted, "Western Powers which should relieve Britain in India must necessarily assume her responsibilities." The Anglo-Saxon civilizing mission should continue—not just in India but "until British scorn of arbitrary government and American love of educated liberty shall encircle the earth."[14]

President Ulysses S. Grant, the man who had denied Seward the opportunity to stay on as secretary of state, echoed his musings on India. During an 1878 tour, the former president enjoyed the hospitality of the Raj. Grant noted that, contrary to his expectations, "a most discreet, able and well-chosen set of officials" administered British rule in the subcontinent. India's best bet for "progress" lay in benevolent British tutelage. Like Seward, he feared that a British withdrawal from India would unloose "the work of rapine and murder and wars between native chiefs" and that "the retrograde to absolute barbarism would be… almost instantaneous." A companion of Grant's noted that Viceroy Lord Lytton's reception in honor of the president was a reminder "of the strong bond that now binds all members of the great Anglo-Saxon race." British rule in India, another concluded, "whatever it may have been in the past, grows more and more beneficent."[15]

No American president of this age was a more vociferous admirer of the British Raj than Theodore Roosevelt. The Anglo-Saxons, he believed, had proved themselves not only the strongest race but also the fittest for the task of civilizing backward peoples. The "best thing" that could happen to such benighted folk was "to assimilate and profit by American and European ideas, ideas of civilization and Christianity." Colonial rule, "in spite of all its defects" was "the prerequisite condition to the moral and material advance of the peoples who dwell in the darker corners of the earth." The British Empire provided the model for Roosevelt as president: "There are plenty of jobs for which I am not competent, but I must say, I should greatly like to handle Egypt and India for a few months."[16] Roosevelt was particularly interested in the British Raj's approach to forestry and irrigation—areas that he regarded as key domestic priorities for his administration. Leading American foresters learned their science from Sir Dietrich Brandeis, the German expert who set up the Indian Forest Department. American irrigators and engineers traveled across India to collect information on the design, construction, and maintenance of the extensive canal system built by British administrators.[17]

Roosevelt's enthusiasm for the Raj stemmed in no small measure from his reading of Rudyard Kipling, whose work he had known even before the author moved to America in 1893. Kipling himself had withering contempt for his wife's country. America, he declared after a few months, was "barbarism—barbarism plus telephone, electric light, rail and suffrage." In 1895, he met Roosevelt and was sufficiently blown over to swiftly include him in a select pantheon of political men of action, which included such British imperial luminaries as Cecil Rhodes, Alfred Milner, and Joseph Chamberlain.

The American turn to empire enormously enthused Kipling. At last the Yanks were taking up "the White Man's work, the business of introducing a sane and orderly administration into the dark places of the earth." Kipling took it upon himself to advise the junior partner in the Anglo-Saxon civilizing mission. Colonies were "like babies," he wrote to one correspondent. "They are all aggravating at first but they are worth it." In February 1899, just as the Filipinos rose in revolt, he published in *McClure's Magazine* "The White Man's Burden." The poem touched all the chords of Anglo-Saxonism—above all, the racial and hierarchical view of the colonized as "half-devil and half-child," whose "sloth and heathen Folly" would wreck the colonizer's noble mission. The poet's own condescension—chiding the Americans to be done with their "childish days"—appears to have grated on his readers. "Rather poor poetry," said Roosevelt to a senior colleague, adding, however, that it made "good sense from the expansionist standpoint."[18]

A couple of years on, Roosevelt was in the White House overseeing the imperial venture in the Philippines. From this vantage point, British rule in India seemed even more admirable to him. India, he said in January 1908, was "the most colossal example history affords of the successful administration by men of European blood of a thickly populated region in another continent.... [I]t is a greater feat than was performed under the Roman Empire." To be sure, the British had made some mistakes, but their rule had been "for the immeasurable benefit of the natives of India themselves." If British control were wound down, "the whole peninsula would become a chaos of bloodshed and violence."[19] American empire, he held, should go a step further than the British in proclaiming its benevolence. When the Filipinos were "fit to walk alone they should walk alone, but I would not pledge myself as to a definite date for giving them independence.... I would certainly try to prove to islanders that we intended not merely to treat them well but to give them a constantly increasing measure of self-government, and that we should be only too delighted when they are able to stand alone."[20] British liberal imperialists like William Gladstone would have applauded.

However, prominent American critics of the imperial adventure invoked India as a cautionary tale. Andrew Carnegie—the owner of US Steel, the first billion-dollar corporation in the world—was outraged that the advocates of empire, professing freedom and democracy, were prepared to crush the Filipinos' desire for independence. Yet his arguments drew on premises strikingly similar to those of the imperialists. "All communities," he wrote in 1902, "however low they may be in the scale, have the germ of self-government." History, he insisted, "teaches that the influence upon the inferior race of such members of a superior race as go to the Tropics, is injurious to both." The key to his argument was "the Tropics." In America a "superior race" had settled on land inhabited by an "inferior race" and done "genuine good...not to the Indians, but to the cause of civilization as a whole." Standing Seward's argument on its head, Carnegie contended that most Americans would not go to a tropical country like the Philippines owing to its climate. At best a few would, and such "contact is ruinous to both races." British empire in India was the perfect example. "The British cannot grow in India," he insisted. British officials "must have seasons out of that climate," and "British children cannot be successfully reared there." Hence, "the races remain apart," and the British could never trust the Indians "not to strike when opportunity offers."[21]

Populist and three-time Democratic Party nominee for president William Jennings Bryan had been a critic of American imperialism almost from the outset. Following the occupation of Manila, he began informing himself about the British Empire in India, which had become a touchstone for American imperialists. In 1906, Bryan traveled to India to see things for himself. His verdict was stark: "British rule in India is far worse, far more burdensome to the people, and far more unjust...than I had supposed." The rulers of India were good men, but they could not settle and strike deep roots in the country. Such officials could not be "expected to know the needs of the people as well as those who share their daily life and aspirations."

Drawing on conversations with leading Indian liberals such as Dadabhai Naoroji and Gopal Krishna Gokhale, Bryan trotted out statistics on the "drain of wealth" from India to Britain. He also seconded their arguments about the extraordinary levels of military spending in India and the languishing of agriculture. "The poverty of the people of India is distressing in the extreme," he wrote. "Millions live on the verge of starvation all the time." The Indian National Congress's moderate demand for "an increased voice in their local affairs" was denied—on the "unsound" ground that "the Indians would necessarily fight among themselves." Bryan's pamphlet *British Rule in India* cut the British to the quick. The Raj promptly banned it as seditious literature. Bryan nevertheless partook of the racial discourse of Anglo-Saxonism. He was, in fact, a supporter of Jim Crow at home. Thus, he called upon Britain's Christian people to extend to India "the doctrines of human brotherhood that have given the Anglo-Saxon race the prestige that it enjoys."[22]

Such calls to conscience cut little ice with American imperialists, who frequently responded by citing another group of Christians. As President Roosevelt claimed, "I have seen many American missionaries who have come from India, and I cannot overstate the terms of admiration in which they speak of English rule in India and of the incalculable benefits which it has conferred and is conferring upon the natives."[23] Indeed, the American missionaries in India were steeped in the same worldview that impelled their countrymen to hanker after colonies abroad.

BETWEEN RECONSTRUCTION AND WORLD WAR I, American missionary activity surged enormously, propelled by new visions of Protestant Christianity that arose in response to the widespread longing for national regeneration. This bout of religious awakening took such diverse forms as Dwight L. Moody's evangelistic revivals, the rise of Pentecostalism, and the advent of the Social Gospel. A faith-based branch of the Progressive movement, the Social Gospel sought to adapt Protestantism to modernity. The past decades had seen an explosion in industrialization, urbanization, and immigration in America. Unprecedented poverty, dismal working and living conditions, and mounting social tensions had accompanied the prosperity of the Gilded Age. Framing this as a moral as well as an economic and social issue, the Social Gospel sought to ameliorate the problems of the underclasses and the down-at-heel. People, it held, were not inherently evil but pushed into depravity by their social environment. By improving this environment, you could improve the person and so unlock the door to Christ.[24]

Although not a direct product of the Social Gospel, the missions were fired by its liberal theology and belief in progress. The missionaries were also influenced by ideas of muscular Christianity that swept across the country in the 1880s. The muscular Christians sought to meld spiritual and physical regeneration. Institutions like the Young Men's Christian Association (YMCA) offered prayer meetings and Bible study with gyms and swimming pools, blending new notions of manliness with key Social Gospel tenets such as self-control and temperance. As such the movement offered the perfect religious counterpoint to the imperial vision of political leaders like Theodore Roosevelt. What is more, the same Anglo-Saxonism and racial condescension that permeated the quest for overseas empire often saturated the vision of paternalist uplift taken abroad by the missionaries. The Reverend Josiah Strong, secretary of the American Evangelical Alliance, the body responsible for Protestant missions overseas, pulled these diverse strands together and articulated a powerful vision for American missionaries: "The world is evidently about to enter a new era....[I]n this era mankind is to come more and more under Anglo-Saxon influence, and Anglo-Saxon civilization is more favorable than any other to the spread of those principles whose universal triumph is necessary to the perfection of the race to which it is destined; the entire realization of which will be the kingdom of heaven fully come on earth."[25]

The missionary enterprise was thus part of the story of American expansion—albeit culturally and ideologically. While some of its leading lights, like Strong, advocated colonialism—Strong wrote his *Expansion* (1900) to justify the subjugation of the Philippines—the missionary enterprise also had ecumenical and internationalist strains. John R. Mott, a YMCA leader and later Nobel Peace Prize laureate, held that his goal was "to weave together all nations." The real project of the missionaries was not to create formal empires that would offer opportunities for proselytization but to recast the world in accordance with Protestant (American) cultural values. In practice, American missionaries were enmeshed in wider transnational networks of religion, charity, and social uplift.[26]

The YMCA's Student Volunteer Movement (SVM) emblematized the crusading spirit in turn-of-the-century America. Formed in the late 1880s in Dwight Moody's birthplace, Northfield, Massachusetts, the SVM initially drew on students from two hundred colleges. Inspired by Moody, 6,000 SVM enlistees pledged in 1891 to accomplish the "evangelization of the world in one generation" and signed up to go abroad as missionaries. Many more would follow in their wake. Although China

was the major destination, the SVM and other Protestant groups identified South Asia as an important area for the expansion of missionary
activity. If the young missionaries resembled their predecessors who set
out from America during the Second Great Awakening, their approach
to evangelization embraced the new modernism and its emphasis on
doing good works as well as saving souls.

Some of the young American missionaries headed to India already
had roots in the subcontinent. Robert Wilder, to take but one example,
was born in Maharashtra in 1863. His father, Royal Wilder, had been a
Presbyterian missionary in India for three decades starting 1846. Robert grew up speaking Marathi as much as English and had little contact
with other European children. He was a frequent visitor, though, to
the palace of the local maharaja, whose wife supported Mrs. Wilder's
attempts at educating Indian women. Robert followed his father back
to the United States and enrolled at Princeton to study theology and
Sanskrit. At the age of twenty-three, he met Moody and convinced the
latter of the potential for harvesting souls in South Asia and of the
need to send an adequate missionary force. In 1893, Wilder went back
to India as secretary of the college department of the YMCA.[27]

Unlike their predecessors, Wilder and his contemporaries faced a
different and evolving matrix of challenges and opportunities in India.
On the one hand, the growth of Hindu revivalism made their mission
more difficult than ever. Hindu revivalism was itself a response to the
fanning of missionaries across India over the past decades and their
frequently intemperate attacks on the religious beliefs of the people.
Between 1877 and 1888, Hindu crowds in the Madras Presidency had
picketed missionary meetings and stoned their houses. By the 1890s,
though, Hindu revivalism had assumed organizational forms and
struck a more confident note. Even as Wilder was making his way back
to India, Swami Vivekananda set sail for America.

At the Parliament of Religions held in Chicago later that year,
Vivekananda delivered a paper on Hinduism and made a considerable
impression on his audience. The poet Harriet Monroe was in the hall

and later recalled that "Swami Vivekananda, the magnificent,…stole the whole show and captured the town." The *New York Herald* called him "undoubtedly the greatest figure in the Parliament of Religions," while the *Northampton Daily Herald* noted that after his opening lecture "thousands would wait for hours to hear a fifteen minute talk from this remarkable man."[28] After this sensational debut in Chicago, Vivekananda undertook a lecture tour across America, holding forth the Vedanta philosophy as the summit of the Indian mind. These lectures and classes were usually well attended, and the Indian monk developed a keen following among Americans, especially women, who saw India's philosophical idealism as an antidote to the tawdry materialism of the Gilded Age. By the end of his stay in America, Vivekananda had founded three Vedanta Societies—in New York, Los Angeles, and San Francisco.[29]

Vivekananda was not interested merely in imparting high Hindu philosophy to American audiences. He also wished to contest the image of India as a hellish heathen land purveyed by the American missionaries. Every country, he argued, had its social evils. But the missionaries had exaggerated India's undeniable cruelties, while airbrushing out of the picture its appreciable aspects. Further, he accused them of indifference to the real plight of India. In one of his earliest talks in Chicago, he bluntly asked, "You Christians, who are so fond of sending out missionaries to save the soul of the heathen—why do you not try to save their bodies from starvation?" Thousands were dying from hunger owing to "terrible famines" in India, but the missionaries were interested in erecting churches. "It is an insult to a starving people to offer them religion."[30] Vivekananda never sounded a defensive note on missionary activity in India. The message of Christ, he claimed, was not inimical to the best ideals of Hinduism. Yet "the great heart of India," he argued, "is today absolutely untouched by missionary effort. Most of the missionaries are incompetent.… How can a man absolutely ignorant of the people and their traditions, get into sympathy with them?"[31]

The American missions were irate about Vivekananda's turn in America. More importantly, they were concerned about the highly exaggerated accounts of Vivekananda's reception and achievements carried in the Indian press. Such was the adulation of Vivekananda back home that when Mark Twain introduced himself as an American to a Hindu monk in India, the first question was about Chicago. In 1897, the Christian Literature Society of India published the pamphlet *Swami Vivekananda and His Guru* to refute the overblown claims of his impact in America. The YMCA in India also encouraged local Christians to refute Vivekananda and his claims on behalf of Hinduism.

They had reason for worry. For after his return to India, Vivekananda set up the Ramakrishna Mission—named for his master but evidently modeled on the Protestant missions. Vivekananda also picked up the discourse on muscular Christianity in America, arguing that India's national revival required biceps as much as the Bhagavad Gita. But over the next two decades, the YMCA and other missionary groups came to understand the importance of working with the lay of the land. Instead of dinning into their audiences the doctrinal claims of Christianity, they should focus on the social message of Christ and on engaging in respectful dialog with the Hindus. A YMCA conference in 1907 concluded, "We ought to avoid, first, disparaging contrasts, however true in themselves, between the effects of Hinduism and Christianity on the lives and societies of peoples; secondly invidious comparisons between Christ and the heroes of Hinduism.... The Hindu mind is naturally Christian and there are valuable assets in it which we ought to turn to our advantage."[32] The publication six years later of J. N. Farquhar's *The Crown of Hinduism* marked an important turning point in the missionaries' approach to proselytization and Indian faiths.[33]

If Hindu revivalism was one challenge to the missionaries, the rise of Indian nationalism was another. Most missionaries started out in India with some variant of racial Anglo-Saxonism and consequent admiration for the British Raj. George Sherwood Eddy, a twenty-five-year-old graduate of Yale University and Princeton Theological Seminary, came to India in 1896 for the Student Volunteer Movement. Soon, he joined Robert Wilder in the college department of the YMCA. Eddy stayed on in India until 1911, when John Mott appointed him the traveling secretary for all of Asia. Toward the end of his stint in India, he wrote an influential book, *India Awakening*, as a guide to other missionaries heading to the subcontinent.

Eddy began by contrasting the Americans with the Indians. The Anglo-Saxons, he wrote, were "infused with the breath of Christianity and toughened with Teutonic vigor ... enriched by a constant growth in freedom and intelligence." The citizens of a "progressive Western nation" and people of "a single race" could not easily comprehend the myriad divisions and weaknesses of the people of India. "We in the West have developed the ideal of individual liberty"—by separating individual from society, society from state, and custom from law. "In India none of these separations have taken place." To be sure, there was "a ferment of new thought.... [T]here is gradually taking shape a grow-ing national movement." This was owing to a "consciousness of Western supremacy." It was heartening to note that "it is not Manu [the ancient Hindu lawgiver], but Mill and Burke that they are reading." The In-dian National Congress sought swaraj, or "self-government," but "the necessity of a long and patient process of producing an intelligent self-governing and self-disciplined people is not yet fully realized." Amer-icans could "sympathize with all lawful desire for self-government in other people," but such peoples would not be ready for self-rule for a while.

Indians were intoxicated with "the new wine of nationalistic spirit," which made them "forget prudence and self-interest." For British rule was in the best interests of the Indians. The Raj had finally established peace, dug canals, laid roads and railway lines, started educating the people, improved their health, and increased their trade. "In a word," Eddy concluded, "Britain has so well governed as to change the most changeless nation in the world." If Britain withdrew, he warned, "India

would welter in blood, with hopeless internal wars.... The clock of India's history would be put back for centuries."[34]

Eddy was in fact among the more progressive American missionaries in India. But this combination of paternal condescension toward the
Indians and unqualified admiration of the British was unlikely to win
the approval of even moderate Indian nationalists. Indeed, as Indian
nationalism gathered steam during and after World War I, its leaders
began to take umbrage at the stance of the American missionaries. B.
G. Tilak and Mohandas K. Gandhi criticized their attempts at mass
conversion of the lowest castes and the "untouchables." Worse, even
converts were abandoning the missions' fold to enter nationalist politics. Their stance on nationalism, some missionaries realized, would
"bring volcanoes down upon the Europeans," especially themselves. In
consequence, they sought either to support a moderate form of nationalism compatible with British rule or to stay out of nationalist matters
altogether.[35]

Then again, the rare missionary strongly supported the Indian national cause. The Reverend Robert Hume, a missionary of the American Board in the western Indian town of Ahmednagar, was born of
missionary parents in Bombay and regarded India as home. He took a
keen interest in the Indian National Congress almost from its formation in 1886. In 1909, he was elected a delegate to the Congress from
both Ahmednagar and Bombay and played an active role in framing
the resolutions it adopted. In 1918, he was the only American invited
to testify before the Montagu-Chelmsford Commission on reforms in
India.[36]

After World War I, especially following Gandhi's ascent to the center stage of the political arena, several progressive American missionaries became more sympathetic to Indian nationalism. Interestingly
Sherwood Eddy was among those who swung to such a position. Touring India during the war, he had advocated the diversion of resources
to social programs in the rural economy. Along with a friend, Eddy
contributed $10,000 to the Christian Central Bank of Madras. "I know

of no better investment today," he claimed. By the early 1920s, he had become a vocal supporter of the Indian nationalists. While maintaining that British rule in India was "the finest instance I know in history of the governing of one people by another," he insisted that Indian self-determination was "desirable, inevitable and just."[37]

Even as missionaries coped with the rise of Indian nationalism, they found several avenues for expanding their footprint in the subcontinent. For one thing, the American missions substantially scaled up their capacity to deliver quality education to meet a burgeoning demand. By the time India became independent in 1947, they were running no fewer than three hundred high schools, twenty colleges affiliated with universities, and sixty teacher-training institutes. This was possible owing to an extraordinary increase in funding for missionary activity in the Indian subcontinent: from $6,000 in 1812 to almost $6 million a year in the 1920s.[38] The missions made a particularly important contribution to women's higher education. The Methodist Episcopal Church had sent Isabella Thoburn to India in 1869. A year later, she established a mud-walled single-room girls' school in the North Indian city of Lucknow. When she died in 1901, the school had grown into a college. Over the following years, Isabella Thoburn College grew under the leadership of Lilavati Singh, a convert and disciple of Thoburn, into a pioneering first-grade college in India.

By the turn of the century, American missionaries had also begun to play an active role in famine relief and combating epidemics. In 1918, as the influenza pandemic swept across India, Ida Scudder, a doctor from a third-generation missionary family with extensive experience of relief work, set up India's first teaching hospital, the Christian Medical College and Hospital, in the southern Indian town of Vellore. The missionaries' involvement in such activities in turn led them to take in thousands of orphans and then to establish several industrial training institutes across the country where these children learned basic mechanical and electrical manufacturing and repair work. The Indo-American Famine Relief Committee of 1900 financed the first such institutes. Aided by the John Deere Company, the mission in the southern Indian town of Kolar manufactured and marketed a light steel plow. Another institute produced a widely used cotton gin. American missions also established agricultural schools as part of famine relief. These schools focused on farm extension activities and gradually began working on other aspects of rural development.

These experiments led the YMCA to begin rural reconstruction work aimed at "building a rural civilization, which should be Christian to the core" and creating "happy, upright, useful citizenship in village life." Some missionaries felt that they should look beyond the Indian Christian community in rural India. The Reverend Sam Higginbottom held that "missionaries should lead India out of economic bondage into economic freedom." Agricultural training was a central component of this undertaking: "It would give the educated non-Christian Indian opportunity to earn a decent livelihood, and to keep his own independence and self-respect." Toward this end, Higginbottom resolved to establish an agricultural institute in the North Indian city of Allahabad. In 1909, he went back to the United States to arm himself with a degree from Ohio State University. During these years, he also toiled to raise $30,000 for the proposed institute. On returning to India in 1911, he purchased a farm of 275 acres and set to work building the pioneering Allahabad Agricultural Institute.[39]

The most elaborate experiment in rural reconstruction got under way at the other end of the country. Duane Spencer Hatch had come to India in 1916 as part of the YMCA. During the war years, he spent some time with the British Indian Army in Mesopotamia under the auspices of the Indian National Council of the YMCA. In the mid-1920s, after taking a doctorate in rural sociology from Cornell, he returned to India and worked with the YMCA in the southern Indian princely state of Travancore. There he set up a rural development association in the village of Martandam.

Hatch came to Travancore with a coherent set of ideas about rural development that he supplemented with painstaking field surveys and periodic monitoring on the ground. "Self-help," he believed, was "the only way of growth to a permanently happier state." But the Indian villager demonstrated helplessness "beyond belief." Rural India relied almost entirely on a "highly centralized Government." Thus, self-help alone would not suffice. "Self-help with *intimate, expert counsel*," he insisted, was "the way up and out" of the "poverty, backwardness, depression and misery of India."[40]

Such experts should, moreover, take a comprehensive view of the problems in rural India. "The Indian villager is not much benefited unless he is helped simultaneously in every phase of his life and in every relationship he bears to others." This called for tackling at once villagers' religious, educational, physical, social, and economic needs. Hatch espoused a tolerant approach to religion: "A truly deeply religious Hindu and a truly deeply religious Christian...work better together because of the common bond of religion." While Christians would naturally have to take the lead in religious matters, he was open to the Hindus leading a session on their scriptures. It was equally imperative to organize other, nonreligious activities on a "whole community basis" in order to have "a unique opportunity denied to any sectarian or denominational body."

Hatch believed that India's poverty was "largely due to failure in sociality" rather than in economics. Hence, he emphasized the need for the cooperative method. "The people have to be persuaded," he held, "to change from their methods of direct antagonism, isolation and competition to the method of co-operation." Lastly, the cooperative method must be combined with the demonstration method. The best form of demonstration, according to Hatch, "is where the learner demonstrates to himself and to his neighbors at his own farm or home a project or a method with the help and direction of the [expert] demonstrator."

Based on these principles, Hatch set up a model rural reconstruction center in Martandam. He chose the location because "we were not strangers here." The YMCA had been active in the area with its village associations, and one of its rural secretaries had spent seven years setting up rural cooperatives of various kinds. Indeed, it remained central to the Martandam experiment. Over a hundred village associations provided unpaid workers for the project. These included "young school teachers, lawyers, farmers, high school boys"—all imbued with "a spirit of service, [and] above the mean of the village in education and enlightenment."

The Martandam Center was housed on a small, one-acre plot. This provided some space for experimenting with various types of grass for cattle fodder and keeping some bees, poultry, and animals. The superior quality of vegetables grown at the center, however, sparked the community's interest. Hatch and his workers also pushed the villagers to attempt crossbreeding of poultry, suggesting that mating "white Leghorn cocks with country hens...brings a great improvement even in the first generation." They also showed villagers how to make fast-color dyes out of bark, roots, and leaves. The center built a library as well as volleyball courts with the help of the local villagers. Gradually, it became a venue for various events and activities—"lectures by prominent persons, exhibitions, dramas, sports meets, scout and health demonstrations, conferences and week-end study groups"—that drew people from other villages in the area.

The Martandam Center attracted the attention of the British authorities as well as of experts from other Asian countries. Hatch was soon launched on a stellar career as a pioneering figure in rural reconstruction and community development. In the early 1930s, Hatch was invited to Philippines to aid and observe US efforts in rural development. Martandam would also serve as an inspiration to another American, Albert Mayer, who came to India after World War II and helped launch the largest community development program in the world. Hatch was himself a transitional figure. He stood at the cusp of the American missionary tradition, with its paternalist emphasis on social as well as spiritual uplift, and an emerging technocratic, social scientific trend that emphasized expertise for the development of backward societies. The latter would have a long career in postcolonial South Asia.

WHILE THE MISSIONARIES' APPROACH to India grew more nuanced after World War I, their earlier impressions of the subcontinent continued to have considerable purchase on the imaginations of many Americans. Their accounts of the horror, evil, and debauched sexuality of the Hindu religion lingered in American minds long after the missionaries had ceased such discourse on India. Particularly influential here were the letters prepared by turn-of-the-century missionaries for Sunday school children in the United States. Their emphasis on "mountains of superstitions," "the heathens in darkness," and the "Hindu mind" would shape American views of India well into the twentieth century.[41]

The missionaries' impressions of Muslims in India were not as well known back home but stood in sharp relief against the image of the Hindus. Missionary accounts depicted Muslims as violent and authoritarian, arrogant and wicked. But for a "strong Christian power" in India, a missionary opined, the Muslims "would have put all non-Muslims to death." Nevertheless, the missionaries also praised their monotheism and respectful attitude toward Christ and even deplored the dilution of their faith owing to the malign influence of the Indian caste system. Traveling through northwestern India just before the Great War, writer and sometime Unitarian minister Price Collier recorded with admiration, "Never have I seen, in a one hour's walk so many lean, upstanding, fearless-looking, fine-featured, eagle-eyed men."[42]

Collier's views were unmistakably filtered through the ideological lenses of the British Raj. The notion of the "martial races," comprising the Muslims of northwestern India as well as the Sikhs and Gurkhas, was the key organizing principle of the Indian army—one that classed most Hindus as effete and unsuited for the rigors of military life. Many Americans were already familiar with this image of the tough and wily

Muslim fighter as compared to the weak and spindly Hindu owing to the popularity of Kipling's stories. It also became something of a staple in Hollywood. Films like *The Black Watch* (1929) turned on a solitary British officer's saving the Khyber Pass with the support of a small Muslim force during World War I.[43] These myths and fantasies would mold American policy toward the subcontinent after the British divided and quit India.

Americans' encounters with India were not always at second hand, however. While American travelers and missionaries made for the subcontinent, smaller numbers of Indians also landed in America. In 1900, a mere 2,031 Indians had legal permanent resident status in the United States. The Indian immigrants fell into three identifiable groups. The first and largest were Sikhs from the Punjab, who had been recruited into the British colonial police in China and the Far East. On retirement, many of them headed to Canada and the United States in search of second careers. Then there were the younger men—predominantly from the Punjab but also other parts of rural North India—who had settled all along the West Coast from Vancouver and Seattle to Portland and San Francisco. Originally hired by the Western Pacific Railroad to build railways lines in the Pacific Northwest, they moved on to work in lumber, construction, and agriculture. The last group of immigrants were students—largely Hindu men with some Sikh and Muslims—at Stanford University, the University of Washington, a few midwestern and East Coast universities, and, above all, the University of California, Berkeley.[44]

Over the first decade of the twentieth century, the US Indian population rose to 4,664—largely as a result of Canadian immigration policies. From 45 arrivals in 1905 and 387 in 1906, Indian immigrants to Canada rose to 2,124 in 1907 and 2,623 in the following year. A swift backlash from nativists and labor outfits resulted in riots against Indians. In response the Canadian government tightened its immigration laws through such requirements as "continuous voyage" from India and effectively barred Indians from migrating to the country. Denied entry into Canada, many Indians turned south to the United States and began working in the lumber industry of Washington.

Soon they faced the wrath of white American workers who feared the competition of Asian laborers willing to work on the cheap. In September 1907, hundreds of white workers descended on the living quarters of the "Hindus"—as all Indians were labeled—in Bellingham and forced some seven hundred to flee across the border. Later that year nearly five hundred workers in Everett turfed the "Hindus" out of the city. When an Indian attempted to buy property in Port Angeles in 1913, real estate agents published a formal agreement not sell to "Hindoos or Negroes" as they were "generally considered as undesirable."[45] Such incidents stemmed from a combustible cocktail of economic and racial anxieties, but they also fed on the prevalent cultural images of India.

The xenophobic antipathy to Indians was part of a larger nativist backlash against Asian immigrants, especially from China and Japan. Leading this campaign was the Asiatic Exclusion League based in San Francisco. Although the numbers entering the United States from East Asia far exceeded those from South Asia, the Indians found themselves in the league's crosshairs. Its first reports on the "Hindoo question" portrayed the Indian as dirty, untrustworthy, insolent, and lustful. In another report of 1910, the league vented its spleen: "We the people of the United States are asked to receive these members of a degraded race on terms of equality.... [W]hat would be the condition in California if this horde of fanatics should be received in our midst." The popular press vigorously stirred the pot of resentment. *Collier's* carried an article on the "Hindu invasion," drawing on the league's estimate of 10,000 Indians in California alone. A piece titled "The Tide of Turbans" in *Forum* depicted Indians as a "dark, mystic race" and warned that the "Hindoo invasion is yet in its infancy; only the head of the long procession has entered the Golden Gate." The government began to take note. The chief investigator of the Immigration Commission on the Pacific coast proclaimed in 1910 that Indians were the most undesirable of all Asians and the peoples of the Pacific states were unanimous in their desire to keep them out.[46]

In February 1914, the US House Committee on Immigration and Naturalization held "Hindu Immigration Hearings." In his testimony, the commissioner-general of immigration insisted "Hindu" immigration was "a menace to the country, and particularly to California." To the litany of stereotypes he added the "scientific" claim that Indians were diseased—afflicted in particular with hookworm. "The question of protection of the white race," one submission to the committee noted, "makes a study of the diseases of these people more important than even their economic or social characteristics. If the eastern immigrants are likely to deplete the vitality of our people, as the Negro has done, it is a far more serious question than if they merely force an unwelcome economic competition upon us." Representative Denver Church of Fresno, California, claimed, "Those of us who come into contact with the Hindus, and I think it is universal, regard them as a menace." Religious prejudice and sheer ignorance compounded this brisk racism. "They have their religion," said Church. "In fact, it seems to be about all there is to a Hindu, his religion." "Is that the Mohammedan religion?" asked the chairman. "As I understand," replied Church.[47]

The committee did not go with the demand for exclusion owing to the small and dropping numbers of Indian immigrants. Church kept up his tirade, warning the House in August 1914 that a "large per-cent" of India's 350 million people were anxious to bring their "superstitious and backward" culture to America: "Heretofore the most terrible of all the gods was the crocodile and in order to appease the wrath of these scaly and saw-toothed monsters, loving but superstitious mothers cast from the banks of the Ganges their helpless offspring into the crocodile's mouth.... With these ideals in mind, it is plain that the ideals of the Hindu will not fit the notions of the West." The imprint of a century of travelers' and missionaries' impressions was unmistakable.

Although Church failed to accomplish his aims, the Immigration Law of February 1917, passed over the veto of President Woodrow Wilson, eventually achieved the exclusion of "Hindus."[48]

Attempts by Indians in America to lobby against exclusion fell on stony ground. Indeed, by the time the law was passed, the community was on the government's radar for its efforts in support of Indian independence. Political activity among West Coast Indians began in 1908 with the arrival of Taraknath Das. A member of the Anusilan Samiti of Bengal, an outfit that sought violently to overthrow the Raj, twenty-three-year-old Das had fled to New York via Tokyo. After taking a degree in Seattle, he worked as an interpreter in the US Immigration Service—only to be fired for his virulently anti-British outlook. Back in Seattle, Das published his journal, *Free Hindustan*, with the avowed purpose of "political education of the masses for revolution." He also gave frequent lectures to Indian students and settlers on the West Coast, using Sikh communal organizations as a conduit for his political work.[49]

Soon other Indian revolutionaries on the run from the British Raj joined Das. The most prominent was Har Dayal, who had resigned a scholarship at Oxford in protest against the education system in India and provided effective leadership to the West Coast radicals. Aided by Das and other Indians, Dayal set up the Ghadar (Revolution) Party and published a weekly newspaper in English as well as several Indian languages. Dayal believed the United States offered the ideal location for launching a revolution for the liberation of India. It was, he wrote, the perfect place "from which a solitary wandering Hindu can send a message of hope and encouragement to his countrymen." America, he noted, had "lifted [the Indians] to a higher level of thought and action. The great flag of the greatest democratic state in the world's history, burns up all cowardice, servility, pessimism and indifference, as fire consumes the dross and leaves pure gold behind."[50]

Dayal's panegyrics for his adopted country did not, however, endear him to US authorities. After a speech to an anarchist rally in San

Francisco, he was arrested and faced deportation as an undesirable alien. Dayal managed to jump bail, fleeing to Switzerland and thence to Germany, where he carried on the mission of the Ghadar Party. The influence of its propaganda remained strong. As an immigration official noted in 1914, "Most of the Indian students...are infected with seditious ideas. Even Sikhs of the laboring class have not escaped their influence."[51]

In February 1915, the Ghadar Party tasted success when Sikh troops of the Indian army mutinied in Singapore. This was followed by an abortive rising in the Punjab, which the Raj ruthlessly put down. Against the backdrop of the world war, the British Empire began to take Ghadar rather seriously. The British had been concerned about Indian revolutionaries in the United States even before the onset of hostilities. In getting the Wilson administration to crack down on them, they faced a peculiar problem in the person of the secretary of state: the notoriously anti-imperialist William Jennings Bryan. As long as Bryan was in office, the British despaired of netting the seditious Indians in America. Unbeknownst to them, though, the US government was keeping a watchful eye on the Indian radicals. In the event, Bryan's departure from office gave the British an opening to press their case for a combined Indian-German conspiracy against the British Empire masterminded by Har Dayal.[52]

Eager to preserve its neutrality and remain above the fray, the Wilson administration took a dilatory attitude toward British complaints against the Ghadar activists. Only after the United States entered the war did the federal government arrest and prosecute several Americans and Germans, including the consul general in San Francisco, and seventeen Indians of the Ghadar Party on charges of conspiracy to violate US neutrality laws. The "Hindu conspiracy" trial tarred Indian immigrants with the brush of secrecy and diabolical plotting and left their poor public image in tatters. It also took a toll on the Indian community on the West Coast and fissured the Ghadar Party. The well-publicized trial stretched out for five months and ended on a sensational note:

with a senior Ghadar leader being shot dead by another Indian defendant in the courtroom, who was then cut down by a US marshal's bullet. The entire episode fixed the public image of Indian immigrants as "traitors"—a particularly dangerous epithet in a time of war.[53]

Among the Indians who felt the heavy hand of the American state was senior nationalist leader Lala Lajpat Rai. A long-standing member of the Indian National Congress, Rai had first visited the United States in 1906. He returned in 1914 on a six-month trip to collect material for a book on America. With the outbreak of war, the British government pressed the Wilson administration to prevent him from returning to India. So Rai was forced to stay on in America until 1919. His book, *The United States of America: A Hindu's Impressions and a Study*, was published in 1916. It received not only acclaim in India but also favorable notice in the United States, including reviews and profiles of the author in prominent publications such as the *New York Times*.

Two aspects of this careful and well-observed account stood out. The first was his treatment of race relations in the United States. Rai had met with the leading African American figures: Booker T. Washington, John Hope, and W. E. B. Du Bois. In the book, he compared African Americans, in terms of status, with the lowest castes in India and with the Indian under British rule. At the same time, he was impressed by their educational progress owing to black colleges like the Tuskegee Institute. Despite institutionalized discrimination, Rai concluded, African Americans were better off educationally than Indians under the Raj. The second noteworthy aspect was his characterization of the American colonial project in the Philippines. Here the Indian nationalist swallowed the American line, if only to draw an implicit contrast with the British rule in India. The American control of the Philippines, he wrote, had "for its sole object the preparation of the Philippines peoples for Self-Government in their own interests and not in the interests of the United States."[54] Theodore Roosevelt would have applauded.

The radicals of the Ghadar Party did not. Unsurprisingly, they regarded Rai as moderate nationalist clinging to the apron strings of the British Empire. Rai, for his part, took a dim view of their desire to liberate India with the support of Germany. At the same time, he was perturbed by Americans' ignorance of Indian politics and their credulity in consuming British propaganda and the accounts of missionaries. Rai believed that American opinion on India mattered both because of Britain's sensitivity about it and because of "how important American influence was destined to be in the affairs of the world." In consequence, he took upon himself "the function of an Indian nationalist ambassador to America whose duty was to inform the American public about the conditions in India."[55] Shortly after the United States joined the war, Rai set up the India Home Rule League of America. He launched a monthly journal, *Young India*, in January 1918 and established the India Information Bureau six months later.

Woodrow Wilson's Fourteen Points, especially his call for settling colonial questions of sovereignty by giving equal weight to the interests of both the concerned populations and the imperial powers, generated a frisson of excitement among Indian nationalists. Rai wrote in *Young India* that the president's postwar vision was "bound to help all subject peoples of the world in their fight for the right of self-determination." He also cabled Wilson personally, stating that his utterances amounted to "a new charter of [the] world's freedom" and would "thrill the millions of the world's subject races." Rai knew that in calling for self-determination, Wilson did not have India uppermost in mind. Nevertheless, he believed that the war had thrown "the Imperial Powers of Europe into the shade," and they would have no option but to fall in with America's plans for the postwar world.[56]

Rai was not alone in thinking of America as a beacon of hope for India and humankind. Poet and Nobel laureate Rabindranath Tagore traveled extensively in America during the war lecturing on nationalism and its evils. He held that the United States, although far from a perfect democracy, was "unhampered and free to experiment for the progress of humanity. Of course she will make mistakes, but out of these series of mistakes she will come to some higher synthesis of truth and be able to hold up the banner of Civilization. She is the best exponent of Western ideals of humanity." During his stay in America, Tagore developed a strong admiration for Woodrow Wilson and wished to dedicate his book on nationalism to the president. The latter's aide, Colonel Edward M. House, sounded out the British envoy and advised Wilson against granting permission on the grounds that Tagore had "got tangled up in some way" with the Indian revolutionaries of the "Hindu conspiracy." The poet was livid but let the slight pass.[57]

By the time Wilson got to the Paris Peace Conference, Indian nationalists were hectically demanding the right to self-determination. Meeting in December 1918, the Indian National Congress adopted a resolution seeking application of the principle of self-determination to India "in view of the pronouncements of President Wilson." The Congress further sought elected Indian delegates to represent the country at the peace conference. The Muslim League, established in 1906 as a representative body of Indian Muslims, also called for recognition of India's right to self-determination and "the immediate opportunity of freely exercising that right." These hopes were belied. But some nationalists, such as Lajpat Rai, insisted that at least there was strong support for India in the United States and that "an extensive propaganda, elsewhere, particularly in America" must supplement India's efforts in Britain.[58]

Meanwhile, developments in the United States continued to cast a baleful shadow on ties with India. A US Supreme Court ruling in 1923 further squeezed the Indians in America. The Court ruled in *United States v. Bhagat Singh Thind* that immigrants from India settled in the United States were not eligible for naturalization as US citizens. Thind himself had immigrated to the United States in 1913 and enlisted in the US Army during the Great War. He had been granted citizenship twice, but on each occasion the Immigration and Naturalization

Service had cancelled his naturalization. The Supreme Court handed down its judgment on the grounds that an Indian could not count as a "free white person." The Immigration Act of 1924 banned admission of all groups that could not naturalize legally in the United States. The ruling firmly shut the door in the face of immigrants from India. Confronting implacable racism and diminishing opportunities, many Indians chose to return home. The plight of the Indian in America was dramatized in 1929 when Tagore abruptly pulled out of a lecture owing to discourteous treatment by immigration officials—behavior that he felt reflected the anti-Indian bias encouraged by the 1924 act. Tagore was thoroughly disenchanted with America. But Americans were ever more interested in India.

IN THE SPRING OF 1930, developments in India riveted many Americans. Mohandas Gandhi had launched the civil disobedience movement, his second massive mobilization of Indians on the principles of nonviolent noncooperation. His famous "March to the Sea" targeted a global audience. This twenty-four-day walk with a band of followers culminated in a symbolic crushing of the colonial salt monopoly when protestors made salt without paying tax. On the eve of this defiance of Britain's Salt Act of 1882 on the seashore of Dandi, Gandhi sent a special message to America that was carried the next day in the *New York Times*: "I know I have countless friends in America who deeply sympathize with this struggle to secure liberty. But mere sympathy will avail me nothing. What is wanted is the concrete expression of public opinion in favour of India's inherent right to independence and complete approval of the absolutely non-violent means adopted by the Indian National Congress."[59]

In the following weeks, Americans read Webb Miller's reports for the United Press of the British crackdown on Indian protestors. Particularly influential was his account of the Congress volunteers' raid on the salt depot in Dharsana. "In 18 years of reporting in 22 countries," he wrote, "during which I have witnessed innumerable civil disturbances, riots, street fights and rebellions, I have never witnessed such harrowing scenes as at Dharsana." Indeed, he was "perplexed and baffled by the sight of men advancing coldly and deliberately and submitting to beating without attempting defense. Sometimes the scenes were so painful that I had to turn away momentarily."[60]

The US consul general in India, Robert Fraser, wrote to the secretary of state that "Gandhi's influence with the masses is unquestionably enormous and his determination to carry through the campaign planned inflexible.... [N]o one who lives in India has any doubt either of his influence or his sincerity." In the wake of Dharsana and other protests, Fraser took a grim view of the crisis. The various incidents, he reported, "indicate conclusively...that Great Britain is confronted potentially with a more serious and dangerous situation in India than has arisen since 1857." Fraser sympathized with the Indian demand for immediate grant of dominion status or self-government akin to that of Canada and Australia: "There is small hope for them in the British idea of advancing step by step towards Dominion Status, up a Jacob's ladder to which there is no end."[61]

The surge of American sympathy for India prompted the British government to step up its own propaganda in the United States. A stream of British visitors—including Sir John Simon, head of the statutory commission for India—toured America in 1930, rebutting the claims of Indian nationalists and setting out their own vision for India's gradual move toward self-government. They succeeded in swaying the traditional pro-British organs of the American press as well as in forestalling any public reaction by the Herbert Hoover administration. But Gandhi had hooked the popular imagination. In December 1930 *Time* put him on its cover as "Man of the Year." Thornton Wilder's 1934 bestseller *Heaven's My Destination* told the story of George Brush, a midwestern traveling salesman who was also a Gandhian. The incongruities of Gandhi's depiction in American popular culture went further. Cole Porter immortalized him in the hit song "You're the Top" for the musical *Anything Goes*:

You're the top, you're Mahatma Gandhi
You're the top, you're Napoleon Brandy.

Interestingly, among the first Americans drawn to Gandhi were Christian advocates of temperance. William "Pussyfoot" Johnson, journalist and activist in the Prohibition movement, traveled to India in the fall of 1921—just as Gandhi was launching his first country-wide noncooperation movement. Johnson insisted that his trip was not politically motivated. Yet he announced his opposition to "whites, particularly Britishers," who "want their rations of whiskey and soda." Gandhi's movement was of interest to him because of its call to boycott liquor shops. Johnson was impressed by what he saw. Gandhi, he con-cluded, had done "more for temperance reform in two years than any other man has been able to accomplish in that time, in the history of the world."[62]

While Johnson was taking stock of Gandhi's efforts at reform, Gandhi invited another American in October 1921 to confer on the state of the nation. Samuel Evans Stokes III came from a Philadelphia Quaker family. Like many progressive Americans at the turn of the century, young Stokes was active in the YMCA. A chance meeting with an American doctor who was treating lepers in India led him to set out for the hills of Simla. There, Stokes served victims of disaster and disease, pioneered the scientific cultivation of apples, embraced the life of a Hindu monk with the name Satyananda, and eventually married an Indian Christian. Throughout he was active in the Indian National Congress, though of a moderate persuasion that called for gradual po-litical reform under British rule. The massacre of Indians in Amritsar, he would recall, "profoundly shocked me." Thereafter, he swung toward the more militant wing of the party and was elected to the powerful All

India Congress Committee. At the meeting in late 1921, Stokes joined several congressmen, including Jawaharlal Nehru, Vallabhbhai Patel, Lala Lajpat Rai, and C. Rajagopalachari, in handing complete control of the organization to Gandhi for the noncooperation movement. Subsequently, Stokes ended up as a guest of His Majesty's Prisons.[63]

Social reform and nationalist politics aside, Gandhi's unique blend of religion and nonviolence attracted a group of ecumenical American Christians. Their interest underscored the many layers of intellectual exchange that constituted America's relations with India. For Henry David Thoreau, whose transcendentalism owed much to his reading of Hindu texts, had deeply influenced Gandhi's thought and practice. Gandhi had read Thoreau's "The Duty of Civil Disobedience" in South Africa in 1907. It resonated deeply with his own evolving ideas of *satyagraha* and practice of nonviolent noncooperation. Indeed, he exhorted his followers to resist unjust laws and be "so many Thoreaus in miniature."[64]

American interest in Gandhi's nonviolence developed in the wake of World War I. The earlier Social Gospel had focused much on the problem of violence. But the enormous bloodletting in the war fostered a radical pacifism, which infused fresh vigor into religious dissent in America. "People in my age group," wrote Christian pacifist A. J. Muste, "have moved, since their graduation from college in pre–World War I days, out of what many regarded as the dawn of the era of permanent peace into what may, with considerable accuracy, be described as an era of permanent war." A group of Christian pacifists coalesced during the war into an antiwar organization called the Fellowship of Reconciliation, which proved the cradle for an extraordinary group of American thinkers and activists, ranging from Norman Thomas of the Socialist Party to Reinhold Niebuhr of the Americans for Democratic Action, a liberal anti-Communist group in the early Cold War. In the aftermath of the war, many of these Christian pacifists turned toward Gandhi for inspiration and instruction.[65]

On April 10, 1921, John Haynes Holmes, minister of the Community Church of New York, rose to deliver his sermon. A Unitarian graduate of Harvard divinity school, the forty-two-year-old Holmes had been interested in pacifism for over a decade. He had spoken out against the war in Europe as early as 1915 and also offered a pacifist program of reconciliation—a position not particularly popular with his congregation. In 1918, he came across a short write-up, by British Quaker Gilbert Murray, of Gandhi's nonviolent campaign in South Africa. Holmes was much impressed by the emerging Indian leader—due not to any understanding of the Indian political situation but to a feeling of moral and religious affinity with Gandhi. Soon Holmes started to learn more about Indian politics. His political education benefited from the knowledge and experience of another Unitarian minister, Jabez Sunderland, who had gone to India in 1895 and 1896. Like many Unitarians, Sunderland had had a particular interest in the thought of Ram Mohan Roy and his Brahmo Samaj reform movement. During his sojourn, Sunderland had traveled across the country, preaching the gospel of religious and social progress and acquainting himself with the problems of India. He even attended a session of the Indian National Congress. Later, during World War I, he struck up a friendship with Lajpat Rai and became an advocate of self-rule for India. In 1919, Sunderland and Holmes penned an essay for Rai's publication on Wilson's program of self-determination.[66]

Holmes's sermon of April 1921 began with a discussion of the Treaty of Versailles. The peace conference had failed in many ways, especially in bringing forward any figure who could be considered the "greatest man" in the world. Holmes went on to talk about three men who might qualify for the position. The first was French novelist Romain Rolland, leader of the peace movement in Europe during the war. Holmes acknowledged Rolland's immense contribution but described him as an idealist. In sharp contrast stood Vladimir Lenin, the man who had transformed Russia but whose tyrannical methods and lack of "ethical or spiritual principle" met with Holmes's disapproval. Finally, there was Gandhi, a man of whom he had heard only a few years before and with whose writings he had limited acquaintance. Nevertheless Holmes observed, "What we have here—under Gandhi's leadership, is a revolution—but a revolution different from any other of which history has knowledge." Four aspects of Gandhi's work stood out: his intention to free India from British rule; his lack of hatred for the British despite this desire; his policy of *ahimsa*, or nonviolence and noncooperation; and finally, and to Holmes most importantly, his search for "the moral and spiritual regeneration of India on the lines of Indian thought, Indian custom and Indian idealism." This meant both the exclusion of Western influence and the breaking down of caste and religious barriers within India. Yet he insisted that Gandhi's was no parochial project: "There must come a leadership of mankind with peace and amity....His idealism therefore transcends the boundaries of race and country, and seeks to make itself one with the highest hopes of humanity." Holmes had no doubt that Gandhi was the "greatest man" in the world.[67]

Holmes's sermon gained wide publicity and was naturally acclaimed in India. In America it brought Gandhi to public attention, though its reception was mixed. The leading Unitarian internationalist, the Reverend Charles Wendte, hit back with an article criticizing Gandhi's aims and beliefs as "reactionary." India, he conceded, had a right to self-rule like other dominions. But if the country closed itself to Western modernity, it would condemn its people to eternal poverty and backwardness. American admirers of the British Empire were quick to warn their countrymen, "Do not lend an atom of support to Gandhism, which is nothing more or less than the most formidable menace to Western culture and a cleverly devised conspiracy against the progress of civilization."[68]

Holmes's apotheosis of Gandhi struck a chord with other Americans. Writing in the *New York Times* a couple of months later, Clair Price declared Gandhi, "a dark little wisp of a man who looks as if he could be picked up in one's arm and carried off like a child," to be "far and away the greatest man living in the world today. He is a philosophic anarchist, a new Tolstoy without Tolstoy's past. He specializes in reducing his wants. He has fasted so long and so often that he is physically a mere shadow of a man. He is an idea, living for a moment in a frail and brittle body." Around the same time, the *New Republic* carried an article titled "Gandhi—an Indian Saint" by W. W. Pearson, which declared that Gandhi was "a saint, a man of austere and ascetic life who follows Truth at whatever cost to himself."[69]

Like the transcendentalists, the Christian pacifists saw India as an antidote to all that afflicted their own society. Applauding Gandhi's movement of truth, love, and nonviolence, Norman Thomas pleaded, "Help us, you of the East to find the better way." Professor Harry Ward of the Union Theological Seminary said that the world would have to choose between Gandhi's soul force or Lenin's physical force. Drew Pearson of the Society of Friends set up another stark choice: Gandhi's retreat from industrialization or Henry Ford's extension of it. Blanche Watson, a leftist, feminist, and pacifist member of Holmes's church, went to India in 1923 and there published an anthology of American writings in support of Gandhi and the Indian nationalist movement. Three years later Holmes serialized Gandhi's autobiography in his own journal, *Unity*.[70]

Richard Gregg was the first American to undertake a sustained engagement with Gandhi's ideas. Born in 1885 to a Congregational minister, Gregg was imbued with a deep religious faith but disavowed all forms of organized Christianity. After studying mathematics and sciences at Harvard, he turned to law. During the war he worked on the National War Labor Board and became a staunch supporter of labor rights. In 1922, he was active in a railway strike, during which he chanced upon the writings of Gandhi. On New Year's Day 1925, he sailed for India to see Gandhi's ideas in action.

During the four years he spent in India, Gregg approached Gandhian thought from a variety of directions. His book *A Preparation for*

Science sought to suggest ways of teaching science that did not equate it with machinery or Western technology. The next book, *Economics of Khaddar*, was an exposition of Gandhi's ideas about the need to fashion a different economy for India's agrarian society. Only toward the end of his stint in India did Gregg start writing about Gandhian nonviolence, a project that would continue into the next decade with a trilogy of books. Gregg's portrayal of Gandhi differed from those of Holmes and other Christian pacifists. While he agreed that Gandhi stood for universal truths, he also insisted that Gandhi's ideas of nonviolence be seen as part of a larger engagement with modernity and an attempt to transcend its iron cage. On returning to America, Gregg became a prominent advocate of India's freedom and helped set up the American League for Indian Independence, one of the many pro-independence groups that sprang up in interwar America.[71]

In the fall of 1931, Holmes traveled to England for his first meeting with Gandhi, who was in London for a roundtable conference on the political future of India. On Holmes's heels was another Christian intellectual, Reinhold Niebuhr. After his years in the Fellowship of Reconciliation, Niebuhr toggled between pacifism, socialism, and Christian realism. Unlike Holmes, Niebuhr did not seek out Gandhi in London, but his assessment of the man was no less reverential. In an article published in December 1931, he presented Gandhi as a world historical, almost transcendent, figure. Against the backdrop of failed capitalism and failing democracy, he saw Gandhi's ideas as a religiously meaningful and politically efficacious way to pursue "equal justice… the most rational ultimate objective of society." Niebuhr wondered "whether there has ever been a more historic moment in centuries than this visit of Gandhi to London."[72]

A few months later, when he wrote his classic *Moral Man and Immoral Society*, Niebuhr had a more robust view of the world and of Gandhi. Neither the religious moralists nor the liberal rationalists had grasped the "brutal character of the behavior of all human collectivities, and the power of self-interest and collective egoism in all inter-group relations." The responsible Christian, he now argued, had to accept the use of force and work toward mitigating its unavoidably evil effects. In a chapter on Gandhi, he presented the Indian as a "prophet" set apart from the "statesman" who had to deal with the world as he found it. In another instance of the tangled intellectual web that bound the United States and India, Niebuhr's ideas resonated with a leading follower of Gandhi. Jawaharlal Nehru read Niebuhr's book in prison and accepted its central premise about the ineluctable presence of violence. "All life is full of conflict and violence," wrote Nehru in his acclaimed autobiography. "Neither the growth of reason nor of the religious outlook nor morality have checked in any way this tendency to violence." Nehru also embraced Niebuhr's contrast between prophets and statesmen—and invoked it whenever independent India was accused of slipping from Gandhian standards of conduct.[73]

For all its importance, Christian pacifism was not the only vestibule through which Americans accessed India. African Americans, for instance, had a very different notion of why India and Gandhi mattered. The leading black internationalist, W. E. B. Du Bois, had argued for decades about the importance of the "color line": imperialism abroad was linked to racism at home. Du Bois had followed Gandhi's noncooperation movement, going so far as to call him "an exceptional soul." In May 1922, following Gandhi's celebrated trial, Du Bois wrote a trenchant critique of the link between imperialism and racism in the Indian context: "White Christianity stood before Gandhi the other day and, let us all confess, it cut a sorry figure. This brown man looked into the eyes of the nervous white judge and said calmly, "It is your business to enforce the law and send me to jail; or if you do not believe that the law is right, it is your business to resign." Can you imagine such a judge resigning? Gandhi is in jail. So is English Christianity."

Nevertheless, Du Bois remained skeptical about strategies of nonviolence or noncooperation for African Americans. Others, like sociologist E. Franklin Frazier, were more scathing about the applicability of Gandhian ideas: "I fear we would witness an unprecedented massacre of defenseless black men and women in the name of Law and Order and there would scarcely be enough Christian sentiment in America to stay the flood of blood." To many black Americans, Gandhi and India had lessons to teach not about nonviolent protest but about anticolonial activity, unity in the struggle against oppression, and exemplary leadership.[74]

While Indian nationalists had accrued some vocal supporters in the United States, they could hardly count on popular support for India's independence. The controversy kicked up by Pennsylvania journalist Katherine Mayo's *Mother India* drove this home clearly. Published in 1927, the book presented a sensational picture of the most degenerate aspects of Hindu society and advanced the case for continued British rule in India. Its contents were entirely consonant with the images of Indian depravity evoked by generations of American travelers, writers, and missionaries to the subcontinent. And the political tone of the tract was wholly in keeping with the idea of Anglo-Saxon racial superiority as well as the necessary and benevolent effects of Anglo-Saxon imperialism. Gandhi famously dismissed the book as a "drain inspector's report." Prominent American friends of India, including Jabez Sunderland, John Haynes Holmes, and Sherwood Eddy, denounced Mayo's apologetics. Yet the book sold an astonishing 256,697 copies, making it the biggest best seller on India. The fiery public debate around it suggested, however, that American views of empire and India were no longer settled.[75] It would take another world war for the United States to make up its mind about South Asia.

3

FIGHTING FOR FREEDOM

I N THE SPRING OF 1940, as German forces scythed through western Europe, India was convulsed with fear. British officials reported "general bewilderment and some depression and nervousness as to the nearing possibility that India may actually be subject to attack." In many parts of the country, rural and urban, people lined up to withdraw their savings from banks and post offices. Such was the degree of alarm that Gandhi urged people not to behave as if "tomorrow there will be no Government." Nevertheless, he too worried that if Britain and France failed, "the history of Europe and the history of the world will be written in a manner no one can foresee."[1]

In the United States the Nazi victories evoked more mixed reactions. As *Life* observed in its June 3, 1940, issue, "The German victories brought shock and deep fear into the United States, but they brought also a consciousness of national strength. The old nations of Europe may fall before the conqueror but the young, strong giant of the West will meet any challenge that Adolf Hitler dares to make." This sense of power also permeated the administration of Franklin D. Roosevelt. A few months later, Adolf Berle Jr., assistant secretary of state and long-time advisor to President Roosevelt, wrote in his diary, "I have been saying to myself and other people that the only possible effect of this war would be that the United States would emerge with an imperial power greater than the world had ever seen."[2]

From the outset, the Americans were confident that they would impose their imprint on the postwar world. This assurance stemmed from awareness of the extraordinary margin of power that the United States could command over its rivals and friends. Indeed, the Americans had begun to plan for the war's aftermath well before they had joined it.

The mid-1930s was the high watermark of American "isolation-ism." As a doctrine, isolationism comprised many strands that commanded varying degrees of public assent. Ruthlessly simplified, it amounted to the belief that the United States, shielded adequately by two oceans, should avoid embroilment in external alliances or wars, that the nation's economic interests overseas were small in comparison with its domestic market, and that it should promote liberal values by demonstration rather than imposition. The Roosevelt administration was sensitive to the currents of isolationism swirling through the American populace. Yet by the time the United States was pulled into the war, public opinion had begun to shift away from isolationism. And the United States began to plan not just to win the world war but to shape the world order afterward.

"We are not isolationists," President Roosevelt had declared in 1936, "except insofar as we seek to isolate ourselves completely from war." At the same time, he maintained, it was a "vital interest…that the sanctity of international treaties and the maintenance of international morality be restored."[3] Once the United States entered the war,

Roosevelt sought to create—after the defeat of Germany and Japan—an international security organization capable of deterring or defeating any country that menaced others with aggression.

An essential complement to this vision of a liberal, law-governed world order was thriving international commerce. Although the United States had pulled out of the London Economic Conference of 1933, a meeting of sixty-six nations to agree on measures to, among other things, combat the Great Depression, and had embarked on an attempt to reflate the American economy via the New Deal, Roosevelt and his colleagues—especially Secretary of State Cordell Hull—remained committed to reducing tariff barriers by the extension of the "most-favored nation" principle. In particular they sought to push this agenda forward in bilateral settings through the Reciprocal Trade Agreements Act of 1934.

This course was not shaped by a straightforward drive to secure foreign markets as part of a renewed "open-door" policy. At the turn of the century, the United States had demanded of the imperial powers carving up China that they respect the principle of equal commercial opportunity in their spheres of influence. The United States had neither questioned the existence of these spheres nor sought anything more than "perfect equality of treatment for…commerce and navigation with such 'spheres.'"[4] Now economic, strategic, and ideological concerns were entwined in various ways in the Roosevelt administration's vision of a liberal, capitalist world order.

As the global economy fragmented into autarkic zones, and as Japan and Germany went on the offensive in Asia and Europe, Roosevelt became convinced that the war was a consequence of the closing of the world economy. After the war, he declared, "The United States must use its influence to open up trade channels of the world in order that no nation need feel compelled in later days to seek by force of arms what it can gain by peaceful conference." Business internationalists were worried about whether "the American capitalist system could continue to function if most of Europe and Asia should abolish free enterprise." A variant of this concern about the feasibility of capitalism in one country was that access to foreign markets was essential to reducing government intervention in the American economy in order to harmonize domestic production and consumption. Hull emphasized both of these aspects when he told a Senate committee in February 1940, "The question of survival or disappearance of free enterprise is bound up with the continuation or abandonment of the trade agreements program."[5]

A State Department report in December 1943 briskly summarized the many reasons for which the Roosevelt administration aimed at promoting a liberal, capitalist world order: "A great expansion in the volume of international trade after the war will be essential to the attainment of full and effective employment in the United States and elsewhere, to the preservation of private enterprise, and to the success of an international security system to prevent future wars."[6] The desire for full employment indicated that the capitalist order envisioned by postwar planners would differ as much from that of the gold standard era as would the international security order from the old balance of power or the League of Nations.

In attaining the purposes of such preponderant power, the Roosevelt administration perceived the British Empire as a major stumbling block. The imperial preference system instituted at the 1932 British Empire Economic Conference in Ottawa, convened in response to the global depression, had erected a high tariff wall around the entire British Commonwealth but allowed low duties on goods traded between countries of the empire. Not only did American exporters find their largest export market fenced by higher tariff rates, but the Americans believed the continuation of imperial preference after the war would encourage other countries to institute similar policies and so keep the world economy divided into blocs. Dismantling this system became a key American objective.

The negotiation of a master lend-lease agreement in early 1941 gave the United States an opportunity to lean on Britain to open up the

Ottawa system. The British delegation led by John Maynard Keynes refused to make any promises.[7] The Anglophile assistant secretary of state, Dean Acheson, tartly observed that after obtaining such vast quantities of American aid, the British must "not regard themselves as free to take any measures they chose directed against the trade of this country." After almost a year of wrangling, the British consented to cooperate in securing the "elimination of forms of discriminatory treatment in international commerce." Prime Minister Winston Churchill nonetheless clarified that this was not tantamount to an advance commitment to repeal imperial preferences.[8]

Colonial monopolies were also one reason why Roosevelt and his advisors sought to prepare the ground for gradual decolonization in Asia and Africa. The continued exploitation of colonial peoples, they worried, could touch off a wave of revolutionary violence leading to further wars. "The colonial system means war," said Roosevelt to his son in 1943. "Exploit the resources of an India, a Burma, a Java; take all the wealth out of these countries, but never put anything back into them, things like education, decent standards of living, minimum health requirements—all you're doing is storing up the kind of trouble that leads to war."[9] This did not, however, mean that Roosevelt and his colleagues regarded all colonial peoples as ready for independence. On the contrary, they shared the turn-of-the-century ideology of the civilizing mission of advanced peoples and their obligation to ensure that their "little brown brothers" were responsibly shepherded into freedom and modernity. As Roosevelt told Churchill in 1943, "In regard to the Far East in general, which means the yellow race, which is far more numerous than the white, it will be to the advantage of the white race to be friends with them & work in cooperation with them, rather than make enemies of them & have them eventually use all the machines of western civilization to overrun & conquer the white race."[10] Hull clarified to a British minister that while the United States sought to provide "encouragement" to colonial peoples, "this was not with any view to their being given, tomorrow or next week, complete independence as separate entities, but to offer them, at some point when they could prove they were capable of independence, the possibility of so conducting their political development that they might be able to hope for this achievement." The American colonial experience in the Philippines provided the template for the Europeans.[11]

Instead of old-style European imperialism, Roosevelt envisioned a process of gradual, supervised decolonization by means of an international "trusteeship" under American oversight.[12] The Americans were also concerned that British, French, and Dutch imperial subjects in Asia would be susceptible to the siren song of Pan-Asian ideas already emanating from Tokyo. In consequence, the new "imperial power" envisaged by Berle that stood ready to dislodge the older ones was self-consciously anti-imperial. This "imperialism of anti-imperialism" was obviously an unstable compound and pulled the Roosevelt administration in contending directions. The president's notoriously evasive style accentuated these ambiguities. As Secretary of War Henry Stimson put it, a discussion with Roosevelt was "very much like chasing a vagrant beam of sunshine around a vacant room."[13]

As with imperial preferences, the American stance on decolonization had to triangulate between the wartime imperatives of defeating Germany and Japan and the postwar objectives of creating a peaceful and prosperous international order buttressed by the United States' unprecedented hegemony. All these considerations shaped US policy toward India during World War II.

ON SEPTEMBER 3, 1939, Viceroy Lord Linlithgow declared war on India's behalf without consulting Indian opinion of any shade. Although Indian political parties ran the provinces of the Raj, the viceroy did not see the need to sound anyone out. Piqued by his refusal to make any commitment on India's political future, the ministries of the Indian National Congress resigned in October 1939. Thereafter the viceroy and the Congress remained at loggerheads. As the latter

refused to offer unconditional cooperation with the war effort, Linlithgow sought to pull together a range of parties and individuals—the
Muslim League, the Hindu Mahasabha, the "untouchables," the princes
of India—opposed to the premier nationalist party.

Linlithgow insisted that the Congress did not speak for all of India.
Indeed, no discussion of India's political future could paper over the
differences between the Congress and these other groups. In particular,
Linlithgow encouraged the leader of the Muslim League, Mohammed
Ali Jinnah, to state explicitly that group's differences with the Congress.
The league's ensuing demand for a separate homeland for the Muslims
of the subcontinent—"Pakistan"—handily helped the Raj keep the
Congress at bay. In Winston Churchill, Linlithgow found a powerful
ally for his policy of rock-ribbed imperialism.

Prior to 1939, the United States had evinced no strategic interest in India. But soon after the war broke out, desk-level officials in
the State Department began arguing, "The Indian attitude towards the
War is of great importance." They told Assistant Secretary of State
Berle—head of the Near Eastern division dealing with India—that
there were "large American interests in India." Meanwhile, most American officials in India looked sympathetically at the Congress's protests
against the viceroy's policy and conduct. By May 1941, the US consul
general, Thomas Wilson, had concluded that the situation in India was
"very serious indeed." The viceroy was a man of "small vision" and too
hidebound to handle the crisis.[14]

The British cabinet was alert to American opinion about India. Indeed, hardly any major decision on India was made without reference
to its impact on public opinion in the United States. To keep a closer
tab on and shape American opinion, the British government proposed
to the State Department in April 1941 the appointment of a senior
Indian official to its embassy in Washington. The State Department
expressed no objection to the proposed "agent-general" of India but
sought and obtained the reciprocal appointment of its own "commissioner" in New Delhi.[15]

The State Department's demand reflected its increasing awareness of India's strategic importance. India had recently joined the lend-lease system, approved by the US Congress in March 1941. The Roosevelt administration knew of India's contribution to the war effort. As the US Treasury noted in May 1941, India had already mobilized over 300,000 men and could "greatly increase" the number. It had dispatched "important forces" to fight in North and East Africa and provided garrison troops for the Far East. The Allied operations in Iraq and the Persian Gulf were based entirely in India. What is more, India had made a "most important contribution" to war supplies. In order to fully mobilize its "enormous basic internal resources," it needed to be able to "import finished and semi-finished manufactures and certain materials." And these could only come from the United States.[16]

Around this time, the State Department was increasingly concerned about the volatile situation in the Middle East. The urgency of dealing with that region pushed to the fore the political problem of India. Secretary of State Hull met the British ambassador and former viceroy of India, Lord Halifax. When Hull raised the possibility of further "liberalizing" moves toward India, Halifax countered that conditions in India were "really very good." Indians had self-government in provinces and been offered seats on the viceroy's council. Despite Gandhi's opposition, Indian sentiment was strongly with Britain. Halifax maintained that his government did not think it "feasible or even necessary now to make further liberalizing concessions."[17]

In the summer of 1941, Franklin Roosevelt and Winston Churchill met at Placentia Bay off the coast of Newfoundland. Although the main objective was to cement the Anglo-American alliance, a statement of war aims—the Atlantic Charter—caught the world's attention. The charter had in fact emerged without much discussion. The British draft of a joint statement had read, "They respect the right of all people to choose the form of government under which they will live; they are concerned only to defend the rights of freedom of speech and of thought without which such choosing must be illusory."

Undersecretary of States Sumner Welles, however, felt that the US Congress and public were unlikely to support such a sweeping pledge to defend rights abolished by Nazi Germany. So Roosevelt suggested removing the second clause and substituting it with "and they hope that self-government may be restored to those from whom it has been forcibly removed." Churchill agreed and added "sovereign-rights and" before self-government. All this obviously referred to European countries under enemy occupation.[18]

Yet the Atlantic Charter took wing in the colonial world. The Burmese premier asked if it applied to his country and dashed off to London to obtain an answer. Hindu nationalist leader V. D. Savarkar wrote to Roosevelt, urging him to state whether the Atlantic Charter applied to India and if the United States guaranteed freedom to India within a year of the war's end. If the United States did not reply in the affirmative, "India cannot but construe this as another stunt like the War aims of the last Anglo-German war." Indeed, the response to the Atlantic Charter was comparable in enthusiasm to that roused among colonial subjects by Woodrow Wilson's Fourteen Points after World War I. But Churchill snuffed out any such suggestion of applying the Atlantic Charter to India. On September 9, he told the House of Commons that the relevant part of the charter applied only to countries under Nazi occupation and did "not qualify in any way" to British rule in India.[19]

The reaction in India to Churchill's clarification was universally critical. Gandhi was witty as usual: "What is the Atlantic Charter? It went down the ocean as soon as it was born! I do not understand it. Mr. Amery [secretary of state for India] denies that India is fit for democracy, while Mr. Churchill states the Charter could not apply to India. Force of circumstances will falsify their declarations."[20] Consul General Wilson told the State Department that Churchill's statement was a "most unfortunate pronouncement" and went "far towards banishing perhaps forever" any goodwill in India. As for the Indian government, he said, there was "no leadership worthy of the name anywhere to be found."[21]

State Department officials urged their superiors to bring the matter to the president's notice. Welles yet again threw a wet blanket on their efforts. He conceded that if the charter had "any real meaning, it should be regarded as all-inclusive" and hence applicable to India. Yet the United States was currently "facing a question of expediency." Halifax had told him that British officials unanimously opposed an immediate grant of dominion status to India, which would trigger "internal dissension in India on a very wide scale" and leave the country totally useless for the war effort. American officials, Welles insisted, were not familiar with the problems of India. Nor did the issue mean "very much to public opinion" at home. Above all, Churchill would feel that the administration was taking advantage of British dependence on America to force its hand against his considered judgement.[22] Thus, anticolonial views had to be set against strategic imperatives—both of using India for the war and of securing the newly crafted alliance with Britain.

In the wake of Pearl Harbor in December 1941, thinking within the administration underwent important changes. Apart from advocates in the State Department, intelligence officials in the Office of Coordination of Information argued that the United States must help arrest the downward political spiral in India.[23] Thus, when Churchill came to Washington two weeks after Pearl Harbor, Roosevelt gingerly broached the question of India. Churchill claimed to have "reacted so strongly and at such length that he [Roosevelt] never raised it verbally again." Toward the end of his trip, the prime minister confidently cabled his colleagues that they would not have "any trouble with American opinion."[24] This judgment would prove premature.

THE FALL OF SINGAPORE on February 15, 1942, alarmed the State Department. Berle argued that they must "immediately get to work," and the "first item on the list ought to be to tackle the Indian problem in a large way." He called for a joint Anglo-American announcement that India would be brought in "as a full partner in the United Nations."

Further, the viceroy should be directed to convene a "constitutional conference" in India. Even if the Congress did not join at this stage, its stance would determine whether or not India cooperated in waging the war. Importantly, Berle noted that President Roosevelt had "indicated his sympathy" for the view that London must promptly recognize India's aspiration to "a freer existence and a full membership in the British family of nations."[25]

The president's sentiment received reinforcement from a variety of directions. A "serious undercurrent of anti-British feeling" flowed among senators, who argued that having done "so much" for Britain through lend-lease, the United States was well positioned to "dictate to England" on its empire. One senator went so far as to declare that "Gandhi's leadership in India became part of America's military equipment." Only accepting "Gandhi's political objective" could secure India's contribution.[26]

The president also heard at first hand from a young and articulate member of the Congress party who had been touring the United States: Kamaladevi Chattopadhyay. Invited to tea by Mrs. Roosevelt, she was pleasantly surprised when the president asked her some questions. He told her,

> You may be aware that I feel strongly on India's right to freedom. It is one of the questions on which Churchill and I have clashed. The war in my opinion has accelerated the urgency of its solution. He gets impatient over what he feels is our inability to see how vital India is to their successful conduct of the war; and irritated over our interfering in their affairs as he calls it. On this, at one point, I had to rather jocularly but appropriately remind him this was natural as at one stage we were in the same position as India now is.[27]

Lastly, intelligence and strategic assessments shaped the president's thinking. The Office of Coordination of Information now held that

India "might well be the decisive element in the war in southeast Asia." Arguing that India "lights a gleam in the eye of the German and the Japanese," the assessment concluded that the "Allied cause *requires* that India should cooperate more vigorously in the war than heretofore."[28]

On February 15, 1942, Roosevelt himself drafted a tough letter to Churchill. After commenting generally on Britain's attitude toward its colonies—out of date by a decade or two—and contrasting it with America's record in the Philippines, Roosevelt wrote that the Indians felt that "delay follows delay and therefore that there is no real desire in Britain to recognize a world change which has taken deep root in India as well as in other countries." There was, he concluded, "too much suspicion and dissatisfaction in India." Hence, its resistance to Japan was not wholehearted.[29] Roosevelt mulled on the letter late into the night. He hesitated to send it, feeling that "in a strict sense, it is not our business." At the same time, India was of "great interest" from the standpoint of conducting the war. Eventually, he decided against sending the letter to Churchill. Instead he asked his representatives in London, John Winant and Averell Harriman, to send him an assessment of Churchill's thoughts on India.[30]

Meanwhile, the British cabinet had stormy meetings about how to deal with the situation in India. At the insistence of Clement Attlee, the senior Labour Party leader in the War Cabinet who would presently be appointed deputy prime minister, Churchill reluctantly agreed to send Stafford Cripps to negotiate a settlement for India. The viceroy was aghast and threatened to resign. In explaining the decision to him, London stressed the "pressure [from] outside, upon Winston from Roosevelt" as a prime factor.[31] The Cripps mission was clearly intended to head off further American intrusion into Indian affairs. It was impeccably timed. Hours later, the Roosevelt administration announced an advisory mission to assist the war effort in India. Significantly, the head of the mission, Louis Johnson, was appointed as the president's special representative.[32]

The next day Roosevelt wrote directly to Churchill. Expressing "much diffidence," he held out for India lessons from American history. Between 1783 and 1789, the thirteen states had formed a "stop-gap government" under the articles of confederation, an arrangement replaced by the union under the US Constitution. Roosevelt suggested setting up a "temporary Dominion Government" in India, headed by "a small representative group, covering different castes, occupations, religions and geographies." This government would have executive and administrative powers over finances, railways, telegraphs, and other "public services." It could also set up a body to consider a more permanent government for India. Having, put forth these radical ideas, Roosevelt wrote, "For the love of Heaven don't bring me into this, though I do want to be of help. It is strictly speaking, none of my business, except insofar as it is a part and parcel of the successful fight that you and I are making."

Cripps's proposal envisioned eventual dominion status for India. After the war an assembly representative of all parties and the princes would draw up a new constitution. Acknowledging the Muslim League's demand for Pakistan, the proposal suggested letting any dissenting province secede. More immediately, Indian leaders would be invited to participate in the war effort. Interestingly, Cripps failed to make headway owing to differences with Congress leaders on the immediate arrangements: the latter sought an Indian defense minister and cabinet-style functioning. Although there were differences on postwar plans, especially the provision for secession, these were not the stumbling block.

By the time Louis Johnson reached Delhi, the Cripps mission was on the brink of collapse. In his first cable, Johnson requested that the president intercede with Churchill to prevent its failure. Although Roosevelt refused to intervene, he wanted to be kept abreast of developments. Thereafter, Johnson worked hectically with Cripps and Jawaharlal Nehru to hammer out an arrangement satisfactory to both sides—but to no avail.[33] Johnson pinned the blame squarely on Churchill's chest. Cripps and Nehru could overcome the problem "in 5 minutes if Cripps had any freedom or authority." London, he wrote, "wanted a Congress refusal."[34]

On the afternoon of April 11, Roosevelt sent a private message to Churchill urging him to postpone Cripps's departure from India for "a final effort." The president apprised Churchill of the mood in America. "The feeling is almost universally held here" that Britain was unwilling to go the distance despite concessions by the Congress party. Roosevelt warned that if the negotiations collapsed and Japan invaded India, "the prejudicial reaction on American public opinion can hardly be over-estimated." But Cripps had already decamped. Churchill sent Roosevelt a soothing reply: "Anything like a serious difference between you and me would break my heart and surely deeply injure both our countries at the height of this terrible struggle."[35]

At Louis Johnson's urging, Nehru wrote directly to Roosevelt, expressing the Congress's continued eagerness "to do our utmost for the defence of India and to associate ourselves for the larger causes of freedom and democracy."[36] After his exchange with Churchill, Roosevelt chose not to reply to Nehru. Gandhi's statements on the United States worsened matters. Even as American troops began to disembark in India, Gandhi told the press that the United States should have stayed out of the war. Criticizing racial policies in that country, he added that Americans were "worshippers of Mammon." The following month, he called the presence of American soldiers in India a "bad job" and the country itself a "partner in Britain's guilt."[37] The British embassy in Washington projected Gandhi's subsequent calls for Britain to leave India as indicative of his alleged sympathy for Japan.

Gandhi's references to racism, however, evoked a positive response from campaigners for equal rights for African Americans. These men and women sought explicitly to link racism in America with imperialism in India. The executive director of the National Association for the Advancement of Colored People, Walter White, orchestrated this campaign. In the aftermath of the Cripps mission, White sounded out influential African Americans, including W. E. B. Du Bois and A. Philip Randolph, about urging President Roosevelt to send an American mission to mediate between the British and Congress party. The mission, he added, should include "a distinguished American negro." Du Bois had already slammed the British empire for having "caused more human misery than Hitler will cause if he lives a hundred lives." "It is idiotic," he wrote in *People's Voice*, "to talk about a people who brought the slave trade to its greatest development, who are the chief exploiters of Africa and who hold four hundred million Indians in subjection, as the great defenders of democracy." White's idea also received the qualified support of Pearl Buck and Wendell Wilkie, the Republican presidential nominee in 1940. Eventually, White wrote directly to Roosevelt, suggesting a commission to India and the drafting of a "Pacific Charter which will assure to all peoples of the world that the era of white domination of colored peoples is ended." Welles, however, criticized the idea on the grounds that "Indians, despite their dark complexion, do not regard Negroes as their equals."[38]

State Department officials were also impressed by the detailed analysis of the Indian political situation by their China specialist, John Paton Davies, who was in India at the time. Like many American diplomats of his age and background, Davies opposed British imperialism. Yet he also felt that the Indians were not ready to take control of their own affairs.[39] Thus he wrote, "It would seem to be both much too late and much too early for an orderly solution to the problem of India." After extensive meetings with political leaders of all stripes, he was deeply pessimistic: "I am not at this juncture persuaded that any interim political formula can be found which will rally the diverse Indian elements behind the United Nations war effort." Any such effort deemed necessary on military grounds should be undertaken "only with the utmost discretion and caution."[40]

In its bid to sway American opinion, the Congress party eventually found some influential allies: American journalists who had descended on India in the summer of 1942. To be sure, not all of them were sympathetic to the Congress's stance. But at least two notable voices weighed in on their behalf: Louis Fischer and Edgar Snow. On returning home, Fischer and Snow wrote important pieces drawing on numerous conversations with Indian and British leaders. These articles at once punched holes in British propaganda about the Cripps mission and presented a sympathetic account of the Congress's predicament. While Fischer's essays focused on the reasons behind the botching of the Cripps mission, Snow focused on its consequences. Cripps's failure, he wrote, had exacerbated Indians' considerable mistrust of the British government. Taking a broader view, he added that the humiliating defeat and withdrawal of British forces from Malaya, Singapore, and Burma had made a hefty dent in the prestige of the Raj. India, he concluded, was the Allies' last bastion. Its fall would endanger China and the Middle East.[41]

The Roosevelt administration found itself pulled in different directions by the desire to burnish its anti-imperialist credentials and by the need to keep the British empire on its side. In a speech on July 23, Hull stated, "There is no surer way for men and nations to show themselves unworthy of liberty than, by supine submission and refusal to fight, to render more difficult the task of those who are fighting for the preservation of human freedom." Although he did not name India in the speech, the target was evident.[42] In private, Hull told the Indian agent-general, Sir Girja Shankar Bajpai, that Gandhi was "evidently doing all in his power to play into the hands of the Japanese by preaching non-resistance and that no practical steps of resistance were being advocated by the other leaders, including Nehru." Yet Vice President Henry Wallace noted that Roosevelt continued to express "a very profound concern about India and a definite belief that England has not handled India properly."[43] But as India lurched inexorably toward another round of mass protests, Washington merely looked on.

Aware of the misrepresentation of his stance by British propaganda in the United States, Gandhi decided to reach out directly to

Roosevelt. Prior to Fischer's return home, Gandhi asked him to carry a letter as well as to convey a verbal message to the president. "I hate all war," wrote Gandhi. But he also knew that his countrymen did not share his abiding faith in nonviolence in the midst of the raging global conflict. Gandhi advanced a straightforward suggestion. India should be declared independent, and the Allies should sign a treaty with the free government of India, which would allow their troops to stay on in the country for the purpose of "preventing Japanese aggression and defending China."[44]

On arriving in America in early August, Fischer sought a meeting with the president to share Gandhi's message as well as his own impressions of the situation in India. Roosevelt was tied up, so Fischer was asked to brief the secretary of state. Fischer, however, wrote again to Roosevelt, emphasizing that the Congress party might lurch toward civil disobedience. "A terrible disaster may be impending in India." Gandhi had explicitly said to him, "Tell your president that I wish to be dissuaded [from civil disobedience]." The viceroy, Fischer added, was hardly inclined to do so.[45]

By this time, however, the Roosevelt administration was not open to intervening in India. The president had no desire to break with Churchill, especially when the Congress seemed set on civil disobedience. He even seemed to have bought into the British argument that any immediate move toward freedom would only lead to a civil war in India. "One thing is certain," Roosevelt noted in a meeting of the Pacific War Council on August 12, 1942, "open hostilities in India will slow up the United Nations war effort."[46] The same day, he wrote to Secretary of Interior Harold Ickes, who was "gravely concerned" about the Indian situation, "You are right about India but it would be playing with fire if the British Empire were to tell me to mind my own business!"[47]

Three days later, as the impending revolt against the Raj gathered steam, Hull pointed out to the president that they had expressed to Britain their "unequivocal attitude" about the need for change in India on the basis of agreement between the government and the Congress party. "Our attitude," he added, "has not been one of partisanship toward either contender." It was not clear that they could do more.[48] The president agreed.

THE QUIT INDIA REVOLT was, as the viceroy noted, the most serious challenge to British rule since the great rebellion of 1857–1858. The Raj responded not only by sweeping the Congress leadership into prison but with a brutal military crackdown across India. It used aircraft to gun down large crowds, lobbed mortars and gas shells at armed rebels and unarmed protestors, and introduced draconian legal provisions to suppress freedom of speech, expression, and congregation. Strict censorship ensured that the American newspapers reported none of this. In any case, the latter had turned sharply critical of the Indian National Congress.

Most Indian sympathizers in the United States felt that India was being unfairly targeted in the American press. As University of Chicago physicist (and future Nobel laureate) Subrahmanyan Chandrasekhar wrote to his father, "I am afraid that many harsh things have been said about her…and India continues to be the most maligned country. All this has been very painful."[49] Groups like the India League and the India Round Table sought to lobby the Roosevelt administration to intervene in the crisis. Over eighty African American intellectuals wrote a joint letter to President Roosevelt urging him to move decisively to resolve the Indian problem. Walter White sent a telegram to the president, claiming "Japan won a great victory in the Pacific Saturday when Gandhi, Nehru and Azad [Congress president] were thrown into prison."[50] Sherwood Eddy, missionary and longtime head of the YMCA in India, offered his services as a mediator and presented a proposal for settlement apparently drafted by Indian Hindus and Muslims in the United States. Several major labor unions passed resolutions calling for American participation in an Indian settlement.

Almost 1,000 people showed up at pro-India demonstrations in New York and Washington, DC, in August and September 1942.[51]

Nevertheless, American public opinion shifted away from the Congress party in the immediate aftermath of the Quit India revolt. Opinion polls by Hadley Cantril in July and August 1942 indicated the changing mood in the United States. In July, 43 percent said that India should get full freedom: 23.7 percent wanted immediate independence, 16.8 percent wanted it after the war, and the rest were unsure. On the other hand, 17 percent opposed granting independence to India, while 34 percent remained undecided. In August 43 percent still favored full freedom for India, but only 19.8 percent thought it should be given immediately, while 20.2 percent felt it should come after the war, and the rest were undecided. Further, those opposed to independence rose to 23 percent, with 29 percent undecided.[52] The results of these polls, shared directly with President Roosevelt, appear to have fortified his "hands-off" policy.

Indeed, the Roosevelt administration was largely impervious to various calls for intervention in India. Adolf Berle told J. J. Singh of the India League that although the United States had "through all our history" been anticolonial, "if we had to choose between the defense of India and the immediate independence of India, we would choose defense." When Senator George W. Norris wrote to Roosevelt that the crisis in India had him "worried beyond measure," the president replied, "The civil disobedience campaign, started at the time when the Japanese army is on their frontier, plainly tends to not the freeing of India, but to its capture by the Japanese, who do not propose to free anybody." He assured Norris that he would take advantage of any suitable opportunity to do something constructive on India, but in meantime "one-sided agitation" was not helpful.[53]

The British, for their part, remained concerned about the state of American opinion. They stepped up their propaganda campaign in the United States, which included such creative measures as a tour by

Henry Polak, a close associate of Gandhi in South Africa. Polak spent fourteen months traveling, lecturing, and writing in America, all the while criticizing his erstwhile friend and praising the benevolence of the Raj. Nevertheless, in late October 1942, Wendell Wilkie enraged Churchill by launching a broadside against the British Empire. "We mean to hold our own," the prime minister famously declared on November 10, 1942. "I have not become the King's First Minister in order to preside over the liquidation of the British Empire."[54]

Churchill had already managed to persuade the Roosevelt administration not to send Louis Johnson back to India.[55] The British Foreign Office, however, felt that they must take more considered steps to keep Americans on their side. The mandarins in Whitehall suggested getting Washington to send "a really high-calibre American in whom we have confidence" as "our best hope of keeping the United States government straight regarding India." The Roosevelt administration promptly agreed and appointed William Phillips as personal representative of the president.[56]

A distinguished career diplomat and friend of Roosevelt, Phillips was the embodiment of the East Coast aristocracy. Everyone, including the British, regarded him as the least likely to go native in India. Still, in his briefing to Phillips, Hull emphasized that Americans could not become "partisans" on India: "We cannot bring pressure, which might reasonably be regarded as objectionable, to bear on the British." Such pressure would result "in a possible disturbance of the unity of command and of cooperation both during and following the war." While the administration hoped that a "practical settlement" would emerge at some point, Phillips should refrain from doing anything that smacked of interference in Indian affairs.[57]

Days after Phillips reached India in January 1943, the imprisoned Gandhi began a twenty-one-day fast to protest British allegations of his role in the violence that had rocked India. Unsurprisingly the viceroy refused to allow Phillips to meet with Gandhi. Over the following days, Phillips watched with mounting disquiet as Linlithgow remained unmoved by all appeals, including the resignation of three Indian members of his executive council. "Reluctantly I am coming to the conclusion," he wrote to Hull, "that the Viceroy, presumably responsive to Churchill, is not in sympathy with any change in Britain's relationship with India."[58] Nor was the State Department much in sympathy with the Congress party. Phillips wrote directly to Roosevelt that the "key to the present problem" lay in Churchill's hands. London must be prepared to "transfer as much civil power as possible *now*, on the understanding that the complete transfer will be made after the war."[59] Roosevelt asked Phillips to convey to the viceroy "our deep concern over the political crisis" and ask him to find some way of keeping Gandhi alive.[60]

Phillips was shocked to find that the viceroy "faced with equanimity the possibility of Gandhi's death." In Linlithgow's view, while it might lead to some disturbance, Gandhi's demise would lead within six months to "a new and improved situation"—but he did not believe that Gandhi would die. Phillips, in the meantime, faced a barrage of requests from Indians and Americans to "do something to save Gandhi's life." C. Rajagopalachari, a close associate of Gandhi who had nevertheless opposed the Quit India movement, was emphatic that the United States should speak out now to prevent a "white against colored complex in the East." Phillips asked the president to "exert friendly pressure" on Britain through its envoy, Halifax.[61]

Hull told Halifax that President Roosevelt was clear that "Gandhi should not be allowed to die in prison." The British refused to respond and instead sought assurance that Phillips would make no public statement on Gandhi in India. Their continued intransigence led Phillips to write yet again to the president. Emphasizing the "nation-wide consternation," he wrote that Linlithgow was wholly indifferent to "the pathos in the appeal of these millions to the freedom of their own country." "Perhaps he is," added Phillips, "a 'chip off the old block' that Americans knew something about in 1772."[62]

In the event, Gandhi came through the fast on March 3, 1943. Phillips used the opportunity to make the case for an active American policy. The Indians, he wrote, were "caught up in the new idea, which is sweeping the world over, of freedom for oppressed peoples. The Atlantic Charter has given the movement great impetus. Your speeches have given encouragement." Phillips recommended that, in order to break the continuing deadlock, the president convene a conference of all Indian leaders, perhaps "presided over by an American who could exercise influence in harmonizing the endless divisions of caste, religion, race, and political views."[63]

Phillips's subsequent travels across India, where he noted "frustration, discouragement, helplessness," reinforced these extraordinary views. The Indian government's suspicion of him and refusal to let him visit Gandhi or Nehru further piqued the American envoy. And the State Department's conservative stance on India compounded his anger. The British, he wrote to Roosevelt, were "sitting pretty." They had been "completely successful" in crushing the Indian revolt. They would make "no effort to open the door to negotiation among the [Indian] leaders." Meanwhile, the Indians were "coming more and more to disbelieve in the American gospel of freedom of the oppressed peoples."[64]

Roosevelt felt that the proposal for an American-convened conference was "amazingly radical for a man like Bill."[65] But he was characteristically evasive in his response. When Phillips returned to Washington for consultations, he found the president unwilling to confront the problem. At his insistence, Roosevelt agreed to recommend to Churchill another British mission to consult "leaders of *all* parties and groups." But he avoided broaching the issue directly. Instead he asked Phillips to meet Churchill, who was also visiting the United States. In their meeting, Phillips told the prime minister of the "unanimous cry for independence" and the Indians' distrust of the British. He asked Churchill to quickly transfer more power to them. An irate Churchill prophesied a bloodbath in the subcontinent if the British left and made it clear that there would be no alteration during the war. Phillips concluded that it was hopeless to expect Churchill to change his mind. So he informed the prime minister that he would probably not return to

India.[66] Roosevelt did nothing to persuade him to go back. Phillips's mission was at an end—as was Roosevelt's interventionist policy on Indian politics.

EVEN AS ITS INTEREST in Indian politics sputtered to a halt, the Roosevelt administration had to focus on the demands of the war. Foremost among these was the provision of economic assistance to India. As with politics, American economic interests and priorities came up against those of the British and the Indians.

On November 11, 1941, President Roosevelt had decided that India could directly receive lend-lease supplies from America. While welcoming the decision, British officials realized that it was pregnant with problems for them. The US proposal to negotiate lend-lease supplies directly with the British-Indian mission in Washington was "something of a bombshell," for it threatened to displace Britain's economic preeminence in India. The United States' economic importance for India was already growing. India's US imports had increased from 9 to 20 percent between 1939 and 1941, while over the same period imports from Britain had fallen from 25.2 to 21.2 percent. Similarly, Indian US exports had risen from 12 to 19.6 percent, while its exports to Britain had fallen from 35.5 to 32.3 percent.[67]

British officials were also aware of the US proclivity to drive a hard bargain. Earlier in the year, while negotiating a treaty of commerce, navigation, and consular rights between the United States and India, the Americans had sought to include a clause that would give private companies from both sides the right to undertake mineral and oil exploration in the other country. They were particularly eager to secure exploration rights in Balochistan. The government of India resisted this clause, claiming that its rights would only be theoretical as no Indian company had the requisite capital to extract minerals or oil in the United States. American officials argued that they had a similar treaty with Britain, which too was only notional since Britain had no deposits of oil or minerals. An agreement with India would amount to actual reciprocity on the part of Britain.

The Americans also demanded a most-favored nation clause providing parity with Britain, explicitly stating that the clause would refer to "the most favored third nation, *including the Kingdom of Great Britain and Northern Ireland.*" The Indian negotiator, Sir Feroz Khan Noon, argued that this would contravene the agreement on imperial preferences between India and Britain. He also observed that inclusion of this clause would exclude the other dominions from most-favored nation status. State Department officials, however, felt that removal of the clause would have deleterious consequences for America's longer-term plans: it "would accord recognition in a treaty to preferential tariff treatment now accorded certain British and Colonial products." Although the United States had recognized imperial tariffs in a trade agreement signed with Britain in 1938, it did so in exchange for a substantial reduction in the tariff. "The recognition of imperial preferences in a treaty is a recognition of a more formal character and the initial compulsory period is for a much longer time." The Indians continued to plead their inability to sign on to this clause but requested a speedy conclusion of the agreement in light of the war. Eventually the Roosevelt administration forbore from pressing its demand and informed Britain and India that despite having hoped the treaty would "embody the most liberal principles of international trade," the United States would refrain from raising this question owing to the "unsettled world conditions."[68] Evidently once conditions had quieted down, the United States would revisit this issue.

With the onset of lend-lease, British officials in the Government of India grew concerned that it might become the thin end of the wedge with which to pry open the system of imperial preferences. Negotiations on the master agreement for lend-lease directly between Britain and the United States had stoked these anxieties. When negotiations began for a similar agreement between Washington and India, the Americans pressed for inclusion of a provision identical to that agreed with the

British. Article VII explicitly committed both sides "to the elimination of all forms of discriminatory treatment in international commerce, and to the reduction of tariffs and other trade barriers." This sought at once to knock down the system of imperial preferences and to prevent the raising of similar barriers in the future by an independent India.

As the negotiations got underway, Indian capitalists sounded the tocsin. G. L. Mehta, president of the Federation of Indian Chambers of Commerce and Industry (FICCI) and future ambassador to the United States, insisted that owing to its nascent industrial status, India could not agree to the removal of tariffs. Leading Indian capitalists with a nationalist orientation had formed the FICCI. From the 1930s, these men had envisaged the creation of an autonomous arena of capital accumulation subject to the dictates of neither British capital nor international investors. Even as they benefited from the wartime spurt in demand, they looked forward to a postwar world in which Indian capital would play the leading part in the industrialization of India. Their views largely synced with those of the Congress party's leadership, barring Gandhi, which was committed to a vision of industry-led development.

So the FICCI adopted a resolution in early 1943 urging the Indian government to hold firm on the issue of tariffs to ensure India's industrial development as well as its fiscal independence. In the viceroy's Executive Council, the Indian member for commerce argued strenuously that failure to do so would be detrimental to India's fledgling industries.[69] Sir Jeremy Raisman, finance member of the council, told Phillips that his own inclination was for minimal barriers to trade, but "the Government feels obliged by strong public opinion to drive as a hard a bargain as possible." The Raj's solicitude for Indian opinion was, of course, conditioned by the fact that the British wanted to keep the system of imperial preferences intact.[70]

State Department officials dealing with economic matters thought the Indian position "fraught with dangers." Any dilution of the master agreement would "give a green light to an exaggerated Indian self-sufficiency program after independence." Moreover, it would undermine the larger American plans for establishing an open capitalist international order after the war. Hence they felt that refusing to water down the lend-lease agreement's provisions "might, on economic and commercial-policy grounds, be well worth the risks of possible adverse political reactions in India." Political analysts in the Near Eastern Affairs Division felt, however, that if an unchanged agreement was rammed through, "it would be immediately and bitterly alleged that the United States and Britain had conspired to force upon India…a tariff policy ruinous to India's future industrial development."[71]

Nevertheless, Assistant Secretary of State Dean Acheson bluntly told Agent-General Bajpai that eliminating the controversial article "would not be feasible." Nothing in it, he claimed, "impaired the sovereign power of any government to enact any legislation." It set out "certain principles…to work out post-war arrangements." Making any exceptions would "destroy the whole purpose of the article," which was indeed "most important from our point of view."[72] Eventually, the negotiations for direct lend-lease had to be shelved, though the United States reluctantly agreed to continue with existing arrangements.

The Indians were piqued that while the Americans preached the doctrine of free trade, their practice departed from it in important respects. In October 1944, the United States began subsidizing cotton exports to the tune of four cents per pound. By diverting excess cotton from domestic to overseas markets, they sought to ensure that the price paid to American farmers stayed at the level pegged by the government. Adoption of this policy by the world's largest cotton producer naturally impacted other countries—especially the second-largest cotton producer, India.

Toward the end of the year, New Delhi sent a note to Washington pointing out that India's cotton markets had "always been 'free.'" India had desisted from taking advantage of wartime disruptions in global markets by boosting its exports. Indeed, it had encouraged farmers to shift from cotton to food crops. The American export subsidies sent cotton prices plummeting in world markets—not just for the high-quality produce, in which India directly competed with US cotton, but also in the lower-quality varieties owing to a knock-on effect "on grounds of sentiment." In other words, traders believed that cotton prices were set to plummet across the board and hence started selling cheap. The implications for Indian farmers were grim: "The present United States policy will disturb the economic balance of India, essentially an agricultural country, by its serious effects on the incomes of Indian farmers, whose return from their produce is already little above a bare subsistence level." The Indian government requested that the Roosevelt administration reduce the subsidy.[73]

In meetings with representatives of India, the Americans insisted that the program was merely a corollary of their domestic policy and that "it was not the intention of the Government of the United States to enter into a competitive cotton price war." They claimed that cotton price movements in the months ahead would bear this out. The Indian government was, of course, concerned less about the Americans' intentions than the consequences of their policy for Indian farmers. But the Americans refused to yield. Instead they suggested that the issue of surplus cotton be taken up in the proposed meeting of the International Cotton Advisory Committee. If the committee recommended holding an international conference on cotton, then India would have an appropriate forum to register its concerns.[74] In the event, the committee did not get its act together until after the war ended.

The Indian government's unwillingness to force a confrontation on this issue underscored the extent to which its war effort relied on American economic assistance. Indeed by 1945, the United States would account for 25.7 percent of India's total imports—Britain lagged behind at 19.8 percent—and for 21 percent of its exports. The major Indian exports to the United States had remained almost the same since the mid-nineteenth century: jute, coir, and lac; rawhides, skins, and rough-tanned leather; cashew nuts and sandalwood. By contrast, machinery, motor vehicles, heavy chemicals, iron and steel, medicines, and packaged foodstuffs dominated US exports to India.[75]

As early as March 1942, the United States had dispatched a technical mission to assess the needs of Indian industry in supporting the war effort. Led by Henry Grady, a former assistant secretary of state, the mission stayed in India for five weeks and in its report, produced toward the end of May, stated, "India is of great strategic importance to the cause of the United Nations." The Grady report was at once a sweeping survey of Indian industry and a sharp indictment of the Indian government. "The Government of India and the industries of India, with few exceptions," the report noted, "were not organized on a war basis." The report made specific recommendations to revitalize all major industries: transportation and communication, petroleum and minerals, iron and steel, shipping and armaments, motor vehicles and machine tools. In conclusion, it emphasized "India's great potentialities for industrial production because of its vast natural and human resources."[76]

The Grady mission's recommendations and plan came with a price tag of $212 million. The Board of Economic Warfare and the State Department supported the plan. Acheson wrote to lend-lease administrator Edward Stettinius that the department wanted the Grady program implemented "in toto." The Joint Chiefs of Staff felt, however, that the program would throw an enormous burden on American shipping, machine tools, and raw materials. Strategic concerns overlaid economic ones. Reacting to the mission's conclusion that "the value...of an India strengthened by a program of this magnitude will be very great," Admiral Ernest King, Chief of Naval Operations, scribbled in the margins, "Especially to England after the war."[77] The State Department argued that the United States should at least support the existing industrial plant to avoid the impression that it was "washing its hands of India," which would have unfortunate political repercussions. The Joint Chiefs agreed to sustain normal requests to maintain India's war effort.[78]

If the Americans were mindful of the benefit to Britain of their economic assistance to India, the Indians—nationalists and industrialists like—were concerned about American inroads into their economy. Nehru saw in Grady's mission the portent of a new attempt to exploit the Indian economy. He told American columnist Raymond Clapper, "There was always such a tendency when a powerful nation came into contact with a weaker one." Wealthy Calcutta businessman G. D. Birla was even blunter in suspecting "imperialist designs" in the mission. Meeting Grady in May 1942, Mehta of the FICCI emphasized that FICCI wanted no more foreign vested interests in India. The country would have to develop new productive capacity under Indian ownership, management, and control. Grady assured them that American capital had no predatory aims in India but on the contrary would be very conservative after the war. The American demands for tariff reductions accentuated Indian capitalists' skepticism, however, and prompted them to oppose the master lend-lease agreement. Toward the end of the war, the Americans and the Indians would once again find themselves at loggerheads over competing visions of the postwar world.

The currency crisis in India during the war also cast into sharp relief the economic asymmetry between India and America. The crisis stemmed from the manner in which Britain financed India's war. Instead of paying New Delhi in real time for its material and military contributions, Whitehall deposited IOUs in an account in London. These "sterling balances" then appeared as assets on the Reserve Bank of India's balance sheet and were used to expand the Indian money supply. This extraordinary monetary expansion led inexorably to galloping inflation with devastating consequences for India.[79]

Owing to increasing inflation, the Indian people began hoarding silver coins and distrusting paper currency.[80] Silver coins came in three denominations: one rupee and eight or four annas (sixteen annas made a rupee). The lack of small change was "disrupting retail trade and causing suffering to the poorer classes," leading to fears that "resulting unrest might cause serious disturbances."[81] Silver (like gold) was traditionally regarded as a store of value and a hedge against inflation. Hence people were not just hoarding silver currency but, in many instances, melting it into bullion. Soon the Reserve Bank's need for silver outpaced availability in the country. Starting in March 1944, coinage would require an estimated 4 million ounces per month. Further, to prevent people from melting silver coins, the Indian government proposed building up a larger stock of 100 million ounces to sell on the market to limit and control the price of silver.

In early June 1943, the Indian government requested that the US Treasury supply under lend-lease 100 million ounces of silver for the stock as well as 20 million ounces for coinage. New Delhi proposed to return an equivalent amount at the end of the war. While the US Treasury was prepared to approve this request, the State Department opposed providing to India the additional 100 million ounces of silver: "Any silver for this purpose should be lend-leased to the British Government and not to the Government of India." The British imploringly told the administration that the matter was "really and increasingly urgent," pointing out India's "grave economic difficulties" and the "grave blow" that would be dealt to the "common war effort."[82] But the State Department refused to budge.

Underlying its resistance were the same paternalistic, racially tinged views that inflected the Roosevelt administration's attitude toward the colonial world. Wallace Murray of State explained to Treasury's Harry Dexter White that "no one could foretell what the set-up in India would be after this war; that a violently nationalistic government made up of Indians themselves might gain power and that it would, in our view, be rash to assume that such a native government, with possibly strong color prejudice against the white peoples of the West, would voluntarily assume [such] obligations." The American position drew the ire of Indian officials. K. C. Mahindra, chief of the supply mission in Washington, told the State Department that he was "astonished and distressed" and that it was "an insult to his country." By doubting India's ability to honor its debt, the United States was "increasing Britain's hold upon India." Agent-General Bajpai pointed out that owing to India's accumulation of sterling balances, it was now a creditor vis-à-vis Britain: "The people of India would be particularly resentful of the demand by the United States that the British Government underwrite a debt of the Government of India."[83]

Faced with this robust response from the Indians, Acheson decided that the United States should compromise. Despite the risk of repudiation by an independent government of India, "nothing but harm can come to the supply arrangements in India upon which our forces depend.... We can see no gain to the United States from giving offense." So it was decided that while the silver would be loaned directly to India, it should be jointly guaranteed by the British government. Despite appeals from London and New Delhi, the Roosevelt administration refused to ship the silver without a joint undertaking by the former. The British eventually agreed to sign a separate bilateral agreement with the United States accepting responsibility for the return of the silver. And so the agreement was sealed—much to the chagrin of Indian officials.[84]

If the currency crisis was one manifestation of inflationary financing of the war, widespread deprivation was another. Spiraling inflation deprived large sections of the Indian people of their ability to purchase food. The most tragic case was the famine in Bengal in which possibly as many as 3 million people perished. By late 1943, the American press began reporting critically on the Raj's negligence and callousness. *Newsweek* reported that so many people were dying daily in Calcutta that "at times the authorities despaired of being able to collect and cremate the bodies." *The Nation* accused the viceroy of failing "to take even the most elementary steps to meet the crisis." *Time* bluntly pronounced, "The Raj has failed."[85]

The Roosevelt administration was well aware of the magnitude of the disaster before the press picked it up. Apart from sending regular reports on the famine from India, Phillips had written directly to the president urging him to take concrete measures to relieve Bengal of its distress: "If only from the point of view of strategy, should we not avoid having a hostile population close to our important base and to our lines of communication?"[86] The Roosevelt administration not only continued its masterly inactivity but also refused to allow the newly launched United Nations Relief and Rehabilitation Administration (UNRRA) to operate in Bengal, although India was one of the forty-four signatory nations (as the main financial contributor, the United States effectively controlled the organization).

Dean Acheson and senior State Department officials justified this refusal with the claim that the UNRRA was only intended provide relief to peoples and places affected by war. The India League of America, led by J. J. Singh, embarked on an intense campaign to lobby the House of Representatives to pass an amendment allowing India to be a beneficiary of UNRRA. Eventually, the amendment went through owing to the efforts of a Republican congressman from South Dakota, Karl Mundt, ably supported by a young Democratic congressman from Montana, Mike Mansfield. But their efforts proved vain as the government of India refused to permit the UNRRA to operate in India.[87]

Worse, even when the British government belatedly and grudgingly acknowledged the devastating magnitude of the famine, the Roosevelt administration shrank from providing any assistance. In April 1944, Churchill wrote to Roosevelt, pointing out the "serious famine" in India and the "gravest warnings" from the viceroy and asking for American ships to move wheat from Australia to India. The president replied that despite his "utmost sympathy" in the matter and "full realization of military, political and humanitarian factors involved," "on military grounds" the United States was unable to divert shipping to India.[88]

The administration's apathy contrasted with the efforts of prominent Americans, including Henry Grady, William Phillips, and Henry Luce, to raise money for famine relief. "Our help today is a moral obligation," they insisted. "Tomorrow it may prove to be a foundation of international goodwill." The *New York Times* made a more pragmatic pitch: "For American businessmen India is one of the mightiest potential markets on the globe, about to enter upon an industrial era that will release the latent energies of one-fifth of the human race. She will want machinery for farm and factory; she will want tens of thousands of products that America can provide. We of this country have a stake in India. For our own well-being, if for no higher reason, we can no longer think of India as being outside our world. We cannot deny her our interest or leave her ills and misfortunes for others to cure."[89]

ECONOMIC PROBLEMS ASIDE, THERE was a war to be won. Here, too, the United States differed seriously with the Indian and British governments on the strategy to adopt in Burma and the resources to devote to it. Sharply divergent political outlooks overlaid these strategic, operational, and logistical discussions. As earlier, the Americans were disinclined to shore up British rule in India or elsewhere, while the British led by Churchill were determined restore the prestige of their empire. Papering over these cracks proved almost as taxing as preparing to take on the Japanese.

The loss of Burma in early 1942 heightened American concerns about China's continued determination to resist the Japanese. The War Department's policy paper was tellingly titled "Keeping China in the War." Chiang Kai-shek would require tangible support in order to buttress his position. It was imperative to reopen the Burma Road, for airlifts alone could not deliver enough supplies over the "Hump" to China. Strategic responsibility for an offensive into Burma had to rest with Britain and India, supported by the American Tenth Air Force and lend-lease supplies.[90] Meanwhile, General Joseph Stilwell, the American commander of Chinese soldiers who had retreated from Burma to India, wanted to train his troops in the latter country.

Some 10,000 Chinese soldiers had escaped overland to India from Burma. The Indian government decided to host them at a capacious camp in the town of Ramgarh in Bihar. From early June 1942, Stilwell designated it the Ramgarh Training Center. Chiang Kai-shek was prepared to fly more troops to India for training. Stilwell had grand plans to train up to 100,000 Chinese soldiers in Ramgarh. But the British would not spring for even half this number.[91] Stilwell, known as "Vinegar Joe" for good reason, cast a caustic eye on the British in India: "'Can't have the dirty Chinks'; Long-range policy: fear of Chinese-Indian co-operation; fear of independent operation; or what not." "Limeys getting nasty about Ramgarh," he noted a few days on. "How many [Chinese] troops, and what for. WHAT FOR? My God! I told them to help our allies retake Burma."[92]

An agreement on the strategy for the reconquest of Burma proved still more elusive. Drawing up the plan, code-named "Anakim," was a protracted affair. The commander in chief of India, Field Marshal Archibald Wavell, deemed the logistical requirements of the operation far too onerous. The Americans felt that the British were exaggerating the problem of resources. At the Casablanca Conference of January 1943, General George C. Marshall came down heavily on them: "Unless operation ANAKIM could be undertaken he [Marshall] felt that a situation might arise in the Pacific at any time that would necessitate the United States regretfully withdrawing from the commitments in the European theatre."[93] American military officers in Delhi thought Wavell's outline plan really consisted of "several pages of well written paragraphs, telling why the mission could not be accomplished."[94]

The Americans felt that British were reluctant to use their resources in India to retake Burma and reopen the road to China. The British seemed far more interested in harboring their strength for a strike at Singapore.[95] Their desire to establish a new South East Asia Command (SEAC) under a British supreme commander seemed a move in the same direction: to recover the prestige of the British Empire. As Stilwell's political adviser, John Davies, trenchantly noted in October 1943, "We have chosen to bring a third-class island kingdom back to its anachronistic position as a first-class empire. We are rejecting the opportunity to move boldly forward with the historical tide."[96]

SEAC was soon dubbed "Save England's Asiatic Colonies." Stilwell's staff sang, "The Limeys make policy, Yank fights the Jap, and one gets its Empire and one takes the rap."[97] Davies pointed out in December 1943 that by participating in SEAC operations, "We become involved in the politically explosive colonial problems.... [W]e compromise ourselves not only with the colonial peoples of Asia but also the free peoples of Asia, including the Chinese." It would therefore be best to restrict involvement in SEAC: "After the recapture of North Burma there comes a parting of ways. The British will wish to throw their main weight southward for the repossession of colonial empire."[98] Like most American officials, Davies's anti-imperialism was shot through with paternalism. As he put it in another note for Stilwell, "However decadent British rule in India may be, most of the Indian nationalistic leaders are themselves more decadent and lacking in aggressive vitality." Nevertheless, he felt that "if arrangements are not made for an orderly turnover of government to the Indians...chaos will ensue."[99]

The SEAC commander in chief, Lord Louis Mountbatten, had his own ideas about the best way to implement decisions made by the Allied leaders at an August 1943 conference in Quebec. The Americans were not impressed. As Stilwell put it, "The Glamour Boy is just that. He doesn't wear well and I begin to wonder if he knows his stuff. Enormous staff, endless walla-walla, but damned little fighting."[100] The Americans made one more attempt to persuade the British to launch a serious offensive on northern Burma. But Churchill refused to consent.[101] So the Allies remained deadlocked on the issue—an impasse only overcome when the Japanese launched their own offensive on India on March 7, 1944, and pulled the Allied forces back into Burma.

BETWEEN 1942 AND 1945, some 200,000 American soldiers came to India. Given this military and economic commitment, the United States was naturally eager to project its contribution in the best possible light. American propaganda in India, however, was a rudderless ship. The Office of War Information (OWI) initially picked journalist and author Robert Aura Smith to head information operations in India. He arrived in India just ahead of Louis Johnson. A "triple bourbon man at lunch," Aura Smith had energy unmatched by organization.

After the arrest of the Congress leadership in August 1942, Aura Smith made a hectic effort to counter the perception that the United States was propping up British rule in India. He hired the J. Walter Thompson (JWT) Agency of New York, which had been operating in India since 1929, to mount a major advertising campaign. The JWT campaign centered on two themes: "America Fights for Freedom" and "America—the Arsenal of Democracy." One advertisement announced, "The 150-year-old constitution of the United States contains a charter of freedom for all mankind, and their president has declared the extension of these fundamental liberties to all men [as] the base of the American people's war-aims." Anyone who wrote in would receive a free copy of the *Life of Franklin D. Roosevelt: Fully Illustrated*. The advertisements on the second theme were equally tactless: "The number of persons engaged in aircraft manufacture in the United States is equal to the total male population of Bombay, Karachi and Ahmedabad combined."[102]

British rulers as well as Indian subjects took umbrage at such condescension. The American consul in Madras pointed out that the campaign would have an "adverse" impact on Anglo-American relations. The consul in Calcutta feared by contrast that "it creates doubts [in Indian minds]...on American political integrity." William Phillips pointed out to Washington that the OWI's campaign had a "cheapness" that did "no credit" but "considerable harm" to American interests in India. Soon Aura Smith was relieved of the job.[103]

His successor, Ralph Block, was another experienced journalist who was also versed in the ways of Hollywood. Block quickly understood that US policy toward India was torn between competing considerations. Yet he felt that India would "influence the affairs of that half of the world in which America will be increasingly dominant culturally and economically." So wartime propaganda should aim to foster a "sympathetic attitude towards the presence of American troops" and avoid limiting "the freedom of characteristic American action in these areas in the future." Toward these ends, they should aim to emphasize the similarities rather than the differences between the United States and India. Instead of focusing on the "froth of American life"—"Hollywood, boogie-woogie, etc."—they should highlight small-town life in America, which was much more salient for the predominantly rural India. Harping on American prosperity might only end up generating envy. "Statements as to our great wealth and industrial power," he insisted, "should take second place to the interesting human details of our common life." Block's ideas would shape American propaganda not only during the rest of the war but for decades afterward.[104]

American propaganda during these years took a variety of forms: radio programs, photographs, libraries, and newsletters. The OWI also produced and screened several documentary films with such titles as *The Grand Coulee Dam*, *The Life of a United States Anthracite Miner*, *Our American Allies*, and *Stop the Rising Sun*. The last centered on the role of African American troops in India but was pulled out of circulation owing to concerns that it portrayed American race relations in an unfavorable light and called into question the United States' avowals of liberty.[105]

The presence of 22,000 African American soldiers was indeed regarded as a "delicate" matter. Not only did African Americans serve in separate military units, but their social life in India was segregated too. In Calcutta, for instance, black soldiers only frequented places like the Cosmos Club, managed by black women from the Red Cross, or the Grand Hotel, where black pianist Teddy Wetherford performed with an Indian band. The US Army sought to muffle criticism by producing a propaganda film—shot in Karachi and edited in Bombay—of "coloured troops, their activities, recreational facilities and mode of living in India." The African American soldiers' experience in India was mixed. On the one hand, many Indians, especially of the upper classes, displayed a "marked attitude of aloofness" and a "superiority complex" toward African American GIs.[106] On the other, black soldiers seem to have gotten on fine with at least some segments of local society. As American military authorities noted, "Negroes frequently are invited to attend native civilian parties to which white troops are not invited. Many Negro soldiers attempt to adopt civilian children as 'mascots.'"[107]

To most American soldiers, India came as a jolt. As an Indian journalist recalled, "Accustomed to seeing India through Hollywood's cameras as a fabulous land peopled by Maharajas and elephants, they were appalled and sickened by the stink and poverty of the place." American soldiers were frequently scathing about the Raj. Seeing the emaciated poor huddled on the streets of Calcutta and peering at the shops, a GI grunted, "If I were they, I'd smash those glasses and help myself to all that's there."[108] Many American soldiers and airmen took a liking to their "native bearers," if in a paternalistic fashion. These locally recruited servants, a GI magazine joked, "make a perfectly lazy man out of a soldier." They often gave funny nicknames to their servants. "Our bearer's name is 'Smokey,'" wrote a GI. "We've forgotten why we call him that, but there are no objections, since his real name is 'Pabitra Mondel.' Aside from his regular duties, Smokey spends most of his time learning GI ways."[109]

Not surprisingly, American servicemen were advised to steer clear of Indian politics. "The political situation in India is not easily understood," warned a handbook for GIs, "and a short stay in India is not long enough to be informed about it." Yet they could not be entirely insulated from the currents of nationalism swirling in India. In an open letter to American officers and soldiers in India, the socialist congressman Jayaprakash Narayan addressed them "as one who loves America only next to his own motherland." Recalling his formative years in the United States—not only in the universities but as a laborer in farms and factories—he wrote, "You are soldiers of freedom....It is, therefore, essential that you understand and appreciate our fight for freedom." Having deftly overturned the tropes of American propaganda in India, he went on to denounce

Britain's claims about the Cripps mission and the unreadiness of India for freedom. Narayan urged his readers, "Tell your countrymen, your leaders and your government the truth about India."[110]

It is difficult to judge whether such appeals had any effect on American soldiers and officers. But the brush with Indian nationalism did indelibly mark the lives of at least some young Americans. Twenty-six-year-old Joan Bondurant was finishing her second degree in music when she volunteered for the war and was sent by the Office of Strategic Services to India in late 1943. As an intelligence analyst, Bondurant decrypted and translated Japanese messages and propaganda. In her spare time she picked up Urdu and Hindi, traveled widely in North India, and befriended many Indians. During these years, she also developed an abiding interest in Gandhi's philosophy of *satyagraha*, or nonviolent resistance. After the war Bondurant returned to India, met the Mahatma, embarked on a career at the University of California at Berkeley, and became America's first academic exponent of Gandhian nonviolence.[111]

IN MAY 1944 GANDHI was released from prison. "It is a most important moment in Indian affairs," William Phillips wrote in his diary. If Gandhi and Jinnah, the Muslim League leader who demanded a separate state for the subcontinent's Muslims, could get together, India's political problems might yet be solved. But such hopes came to nothing.[112] Emboldened by British support and the growing clout of the Muslim League during the war, Jinnah insisted on Pakistan, and his talks with Gandhi proved abortive. The British, for their part, refused to make any political overtures toward the Congress until after Germany's defeat in May 1945. Then too, an all-party conference called by Lord Wavell, now viceroy, for the summer of 1945 fell through owing to Jinnah's demand for parity with the Congress in any postwar dispensation.

The United States continued with its cautious approach toward India. On January 29, 1945, Acting Secretary of State Joseph Grew publicly stated that the United States had continued to follow Indian affairs sympathetically and was prepared to assist, if required, in bringing about a settlement. The British declined to take notice of the statement. But Indian opinion was once again stirred. In fact, Gandhi had already encouraged Nehru's sister, Vijayalakshmi Pandit, to travel to the United States.[113] Pandit's daughters were enrolled in Wellesley College, and she used the trip not just to visit them but to present the Congress's case for Indian freedom. Eleanor Roosevelt invited her to tea, while William Phillips hosted a dinner in her honor. But her forceful advocacy unnerved the administration. None less than Mrs. Roosevelt wrote to the secretary of state, pointing out that while most Americans sympathized with the Indian nationalists, it was "dangerous to stir up feeling against Great Britain" at this time.[114]

The usually liberal First Lady's reference to timing was significant. At the recently concluded Yalta Conference between the United States, Britain, and the Soviet Union, President Roosevelt had shrewdly manage to corner Churchill on the question of UN trusteeship. Although the agreed-upon formula did not directly apply to European empires, it included their League of Nations mandates and provided for voluntary transfer of territory into a trusteeship system. This ensured that the successor to the league, the United Nations, could serve as a platform to arraign the British Empire.[115] While Churchill had unwittingly given in, the Americans were concerned that the British would backpedal on the agreement. The trusteeship plan in the new international organization was Franklin Roosevelt's swansong. Eight days after Mrs. Roosevelt's letter on Pandit, the president was dead.

Meanwhile, the Allied countries convened for a conference at San Francisco from April to June 1945. India had not been party to the preliminary discussions on the successor to the League of Nations—especially those at Dumbarton Oaks in late 1944 between the United States, Britain, the Soviet Union, and China.[116] Yet it was the only colonial entity invited to San Francisco. This reflected both its contribution to the war and its presumed postwar importance.

The government of India nominated a trio of knighted non-nationalists to represent India at San Francisco. The Indian National Congress was predictably outraged. Speaking to the press, Gandhi harked back to the views that he had taken when Churchill denied the Atlantic Charter to India. Thus he insisted, "Exploitation and domination of one nation over another can have no place in a world striving to put an end to all wars." Complete independence for India was an essential first step toward peace. This would demonstrate to all colonized peoples that their "freedom is very near and that in no case will they henceforth be exploited." "Either India at San Francisco is represented by an elected representative," he said, "or not represented at all."[117] The government went ahead regardless.

During the conference, the question of India's independence brought together diverse groups and personalities that pressed the new United Nations to grant independence to India as well as justice and equality to all colonial subjects.[118] In a flurry of public speeches in San Francisco, Pandit lambasted the British government for speaking with a forked tongue—freedom for the world and servitude for India—and urged the United States to give full effect to the Atlantic Charter. Much to the discomfort of Anglo-American officials, Pandit also circulated a memorandum to all conference attendees: "The recognition of India's independence now will be a proclamation and assurance to the whole world that the statesmen of the United Nations, assembled in this solemn conclave in San Francisco, have in truth and in honour heralded the dawn of a new better day for an all but crucified humanity."[119] Nothing came out of it, but the San Francisco conference foreshadowed the differences between India and the United States on decolonization in the years ahead.

Equally disappointing for Indian nationalists was their country's participation in the Bretton Woods conference of July 1944, which set up the International Monetary Fund (IMF) and the World Bank. India was invited to this conference owing to its economic contribution to the war.[120] A measure of this was its status as a creditor to Britain:

India would amass, by the end of the war, £1.3 billion in sterling balances in London. The accumulation of such an enormous amount by so poor a country also underlined the extraordinary privations imposed on India during the war. In consequence, Indian nationalists of all hues intended to use these sterling balances for the postwar reconstruction and development of the country. The famous "Bombay Plan" drawn up by leading Indian industrialists explicitly envisaged financing a chunk of the plan by drawing on these balances. The British government feared that if India converted even a part of this amount into dollars, the pound sterling would collapse. So it sought either to write down a large portion of the sterling balances or to release them gradually to India. Pronouncements to this effect by prominent British leaders, including Keynes, had already alarmed Indian nationalists.

The Indian delegation at Bretton Woods, led by Jeremy Raisman, finance member of the Executive Council, included C. D. Deshmukh, governor of the Reserve Bank of India; Ardeshir Shroff, an author of the Bombay Plan; and Shanmukham Chetty, later independent India's first finance minister. Prominent on their agenda was securing an equitable, multilateral settlement of sterling balances. Shroff and Chetty were particularly worried about a bilateral settlement with the British.

As the largest holder of sterling balances, India proposed an amendment, calling on the IMF to "promote and facilitate the settlement of abnormal indebtedness arising out of the war." The Americans staunchly opposed this, however. If freighted with settlement of wartime debts, the "new experimental machinery" being fashioned at the conference "would certainly have a much less prospect of success and survival.... [T]he amounts involved are so great that they far exceeded the entire operation of the Fund."[121]

Shroff argued that they only sought the "settlement of a reasonable portion." These would be deployed for India's development plans while Britain rebuilt its capacity for exports to India. By refusing to grant India's request, he said, "You are placing us in a situation which I compare to the position of a man with a $1 million balance in the bank but not enough sufficient cash to pay his taxi fare....Do you expect to fulfil the main objectives of this Fund if you allow large countries to be festered with this sort of poverty?" Keynes insisted that the sterling balances were "a matter between those directly concerned." He would accord no role to the IMF in the matter; nor would he offer any assurance to India on convertibility of sterling into dollars or gold. He merely stated that Britain would "settle honourably what was honourably and generously given."[122]

The Americans stuck to their earlier position, claiming for good measure, "Wartime indebtedness can be amicably settled by the countries directly concerned." This slotted in smoothly with the position espoused by the British. The Americans' desire to ensure open international trade after the war, however, drove their stance. Washington believed that most of the blocked sterling balances should be written off, and the rest should be unfrozen. As a State Department official explained, "The barriers and discriminations against American trade in the sterling area are due basically to the shortage of dollars and the consequent blocking of sterling." He added that the "success of any international post-war program for reducing trade barriers and removing discriminations will depend on finding some means of unblocking these funds."[123]

In short, India's aspirations to use the sterling balances to foster its development came up against the American determination to ensure an open global economy. The Indians' disappointment was palpable. Shroff bluntly stated, "It may be unfortunate that situated as we are politically, perhaps the 'big guns' in the conference may not attach importance to a country like India." But, he added, ignoring a country of the size, population, and resources of India would not bode well for the international cooperation that the IMF sought to achieve. Nor did it portend well for the United States' future relationship with independent India.

4

BETWEEN EAST AND WEST ASIA

IN LATE 1951, CHESTER Bowles—a former governor of Connecticut and prominent liberal Democrat—asked President Harry Truman if he might serve as ambassador to India. The president, Bowles recalled, was "appalled" by the idea of anyone wanting to go there. "Well," Truman said, "I thought India was pretty jammed with poor people and cows wandering around the streets, witch doctors and people sitting on hot coals and bathing in the Ganges and so on, but I did not realize that anyone thought it was important."[1] Truman had been at the helm of the United States for six years, and his comments encapsulated the political, economic, and cultural lenses through which his administration viewed South Asia. But these views were part of a grand strategy for American preponderance that was well in place by 1951.

When Franklin Roosevelt died in harness in April 1945, Truman inherited and embraced the postwar objectives and plans drawn up by the previous administration. These were inchoate and far from settled, but the broad contours were clearly etched: a liberal capitalist order under American hegemony, based on nonaggression, open trade and access to raw materials, orderly decolonization, and participation in international organizations. Within a year after the war ended, this vision of a new world order faced hurdles on two fronts. First, the dissolution of the wartime alliance and the onset of the Cold War meant that the Soviet Union emerged as a potential challenger to American global dominance. Second, the economic impact of the war on the United States' European allies as well as the defeated enemies proved much worse than anticipated. The two major problems were linked. While the Americans never doubted their margin of superiority over the Soviet Union in every index of power, they believed that the economic travails of western Europe and Japan would allow Moscow to make inroads into these countries via their Communist parties. Kremlin control of the core industrial countries of Eurasia would result in an accretion of Soviet power and a relative diminution of American superiority.

To preserve American dominance, the Truman administration adopted a grand, two-pronged strategy.[2] The first prong sought to contain the USSR's power and roll back its influence. The strategy of "containment" was not merely defensive: the Truman administration wanted to win the Cold War. The other prong aimed at fostering the economic revival both of America's western European allies and of Germany and Japan. Toward this end, the United States sought to integrate these core industrial economies with those of the peripheral countries. Thus, securing the Middle East became important to ensure the uninterrupted supply of energy to western Europe. Similarly, controlling commodity-rich Southeast Asia was seen as crucial to Japan's economic prospects. This strategy of "integration" also necessitated a reconsideration of other, related objectives identified during the war.

For one thing, while the United States never gave up its determination to ensure an open trading system, it agreed to go slow in light of the economic frailness of western Europe. As earlier, the American policy did not reflect a straightforward desire for an "open door" for exports. In fact, economists in the administration emphasized that the prosperity of the American economy did not depend on preserving the current volumes of exports. The main concern was that a turn toward autarky abroad would make it difficult for the United States to maintain its free market economy at home. Capitalism could not flourish in one country. And the possibility of western European economies coming under Communist influence now outweighed concerns about the persistence of closed trading systems adopted by European imperial powers. In particular, the United States cut Britain slack and refrained from demanding an immediate dissolution of imperial preferences or the sterling bloc—although it sought to push Britain steadily in that direction.

Related to this was modulation in Washington's views about decolonization. While never for swift decolonization, the Americans now felt that the economic recovery of western Europe depended on imperial ties, especially with commodity-producing tropical countries. At the same time, the strategy of integration did not imply unconditional support for European imperialism. If nationalists could be trusted to keep the Communists and, by extension, the Soviet Union at bay, the United States was prepared to insist on transfer of power. But where the Communists were the dominant anticolonial force, the United States was willing to allow the reimposition of imperial control. These considerations led the Americans to force the Dutch out of Indonesia, even while allowing the British and the French to take control of Malaya and Indochina.[3]

In the immediate aftermath of the war, the Truman administration's grand strategy chimed well with Britain's own plans for India. The Labour government led by Clement Attlee wished to rid itself of the incubus of governing India (and Palestine) and to refashion the imperial system. Mainly strategic considerations influenced White-hall's South Asia policies. The large standing army, the vast reservoir of military manpower, India's importance in defending the Middle and Far East: all of these mandated preserving Indian unity and ensuring India's continued presence in the Commonwealth.[4]

South Asia did not rank high in Washington's short-term priorities. It was neither industrially advanced nor a producer of key commodities like oil or rubber. It supplied certain raw materials—mainly cotton and jute—to Japan and was potentially a large market for Japanese goods. The United States also saw it as "a major source of raw materials, investment income, and carrying charges for the UK, thus strengthening the UK's and Western Europe's effort towards economic recovery essential to US security."[5] In American eyes, too, the subcontinent mattered primarily because of its military manpower and its geographic location between the Middle East and Southeast Asia. Unsurprisingly, in this context, the Truman administration supported Britain's efforts to ensure the emergence of a united, independent India and a peaceful transfer of power.

But the demand for a separate homeland for the subcontinent's Muslims, "Pakistan," had gained considerable traction during the war years, owing both to the imperial power's support for the Muslim League and its stalwart leader, Mohammed Ali Jinnah, and to the Indian National Congress leadership's incarceration following the Quit India revolt. The elections held in the winter of 1945–1946 indicated a surge in support for the Muslim League among the Muslim electorate of India. A three-member Cabinet Mission sent by London sought to come up with an arrangement that would keep India united: essentially a federation of Muslim and Hindu provinces with a weak central government. Both the Congress party and the Muslim League opposed various provisions of this rather complicated proposal. Meanwhile, violence between Muslims, Hindus, and Sikhs escalated in the two large provinces that would be partitioned: Bengal and Punjab. By March 1947, the British government saw clearly that it would have to work on an accelerated timetable: divide and quit in just about five months. This touched off a spasm of violence, especially in the Punjab, which left at least a million dead and many more displaced. The partition of India and Pakistan in mid-August 1947 was accompanied by one of the deadliest bouts of ethnic cleansing in the twentieth century.

AGAINST THIS BACKDROP, a wide-ranging analysis by the Truman administration in September 1947 placed South Asia below western Europe, the Middle East, and East Asia in terms of American interests. Nevertheless the first formal paper on the area prepared by an inter-departmental committee noted its potential to "dominate the region of the Indian Ocean and exert a strong influence also on the Middle East, Central Asia, and the Far East." The paper went on to warn, "The loss of the U.S. access to the raw materials and present and possible pro-ductive capacity, manpower and military bases of this area, or Commu-nist control of the areas and its vast population, would gravely affect the security of the U.S."[6] In consequence, it was imperative to ensure South Asia's favorable orientation toward the United States. Yet when it came to prioritizing and allocating resources, the Truman adminis-tration preferred to let Britain take the lead in the region.

From the outset, the Americans discerned different interests in Pakistan and India. They saw the former as more important from a military-security perspective owing to its large pool of manpower from the so-called martial classes and potentially important bases close to Soviet Central Asia. India, on the other hand, they regarded as "the natural political and economic center of South Asia."[7] What is more, the two new states had rather different external orientations.

Barely three weeks after independence, Pakistan's Governor-General Jinnah declared at a cabinet meeting, "Pakistan [is] a democ-racy and communism [does] not flourish on the soil of Islam. It [is] clear that our interests [lie] more with the two great democratic countries, namely, the U.K. and the U.S.A., rather than with Russia." American diplomats in Karachi promptly reported this sentiment to Washington. In another cabinet meeting four days later, Jinnah maintained the importance of an alliance between the United States, Britain, and Pakistan: "The safety of the North West Frontier [is] of world concern and not merely an internal matter for Pakistan alone."[8] To American journalist Margaret Bourke-White, Jinnah claimed, "America needs Pakistan more than Pakistan needs America." Pakistan was the "pivot of the world, for we are placed on the frontier on which the future position of the world revolves." "Russia," he added, "is not far away."[9]

By contrast, independent India had very different international priorities. Jawaharlal Nehru believed that India was "potentially a Great Power.... [S]he will have to play a very great part in security problems of Asia and the Indian Ocean, more especially of the Middle East and South-East Asia." At the same time, he held, "India should adopt an independent attitude with no marked alignment with any group.... India should play a much more independent role in foreign affairs."[10] In his first speech as head of the interim government in September 1946, Nehru declared, "We propose, so far as possible, to keep away from the power politics of groups aligned against one another, which have led in the past to world wars and which may again lead to disasters on an even vaster scale."

Nonalignment would indeed become a cornerstone of India's foreign policy. But the more immediate concern for Britain and America was the range of disputes in which the two successor states of the Raj rapidly became enmeshed. None was more important or more intractable than their conflict over the princely state of Jammu and Kashmir.

The contest over Kashmir involved the vital interests of both India and Pakistan. These stemmed from its strategic location atop the plains of the Punjab, athwart the trade route from Central Asia, and abutting Afghanistan and China. For Pakistan, Kashmir was also important from an economic perspective—not least because the rivers flowing through it sustained Pakistan's agriculture. Subsequently, Kashmir became invested with the hopes and fears of India and Pakistan. In the aftermath of partition, Gandhi and Nehru regarded Kashmir's presence in the union as a powerful affirmation of India's secular identity. As Nehru observed, "If Kashmir went, the position of Muslims in India would become more difficult. In fact, there would be a tendency of people to accept a purely communal Hindu viewpoint. That would mean an upheaval of the greatest magnitude in India."[11] To the Pakistanis, however, Kashmir's accession to India portended the eventual annulment of partition.

Kashmir was one of India's largest "princely states," or entities not directly governed by the British. As independence and partition approached, Lord Louis Mountbatten advised the princes to join either India or Pakistan based on their geography and the religious composition of their populaces. As the Hindu ruler of a Muslim-majority state, Hari Singh, the maharaja of Jammu and Kashmir was on the horns of a dilemma. Geographic contiguity and religious composition suggested that accession to Pakistan would be the natural course to adopt. But Singh was loath to join a self-professed Islamic state. Yet his subjects might resent a decision to accede to India. So the maharaja tarried. He signed a standstill agreement with Pakistan and offered one to India, but made no moves toward accession. All along, he desperately hoped that Kashmir might yet manage to remain independent.

Given Kashmir's strategic importance, the Pakistanis naturally feared that its going to India would jeopardize their security. Pakistani officials told Jinnah that they had no option but to turf out the ruler. For this, Pakistan had only to "supply arms and foodstuffs to the tribes within and without the State." Indeed preparations were already underway.[12] On October 22, 1947, a tribal levy of nearly 5,000 men recruited from the frontier tracts seized key towns in the Kashmir Valley and surged toward Srinagar. Two days later, a beleaguered maharaja formally offered to accede to India and asked Delhi for military assistance. Nehru was certain that the invasion "could not have taken place without 100% assistance of Pakistan authorities." The Indian government airlifted troops to Srinagar the next morning. It also agreed to accept Kashmir's accession subject to the outcome of a plebiscite when conditions permitted.[13]

Over the following weeks, the Indian army sought to repel the invaders from the Kashmir Valley. Simultaneously, Indian and Pakistani leaders sought to negotiate their way out of the escalating conflict. In principle India's offer of a plebiscite to ascertain the wishes of the Kashmiri people pointed toward a practical solution. But in practice the discussions foundered on the question of the conditions for holding a plebiscite. Nehru insisted the Pakistanis had to pull all the raiders out of the state, following which the Indian army would withdraw, and only then would a plebiscite be held under UN supervision. By late December 1947, the Indians realized that their forces could only push the tribesmen out by crossing the border in Punjab. This would, of course, amount to a declaration of war on Pakistan. In order to stave off this choice, Nehru took the Kashmir dispute to the United Nations and charged Pakistan with aggression.[14]

So far the Truman administration had taken only episodic interest in these distant happenings. India's referral of the dispute to the United Nation compelled Washington to pay more attention. In time, the Americans realized that the conflict between India and Pakistan would threaten their ability to pursue a regional policy that sought good ties with both countries. It would also give the Soviet Union an opportunity to meddle in the subcontinent. Feeling "spread out very thinly," however, the United States felt Britain should take the lead in this case.[15]

While both the United States and Britain sought a speedy settlement of the Kashmir dispute, additional, and more immediate, considerations preoccupied London. From Britain's standpoint Kashmir tied in with the problem of Palestine. The latter's descent into war and ethnic cleansing meant that Britain could not risk opposing Pakistan on Kashmir. In pulling out of Palestine, it had already alienated the Arabs. The perception that the British were supporting India on Kashmir might further inflame Muslim opinion—and further complicate their position in the Middle East.[16]

At the UN Security Council, the British delegation brushed aside India's complaint and asserted that fighting could only stop if arrangements for a fair plebiscite were reached. This would entail inducting Pakistani troops into Kashmir and establishing a "neutral" administration.[17] The Americans recognized that the British proposals were strongly tilted toward Pakistan. Secretary of State George C. Marshall thought it "highly doubtful" that India would acquiesce to this plan. Indeed, the British proposal excluded "any possibility [of a] compromise solution." Nevertheless, Washington went along with the British partly to avoid presenting "competitive formal proposals" and partly in deference to the "wealth of their experience" in the subcontinent.[18]

The opening Anglo-American stance complicated the discussions on Kashmir. Nehru concluded that the United Kingdom and the United States had "played a dirty role."[19] Faced with staunch opposition from India, the British sought to modify its proposals. In the ensuing lengthy and contorted diplomacy at the United Nations, India and Pakistan could only agree to confer with a five-member UN Commission on India and Pakistan. Although the Truman administration had little faith in the United Nations' ability to handle such matters, it agreed to participate in the commission.

The UN commission landed in Karachi on July 5. Foreign Minister Zafrullah Khan threw the "first bombshell": three Pakistan army brigades were already fighting in Kashmir.[20] In Delhi, the commission found the Indians indignant and opposed to discussing a plebiscite until Pakistan's aggression was condemned. By this time, in fact, Nehru and his senior colleagues were veering toward a partition of Kashmir rather than a plebiscite. The Pakistanis, however, resolutely opposed the idea of partitioning Kashmir. So the commission reverted to the idea of holding a plebiscite.

On August 13, 1948, the commission adopted a three-part resolution. Part 1 called for a cease-fire. Part 2 outlined the principles for a truce agreement: first, Pakistan would remove its troops from Kashmir and secure the withdrawal of tribesmen and Pakistani nationals;

thereafter, India would withdraw the "bulk of its forces" in stages. Part 3 stated that upon acceptance of the truce agreement, both countries would enter into consultations with the commission to determine conditions for settling the future of Kashmir "in accordance with the will of the people."

India deemed this resolution acceptable, but Pakistan effectively turned it down, calling for a reversion to the older proposals. A few weeks later, Jinnah succumbed to illness. Prime Minister Liaquat Ali Khan was in no position to make concessions on Kashmir. When he met Nehru in London later that year, Liaquat made clear that Pakistan would neither unreservedly accept the commission's resolution nor consider partition of the state along the current lines of engagement. Nehru, for his part, would not budge.

As Marshall delicately observed after a meeting in October, Nehru "found it difficult when his turn came to talk about Kashmir in a moderate way." The Pakistanis were less emotional but no more open to compromise. They "flatly refused" to entertain any suggestion of partitioning Kashmir. "It seems clear," concluded the US ambassador to the United Nations, "that a stalemate exists between the two Governments on the Kashmir question and that neither is willing to make concessions which are obviously necessary if a peaceful settlement is to be achieved."[21]

The commission presented its interim report to the Security Council on November 19, 1948. The United States and Britain agreed that to obtain Pakistan's acceptance of the August resolution, it was essential to appoint a plebiscite administrator and draw up the details of a plebiscite. With the council's approval, the commission began consultations. Displeased with the commission's attempt to hammer out proposals for a plebiscite, the Indians argued that this process could only begin after the truce agreement was in place. Nor would India agree to even consider a plebiscite without Pakistan pulling out its troops, which privately Nehru believed it "almost impossible for them [Pakistan] to [do]." He reluctantly agreed to consider the commission's proposal mainly because "an adverse decision of the Commission might prove harmful to us." In any event, this paved the way for a cease-fire in Kashmir from January 1, 1949.[22]

THE UNITED STATES FOLLOWED these developments with growing disquiet that stemmed from a variety of sources. For one thing, the Americans worried about their deteriorating position in Asia. Chiang Kai-shek's regime in China was moving inexorably toward defeat. Indochina and Indonesia were in the throes of bitter colonial conflicts. And another round of fighting in the Kashmir dispute would considerably aggravate Washington's Asian problems. In 1948, when Indian and Pakistani troops fought in Kashmir, the Truman administration had imposed an informal arms embargo on both sides. Since both countries had American equipment received under lend-lease during World War II, the ban on sales of spares and ammunition as well as weapons pinched them hard. Despite repeated requests from India and Pakistan, Washington refused to lift the embargo until they reached the cease-fire agreement. Renewal of fighting in Kashmir would necessitate adoption of a similar policy, which both sides would resent.

Further, the Americans rightly held that India was stonewalling various proposals owing to its unwillingness to hold a plebiscite in Kashmir. Yet American attempts at leaning on India threatened to backfire. At one point, Nehru told the US ambassador in India, Loy Henderson, that "he was tired of receiving moralistic advice from the U.S. India did not need advice from the U.S. or any other country as to its foreign or internal policies....So far as Kashmir was concerned he would not give an inch. He would hold his ground even if Kashmir, India, and the whole world would go to pieces."[23]

Nevertheless, in the context of wider Asian developments, the Truman administration came to see India as ever more important. In mid-August 1949, the new secretary of state, Dean Acheson, told Truman, "Mr. Nehru is today and probably will be for some time the dominant political force in Asia." Defense Secretary Louis Johnson in turn told Acheson that Nehru was "one of the best and potentially one of the strongest friends of the United States in the whole of Asia." The Central Intelligence Agency held that India alone could "compete with Communist China for establishing itself as the dominant influence in Southeastern Asia." The president himself told Walter White of the National Association for the Advancement of Colored People (NAACP) that he regarded India as the key to the evolving situation in Asia.[24]

Yet Nehru's well-publicized visit to the United States later that year yielded no tangible outcome on either Kashmir or wider Asian matters. In particular, his views on Communist China clashed sharply with those of the administration. Despite Nehru's old friendship with Chiang Kai-shek, India was one of the first non-Communist countries to recognize the People's Republic of China (PRC). Nehru was also among the earliest statesmen to argue that the enlarged Communist bloc was not a monolith. Nehru thought it imperative to bring China into the international system rather than try to isolate it: "I could not imagine a great country like China being submerged in a way in the U.S.S.R. or to become just a dependent member of the Soviet system....China was a great power and bound to function as such."[25]

Over the following months, India emerged as a vocal champion for allowing the PRC to take China's seat in the United Nations instead of Chiang's Republic of China. At one point, when State Department officials floated a trial balloon about India taking China's place on the Security Council, Nehru quickly deflated it, insisting that India could not be party to any attempt to deprive China of its rightful spot. Not surprisingly, a National Security Council report on US policy in Asia concluded, "It would be unwise for us regard South Asia, more particularly India, as the sole bulwark against the extension of communist control in Asia."[26]

KASHMIR WAS NOT THE only regional dispute that Washington had to handle. Pakistan was also at loggerheads with its western neighbor,

Afghanistan. For nearly three decades, Afghanistan had periodically courted the United States—to little avail. The Third Anglo-Afghan War of 1919 had led to the formal independence of Afghanistan. However, in keeping with its long-standing strategy of maintaining Afghanistan as a "buffer state" against Russian expansionism, Britain had continued to regard the country as falling under its "sphere of political influence." At the same time, Britain had withdrawn its economic subsidies to Afghanistan. The new amir, Amanullah Khan, had embarked on a rapid modernization of the country. Even as he enforced a series of ambitious social and economic reforms, Amanullah looked abroad for technical and financial assistance.

In July 1921 a mission from Kabul arrived in Washington seeking diplomatic recognition from the United States and its participation in the development of Afghanistan. The Afghans were eager to meet President Warren Harding and hand him a letter from Amanullah. Warren met with the delegation and also replied politely to the amir—"Great and Good Friend"—that establishment of diplomatic ties "must be reserved for further consideration." Two main considerations shaped the American stance. Although Afghanistan had established ties with several European countries, including Soviet Russia, Britain was sensitive about "any special agreements with Afghanistan." In any case, commercial opportunities for American businesses were "extremely limited." Indeed, there was "little or no opportunity for trade" except in such semiprecious stones as sapphires or lapis lazuli.[27]

Political and economic reasoning apart, US policy toward Afghanistan was filtered through an orientalist cultural prism constructed primarily of images drawn by Rudyard Kipling, Josiah Harlan, and American missionaries in South Asia. As a State Department official told Congress in 1930, "Afghanistan is doubtless the most fanatic country in the world today.... There is no pretense of according Christians equal rights with Muslims.... [The Afghans] detest taxation and military service and welcome chaos and confusion which enables them to do ... as they see fit on helpless communities and passing caravans....

No foreign lives in the country can be protected and no foreign interests guaranteed." As William Phillips, then undersecretary of state, succinctly put it, American reluctance stemmed from "the primitive condition of the country, the lack of guarantees for the safety of foreigners...[and] the absence of any important interests."[28]

Owing to repeated requests from Kabul, Washington accorded diplomatic recognition in 1934. But the United States declined to set up a mission in the country. As they did with the rest of the subcontinent, American views of Afghanistan significantly changed with the onset of World War II. Even as German tanks rolled into the Soviet Union in June 1941, an American diplomat in Iran visited Kabul and recommended that Washington immediately establish a permanent mission: "The U.S. should accept the hand of friendship offered it by this small and independent nation....[T]his is an opportunity which should not be missed of establishing ourselves solidly in a strategic position in Asia." Less than a year later, Cornelius van H. Engert arrived as the first American minister to Afghanistan. His first task was to establish an alternate route for lend-lease supplies to Russia and China by constructing a mountain road through the Khyber Pass and the Wakhan Corridor—a Stilwell Road via Afghanistan. Although this ambitious plan fell through, Engert succeeded in procuring American supplies for Afghanistan. By the end of the war, the British resident reported, the Afghans were "praising everything American."[29]

As with the rest of the subcontinent, Afghanistan seemed to recede in importance during the early years of the Cold War. Already a wartime intelligence report had emphasized that while Afghanistan was favorably oriented toward the West, its population was uneducated and rife with disease. Although hardy and skilled at guerilla warfare, the Afghans were "poor material for a disciplined army." Further, Afghanistan had few strategic resources to offer the United States. It had no major industries, few skilled laborers, and no minerals of vital importance. Nor did it have any asphalt roads or railways, and its airports were "little more than cleared fields." As earlier, the Americans saw Afghanistan as culturally as well as economically backward—"probably the most fanatically Mohammeden country left in the world today."[30] Even within South Asia, then, Afghanistan ranked at the bottom.

Nevertheless, the Truman administration was forced to pay attention to Afghanistan owing to its thorny relationship with Pakistan. The two neighbors were at loggerheads from the moment Pakistan was born. The dispute centered on the status of ethnic Pashtuns in the North-West Frontier Province (NWFP) and the 1896 Durand Line marking the boundary between Afghanistan and British India. When the British announced the partition of India, they also declared that a referendum would decide the future of the NWFP, a Muslim-majority province ruled by a Congress government under Dr. Khan Sahib and led by his brother, Abdul Ghaffar Khan.

Nehru and other Congress leaders reluctantly reconciled themselves to the loss of this province. They did not want to create an appendage of India on the wrong side of Pakistan—notwithstanding the geographic anomaly of Pakistan, separated into western and eastern wings by over a thousand miles of Indian territory. But the Pashtun Congress leaders were loath to join Pakistan, which they believed the Punjabis and elite migrants from India would dominate. So the Khan brothers demanded that the referendum be a choice between Pakistan and an independent "Pashtunistan." Britain's refusal led them to boycott the referendum, which delivered the NWFP to Pakistan.

Ahead of the referendum, the Afghan government told Britain that it had never accepted the legality or legitimacy of the Durand Line. Now that the British were departing from the subcontinent, the Pashtuns of the NWFP and adjoining tribal areas must be allowed to unite again with their kinsmen in Afghanistan. London and New Delhi refused to entertain such demands, insisting that Kabul had no skin in the game. At the same time, British officials believed that Afghanistan should continue to serve as a reliable buffer between the subcontinent and the Soviet Union. Hence, they insisted that all their treaty obligations, including the Durand Line, would devolve to the new state of Pakistan. After demurring for a bit, Jinnah accepted that Pakistan would be the legatee of these treaties.

Although Afghanistan welcomed the creation of Pakistan, it demanded that the Pashtun areas be designated as a "sovereign province." Kabul initially voted against Pakistan's entry into the United Nations, though it subsequently recognized Pakistan and sent an ambassador. Nevertheless, Afghanistan's irredentist stance on "Pashtunistan" remained a major source of friction with Pakistan. In July 1949, a *loya jirga*, or grand assembly of tribes, formally repudiated the Durand Line and all other treaties with Britain. The next month, Afridi tribesmen on both sides of the line announced the establishment of an independent Pashtunistan. Kabul's recognition of this entity led to a serious face-off with Pakistan. Over the following year, Afghan and Pakistani forces clashed along the Durand Line. Pakistani planes bombed Afghan villages close to the border. The Pakistanis also cut off all trade and fuel supplies to Afghanistan.[31]

The Truman administration thus faced a dispute between Afghanistan and Pakistan that was strikingly symmetrical to the one between Pakistan and India. Very like the Pakistanis, the Afghans sought arms from the United States—and on similar grounds. They insisted that they needed these weapons primarily to maintain internal security. But they also wanted to make a "positive contribution" in an "inevitable" war between the United States and Soviet Union. The Afghan minister of national economy, Abdul Majid Khan, admitted, "When war came Afghanistan would of course be overrun and occupied," "but the Russians would be unable to pacify the country. Afghanistan could and would pursue guerrilla tactics for an indefinite period." The key was ensuring they were "properly armed and convinced of U.S. backing."[32] These were prescient words, but three decades would pass before an American administration responded to such pleas.

The Truman administration deemed Afghanistan's stance on the Pashtun issue "highly unreasonable" but nonetheless wished to forestall further escalation of the crisis. Chastened by the experience of

Kashmir, it decided to keep the issue out of the United Nations and to avoid joint action with the British. In November 1950, Washington approached both Kabul and Karachi expressing concern that the prevailing tension "creates [a] situation favorable [to] Soviet intrigues and subversion." The United States offered to act as an "informal 'go-between'" to help resolve the dispute. As a starting point, the Americans suggested that both sides cease hostile rhetoric and actions on the ground and nominate representatives for "informal, exploratory discussions" with no agenda or preconditions.[33]

The Afghans readily agreed, but the Pakistanis were most reluctant. The American proposals would, they claimed, lead "to interminable discussions with no chance of solving the basic problem." Indeed, the Afghans would construe their readiness to talk as a weakening of their position on the matter. Instead, the Pakistanis urged the United States to endorse the sanctity of the Durand Line. But the Americans "emphasized we did not believe it timely for us to make any such statement at present." Nor would they commit to making such a pronouncement in the future.[34] Given the American stance, the Pakistanis refused to get on board.

When pressed again some months later, the Pakistanis claimed to have "proof that India was subsidizing Afghanistan to promote unrest in the tribal areas." Indeed, "if the Kashmir question were settled, Afghanistan would immediately abandon its sponsorship of Pushtoonistan." When the Pakistanis expressed dismay at American unwillingness to come out in support of the Durand Line, US officials insisted, "We could hardly make [such] a pronouncement…as the Afghans would then doubt our good faith." The Americans did not question the validity of the line. Nor did they support Afghanistan's ethnic claims on all Pashtuns. Indeed, in conversations with the Afghans they bluntly said, "The principle of self-determination was one enunciated by President Wilson but…this principle was not applicable in the present world." Yet they wanted Pakistan to agree to their proposals and so ensure a speedy withdrawal of Afghanistan's claims. The Pakistanis remained adamant in their refusal to discuss the Durand Line or Pashtunistan. After waiting for months, the Afghans also dug in their heels, insisting that the central problem between the two countries was the status of trans-Afghan Pashtuns. By the end of September 1951, the Americans wearily concluded that their proposal could "no longer usefully serve as a basis for improving Afghan Pak relations."[35]

MEANWHILE, INDIA AND PAKISTAN were balancing on the brink of another war in Kashmir, primarily due to misperceptions of each other's aggressive intent. As the situation brimmed with risks, the United States made simultaneous diplomatic approaches to India and Pakistan. Expressing grave concern over the recent events, it argued that a single spark—a violent communal incident or a misperception—could lead to a conflagration. Washington thus urged both governments to pull their troops back and tone down the rhetoric.[36] Neither side responded positively to the American message. Nehru considered the intervention wholly unwarranted but in keeping with US support for Pakistan on Kashmir. Nevertheless, he believed, "In the final analysis... it is thoroughly understood in the U.K. as well as the U.S.A., that India counts far more than Pakistan."[37]

On the morning of October 16, 1951, Liaquat Ali Khan was scheduled to address a large public gathering. As Pakistan's prime minister rose to deliver his speech, an assassin's bullets cut him down. Liaquat's tragic death, however, helped Pakistan and India pull back from the brink of war. All the same, the crisis convinced the Pakistani leadership of the need to obtain arms and external security guarantees to avoid being steamrolled by India in all areas of contention, particularly Kashmir. Indeed, even as the crisis raged, Pakistan had decided to intensify efforts in this direction. On August 25, 1951, Liaquat had written to Acheson indicating Pakistan's desire to procure arms. At the time of his death, Liaquat was hopeful that, unlike earlier, the Americans would now accede to Pakistan's requests. His optimism reflected the wider shift underway in US relations with South Asia.

Fourteen months before Liaquat's assassination, on June 25, 1950, North Korean troops had crossed the thirty-eighth parallel and attacked South Korea. By the end of the month, the Truman administration had committed ground, naval, and air forces to a part of Asia that it had not reckoned of vital interest. Over the following year, the fortunes of war ebbed and flowed in unanticipated ways: retreat of US and South Korean troops to the Pusan Perimeter; General Douglas MacArthur's bold landings at Inchon; the heady advance northward to the Yalu River; the entry of Chinese troops and retreat of the UN Command to the neck of the peninsula. By the time the front had stabilized in the spring of 1951, the United States was convinced that a monolithic, global Communist bloc challenged its preponderance. American officials also believed that the war had "greatly increased [the] strategic importance of the subcontinent."[38]

Given New Delhi's greater political heft, Washington gravitated toward India in the initial stage of the war. India voted in favor of the UN resolution, introduced by the United States, condemning North Korea's aggression. Although the vote had been cast without reference to New Delhi, Nehru publicly affirmed that "the North Korean Government had committed aggression on a large scale on South Korea." When a second resolution, asking states to contribute troops to repel the attack, was tabled, India abstained. The Indian government issued another statement supporting the need to resist aggression but also affirming that there would be no change in its nonaligned foreign policy.[39]

In the days ahead, it became clear that the Nehru government had a different set of priorities from the Truman administration. While Nehru acknowledged the North Korean aggression, his main concern was that Washington's military response, coupled with its refusal to recognize the People's Republic of China, might result in the latter entering the war on the side of North Korea. On July 12, Nehru sent personal messages to Acheson and Joseph Stalin suggesting that the PRC be admitted to the United Nations and that the Soviet Union cease boycotting the Security Council. Annoyed by Nehru's activism, Acheson firmly replied, "We do not believe that the termination of the aggression in northern Korea can be contingent in any way upon the determination of other questions which are currently before the United Nations."[40]

The Truman administration nevertheless found it expedient to keep Nehru on the right side. For New Delhi could also serve as a diplomatic conduit to Beijing. On July 25, Acheson wrote again to Nehru, asking him "to persuade the Peiping authorities that their own interests require that they avoid intervention in the Korean situation."[41] Nehru agreed to send this message on to Beijing, though he was skeptical of the outcome. "The United States policy," he wrote to his sister and ambassador in Washington, "is the one policy which will make China do what the United States least wants." The Chinese, too, used their contacts with India to warn the Americans. As UN forces stood ready to cross the thirty-eighth parallel into North Korea, PRC premier Zhou Enlai repeatedly told the Indian ambassador, K. M. Panikkar, "If America extends her aggression, China will have to react."[42]

Nehru urged both Beijing and Washington to exercise restraint. The Americans dismissed Panikkar as "panicky" and held that the Chinese were giving him the works. In a bid to stave off a wider conflict, India also voted against a General Assembly resolution calling for the unification of Korea. Nehru's moves elicited a heap of opprobrium from the American press as well as the administration. Even as US-Indian relations nose-dived, Chinese forces entered North Korea and began rolling back the American offensive. Nehru's accurate prognosis of Chinese intention, however, won him no brownie points with the administration. India continued to play a role on the margins during the remainder of the war. And the United States found it an occasionally useful interlocutor with the PRC. Nevertheless, the two continued to diverge sharply on Asian affairs.

These differences came to the fore in the summer of 1951 during the conclusion of the peace treaty with Japan, formally ending World War II in Asia and the Allied occupation of Japan. The Soviet Union had refused to sign the treaty in San Francisco, while China was not invited. India was conspicuous by its absence—not least because of its role in the defeat of Japan. Nehru opposed the treaty on several counts. Without Russia and China, he believed, no treaty could be stable. He was also concerned about the failure to return the Ryukyu and Bonin Islands to Japan and Taiwan to China. Above all, he opposed the perpetuation of American military bases in Japanese territory.[43] India refused to sign the San Francisco Peace Treaty and instead concluded a separate treaty with Japan the following year.

The Americans were indignant at India's refusal to ink the accord. Ambassador Henderson felt that it was entirely in keeping with Nehru's policy of "eventual exclusion from mainland and waters of Asia [of] all Western military power and what he would consider Western political and economic pressures." Nehru, he concluded, sought an "Asia for Asians" under the banner of anti-Western nationalism.[44] President Truman, according to John Foster Dulles, upon reading India's note on the draft treaty provisions, "spent a sleepless night pacing his room, and filled the margins with irate comments: 'So what' and 'Oh Yeah.'" This was too polite by the president's standards. Truman had scribbled, "Evidently the Govt of India has consulted Uncle Joe and Mousie Dung of China!"[45]

When Henderson told Nehru that the administration believed India's policy was "to try to separate Japan from USA," Nehru replied that this "novel suggestion" had never occurred to him. He maintained, however, that "there could be no peace in the Far East if China was excluded from the settlement."[46] Nehru publicly insisted that he was "not for pan-Asianism. Asia is far too big and varied for that [and] has a variety of peoples."[47] But the Truman administration continued to look askance at India.

As India's stock dipped in Washington, Pakistan's rose. Following the outbreak of the Korean War, the Truman administration grew anxious about defending the Middle East from an attack by the Soviet Union. Senior officials knew that India could not be persuaded to participate in this enterprise. But they thought that Pakistani troops could make a crucial contribution, particularly as Pakistan had initially been willing to send troops to Korea. Days after war broke out, the United States had requested that Pakistan send an army brigade to Korea and offered to equip the force with modern weapons. Liaquat made all the right noises but eventually declined to send the troops. Pakistan's major security concern, he clarified, lay with India. If the United States could allay it, then Pakistan would be ready to do its part in containing the Soviet Union.

From late 1950, the United States and Britain conferred regularly on arrangements for the defense of the Middle East. Pakistan featured prominently in these discussions, though no one had much of a clue about how exactly it could contribute. Assistant Secretary of State George McGhee's exchange with British officials in April 1951 was typically inflationary in its strategic assumptions. Pakistan's contribution, McGhee argued, "would probably be the decisive factor ensuring defense of the area." The British nodded deeply in agreement—"probably not possible without effective support of Pakistan."[48] Washington and London differed, however, on how best to secure Pakistan's participation. State Department officials like McGhee believed that Karachi must receive a security guarantee as quid pro quo. But the British were more mindful of the potential response from India. Given India's importance in the Commonwealth as well as the scale of British commercial interests in India, the British were unsurprisingly leery of alienating New Delhi.[49]

Although the Truman administration no longer followed Britain's lead in the subcontinent, it too balked at Pakistan's demands. In May 1951, Liaquat told the US envoy "bluntly that now is the time for decision." Pakistan was ready "to move with [Washington] not only in Korea but also in the Middle East and to commit themselves irrevocably." But the United States "must give [Liaquat] a commitment that will assure his people." Washington "must support him against Nehru's defiance of the UN...in Kashmir." Similarly, the United States should bring its "influence to bear in Afghanistan and put an end to...Pooshtoon nonsense." Acheson put his foot down and declined to provide "complete and unqualified support on Kashmir and Pushtoon issues." Liaquat's proposals were unacceptable because they would result in "complete alienation" of India and Afghanistan and impose "limitation on US freedom of action re complex present and future issues in Asia."[50]

At the height of the Kashmir crisis later that year, Liaquat wrote to Acheson requesting military equipment and indicating concerns about global developments. Clearly the Pakistanis were now willing to settle for less. Two days after Liaquat's assassination, a Pakistani military mission arrived in Washington. The leader of the delegation explained that his aim was "to get as much military equipment as he could." The list included a request for 250 tanks. He also expressed Karachi's willingness to participate in arrangements for defending the Middle East, even if the United States was unwilling to guarantee Pakistan's security against India. In November 1951, Washington finally approved the sale to Pakistan of a portion of the equipment requested.[51]

THE TRUMAN ADMINISTRATION'S ECONOMIC policies toward South Asia took equally long to crystallize. In the initial aftermath of the war, the Americans held that the "Indian import licensing system and exchange control [were] among the chief deterrents to a free-flowing trade between the United States and India."[52] Hence, they sought to dismantle imperial preferences and the sterling bloc. With the dawn of the Cold War, however, Washington was prepared to go slow on its plans for an open capitalist world order. The economic revival of Britain and Europe assumed priority. This impinged on South Asia in a couple of ways.

First, the United States was open to the continuation of the sterling bloc for some more years. At the same time, though, it pressed Britain to liquidate the wartime sterling balances as a prelude to returning the sterling to full convertibility and winding up the sterling area. This affected both India and Pakistan because it at once allowed Britain to wipe out a third of their sterling assets by devaluation of the pound and ensured that Britain could put them on a dollar ration. American policy, in short, hampered Indian and Pakistani access to vital foreign exchange reserves.

Second, as it did with other countries on the periphery, the Truman administration sought to integrate India and Pakistan with the economies of Britain, western Europe, and Japan. Washington saw them mainly as suppliers of commodities and as potential markets for finished goods from the core industrial economies. India, in particular, represented a huge market for consumer goods and an important source of strategic raw materials for the United States.

The Americans were aware that countries like India and Pakistan wished to industrialize. But they held that the road to industrialization ran through further specialization in unfinished and semifinished raw materials. As these activities grew larger in scale and more mechanized, they would also become more profitable. Greater exports of such materials would help finance the development of light industry, focusing on the production of manpower-intensive products like textiles and footwear. As influential Harvard economist Alvin Hanson put it in a wartime report, countries on the periphery had "legitimate goals," but they should aim at "a moderate degree of industrialization consistent with their resources, especially the manufacture of light consumer goods."[53]

To be sure, the development of such light industries would in due course limit the opportunities for small American exporters of consumer goods. But the export of heavy machinery to peripheral countries and opportunities for American business to invest in their light industries would more than offset these losses. As the early theorists of such "import substitution industrialization" noted, the key bottlenecks were capital and foreign exchange.[54] To encourage the flow of capital investment from the United States, these countries had to ensure favorable tax regimes, remove laws discriminating against foreign investors, and sign a treaty of friendship, commerce, and navigation drawn up in consultation with American businessmen of the National Foreign Trade Council. To conserve foreign exchange, these countries could adopt moderate import controls. To foster the development of their home-grown industry, they could also resort to limited tariff barriers—so long as they were carried out "under the direction of international experts" and consistent with longer-term plans for an open world economy. These ideas underpinned the Point Four Program announced by President Truman in his January 1949 inaugural address.[55]

In the fifty years preceding independence in August 1947, the Indian economy had grown on average by just about 1 percent. Over the same period, the Indian population grew at a little over 1 percent. In other words, the per capita income of India during the late colonial period was stagnant. Inflation, deprivation, and famine had also ravaged this large, populous, and poor country during World War II. The postwar slump aggravated the travails of the Indian economy. But wartime exigencies had also forced India to adopt a model of industrial development rather similar to import substitution. Ahead of independence, therefore, Indian capitalists were primed to pursue rapid, autonomous industrialization. While they recognized the need for foreign goods, capital, and expertise, they were determined not to allow foreign control of Indian industries. The Bombay Plan of 1944 had already outlined their vision for growth in independent India. And important sections of the Congress party, including left-of-center leaders like Nehru, supported it. Pakistan inherited a much smaller share of united India's industries, but the capitalists associated with the Muslim League also aspired to quick industrialization.

The economic vision of the Truman administration collided with the aspirations of India and, to a lesser extent, Pakistan. As the subcontinent moved toward independence, export-oriented American businesses looked forward to tapping the huge Indian market. Robert Alfredson of Pal Blades, manufacturers of cutlery and safety razors, spent two and a half months in 1947 scouting possibilities in India. At the end of his trip, he concluded, "India can be a highly profitable market for American industry. There is almost nothing...which could not be sold in India."[56] But the Indians did not want to bring down the tariff walls. Indian and American representatives clashed during the formulation of the Havana Charter for the International Trade Organization, the precursor to the negotiations on the General Agreement on Trade and Tariffs. The Indians defended the right of the developing countries to take protectionist measures to safeguard their national industries and to implement discriminatory measures against foreign capital.

While the Americans could put up with moderate tariffs, they strongly objected to the barriers to investment. The Indian businessmen in the Federation of Indian Chambers of Commerce and Industry (FICCI), however, had been loath to open the doors to American capital. Since the war years, they had lobbied the Indian government to ensure that the Americans did not supplant the British in dominating the Indian economy. They argued against the entry of foreign firms not only in heavy, basic industries but also in the production of consumer goods. It was better, they insisted, to import consumer goods not yet produced in India than to allow their production by foreign companies in the country. In their view, India needed foreign technical assistance and managerial talent more than capital. In any case, the effective control of such enterprises had to remain in Indian hands. In a report to the Indian government in January 1947, the Advisory Planning Board reflected these views.[57]

The Americans were not pleased. The next month, the head of the American economic mission in India, Westmore Wilcox, wrote directly to Nehru seeking increased opportunity and better terms for American investment in India. He also suggested a twenty-year ban on the nationalization of American companies. Then the Indian government would buy out American shareholders at a price determined by the company. Wilcox also hinted that US government loans to India might be tied to a liberal foreign-investment policy. Nehru replied that India would "gladly welcome help from abroad" in its industrialization. "But we are equally anxious to prevent any foreign control of Indian industry." India realized the importance of creating value for foreign investments, but "where there is any question of control by foreign interests, there is likely to be great opposition in India." Nehru emphasized that American involvement in the development of India must be "within the terms of our own policy and with full freedom for us to do what we consider proper."[58]

In April 1948, the Indian parliament adopted an Industrial Policy Resolution, which introduced a state monopoly on railways and the defense industry and asserted the primacy of the state in six other areas: coal, iron and steel, aircraft manufacture, shipbuilding, telegraph and wireless equipment, and mineral resources. While all other areas were open to the private sector, the state reserved the right to regulate those of special importance: automobiles and machine tools, heavy chemicals and fertilizers, textiles, and cement, among others. The resolution observed that foreign capital was essential for acquiring capital goods and technical knowledge. As foreign equity was concerned, however, the effective control and majority capital would have to be Indian. These rules could only be relaxed in exceptional cases in the national interest.

The Americans naturally found these conditions rather unattractive. "Speaking for the capitalists of my own country," observed Ambassador Henry Grady, "I can say that while under proper terms and conditions they are willing to lend money to this country and to other countries, they are not prepared to beg that their capital be received."[59] He was right: American capital had far more profitable venues at home and in western Europe. Grady also found India's policy schizophrenic. It was inconsistent, he argued, for the Indians to complain that foreign capital was not flowing in when they were adopting policies that would have no effect other than to keep it out.

The lack of adequate foreign capital flows registered painfully on the Indian government when it faced a dollar crunch in early 1949.

By March, New Delhi had already drawn its entire annual quota of $100 million from the International Monetary Fund (IMF). At best, the fund could provide a lump sum to help get it through the liquidity crisis. Against this backdrop, the Indian finance minister announced in Parliament that American capital and enterprises were welcome to collaborate with Indian firms. The following month, the prime minister stated, "Indian capital needs to be supplemented by foreign capital not only because our national savings will not be enough for the rapid development of the country on the scale we wish, but also because in many cases scientific, technical and industrial knowledge and capital equipment can best be secured along with foreign capital."[60]

A series of measures followed aimed at allaying American concerns: treatment of foreign enterprises on a par with Indian ones, no restrictions on withdrawal of foreign investments, unhindered repatriation of profits except on foreign exchange considerations, and fair and equitable compensation for any foreign company acquired by the government. Above all, in September 1949, the government announced that to ensure "maximum possible influx of foreign capital in the shortest possible time," it was open to allowing foreign majority ownership and, in some cases, even non-Indian effective control, especially in the formative stages of a venture.

The last announcement came ahead of Nehru's visit to the United States in October 1949. In fact, it followed a series of discussions between the two sides during the previous August and September. The Americans noted "a serious divergence of views over the investment issue." But their negotiators felt that India's position was weakening, and they advised "postponing further discussions for several months since there is a reasonable possibility that a more favorable attitude toward the main negotiating issues may develop within the Indian government in the near future."[61] But New Delhi did not have much legroom for further concessions. In response to the September announcement, Indian capitalists in the FICCI issued a statement demanding strict adherence to the Industrial Policy Resolution of 1948 and even suggested reverting to the yet more restrictive framework suggested by the Advisory Planning Board.

The Indian government's Industries (Development and Regulation) Act of 1951 deepened American fears about state interference in the management of private enterprises. The data spoke for themselves. Between early 1948 and mid-1952, the Indian government approved 108 new joint venture projects, of which only 13 were American (British capital accounted for 69). The major chunks of American private investment in India were in the oil industry. Then, too, the Indian government had to make huge departures from stated policy to attract US companies into a sector that it considered strategic. Take the Standard Vacuum Oil (Stanvac) refinery near Bombay. New Delhi agreed that the company would not be nationalized for twenty-five years, that Indian capital would not exceed 25 percent, that annual profits could be repatriated in dollars, that the company could use its own tankers to import crude oil, and that these imports would be free of customs duty for ten years.[62]

Not surprisingly, then, India refused to conclude a treaty of friendship, commerce, and navigation with the United States. The Americans had sought such an agreement since they began dealing with India over lend-lease in 1942. But it had been shelved owing to Indian capitalists' concerns about American domination. Grady sought to move the discussions forward during his tenure. But Nehru would not be hustled. "The question of economic domination of India by the U.S.A.," he wrote to the foreign secretary, "is not one that frightens me although one should be careful not to encourage it." The real question was how far such an agreement might "come in the way of the general development of our economic policy...laid down in the Government's industrial policy statement." The "safest policy," Nehru concluded, was "to be friendly to America, to give them fair terms, to invite their help on such terms, and at the same time not to tie ourselves up too much with their world or their economic policy."[63]

The Truman administration proposed a fresh draft in the wake of his "Point Four" speech, but the Indians were unwilling to conclude the agreement. Nor were the Pakistanis willing to sign up, although American economic interest in that country was less. Returning from a trip to South Asia in early 1950, George McGhee summed up Washington's frustration: "Present policies of the two governments, as we understand them, involve nationalization of certain key industries and rather extensive and restrictive controls over other major elements in their economies which we associate with the methods of socialism.... The real need of India and Pakistan for industrial development is equity capital, not loans."[64] Ambassador Loy Henderson was even blunter in conversation with the governor of the Reserve Bank of India. The recent concessions made by India were not good enough. American investors justifiably believed that "they were not really wanted in India and that those concessions...had been granted with reluctance." But, he added, "American investors were not to be tempted to go into a field where they were likely to be considered as a temporary necessary evil." Governor B. N. Rau replied that liberalizing Indian policy further would not help either. For the Americans had an automatic "suspicion of the real attitude of India toward foreign investments which could not be removed by mere announcements."[65] Indeed, the gulf between the two sides would persist for decades.

Beyond the unavailability of American direct investment in India, New Delhi's problem was also its inability to access India's sterling balances in London and use them for imports from the United States for its own program of industrialization. This was a consequence both of Britain's unwillingness to allow India unfettered use of its own foreign currency reserves and of the US desire for an early end to the sterling bloc, even if it meant writing down the balances owed to countries like India. The Americans periodically urged Britain to do so and, in effect, encouraged the devaluation of the pound in 1949. During his visit to the United States that year, Nehru put India's case eloquently: "Those sterling balances represent many things. They represent the goods which we produced and sold to America, to England, sold for dollar and sterling, sold for lesser than market price. They represent the lack of necessaries of life which India had to put up with, even food. They represent the final culmination of that great tragedy, the Bengal famine, in which three million people died....So, when you think of those sterling balances about which there is often so much discussion, think of the price that India paid for them in blood and suffering." Still, as during the Bretton Woods conference, the Americans saw no reason to intercede on India's behalf.

Ironically, India was forced to turn toward the IMF in 1949 to cope with its dollar crunch. What is more, it had to ask the United States not to oppose its application for increased dollar withdrawals. To cap it all, American officials discerned an opportunity for "expediting settlement of [the] Kashmir crisis." As an aide to the president's special adviser, Clark Clifford, noted, "India has serious balance of payment problems. If the United States should wish to exert pressure at this time to achieve a solution of the Kashmir question, it is in an excellent position to do so by instructing the US Executive Director of the Bank and the Fund that it is not favorably disposed toward the request to draw additional dollars from the fund, or to obtain a loan from the Bank."[66]

The administration wisely desisted from such a course. In fact, later that year India received a World Bank loan of $35 million to finance part of an $84 million program to upgrade the Indian railways. The president of the bank recommended the loan on the grounds that India was using its sterling balances for development and that the "allocation of the released [sterling] balances for development expenditures was not as large as had been expected."[67]

In this context, India came to rely increasingly on foreign aid to finance its economic development. But such aid was not forthcoming. As early as July 1947, an interdepartmental committee had concluded that the situation in India was "not now, nor is likely to be within the next five years, so critical as to necessitate special appropriations of American public funds in order to safeguard United States security by extraordinary measures of financial aid to India."[68] This reflected the scale of the administration's commitments to Europe and the limited importance attached to South Asia.

From late 1947, Grady sought to make a robust case for India. In particular, he wished to ensure American involvement in the river valley projects (modeled on the Tennessee Valley Authority) launched by Nehru. In discussions with Indian cabinet ministers, he proposed contracting an American engineering firm for at least one of these projects and suggested that cheap financing might be available through the Export-Import (EXIM) Bank of the United States. Grady urged his friend Stephen Bechtel of the Bechtel International Corporation to participate in the construction of a dam. "As you know," he wrote Bechtel, "one of the reasons I came here, in fact, the principal reason, was to endeavor to keep India in our camp.... We can demonstrate our system is better by helping India in an unselfish way to develop her own resources." Bechtel directed Grady toward the Morrison-Knudsen Corporation that operated in India and even accompanied the ambassador for negotiations with the Indian government. Grady urged Nehru to just hand over one project to Morrison-Knudsen and see "how fast the dirt will fly."[69] The prime minister had concerns about how much employment the project would generate, given the Americans' reliance on heavy machinery. But the idea eventually foundered owing to a lack of funding from the EXIM Bank.

Grady's successor, Henderson, made another strong pitch ahead of Nehru's visit for an aid package worth $500 million for India. The British enthusiastically endorsed the idea, but the State Department shot it down. In the late 1940s Washington deemed requests for aid from India problematic. The first consideration was ideological: American officials believed that peripheral countries like India did not warrant US government aid. As a State Department policy summary put it, "We regard private investment as the principal means of U.S. financial assistance to India in the development of its economy." Then there were political considerations. The State Department was "reluctant" to endorse India's policy of "overt neutrality." Finally the Americans believed that providing economic aid to India was "almost hopeless" "so long as [the] running sore of the Kashmir problem was eating into India's financial position and undermining the political economic stability of southern Asia."[70]

Pakistan's requests for aid fared no better. As a new breakaway state created under adverse circumstances, Pakistan desired American economic assistance from the outset. In his first meeting with Ambassador Grady, before Pakistan formally came into existence, Jinnah was "most cordial, expressed great admiration for the U.S. and said he was hopeful U.S. would aid Pakistan in its many problems."[71] Soon after independence, Pakistan affirmed its pro-West orientation. Jinnah also sent an emissary to Washington requesting a $2 billion loan. The Americans, however, pointed out that the administration could not extend foreign credits of such magnitude without congressional approval. Instead they advised Pakistan to identify projects that might "qualify for financing by the Export-Import Bank or ultimately by the International [World] Bank." Eventually, the Americans offered a mere $10 million for relief and rehabilitation of refugees pouring into Pakistan from India.[72] Aid to Pakistan was tricky in other ways too. For one thing, the Pakistanis sought more military than economic aid. For another, the Americans believed that providing aid to Pakistan while denying it to India would needlessly complicate their regional policy.

The provision of aid to the subcontinent acquired salience within the administration toward the end of 1950. A peculiar concatenation of droughts and floods had laid to waste over 2.5 million tons of food crops in India. Coming on the heels of the foreign exchange crisis, this massive shortfall pushed the country to the brink of famine. Nehru had no choice but to gulp his pride and ask the United States for 2 million tons in food aid. Several prominent American figures and organizations came out in support of India's request: Eleanor Roosevelt, Pearl Buck, Walter White of the NAACP; the YMCA, the National Council of Churches, the National Lutheran Council, and the Friends Service Committee. Many of them had long been associated with or espoused the cause of India—most recently during the 1943–1944 Bengal famine. But in the context of a Cold War that was turning increasingly hot in Asia, the case for food to India proved rather more difficult to make.

"Nehru is out giving us hell of a time, working against us and voting against us," complained Tom Connally, the powerful Democratic chairman of the Senate Foreign Relations Committee. Senior State Department officials felt, however, that if they failed to assist India, "elements inimical to the United States and the Western world generally will be strengthened."[73] At the same time, they sought to use the opportunity to nudge India's foreign policy in the desired directions. Meeting Ambassador Vijayalakshmi Pandit on December 29, Acheson mentioned that "India's attitudes" on two foreign policy matters would be of importance in getting the US Congress to act on food aid. The first was settlement of the Kashmir dispute. "If this were done," he said, "the people of the Hill would be favorably impressed." The second was Korea: "Members of Congress would ask whether India understands the depth of the danger we now face." McGhee, who was also present at the meeting, assured her that "the question of an all-out alignment [with the United States] did not necessarily arise," though he asked if India might consider "mutual defence arrangements." Pandit responded guardedly but emphasized that the aid should not come with strings attached: "Statements might be demanded which India could not make."[74]

In the event, Truman weighed in with a message to Congress urging 2 million tons of wheat in food aid to India and emphasizing the need to keep New Delhi on the right side in the struggle against world communism. Still, hearings in the House and Senate proceeded slowly, and the exchanges were often sharply critical of India's foreign and economic policies. The US Congress sought to tie repayment of the $190 million loan to provision by India of strategic minerals, especially Monazite sand, embargoed since 1946.[75] Nehru bristled at this and other arrangements pertaining to the delivery and distribution of the food. The proposed legislation sought, he told Ambassador Pandit at one point, "practically [to convert] India into some kind of a semico-lonial country or at least a satellite in the economic sense…I realize completely the consequence of our refusal of this gift. Nevertheless, I cannot bring myself to agree to this final humiliation."[76]

The administration managed to finesse these differences, and President Truman signed the wheat loan legislation on June 15, 1951. Nehru welcomed it as a "generous gesture." But the entire episode had underscored the political, economic, and ideological crevasse that had opened up between the United States and India.

By the time the wheat loan was authorized, the administration's aid policy toward South Asia was coming into focus. In May 1950, the US Congress approved a program based on Truman's Point Four proposals. Although the president dubbed it a "bold new program" to assist underdeveloped countries, the total appropriation was only $35 million—of which India's allocation was a measly $4.5 million. The comparison was stark not just with the $2.85 billion given to west-ern Europe under the Marshall Plan but also with the $194 million in aid to Korea, Southeast Asia, and Taiwan. A month later, McGhee proposed a program of developmental projects for South Asia to the tune of $200 million. When presented to Truman this became part of a $300 million initiative for South Asia, the Arab States, and Iran. None of this, however, was sent to Congress before May 1951, and by then the proposals had considerably shrunk. The administration sought just over $78 million for South Asia: $65 million for India, $12.5 million for Pakistan, and $700,000 for Afghanistan, Ceylon, and Nepal. The Congress axed some of this and eventually appropriated only $54 million for India.[77]

EVEN AS THE ADMINISTRATION embarked on a modest aid pro-gram for South Asia, Truman appointed Chester Bowles as ambassa-dor to India. An archetypal, liberal New Dealer, Bowles had sought out the post in India. He discussed his choice and credo eloquently in a letter to a close friend in January 1952: "The single force capable of dealing with the Communist forces in Asia is the United States, *operating within its best liberal traditions.* This calls for an America willing to share its wealth with countries which are willing to do their own share; an American free of racial prejudices and willing to accept men of all creeds and colors as their equals; an America keenly aware of the problems of defense but equally aware that we cannot buy security with bombs."[78]

In thinking about the development of the periphery, Bowles shared the widely held notion that Third World countries should focus primarily on agriculture and then on producing light consumer goods: apparel, sewing machines, bicycles, and radios. "How I would love to see Sears and Roebuck come out here," he told a State Department official, "and really tackle the problem of inexpensive distribution of consumer goods, keyed to the Indian market."[79]

Owing to his New Deal background and convictions, however, Bowles saw only a limited role for foreign private capital in the early stages of development. This did not mean that he passed up opportunities for American capital in India: on the contrary, Bowles, himself, had prevailed on the Indian government to make concessions to attract American investment in oil refining. Yet he held that the main requirement of underdeveloped countries like India was foreign exchange and that foreign aid, including food aid, would be an important source of this.

Bowles's arrival in India coincided with the launch of its first five-year plan. This plan departed from earlier ideas and blueprints for rapid industrialization envisaged by Indian capitalists as well as the nationalists. It by no means abandoned them, however; they would make a strong comeback in the second five-year plan. But chastened by the chronic food shortages of the past decade, the Indian planners chose to concentrate on agriculture. About a third of the outlay in the public sector targeted agriculture, irrigation, and community development. By increasing productivity, the government hoped to attain self-sufficiency in food and other commercial crops like cotton and jute. Only 8.4 percent of the public-sector outlay went to the industrial sector. The government planned to finance the total public-sector expenditure of nearly 21 billion rupees by mobilizing domestic resources. Of this, 4 billion would be needed in foreign exchange—an amount that the planners hoped to meet with sterling balances and foreign aid.

Insofar as the plan emphasized agriculture, it met with US approval. Nevertheless, Bowles harbored deep reservations about Nehru's commitment to a mixed economy and believed that India needed shepherding toward a proper liberal, capitalist path of development. Following the wheat loan, the two sides had successfully negotiated a bilateral economic cooperation agreement in January 1952. This led to the establishment of an Indo-American Technical Cooperation Fund, financed initially by the $54 million approved by the US Congress and matched by a Special Development Fund to which the Indian government contributed an equivalent amount in rupees. These funds would finance the first set of joint development projects.[80]

In deploying these funds, Bowles championed a Community Development Program (CDP) that would set India on the road to liberal capitalist modernity. Drawing on an ongoing experiment in community development in North India's Etawah district, Bowles envisaged a major CDP to expand agricultural extension, raise health and literacy standards, and improve rural living conditions. He quickly developed a rapport with Nehru and convinced him to endorse his ideas for a "dynamic, cooperative effort to raise living, health and literacy standards in all parts of India."[81] In its initial stage, this program would cover fifty-five community projects, each with three hundred villages and 200,000 people—in all encompassing 11 million Indians. In the years ahead, India would become by far the largest site for applying notions of community development. In the beginning, however, the CDP relied on two other sources of expertise and assistance.

Since late 1950, the Ford Foundation had been looking for an appropriate entry point into South Asia. In considering its role, Ford built on the earlier experience of the Rockefeller Foundation but adapted it to the demands of the postwar world: American preponderance, communist challenge, and the aspirations of decolonizing countries. The first president of the Ford Foundation was Paul Hoffman, formerly head of Studebaker Corporation and administrator of the Marshall Plan. "We have learned in Europe," Hoffman held, "what to do in Asia, for under the Marshall Plan we have developed the essential instruments of a successful policy in the arena of world politics."[82] The State Department's Near East and South Asia Desk had welcomed foundation programs in India and Pakistan as "an indication of paramount American *private* interest" and suggested agricultural policy and raising of per capita farm income as an important area of focus. A trip to the region in August 1951 convinced Hoffman that Prime Minister Nehru "greatly needs understanding, sympathy, and help from the people and governments of other free nations." Hoffman was particularly taken in by the Etawah experiment in community development and saw "no reason why all 500,000 of India's villages could not make a similar advance."[83]

Nehru, for his part, felt that a Ford-funded pilot CDP would help gauge the potential for scaling up the program in other parts of India. New Delhi invited the Ford Foundation to set up office in India and collaborate on mutually agreed initiatives. Hoffman persuaded a young and dynamic official from the Office of Foreign Agricultural Relations, Douglas Ensminger, to head the foundation's activities in South Asia. From November 1951, Ensminger and his colleagues got down to understanding the challenges and modalities of community development in India. When Hoffman's old friend Chester Bowles advocated an expansive CDP, Ford pitched in with a $2.9 million grant to establish regional training centers for village-level workers.[84]

Nehru, Bowles, Hoffman, and Ensminger all sought to build on the model of the Etawah project, conceived and directed by a young American architect. Albert Meyer was part of a small but influential group of communitarian planners in the United States that included Lewis

Mumford, Clarence Stein, and Catherine Bauer. Meyer came to India during World War II to build airstrips in the Northeast. At the end of the war he met and established an intellectual affinity with Nehru. He would later recall "intimate talks until far into the night" about model villages and the prospect of applying communitarian ideas to India. Nehru enjoyed considering not this or that aspect of human welfare but "a whole with various aspects inter-linked" in order to "build up community life."[85]

At Nehru's invitation Meyer returned to India after the war and set about studying various attempts at rural development. Gandhi and his followers had, of course, engaged in constructive work in Indian villages since the early 1930s. While Meyer "revered" Gandhi, he also felt "their approach assumes the existence of more saintly people than the world contains." He wondered, "To what extent can the village remain self-contained…without excessive material loss?" Nor was he sure that the local cottage industries and crafts promoted by Gandhi were a "viable mode of production." Meyer also examined the efforts of the missionaries, noting their technical contribution to rural development, especially with hospitals, agricultural institutes, and elementary and secondary schools. But these were too few to make a broader impact. He also felt that villagers' disinclination to work with the missionaries, a lack of urgency stemming from a faith in providence, and an aloofness from the state hampered these efforts. Spencer Hatch's rural work in Martandam was another point of reference for Meyer.[86] All this was apt, for Meyer and the development specialists who followed in his wake were heirs to the old American missionary tradition in South Asia: they were missionaries of modernity.

Nehru's colleague and the premier of Uttar Pradesh, G. B. Pant, invited Meyer to set up a pilot project in the district of Etawah. Here Meyer undertook a range of activities: distribution of seeds and provision of better livestock, vaccination and inoculation, hygiene, sanitation, and upkeep of public utilities. Meyer's distinctive contribution lay in his emphasis on a bottom-up, grassroots approach to development.

His army of village-level workers constantly consulted with the villagers and elicited their views and needs—even if these were not based on any scientific measure. Meyer also encouraged open, communal deliberations that did not accord primacy to official and bureaucratic hierarchies. The results in certain parts of Etawah were striking. Using their own materials villagers built roads and culverts, schools and libraries, sanitary wells and hand pumps, brick kilns and cooperative ventures. Meyer and Etawah shot to fame not just in India but also in the United States. *Time, Life,* and the *New York Times* magazine, among other publications, covered the project. Even President Truman singled it out in his speeches.[87]

While Meyer acquired international prominence in India, another American toiled in obscurity in the most inaccessible parts of Pakistan. John Clark was a geologist who also came to the subcontinent during World War II. As a reconnaissance engineer on General Joseph Stilwell's staff, he had spent considerable time exploring the frontier between the Xinjiang province of China and the Himalayan ranges. In late 1949, he raised a few thousand dollars and set off for Hunza in the Gilgit province of the undivided state of Kashmir—now under the control and administration of Pakistan. "My object" wrote Clark, "was to attempt to show the members of one Asian community how they could use the resources they already possessed to better their own lives."

Ironically, Clark's vision of rural development took inspiration from what he had seen of Soviet efforts in Xinjiang, when the province was for all practical purposes under their control. The Russians had set up schools in every village, built simple gravel roads as well as all-weather roads with wooden bridges, and introduced small, portable steam engines, electric plants, flour mills, and sawmills. In Hunza, Clark sought to show the people that "within their own efforts lay their hope of the future...and that they did not need Communism." Admittedly "one man could not stop Communism in Asia," but Clark felt that "one properly managed project like mine could free several thousand

Asians from its menace, and could act as a sort of pilot model for larger efforts."[88]

The Pakistanis permitted Clark to try out his experiment in Hunza if only because they were in no position to do anything for that remote province. Over the next twenty months, Clark set up a medical dispensary, built schools and drew up the curriculum, prospected for marble and minerals, introduced handmade machinery such as pipes and lathes, organized a handcraft school, and promoted trade between the valleys—all with no financing from either the US government (which had flatly turned him down) or the Pakistan government (which had none to offer). But crucially, his efforts drew on the support and resources of the local hamlets and villages of Hunza.

Here was rather a different American vision of community development—one that emphasized private initiative rather than state patronage. At the end of his stint, Clark urged, "Stop at once the ruinous system of large, direct gifts from the American government to Asian governments." Instead the United States should "work entirely through the established private agencies"—philanthropic foundations. "No twenty-million dollar steel mills," he insisted, "but rather twenty-thousand-dollar projects in a thousand villages." In fact, the Ford Foundation had approached the Pakistani government with a community development project, but the Pakistanis had not been keen on it. Nevertheless, later in the decade Pakistan would become the testing ground for another project in rural development—in the province of Comilla in East Pakistan (later Bangladesh).

IN HIS FAREWELL ADDRESS on January 15, 1953, Harry Truman said, "History will remember my term in office as the years when the 'cold war' began to overshadow our lives. I have hardly had a day in office that has not been dominated by this all-embracing struggle—this conflict between those who love freedom and those who would lead the world back into slavery and darkness."[89] South Asia was not a key battleground in the Cold War. Nevertheless, the imperatives of America's grand strategy impinged on the region. As the curtains came down on the Truman administration, there was growing strategic convergence between the United States and Pakistan. The United States and India, by contrast, stood increasingly apart owing to their differing views on the Cold War in Asia and India's unwillingness to play the economic role assigned to peripheral countries in the American script. The cultural lenses through which Americans viewed the subcontinent exacerbated these differences.

Religion and race had been crucial in shaping American images of South Asia over the past century and more. Neither had been fixed or unchanging components of the American cultural repertoire, but they imbued Americans with a remarkably durable sense of hierarchy. In the postwar years, religion did not have the same salience in American engagement with South Asia, but it remained important.

As Truman's parting speech suggested, many Americans saw the Cold War as a spiritual contest between the forces of light and darkness. To an ardent cold warrior such as Loy Henderson, India's reluctance to stand by the United States in this "holy war" was an extraordinary moral failure. But it fit well with the older images purveyed by missionaries about the Hindus' lack of masculinity and vitality. A State Department study in 1952 concluded that Pakistani Islam "presents a more effective deterrent to the acceptance of communist doctrines than Hinduism." Hence Pakistan was a more reliable partner in the global crusade against communism.[90] The impress of the older missionary ideas was evident in yet another way. The emerging ideas of development reflected the missionaries' image of the subcontinent as a backward region awaiting redemption. American experts who began trooping into the subcontinent also drew and built on earlier efforts at social uplift by the missionaries. So did the American philanthropies that supported the new developmental missions.

These developmental hierarchies of modernity also mirrored the older hierarchies established by notions of race. To be sure, modernization theory had yet to be fleshed out in all its scientific trappings. But its debt to increasingly discredited ideas of race was obvious. The overt biological racism of the prewar years was clearly on its way out—challenged both by developments in disciplines like physiology and social anthropology and by the experience of World War II when Americans found themselves fighting against a regime that was racist all the way down. In the aftermath of the war, Americans increasingly frowned on racial prejudice, though real change was slow in coming. Nevertheless, race remained a key prism through which US policymakers perceived the non-Western world.

Apart from tincturing notions of development, race structured American views of South Asia along two axes. First, while stripped of racial language, the sense of hierarchy stemming from racial superiority remained in place. Even those favorably inclined toward the region partook of an unmistakable paternalism. This was evident in American dealings with India. The United States of course saw nonalignment as problematic for political reasons, but the issue acquired an edge owing to Americans' frustration at their inability to control a country that they deemed inferior to them in every imaginable way. In consequence, American officials frequently viewed the Indians as deviant, misbehaving children.

Thus, Henderson regarded Nehru's criticism of the United States for propping up colonial powers like the Netherlands in Asia as an expression not just of his "animosity" but also of his "lack of stability."[91] The briefing for Secretary of State Marshall ahead of his 1948 meeting with Nehru noted that India's foreign policy was "indicative of its political and international immaturity and feeling of self-righteousness"—characteristics "shared and epitomized by Prime Minister Nehru." Prior to Nehru's visit to the United States the following year, Henderson wrote, "With all his complexity, Nehru still has in him the makings of a small boy." Diagnosing the reasons for the growing rift between India and the United States, Henderson wrote to Acheson, "Indian leaders, particularly Nehru, have been cajoled and treated as spoiled children so long by other members of the [British] Commonwealth that they have tendencies to become outraged when their schemes are opposed." They must become "sufficiently adult," especially the "vain and immature" Nehru.[92]

The Indian prime minister's hauteur particularly grated on American officials because it inverted their conceptions of hierarchy. "Nehru came to America," recalled George McGhee, "with an apparent chip on his shoulder toward American high officials, who he appeared to believe could not possibly understand someone with his background." Dean Acheson claimed that Nehru spoke to him "as Queen Victoria said of Mr. Gladstone, as though I were a public meeting."[93]

Race structured American perceptions of South Asia along another axis by fueling anxieties about racial prejudice in the reverse. Alarmist notions of Asian "racial chauvinism" or "reverse color prejudice" underpinning a "revolt against the West" had considerable purchase on US policymakers. These anxieties predated the war but were sharpened by the Japanese wartime rhetoric of pan-Asianism. Other European empires in Asia shared such concerns, which served as a trope to delegitimize nationalist movements or postcolonial states that challenged long-established hierarchies.[94]

Henderson held, for instance, that Indians' complaints about racial discrimination by Western powers were bogus. Nehru, he told Acheson in early 1951, was "constitutionally unhappy when he [was] not leading some cause of downtrodden peoples, particularly of Asian or colored peoples, against real or imagined oppression." His successor, Chester Bowles—who held more enlightened, if gradualist, ideas about the need for racial equality at home—felt that Indians had an "almost psychopathic suspicion of Western intentions, and…deep resentment of our prejudices towards the colored races."[95] Graham Parsons, a senior official in the embassy in New Delhi, similarly observed, "Those who deal with India…are seldom permitted to forget for any length of time the absorbing interest that Indians have in racial discrimination… in our own country."[96]

Concerns about Western racism were not restricted to India, however. State Department officials noticed popular interest in this issue across the subcontinent. Nonofficial visitors to the region also picked it up as a hot-button topic. After touring India and Pakistan in late 1952, Norman Cousins of the *Saturday Review of Literature* found "race prejudice and discrimination" was the "number one" topic of discussion about America. Indeed, defense of America against charges of racism became a dominant theme of US propaganda in South Asia. The State Department sent several prominent intellectuals and activists to the subcontinent on speaking tours. Walter White of the NAACP came out in 1949 to present his vision of liberal anticommunism as a progressive creed at home and abroad. "As an American negro," he said in Karachi, "I am deeply aware of the grave shortcomings of my own country." But he insisted that "under democracy, minorities can fight against injustice.... [W]e are making progress." A young Pakistani in the audience responded, "You talk a great deal about your American type of democracy. But we all know what it means. We know that if a colored man even looks at a White woman in the United States, he is lynched." When Ralph McGill, the liberal white editor of the *Atlanta Constitution*, told an Indian railway guard that he was from the American South, the man promptly asked, "They [African Americans] can't walk on the sidewalks can they? Or go in the shops?" When McGill said that much of what "you read here is exaggerated," the Indian persisted, "I read about a lot of them getting shot by men in masks." McGill noted that the Indian had picked this up from left-leaning newspapers, which took an anti-American and pro-Soviet line.[97]

Anxieties about reverse racism thus meshed with traditional Cold War concerns. A regional meeting of American diplomats in early 1951 recommended that "anti-Westernism springing from color and race prejudice should be combatted by maintaining the present volume of counter-propaganda through an information and cultural approach which admits the existence of a color problem in the United States but points out that we are doing something about it." The group also recommended having in American establishments in the region "a few additional American negroes." Similarly, "charges of United States support for imperialism and colonialism in Asia should be attacked through a carefully formulated public relations program." This should include an increase in "friendly discussions with influential individuals and groups in South Asia, such as labor organizations as well as with the 'grass roots.'" Private agencies, including American philanthropies and universities, should be encouraged to undertake activities that could "usefully supplement, or, under certain political conditions, supersede those of United States official agencies."[98]

The number of United States Information Service (USIS) personnel in the subcontinent was just over 450, with almost 350 posted in India. Congressional cuts in funding prevented expansion as envisaged by the State Department. But senior officials in Washington were also concerned about the US propaganda strategy in India. Some believed it "not sufficiently subtle": "We are trying to 'sell' America rather than show American interest in Indian problems and Indian traditions." McGhee noted the "difficulty of doing business with Nehru and of Nehru's dissent from our policies, especially with reference to the Far East and development of collective security." Others, however, felt that "we could succeed with the Indian people, even if we could not succeed with Nehru; but, that given time, we could even succeed with him."[99] In his farewell meeting with Nehru later that year, Henderson sought to clarify that US information activity in India was not aimed at interfering in domestic affairs. "What the U.S.I.S. wanted to do was to put down their own positive points of view in order to counteract Communist propaganda in India." Some Indian newspapers were "attacking America all the time." Also, Indian bookstores were "full of communist pamphlets and literature." US publicity was absent "while Communist publicity was obvious."[100]

No sooner had Bowles taken over than he determined to overhaul US propaganda. The Americans had experience in dealing with Communist ideology in western Europe, which was not particularly useful in the Indian context: "In India we are dealing with sensitive people somewhat unsure of themselves, proud of their new freedom, and inclined to look on us as bragging white men." Nevertheless, he believed that these attitudes could be "broken down with a surprising speed" if the United States presented its "own beliefs with honest humility." Instead of "black and white statements about the cold war," they should help the Indians reason out the "world conflict in their own minds."[101] While American officials shared Bowles's cultural assumptions about the region and its peoples, neither the Truman administration nor its successor was prepared to follow his prescriptions.

5

ALLIES AND AID

Dwight Eisenhower shared the grand strategic preoccupations of his predecessor. Unlike Harry Truman, though, he had thought long and hard about American strategy prior to entering the White House. At the heart of Eisenhower's worldview was an expansive conception of American security that explicitly went beyond the defensive notion of containment. As he wrote in his diary in January 1952, "It is necessary to recognize that the purpose of America is to defend a way of life rather than merely to defend property, territory, homes or lives. As a consequence of this purpose, everything done to develop a defense against external threat...must be weighed and gauged in the light of probable long-term, internal, effect."[1] In Eisenhower's mind strategic and economic considerations were inextricably intertwined. America sought a preponderance of power in order to sustain a liberal, capitalist global order, which in turn was essential to maintaining such a system at home.

This "Great Equation," as Eisenhower at times referred to it, acquired a particular salience owing to his fiscal conservatism. On the campaign trail, Eisenhower had been critical of the burgeoning defense budget under Truman and asked if it was sustainable. "We must achieve both security and solvency," he insisted. "In fact, the foundation of military strength is economic strength. A bankrupt America is more the Soviet goal than an America conquered on the field of battle."[2] Thus, while Eisenhower agreed with the aims of Truman's national security policy and the need to maintain a dominant position in the Eurasian heartland, he did not believe that these called for an increasing American military buildup. Instead, the Eisenhower administration's "New Look" strategy emphasized different and more affordable means of ensuring the preponderance of American power.

On the one hand, the strategy relied on the deterrent capabilities of America's nuclear arsenal. The United States would respond to any aggression in western Europe with massive, retaliatory nuclear strikes. Eisenhower believed that the Soviet leadership was rational and focused on self-preservation. Hence the threat of massive retaliation would check its aggressive instincts. On the other hand, the Eisenhower administration set greater store by the role of allies. By strengthening and expanding US bilateral and multilateral alliances, Eisenhower sought to encircle the Communist powers and scale back America's military commitments. By substituting allied manpower for American forces in various regional defense networks, he also hoped to lighten the United States' growing fiscal burden. A greater emphasis on propaganda, public diplomacy, psychological warfare, and covert action supplemented these military means. Eisenhower believed that the ideological and cultural competition was as central to winning the Cold War as the strategic and economic struggle.

All this led in the context of Asia to a series of bilateral and multilateral security alliances aimed at securing the Far East, Southeast Asia, and the Middle East. While South Asia was not the focus of any such arrangement, its location, size, and population ensured its importance to the administration's "pactomania." The region also acquired salience owing to the growing strength of nationalism across the colonial world and the spurt of decolonization from 1957. The "Third World" as an entity was imagined into existence during Eisenhower's years in office. And crafting effective policies toward it proved rather challenging.

The problem was particularly acute owing to the new Soviet leadership under Nikita Khrushchev, which sought to expand Moscow's influence in these countries with the infusion of economic aid and technical assistance. In November 1955, the Central Intelligence Agency (CIA) warned of a "grave danger" that the new Soviet policy would "create an even more serious threat to the Free World than did Stalin's aggressive postwar policies."[3] In his second inaugural address, Eisenhower warned that international communism "strives to capture to exploit for its own greater power, all forces of change in the world, especially the needs of the hungry and the hopes of the oppressed."[4] The United States needed to unloose its purse strings—despite the president's fiscal prudence—for the development of the Third World. A budget-conscious Congress, however, was unwilling to walk all the way with the president. In consequence, Eisenhower's policy toward South Asia was pulled in different directions.

FROM THE OUTSET, THE Eisenhower administration displayed an affinity for Pakistan and took a sterner view of India's nonalignment. The new secretary of state, John Foster Dulles, had already clashed with New Delhi while negotiating the San Francisco Peace Treaty that ended World War II in Asia and the Allied occupation of Japan. Even more than many of his contemporaries, Dulles viewed India through the prism of race and religion as well as in terms of politics and strategy. "The Chinese communists," he wrote in a memorandum on the Japan treaty, "using the old Japanese war slogan of 'Asia for Asiatics,' are attempting to rally all of Asia to rise up to eject violently all Western influence. India shows a tendency to move in that direction." This would only lead, Dulles warned in a speech to the National Council of Christians and Jews in late 1951, to an "Asia for Russians."[5] The venue of the speech was no coincidence. A devout ecumenical Christian from a family of Presbyterian missionaries—his grandfather had worked in India and Ceylon—Dulles saw the Cold War as a crusade and regarded neutrality in the conflict as a profound moral and spiritual failing.[6] By contrast, he took to Pakistan after his first visit to the country in 1953: "Pakistan is one country that had [the] moral courage to do its part [in] resisting communism."[7]

The administration's leanings were evident in its early stance toward India and Pakistan. Dulles took the knife to Chester Bowles's recommendation to send $200 million in aid to India during fiscal year 1954. "I doubt that this amount is either justified by facts," said Dulles, "or could be justified by Congress."[8] At his instruction, the State Department pared down India's allocation by $60 million. Dulles was not displeased when Congress scaled it down by another $30 million. Along with aid to India, he also rid the administration of Bowles and replaced him as ambassador with George Allen.

At the same time, when Pakistan appealed to the United States for 1 to 1.5 million tons of food grain to meet with a potentially grim situation, the administration responded with alacrity. Assistant Secretary of State Henry Byroade wrote to Dulles, "Pakistan is potentially an important contributor to Middle East defense and is strategically located between free Asia and the Middle East." The country was already facing internal unrest following the death of Liaquat Ali Khan—unrest that would escalate if the government failed to provide food. Dulles agreed that Pakistan was facing a "desperate food situation." Famine relief through a dollar loan would necessitate diversion of resources from development and "seriously retard" the country's economic growth. Pakistan, he wrote to the president, "most friendly to us, needs immediate assurance of our aid." He "strongly" urged that this aid be in the form of a dollar grant instead of a loan.[9] Within two months, Eisenhower had signed the bill providing Pakistan with a million tons of wheat. The celerity with which Pakistan received food aid contrasted noticeably with the Truman administration's approach to India a couple of years earlier.

Concurrently, the administration was examining older plans for the defense of the Middle East. The Anglo-American position in the region seemed to be steadily slipping. The stalled negotiations between Britain and Egypt over the future of British military bases in Cairo and Suez had also placed on ice the ideas for a Middle East defense organization centered on Egypt. While Eisenhower refrained from disavowing his predecessor's commitment to such an organization, his administration began actively considering alternatives. Following his trip to South Asia and the Middle East in May 1953, Dulles held that "Pakistan would be cooperative member of any defense scheme that may emerge in Middle East." He was so "impressed with appearance and spirit of what we saw of armed forces and their leaders" that he felt the United States "need not await formal defense arrangements as condition to some military assistance to Pakistan."[10]

Dulles's conclusions were significant not just for Pakistan but also for the tightening military-bureaucratic axis that was supplanting Pakistani politicians. The men who had impressed Dulles, especially army chief General Ayub Khan, had their own ideas about what their country needed and had recently replaced the prime minister of Pakistan with a more pliant candidate. Ayub had told Dulles that the United States "should not be afraid to openly aid those countries which have expressed a willingness, and even desire, to cooperate." He emphasized Pakistan's potential "both in manpower and bases" and insisted that his country was "extremely anxious to cooperate with the United States."[11] The relationship with the United States was, of course, critical to strengthening the military's hold over the polity. The emerging external nexus with the United States would in time enable the army to thoroughly undermine democratic politics in Pakistan.[12]

His visits convinced Dulles that the older concept of Middle East defense, with its nucleus in Egypt, was "certainly finished." Instead, the Americans should pull Pakistan, Iran, Iraq, and Turkey—the so-called northern-tier states—into a regional alliance, which would be much stronger, he argued, than a defense organization centered on Egypt. Dulles's views on Pakistan were not just strategic but cultural. He was "immensely impressed by the martial and religious characteristics of the Pakistanis." The country could therefore serve as a "potential strong point" in a regional alliance.[13]

The image of a virile, strong Muslim evoked by Dulles had a long pedigree in American perceptions of the subcontinent. The notion of "martial races," in particular, had been imbibed from Rudyard Kipling. Dulles's conversation with Walter Lippmann illustrates the extent to which such cultural images structured strategic conceptions. "The only Asians who can really fight are the Pakistanis," insisted Dulles. "That's why we need them in the Alliance. We could never get along without the Gurkas." When Lippmann pointed out that the Gurkas were not Pakistanis, Dulles replied, "Well they may not be Pakistanis but they're Moslems." Lippmann persisted that they were not Muslims but Hindus. Dulles shrugged this off, saying, "No matter."[14] Unsurprisingly, therefore, the Eisenhower administration never quite managed to answer key questions about how exactly Pakistan would contribute to the defense of the Middle East and how much military aid it needed to fulfill this fuzzy role. Its officials could only point to the large potential military manpower in Pakistan, the possibility of acquiring bases in the future, and the need to ensure that Pakistan did not embrace neutralism. The chairman of the Joint Chiefs of Staff, Admiral Arthur Radford, conceded that planners in the administration had not come to grips with the critical issues.

Meanwhile the Pakistanis grew impatient at the delay in providing them military equipment. Ayub visited the United States at the end of September 1953. In his meeting with Dulles, Ayub bluntly said that he had a single-point agenda of procuring weapons and griped about the slow bureaucratic machinery in Washington. In a bid to hasten things along, the Pakistanis leaked the plans for a military alliance to the *New York Times*. A couple of days later, the Pakistani press reported that Washington was considering a military assistance program to the tune of $25 million. New Delhi was predictably outraged and warned the United States against an alliance with Pakistan.[15] India's reaction strengthened Pakistan's case. When Vice President Richard Nixon visited Karachi in December 1953, Pakistani governor-general Ghulam Mohammed told him that a US delay in sending arms to Pakistan would "make Nehru more difficult to deal with on the Kashmir issue." Indeed, he emphasized, "were the U.S. not to grant aid now, especially in view of all the publicity, it would be like taking a poor girl for a walk and then walking out on her, leaving her only with a bad name."[16]

Some American officials did argue against the impending alliance with Pakistan. From New Delhi, Ambassador Allen pointed out that India's response would be "bitter and vigorous and [would] color and perhaps change the course of United States–India relationship for a long time to come." Senior desk-level officials in Washington also observed that the alliance would imply that "we had considered India's cold war and hot war importance and had decided that the smaller and much weaker country of Pakistan was more useful to us." "India is the power in South Asia," they insisted. "We should make it our ally rather than cause it to be hostile to us. Pakistan is distressingly weak." The British government was already concerned about the drift toward Pakistan under Truman. The Eisenhower administration kept its special ally in the dark until the decision to forge an alliance with Pakistan was almost sealed. The British were concerned that "in return for the uncertain prospect of future assistance from Pakistan, the United States proposal will spoil the more immediate prospect of improved relations between India and Pakistan, which can provide the only real basis on which a strong Pakistan, capable of playing a valuable role in western defence, can be build." They told American officials that they did not like the proposal but would not stand in the way, owing to the implications of doing so for their ties with Pakistan.[17]

At one point, Eisenhower himself counseled caution. Partaking of the same paternalism that informed his predecessor's approach to South Asia, he wrote to Dulles in mid-November 1953, "This is one area of the world where, even more than most cases, emotion rather the reason seems to dictate policy. I know you will be watchful to see that we do not create antagonism unnecessarily." Dulles insisted, however, that this was "a situation where emotion ruled and where it is difficult to help one without making an enemy of the other."[18] Nixon argued vigorously against succumbing to concerns about India. "Pakistan is a country I would like to do everything for," declared the vice president. "The people have less complexes than Indians. The Pakistanis are completely frank even when it hurts. It will be disastrous if the Pakistan aid does not go through."

In January 1954, Dulles sent his final recommendations to the president. Recalling previous plans for limited military assistance to strategically located countries prepared to "stand up" to the Soviets, he noted that Pakistan and Turkey were ready to enter into an alliance. This was conditional on the United States providing military aid to Pakistan. Admittedly, there would be "quite a storm from India," but Dulles believed Washington could "ride out the storm without fatal effect on U.S.-Indian relations." In closing, he argued, "We can get a great deal by going ahead." But refraining from doing so would be "disastrous both to our relations with Pakistan and to the position of the present pro-American Pakistani Government. It would probably also be disastrous to our standing with other countries of Asia, who would assume we had backed down in the face of Indian threats."[19] This was not the last time the United States invoked such reputational concerns to justify a tilt toward Pakistan. It is perhaps no coincidence that President Nixon would deploy similar arguments during the South Asian crisis of 1971.

At a meeting on January 5, Eisenhower agreed in principle to go ahead with military aid for Pakistan. He stated, however, that he would only sign off on it if the administration could "present this in a reasonable way, which would allay the apprehension...that we were trying to help Pakistan against India." The administration should emphasize that this was part of a regional security project "initiated by Turkey and Pakistan" and that it was willing to offer similar military aid to India.[20] Nine days later the president gave his final approval to the initiative. Even at that moment, he worried about India's reaction and insisted that all efforts be made to smooth ruffled feelings in that country. On February 25, 1954, Washington formally announced its decision to provide Pakistan with military assistance.

THE NEWS OF A POSSIBLE US-Pakistan alliance had already touched off the tocsin in New Delhi. By signing such an agreement, Jawaharlal Nehru wrote to his Pakistani counterpart, "Pakistan enters definitely into the region of cold war." To his close advisors, he confided, "The US imagines that by this policy they have completely outflanked India's so-called neutralism and will thus bring India to her knees. Whatever the future may hold, this will not happen."[21] While the former was certainly an objective of the Eisenhower administration, aid to Pakistan was not intended to cut India down to size. But to Indians this seemed obviously the case. The only question was how to respond to this dramatic development.

Foreign Secretary R. K. Nehru held, for instance, that the Americans sought "to provide the Pakistan Army with modern weapons which would be superior to those possessed by us." US military assistance would entail "a complete change in the balance of forces" in the region. Within the Indian government, senior officials argued that they could not allow an upset in the military balance with Pakistan. They must use "all means" to "preserve the status quo and safeguard our national security, which is being threatened by external forces." This might include concluding "non-aggression pacts with the Soviet and Chinese," obtaining and developing weapons with Moscow's "collaboration and assistance," and even considering an offer of arms from the United States if provided "without any strings attached." Prime Minister Nehru, however, objected to going down this route: "I do not think we can deal with this developing situation in a military way, by trying to keep pace with Pakistan....I am entirely opposed to taking direct aid for military purposes from the US, or any other country. There is no such thing as 'no strings attached' when such aid is taken."[22] India, he insisted, had to remain confident in its ability to meet any developing threat without forsaking its foundational principles.

Ambassador Allen delivered a letter from Eisenhower to Nehru on February 24, explaining the rationale in terms of a regional security pact between Turkey and Pakistan and offering a similar deal to India. Nehru read the letter. "At [its] conclusion he smiled, studied his cigarette for few moments, then said in pleasant and almost confidential tone, 'I have never at any moment, since [the] subject arose two or three months ago, had any thought whatsoever that [the] US Government, and least of all President Eisenhower, wished to do any damage to India.'" He was disturbed not by US motives in aiding Pakistan but by the consequences of the decision. It was bound to complicate India's ties with Pakistan and might even aggravate relations between Hindus and Muslims in India.[23]

In public Nehru spoke scathingly about the US-Pakistan alliance, insisting that its fallout was "bound to be unfortunate." Shortly after the pact was announced, he sought the removal of all US nationals serving as members of the UN observation group in Kashmir. "No person coming from that country," he told the UN secretary-general, "can be considered as disinterested or impartial by us."[24] Nehru was also pointedly critical of the creation of the Southeast Asian Treaty Organization (SEATO) and the inclusion of Pakistan in this alliance. Washington regarded India's concerns with the customary condescension and paternalism. A panel put together by the White House dismissed the Indians as "petulant" and their response to SEATO as symptomatic of the country's "immaturity" and "fragile mental health."[25]

Nevertheless, the United States had to reckon with India's own policies in the wake of the US-Pakistan pact. The provision of weapons to Pakistan came in handy to Nehru as he dug in his heels on the Kashmir dispute. By early 1956, the Indian prime minister was openly stating that the conditions for holding a plebiscite in Kashmir would never be met: "As a practical person, I think that [a plebiscite] is leading us to a blind alley."[26] The Americans also watched with concern as India concluded an agreement with China on trade and transit in Tibet. The text of the agreement was prefaced by the *panchsheel*, or the "five principles of peaceful coexistence," which suggested that nonaligned India was trying to find a modus vivendi with Asian communism. Above all, the United States worried about the possibility of India's nonalignment morphing into "Asia for Asians." The Americans would have been a lot more concerned had they been privy to Nehru's conversation with Mao Zedong during his visit to Beijing later that year. Invoking the negative imagery of American missionaries in the Indian (and Chinese) imagination, Nehru observed, "A man like Dulles is a great menace. He is a Methodist or Baptist preacher who religiously goes to Church, and he is narrow-minded and bigoted. He thinks everyone must agree with him, and a man like him might take any move."[27]

The April 1954 Conference of South Asian prime ministers in Colombo, which included India, Pakistan, Ceylon, Burma, and Indonesia, accentuated American concerns about a developing pan-Asianism. At one point, Nehru lost his temper with the Pakistani prime minister, claiming that further discussion on Asian affairs was useless "with America represented here." The Pakistani leader gave as good as he got, calling Nehru and Indians "stooges of Chinese and Russian imperialism." But the Americans disliked the tenor of the conference, which suggested that colonialism was a greater danger for Asia than communism.[28] The five prime ministers met again at Bogor in Indonesia toward the end of year. This meeting, the Indians noted, was "marked, on the whole, by a general spirit of agreement and willingness to meet one another's point of view." Yet, when the Indian delegation suggested including the *panchsheel* principles in the joint communiqué, the Pakistanis resisted on the grounds that the UN Charter already embodied them. "It was obvious," the Indians concluded, "that Pakistan is not very happy at India's lead in creating a peace area in the world on the basis of the PANCHASHILAS [*sic*]."[29] In fact, the Americans were more concerned on this score.

At Colombo, the Indonesian premier had mooted the idea of a larger Afro-Asian meeting. This conference was eventually convened in Bandung the following year. Although it included several American allies—including Pakistan, Turkey, Iraq, Thailand, and the Philippines—the Eisenhower administration was uneasy about the gathering. For one thing, not a single Western country was present. For another, China had been invited at the recommendation of India. The American press picked up both points. Walter Lippmann wrote, "The list of states they did not invite makes it very evident that this is no mere attempt to make a neutral bloc or a third force in between the giant military powers. Red China is no neutral and no third force. What this is, to put it plainly, is the most ambitious move yet made in this generation to apply the principle of Asia for Asians." Dulles too harbored such anxieties. He feared that "if the nations invited to Bandung acquired the habit of meeting from time to time without Western participation, India and China because of their vast population will certainly dominate the scene." Ideas like the *panchsheel* were pernicious in this context. As earlier, the Americans were also nervous about reverse racism. The Bandung conference, Dulles felt, "might establish firmly in Asia a tendency to follow an anti-Western and 'anti-white' course, the consequences of which for the future could be incalculably dangerous....If at the conference only bad things in the record of the West are emphasized, it would be easy to give impetus to an 'Asia for Asians' movement."[30]

Even as Indian and Chinese leaders shared the spotlight in Bandung, the Soviet Union under Nikita Khrushchev was pushing its own policy of "peaceful coexistence." Unlike Joseph Stalin, who regarded independent India as a stooge of Western empires, Khrushchev sought to cozy up to nonaligned countries. A couple of months after Bandung, Nehru visited the Soviet Union and was feted as the leader of a large, progressive country. Khrushchev and Soviet premier Nikolai Bulganin visited India later that year. The Soviet leader came out in support of India's stance on Kashmir. "The question of Kashmir as one of the constituent states of the Indian Union," he declared, "has already been decided by the people of Kashmir."[31] Of greater concern to the Americans was the ensuing flow of financial aid and technical assistance from Moscow to New Delhi. The Soviets supported several prominent projects in India such as the Suratgarh State Farm, the thermal power station in Singrauli, and, above all, the Bhilai steel plant, which Khrushchev extolled as "the Indian equivalent of our Magnitogorsk."[32] By enthusiastically supporting such heavy industrial projects, the Soviets sought to differentiate their vision of development for the Third World from that of the United States and its promotion only of light, consumer goods–oriented industry.

India was not the only South Asian country that appeared to edge closer to the Soviet Union following the American alliance with Pakistan. In October 1954, the Afghan deputy prime minister met with Dulles and expressed his country's concerns about the "new and difficult situation" in which it found itself. US military aid to Pakistan and other northern tier countries had left "Afghanistan particularly exposed to the threat of its northern neighbor." The US-Pakistan alliance was also problematic from the standpoint of the unresolved "Pashtunistan" dispute between Afghanistan and Pakistan. Owing to both these concerns, Afghanistan requested military and economic aid from America.[33] Toward the end of the year, Dulles informed the Afghan ambassador that the administration would not meet his country's requests. Military aid to Afghanistan at this juncture would "create problems for it which would not be offset by the strength such aid might create." Nor were the Americans minded to provide greater economic aid. As for Afghanistan's dispute with Pakistan, Kabul would be better off seeking an overall improvement in ties by increasing trade and commerce rather than aiming at a resolution of the Pashtun problem.[34]

This brusque rebuff by the United States left the Afghans smarting. Afghan Prime Minister Sardar Mohammed Daoud was determined, however, to pursue his vision of rapid, centralized modernization of the country. Daoud swiftly turned toward the Soviet Union. In January 1955, he concluded an agreement with Moscow to train and equip the Afghan officer corps. Later that year, Khrushchev and Bulganin stopped in Kabul on their way back from India and held out an aid package of 150 million rubles a year. What is more, the Russians openly supported their hosts on "Pashtunistan": "We sympathize with Afghanistan with respect to its policy on the Pakhtunistan [sic] Question. The Soviet Union supports a just solution to the Pakhtunistan problem, which will not be possible without consideration of the vital interests of the people of Pakhtunistan." Soviet engineers soon arrived to build asphalt and cement factories, roads, and river port facilities. Soviet economists drew up the first five-year plan for Afghanistan in 1956. Over the following decade, the Russians managed to make deep inroads into Afghanistan, though they did not entirely supplant American and West German aid and expertise in the country.[35]

The Eisenhower administration might have worried less about the adverse fallout of its alliance with Pakistan if it had delivered tangible benefits. On the contrary, the perils of making policy on the basis of cultural fantasies were soon apparent. Faced with importunate demands from the Pakistanis, Ambassador Horace Hildreth observed that in crafting US policy toward Pakistan important factors "may not have been appraised and analyzed in advance." "The unanswered questions," he continued, "relate to the degree of importance which the United States may attach to these objectives, in the light of our worldwide commitments, and to judgments of Pakistan's abilities to attain these objectives. Out of the answers to these questions must come the decision as to what the United States investment in Pakistan should be." In an incisive analysis of Pakistan's political, economic, and security challenges, Hildreth insisted, "Our investment should be scrutinized with unrelenting care. Prospects of returns must be compared with those expected from India and from Pakistan's Middle Eastern neighbors."[36]

The ambassador's critical assessment made no impression on the thinking of the secretary of state. But it did force the administration to get its act together on the package for Pakistan. In October 1954, the Americans handed the Pakistanis a detailed note on provision of $171 million in military aid over the next three and a half years and of $105 million in economic aid. The Pakistanis, however, continued to complain both about the quantity of aid and the speed of delivery. Their grievances soared when they learned that owing to funding and delivery problems, completion of the military assistance program would take twice as long. Washington, for its part, was mortified to learn that outfitting five and a half Pakistani divisions would require $301 million rather than the estimated $171 million. Such funds were simply not forthcoming from the tightfisted Congress. "I personally would lose my trousers," fumed Ayub Khan. "I've stuck my neck out for the Americans. But I can't go on doing it, because you've gone back on your word."[37]

To ensure Pakistan's pro-American orientation, the Eisenhower administration agreed to breach the $171 million ceiling. Revised estimates in May 1956 placed the cost of the military assistance program at over $400 million. If Americans agreed to absorb the maintenance costs, the program would amount to anywhere between $765 million and $1.1 billion for 1958 to 1960 and between $130 million and $235 million for every year thereafter. Little wonder that by the end of his first term, President Eisenhower came to feel that "our tendency to rush out and seek allies was not very sensible." The heavy military commitment meant "we were doing nothing for Pakistan except in the form of military aid.... [T]his was perhaps the worst kind of a plan and decision we could have made. It was a terrible error, but we now seem hopelessly involved in it."[38]

IN THE WAKE OF Khrushchev and Bulganin's dramatic passage through South Asia, the Eisenhower administration began a quiet but thorough reconsideration of its policy toward the region. In particular, the president was eager not to lose nonaligned India to the Soviet Union. The American alliance with Pakistan was obviously the sorest point in ties with India, but there were other issues too. In December 1955, the administration stepped on New Delhi's toes when it got entangled in the dispute between India and Portugal over the latter's colonial enclave in Goa. After a meeting in Washington, the Portuguese foreign minister and Dulles issued a joint statement dealing mainly with the North Atlantic Treaty Organization but also including a reference to Goa as a "province" of Portugal. This set off a firestorm in India—not least because Khrushchev had recently affirmed Moscow's support for India's claim on the state. The new American envoy in New Delhi, Sherman Cooper, advised an official apology. Dulles would have none of it. The statement, he told Cooper, was not an endorsement of Portuguese claims but a response to "the campaign to promote hatred which was being waged by the Soviet leaders in India."[39]

The Indians were irate. Meeting Dulles a couple of months later, Ambassador G. L. Mehta noted that the larger divide between the two countries could be summed up "under three 'C's—Communism, China and 'colonialism.'" As far as bilateral ties were concerned, he bluntly stated, "the two most serious mistakes on the U.S. side...were military aid to Pakistan and the U.S. attitude in regard to Goa."[40] These differences stemmed from the political, strategic, historical, and cultural gulf that separated them. But personalities gave these larger factors an edge.

If the Indians could hardly abide Dulles, Nehru's close colleague, V. K. Krishna Menon, repelled the Americans. Dulles and other officials had dealt with Menon in the context of Korea and Taiwan and come away with the impression that he was sympathetic to the Communists. More importantly, the razor-tongued Menon scarred them. His performances at the United Nations, especially his extraordinarily long filibusters on Kashmir, and his frequent barbs on America were hardly calculated to smooth ties. Socialist Norman Thomas, an old American friend of India, told the Indian ambassador, "Krishna Menon has not helped at all in America. A good many Americans who might not have liked all his opinions would have taken them better if they had been otherwise expressed."[41] Menon's attempt to convince the United States to talk directly to China infuriated even the usually calm Eisenhower. As the president confided to his diary in July 1955, "Krishna Menon is a menace and a boor. He is a boor because he conceives himself to be intellectually superior and rather coyly presents to cover this, a cloak of excessive humility and modesty. He is a menace because he is a master at twisting words and meanings of others and is governed by an ambition to prove himself the master international manipulator and politician of the age."[42]

Nevertheless, Eisenhower sought to pick up the pieces with India. Nehru, he told Dulles, was "more swayed by personality than by logical argument." Hence, their ambassador to India should "do everything possible to win the personal confidence and friendship of Nehru." In March 1956, Dulles visited India again. Ahead of this trip, he struck a conciliatory note with the Indian envoy in Washington. It was "surprising and regrettable," he said, that two countries sharing political ideals should have differences. These were, of course, real; yet "despite [them], we should respect each other."[43]

In New Delhi, Dulles had extensive and frank discussions with Nehru. These conversations threw into relief the yawning gap between the two sides on Asian affairs. But they also helped them plumb the depths of each other's feelings on various issues—none more so than Pakistan. Dulles gained the "distinct impression" that India had an "almost pathological fear of Pakistan." While he knew that the Indians did not like the US alliance with Karachi, "I never appreciated before the full depth of their feeling." While the United States could not alter its tie with Pakistan, "I do think that we must try to handle it in ways which will give maximum assurance to India that our military aid will only be used for purely defensive purposes." At the same time, he conveyed to Nehru the administration's concerns about where India's relationship with the Soviet Union might be headed. Dulles later reported to Eisenhower that when Nehru said India was contemplating a Soviet offer of military transport aircraft, "I could only tell him frankly that I felt it would greatly vex our relations" and, in particular, would "make it almost impossible" for the administration to provide economic aid to India. Despite these tough conversations, Dulles could sense a thaw: "He [Nehru] had completely cleared his calendar for the two days of my visit. The first day we had three and one-half hours together just the two of us, in a most intimate way. I was amused that towards the end of the conference he was sitting on the back of the sofa with his feet on the seat. We really took our hair down."[44]

Dulles also carried with him an invitation from Eisenhower for Nehru to visit the United States. Over the following months, the two leaders kept up a regular correspondence. Their exchanges reflected a gradual reduction in friction and differences owing to a series of developments—above all, the Anglo-French-Israeli aggression in Suez, with which Eisenhower dealt firmly, and the Soviet invasion of Hungary, which Nehru criticized. India also refrained from purchasing Soviet arms and instead bought aircraft from Britain. The Americans, for their part, softened their stance on nonalignment, which they had hitherto castigated as immoral. Eisenhower explained to his archconservative brother Edgar that "the concept of neutrality for a nation does not necessarily mean that a nation is trying to occupy a position between right and wrong." The United States itself had followed this course for the first 150 years of its existence.[45]

The Indians took note of this subtle shift in the American position. In a lengthy assessment, Ambassador Mehta told New Delhi, "There has been a noticeable change in tone and emphasis....U.S. foreign policy has, in fact, been undergoing a reappraisal for some months." "The main reason is, no doubt," he continued, "the shift in Soviet policy and emergence of what is termed an 'economic cold war.'" But there was more to it. Dulles's meetings with Nehru had "made some impression on him." He now maintained that the United States respected the right of countries to remain nonaligned and that such policies would not affect American friendship for and desire to help them. The president's own attitude toward nonalignment had "apparently undergone a radical change." There was also a growing recognition that "the military posture of the United States [had] been overdone" and an increasing "emphasis on economic and social cooperation and technical assistance."[46]

Nehru's visit to the United States in late 1956 proved rather more successful than his previous one seven years before. Eisenhower and Nehru acknowledged their differences but nevertheless struck up an easy personal relationship. The Indian leader only briefly mentioned Pakistan and said almost nothing about aid to India. Yet Nehru and Eisenhower came away with a deep appreciation for each other's worldviews and policy positions.

Two weeks after Nehru's departure, the president approved NSC 5701—a new statement of policy toward South Asia. This document held that the Soviet Union was "engaged in a vigorous and open, diplomatic, propaganda, and economic campaign to increase its influence in the area." As the prime target of Soviet policy, India posed "an undeniable dilemma for U.S. policy." India's nonalignment frequently brought it into conflict with the United States, and a stronger India might become an even more powerful advocate of positions that cut against American interests. "Nevertheless," the paper insisted, "over the long run the risks to U.S. security from a weak and vulnerable India would be greater than the risks of a stable and influential India. A weak India might well lead to the loss of South and Southeast Asia to Communism. A strong India would be a successful example of an alternative to Communism in an Asian context."[47]

The deterioration of Sino-Indian relations over the next two years gave the Eisenhower administration an opening to set aright its political relations with India. The bonhomie in India-China relations witnessed around the Bandung conference proved short-lived as the boundary dispute between them began to cast a shadow. Until 1958, both sides sought to brush the problem under the carpet in the interest of improving bilateral ties and reaching a settlement in the future. But the sheer scale of the dispute all along India's frontiers with China ensured that it could not be disregarded. Initially, both sides took to publishing official maps depicting their claims but refused to address the massive difference head on. Both also sought to quietly extend their administrative control along the frontiers, though the Chinese moved more swiftly and decisively.

By 1958, the Chinese had not only occupied a considerable portion of the Aksai Chin plateau abutting Kashmir but also constructed a road through the area linking Xinjiang with Tibet. This road was crucial in maintaining their military presence in Tibet. India's decision to diplomatically challenge this move set the stage for a prolonged, testy exchange regarding boundary claims and a rapid slide in bilateral ties. By the summer of 1959, Indian and Chinese troops were in a tense face-off all along the border. Unsurprisingly clashes ensued. On two occasions, the Chinese attacked Indian posts and patrols, leaving several Indian soldiers dead. Subsequent negotiations between Nehru and Chinese premier Zhou Enlai went nowhere.

The disputed boundary was not, however, the sole reason for this deterioration in ties. Equally important were Chinese concerns about unrest in Tibet and about the links between rebels and external powers, especially India and the United States. A rebellion in the Kham province had kicked off in 1956, and some rebels fleeing Chinese retaliation escaped into Sikkim and India. The Khampas did not seek any material assistance from India, but they did establish contacts with Taiwanese Kuomintang agents in the border town of Kalimpong. The Chinese understandably suspected that the Kuomintang agents were in cahoots with the CIA.[48] In fact, Zhou Enlai broached this issue directly with Nehru.

The CIA had contacts with prominent Tibetan émigrés, including the Dalai Lama's elder brother Gyalo Thondup, going back to the Chinese occupation of Tibet in 1950. The agency began seriously thinking of assisting the Tibetans in September 1956, after the Kham rebellion was underway. The CIA's attempts to reach out to the Dalai Lama failed, but it worked with Thondup and other émigrés in India to identify a group of six young men to be trained as fighters and signal operators before being parachuted into Tibet. In March 1957, this small group of Tibetans was taken from India to East Pakistan and thence to Saipan in the Mariana Islands. Four months later they were inserted into Tibet. They and the CIA's materiel assistance did not make much difference to the Khampa rebellion. But when the Dalai Lama decided to flee Lhasa in March 1959, two of these fighters linked up with his party and informed the CIA of his departure.[49] India's decision to offer him asylum incensed the Chinese, who concluded that New Delhi had actively worked, perhaps with the CIA, to get the Dalai Lama out of Tibet.[50] The conjunction of the Tibetan crisis with the boundary dispute placed India and China on a collision course.

In the aftermath of the Dalai Lama's entry into India, the CIA grew more circumspect about operating in or near Indian territory. In September 1959 the agency shifted its base for operations in support of the Tibetan rebels from East Pakistan to northern Thailand to avoid the need to fly over Indian territory.[51] Nevertheless, from 1960—if not earlier—the Indian government apparently knew of the CIA's assistance to the Tibetan rebels and chose to turn a blind eye.

All this ensured that Eisenhower's visit to India in December 1959 went exceedingly well. Nehru welcomed him "at this special hour" as a great man holding the banner of peace. In their discussions, Eisenhower expressed his understanding of India's nonaligned policy and said that this need not stand in the way of close friendship between their two countries. He also sought Nehru's views on the evolving situation with China and suggested that India and Pakistan might come together to resist Chinese aggression. Nehru made clear his dismay at China's tough behavior but also insisted that India could hold its own so long as Pakistan did not stab it in the back in the event of a confrontation with Beijing. Eisenhower promptly assured him that the United States would come down heavily on any attempt by Pakistan to benefit from India's problems.[52] The threat from China also provided the backdrop against which Nehru and Eisenhower discussed India's economic plans.

ECONOMIC AID TO INDIA was the principal means by which the Eisenhower administration aimed to achieve its objectives. India had unveiled its second five-year plan in February 1956. Vetted by the Ford Foundation and other American experts,[53] it was a lot more ambitious than the previous plan. The remarkable success of the US-supported Community Development Program shaped the document's background assumptions. The production of food grains had risen continuously from 51.2 million to 68.7 million tons between 1951 and 1954. The planners assumed therefore that India's chronic food problem was all but resolved. So, while the first plan had focused on agriculture, the second shifted gears toward industry. The second plan indeed consummated the industrialization ideas brewing in India since World War II.

The plan called for a total outlay of 72 billion rupees, or about $14.7 billion—more than double the amount spent under the first plan. Unlike the previous plan, which allotted only 7.6 percent of the outlay to industry, the second plan set aside 18.5 percent of the overall expenditure. By contrast, the allocation for agriculture and irrigation slid from 34.6 to 17.5 percent. Although the actual expenditure on agriculture was slightly more than during the first plan, the government's priorities were unmistakable. The optimistic assumptions about food output and the consequent downgrading of agriculture would soon be put to the test. The plan also rested on somehow bridging a financial deficit of $2.5 billion—including almost $1.7 billion required in foreign exchange to pay for imports of capital equipment for industrialization.

Even after counting multilateral (World Bank and International Monetary Fund) and bilateral (United States, Soviet Union, and United Kingdom) foreign assistance, India would fall short by over $1 billion.

This provided an opportunity for the United States to step up assistance and bolster its ties with India. Ambassador Cooper suggested a threefold aid package. First, the United States should promise $500 million in development loans over the duration of the plan to help New Delhi close its foreign exchange gap. While this would not entail much of an increase in the annual aid to India, it would require a multiple-year plan and commitment. Second, he advised the administration to accept a long-term moratorium on the repayment of $120 million in silver shipped to India during World War II. And third, he recommended the provision of $300 million in surplus agricultural commodities under the PL480 program whereby the United States shipped such commodities to "friendly" nations on favorable terms. This would allow India to pay for the import of these commodities in its own currency and so save foreign exchange.

Cooper's plan was watered down in Washington. Vice President Nixon insisted that "it was extremely important that we not appear to court neutrals and to abandon our allies." The Treasury refused to accept a moratorium on the silver. The State Department recommended a five-year program of $75 million a year, which the administration modified into a recommendation to Congress of $70 million in development assistance and $10 million in technical assistance during 1956. Congress eventually appropriated a total of $75 million for India. The White House managed, however, to supplement this package by concluding in August 1956 a $360 million PL480 agreement to be implemented over three years.[54]

By the time Nehru visited the United States, the administration was taking a strategic view of foreign aid to India. This was indeed the elephant in the room during Eisenhower's extensive conversations with Nehru. Soon after, NSC 5701 stated, "The second five-year plan provides at present the best vehicle for action to promote U.S. interest in an independent and stable India." American officials also saw aid to India in the light of China's own five-year plan for a "great leap forward." Thus the National Security Council (NSC) document insisted, "The outcome of the competition between Communist China and India will have a profound effect throughout Asia and Africa."[55]

Neither the Americans nor the Indians had anticipated the magnitude of New Delhi's foreign exchange problem. By late 1957, the country faced a severe crunch that threatened to derail the economy. The Indian planners had projected a manageable balance-of-payments deficit of about $550 million for the five-year period, but the aggregate deficit had already touched $400 million in the first two years of the plan. In mid-1957, the Americans estimated India's dollar gap for the remainder of the planning period at between $700 million and $900 million. The crisis grew out of a combination of factors: spiraling costs of iron, steel, and capital goods; dysfunctional controls over import licenses, leading to surging private imports; and rising defense expenditure in the wake of US military aid to Pakistan.

Shortfalls in food production aggravated the crisis. The planners had assumed that annual production would rise from 65 million to 75 million tons during the five-year period, with a minimal increase in outlay for agriculture. But this target proved insufficient to meet the needs of a rapidly growing population and increasing urban demand. In late 1956, the food target was pushed upward to 80 million tons but without an increase in the allocation for the rural sector. Nehru and his planners sought to cope with this situation by calling for cooperative agriculture to boost output. But the landed interests that controlled the Congress party refused to countenance the idea, forcing the government to fall back on the Community Development Program. Worse, due to the failure of monsoons in North India, food production plunged to 62.5 million tons. By September 1957, Nehru had no option but to send his finance minister to Washington, requesting an American loan of $500 million to $600 million.

The request from India coincided with the onset of a recession in the United States. The White House was already at loggerheads with the Congress over its foreign aid program. In this scenario, securing additional aid for India was tricky. Given the current mood of Congress, Dulles quipped, he did "not think that boosting India [would] be a popular pastime." The secretary of state was open to the idea of giving more to India—not least because the Communist Party of India had recently won the elections in the southern state of Kerala. Nevertheless, he told the president that requesting special legislation for India would invite "spectacular defeat in Congress."[56] The Eisenhower administration cast about for ways to help India without having to approach Congress for a special loan. Ultimately, it decided to splice together a $200 million loan from the Export-Import (EXIM) Bank of the United States and $75 million from the newly established Development Lending Facility, a US government credit agency.

On January 16, 1958, the administration announced the immediate provision of $225 million for India, with promise of more to come. Indeed, American grants and loans to New Delhi—less the EXIM Bank loan of 1957—grew from $89.8 million in 1958, to $137 million in 1959, to $194 million in 1960. To ensure best utilization of these funds, the United States took the lead in devising a consortium of the five main donors to India—Britain, Canada, Germany, Japan, and the United States—under the umbrella of the World Bank. In May 1960, the administration also concluded a four-year $1.276 billion PL480 accord with India—the largest by far of such agreements under the act.[57]

Beyond the geopolitical context, changing ideas about economic development enabled this momentous policy shift. In the first place, American policymakers had to acknowledge that flows of private investment from the advanced industrial countries could not be the primary engine of economic growth in the Third World. In the case of India, private investment by American firms had always been a nettlesome issue. In its early months, the Eisenhower administration had circulated another draft of a treaty of friendship, commerce, and navigation focused all but exclusively on investment. But the Indian government was not keen on such an agreement.

Indian officials believed that American companies abroad "set up enterprises which are replicas of their own American plants, but India and other countries are geared to an entirely different cost and price structure. Therefore under this system American goods are produced abroad not for the masses but the select few." They argued that India would be better off seeking specific technical assistance from American companies rather than inviting them to set up shop in India. Not surprisingly, American private investment in India was down to a trickle—no more than $30 million between 1947 and 1954. General Motors, which had been operating in the subcontinent for years, had even wound down its establishment.[58]

The foreign exchange crisis of 1957 forced the government to moderate the rules to attract foreign investment. New Delhi guaranteed foreign investors the right to unlimited repatriation of profits in dollars. Two years on, it even agreed to compensate foreign companies in the event of nationalization. At the same time, the Indian government announced a series of tax incentives for foreign investors and concluded a double taxation treaty with the United States. Nevertheless, the regulations for foreign control of enterprises in India remained firmly in place.

Second, the Americans had to come to terms with the fact that countries like India would want to pursue a mixed economy—a system that smacked of socialism to many. In April 1956, India adopted a new industrial policy resolution aimed at achieving a "socialistic pattern of society." It went beyond the 1948 resolution in extending the role of the state in the development of basic and heavy industries. The new policy did not, however, contemplate nationalization of already existing private concerns in sectors now brought under the purview of the state. In other areas, private enterprises could operate in conjunction with the state or entirely on their own. The new industrial policy drew criticism from the World Bank, whose American president, Eugene Black, wrote to the Indian government that by subjecting private enterprise to too many controls, it was not using its capacity for the economic development of the country. The Bank advised India to seek technical cooperation and financial assistance from foreign private enterprise by offering attractive terms. Nehru shrugged this off as the traditional opposition of Americans to all measures aimed at strengthening the public sector.[59]

Lastly, the Americans had to concede that their preferred economic model of industrialization for the Third World—gradual buildup of light, consumer goods industry—might not live up to the expectations of the leaders and peoples of these countries. India's second five-year plan heralded its desire to accelerate toward industrial modernity. It also sought to adopt a model of heavy import substitution industrialization.

To a remarkable degree, Eisenhower came around to accepting each of these premises in supporting India's economic development. In an NSC meeting in January 1957, Secretary of Commerce Sinclair Weeks pointed to the need for greater private investment—rather than government aid—to India. The president "stated firmly that if in our dealings with other nations the United States tries to impose its own economic system, the result would shortly be self-defeating." The United States "cannot argue with friendly nations about the wisdom of their form of government." Furthermore, every country in the world, "not excluding the United States itself, has certain elements of Socialism in its government and in its economy." In a country like India, where per capita income was less than $200 a year, it was "obvious" that "only government credit could do much to achieve the economic benefits that the country required. In point of fact, it was fatuous to imagine that private enterprise alone could achieve India's economic objectives."[60]

Secretary of Treasury George Humphrey, perhaps the most conservative member of the cabinet, argued that the United States could not expect India to use its aid for the development of private enterprise in that country. Government-owned steel plants in India had an unfair advantage over private steel industry. He asserted, "The difference between Socialism and Communism was mighty thin. The results were the same.... [W]e are making use of our own capitalist system to promote Socialism abroad." Eisenhower replied that "he simply could not agree.... [W]e had quite a lot of Socialism right here in the United States." The president then asked Humphrey "if he had ever read the new Indian Five-Year Plan." He had not. Eisenhower went on to list "certain highlights of the Five-Year Plan." Barring some seventeen large industries, he observed, the private sector had a free run in India. Humphrey insisted, however, that all of these seventeen industries "could be easily developed by private resources if only the right kind of climate prevailed in India." Eisenhower rebutted that "he could not possibly agree": "Nehru had on his hands a population of some 350 million people, many of whom were living on the verge of starvation. No government in India could stand aside and ignore such a situation." Finally, Eisenhower pulled out his trump card: "If we ourselves did not aid countries like India, we could be sure that Soviet Russia would do so." And there the matter rested.[61]

Several sources influenced this extraordinary shift in Eisenhower's thinking from the traditional, Republican "trade not aid" stance. Harold Stassen, director of the Foreign Operations Administration, had advised Eisenhower since 1954 that only a long-term effort to promote not just agricultural but industrial development could contain Asian communism. "It will be a long-term struggle," he said, but "acceleration of industrialization is an indispensable part of a successful program." Then there was the president's own curiosity. In 1955, he read an article in the *Economist*, "India's Progress and Planning," which argued that owing to India's lack of capital and expertise, as well as its burgeoning and poor population, an enlarged public sector was a necessity rather than a dogma. Describing the article as "instructive," he asked Dulles to "pick it up and read it" and sent copies to Stassen and others in the administration.[62] Another influence was Ford Foundation head Paul

Hoffman. Owing to the foundation's deep involvement in India's development, Eisenhower took seriously Hoffman's views on the Indian economy and its requirements. In fact, at one point Eisenhower even wanted to appoint Hoffman as his ambassador in New Delhi.

The Ford Foundation also influenced the wider discourse around foreign aid in an indirect way. Since 1953, the foundation had supported the work of the Massachusetts Institute of Technology's Center for International Studies. The center's prime movers were Walt Rostow and Max Millikan, both liberal cold warriors who believed that the American social sciences had their work cut out in the struggle against global communism. In their proposal to the Ford Foundation, they pointed out that America's ability "to help the nations of the free world achieve political stability by helping them to expand their productivity and standard of living" was one of Washington's "strongest psychological weapons" in the Cold War.[63] India bulked large in this vision. Rostow and Millikan were eager to establish a research center in the country. On receiving grants to the tune of $1 million, they roped in leading development economists Wifred Malenbaum and Paul Rosenstein-Rodan to work in India—in collaboration with Douglas Ensminger and the Indian Planning Commission. Simultaneously, their ideas began to circulate in the Eisenhower administration.

Rostow and Millikan advanced a liberal model of development for the Third World.[64] This approach rested on the notion that economic growth required the "diffusion" of capital, technology, and culture from developed to backward nations. Rostow identified five "stages of development" in Western historical experience, which he then proceeded to universalize. All societies, he argued, must pass from the "traditional stage," when economic aid helps a country accumulate savings and technical knowledge, to the "preconditions for takeoff," and thence through the "take-off" and "drive for maturity" stages, to arrive at "self-sustained economic growth." At this terminus, a substantial chunk of the population would have access to consumption goods beyond the necessities of survival. This process of diffusion, Rostow held, took place through capitalist investment and trade, but it had to be supplemented by timely doses of Western economic and technical aid. Rostow and Millikan were not concerned about "ideological issues" such as government control and private enterprise: both had their place in any growth strategy. India, they believed, was the perfect candidate for development by stages and could fruitfully absorb large quantities of American aid.

Although "modernization theory" challenged some of American policymakers' ideological assumptions, it slotted snugly with other aspects of their worldview. Shorn of social sciences jargon, the ethnocentric and hierarchical views of "modernization theory" fit well with American cultural images of Asian societies. "Condescending and paternalistic," writes historian Michael Hunt, "development theory also carried forward the long-established American views on race."[65] All the same, it also had considerable purchase on Third World leaders like Nehru, who bought into its "stage-ist" view of history as well as its policy prescriptions.

Rostow's *Stages of Economic Growth*—modestly subtitled "A Non-Communist Manifesto"—was not published until 1959, but his and Millikan's ideas were already influencing the Eisenhower administration's thinking on foreign aid. When an aide sent the text of a talk by Rostow to the president, Eisenhower wrote back, "I quite agree with your verdict on Professor Rostow's talk…and I am grateful to you for giving me an opportunity to see it."[66] Their ideas also informed the resolutions introduced in the US Congress by a young senator, John F. Kennedy, along with Sherman Cooper, the erstwhile envoy to India. Describing the "development gap" as equally dangerous as the "missile gap," Kennedy called on the administration to assure India of its assistance in the fulfillment of the second five-year plan as well as the effective formulation of the third plan.[67]

By the end of the 1950s, modernization theory was well on its way to becoming the dominant discourse on Third World development. To be sure, the older ideas continued to be aired, but their purchase on policymakers was much weaker. In the wake of the Kennedy-Cooper resolutions, conservative economist P. T. Bauer published, under the aegis of the American Enterprise Institute, a scathing analysis of US aid to India. Bauer criticized several aspects of India's second five-year plan: the massive expenditure on industry, the comparative neglect of agriculture, the restrictions on import of consumer goods and establishment of private enterprises, and so on. By increasing its aid to India, he argued, the United States "would make it inevitable that the country is pushed further in the direction of the establishment of a completely socialized economy, in the direction of an economy in which the range of choice of individuals is severely circumscribed both as consumers or producers, and in which the state is all powerful." US aid, Bauer insisted, should be used to reorient India's economic trajectory "away from acts of emulation of the pattern of the Soviet world."[68] But his was a voice in the wilderness.

As earlier, India was not the only site in South Asia testing and implementing ideas of modernization. Nor was it the only country of concern to Washington. Afghanistan's growing dependence on the Soviet Union began to gnaw at the Eisenhower administration—never mind its earlier insouciance about the country. To claw back some influence, the United States began focusing on a project that had languished for a while in Afghanistan. The Helmand Valley project was a typical effort at modernization in the American mold. Modeled on the Tennessee Valley Authority, the Helmand River dam would at once cater to irrigation, electricity, and farm extension. It was, in fact, the first such project undertaken by the Americans in the subcontinent.

At the end of World War II, Afghanistan had accumulated an export surplus of $20 million in foreign exchange. The bulk of this was diverted to the development of the Helmand and Arghandab River valleys. In 1946, the Afghan government contracted the Morrison-Knudsen Company of Idaho to build two dams and canals as well as to train Afghan personnel in their maintenance. Kabul sought both to turn the desolate southwest of the country into its granary and to extend the central government's sway into distant provinces of the country. The high modernist vision of the Afghan state would be inscribed on the site of the dam.

The administrative and operational complexities of the project proved bewildering. Within a few years, the funds allocated to the project were at an end, but the construction had barely begun. Meanwhile, the trade war with Pakistan, which followed the "Pashtunistan" dispute, had emptied Kabul's foreign exchange coffers. In 1949, the Afghan finance minister went to Washington with a request for $118 million in aid to finance several interlinked projects. But the Truman administration held out nothing more than a $21 million loan from the EXIM Bank to fund the Helmand Valley project, which was of course being undertaken by an American firm.

A series of problems, however, continued to mire the project. Land reclamation, for instance, proved exceedingly difficult, given the state of farm equipment used by the Afghans. Afghan plows, a report noted, were no more than "iron-pointed sticks...pulled by slow moving oxen." The farmers sowed by hand and had no equipment to control weeds. The "saw-toothed sickle" used to harvest the crop was "the flint sickle of the neolithic peoples, living 12,000 years ago."[69] Social challenges compounded technological problems. Through the Helmand Valley project, the Afghan state was attempting to force the nomadic tribes in the area to settle down. But they were not inclined to oblige. Then there were geographical and geological problems. The dam held more water than could be used, and there were no markets for the electricity generated. Weeds infected the canals, and silt clogged the dam feeders. Above all, salts and alkaline agents contaminated over a third of the total area and prevented effective cropping.

The Afghan government set up a Helmand Valley Authority to coordinate the financing and execution of the project. But disbursal of the EXIM Bank loan dragged, and the project was bogged down in allegations of corruption. Morrison-Knudsen, for its part, decided to go slow. By 1954, the Eisenhower administration had concluded that the project had drained considerable sums with little to show for them. The EXIM Bank pitched in with another loan to prevent the project from going under, but its ungenerous financial terms affronted the Afghans. The Americans, however, were apt to dismiss Afghan concerns as reflections of a backward people's inability to understand the functioning of a modern bureaucracy.

Only after Prime Minister Daoud turned to the Soviets did Washington focus its gaze on Kabul. The Eisenhower administration tasked Tudor Engineering Company with reviewing the Helmand Valley project. The authors of the resulting report did a patchy job and pinned much of the blame for delays on Afghan contractors. The Afghan government also came in for the rap owing to its "unrealistic expectations" of the speed of construction. All this was rather convenient, for Tudor was an affiliate of Morrison-Knudsen. Having whitewashed the past, the report went to paint a rosy future. There was "already proof of substantial benefit" to the country from the project, which would bring $24 million into the Afghan treasury from 1964. The State Department endorsed the report's conclusions and came to believe that the project was indeed a success.[70] In the event, the dam was constructed by 1960, and the United States continued to support projects associated with it for years afterward.

The Eisenhower administration also funded several smaller projects in the country, the most prominent being the airport in Kandahar. In 1960, historian Arnold Toynbee landed there and drove on the new blacktop road to Lashkar Gah, a modern planned city that housed the headquarters of the Helmand Valley Authority. Lashkar Gah, known locally as the New York of Afghanistan, also prided itself on a multipurpose hospital, the only coeducational school in the country, and a beautiful alabaster mosque. Traditional Afghanistan, Toynbee felt, was nowhere in sight. "The domain of the Helmand Valley Authority," he wrote, "has become a piece of America inserted into the Afghan landscape.... The new world they are conjuring up out of the desert at the Helmand River's expense is to be an America-in-Asia."[71]

Meanwhile, another sliver of American modernity was visible in neighboring Pakistan. The Korangi project aimed to create a satellite town southeast of Karachi for hundreds of thousands of refugees who had come from India during partition. Billed as the largest slum clearance and urban development project in Asia, it received funding in October 1958 from the US Agency for International Development and the Ford Foundation and contracted with a foreign company. Work began at a brisk pace. By the following summer, the first lot of 15,000 houses was ready, and General Ayub Khan handed over the keys to the residents in a well-publicized ceremony.

Lauded as showcasing Pakistan's modernization, Korangi attracted much international attention. It was designed to house a range of civic amenities as well as industrial facilities, to attract middle-class professionals and families, and eventually to become a "balanced" and nearly self-contained urban community. These modernist hopes proved easier to articulate than realize. The neat houses masked the lack of or shortfalls in basic necessities. Water was scarce and available only from improvised taps. There was neither sewage nor electricity. Most importantly, transport links to Karachi were poor and patchy. In consequence, few working people chose to live in Korangi. In effect, it was a wasteland in the making.[72] But this lay in the future. The Eisenhower administration was understandably pleased with the project—not least because the new military dictator of Pakistan had executed it.

Sites like Korangi and Helmand Valley mattered to the United States because they advertised its readiness to compete with the Soviet Union in the battle for the hearts and minds of the Third World. But in waging this battle of the Cold War, the Eisenhower administration relied on other, overt and covert methods. Propaganda and intelligence operations were an integral arrow in the administration's quiver in securing its influence in South Asia. These activities had been conducted in the region for over a decade, but under Eisenhower they acquired unprecedented importance.

As with economic policy, concerns that the Soviets already had an upper hand galvanized American efforts in the psychological arena. During the Truman years, public diplomacy in South Asia—especially India—had not made much headway: the lack of its own infrastructure hampered the Voice of America, while the films of the US Information Service (USIS) had not elicited much interest. Efforts at countering perceptions of American race relations, consumerism, and imperialism had at best been halting. As Loy Henderson had griped to Nehru in his farewell meeting, the Communists by contrast seemed to have the free run of India.

The consummation of the US-Pakistan alliance made American public diplomacy in the region ever more difficult. On the one hand, American attempts to portray the alliance as solely aimed at the Communist bloc miscued in India. As Ambassador Allen reported, the Indian public as well as officials regarded American propaganda as inherently deceitful. On the other, the attempt to downplay the alliance irritated the Pakistanis, who already felt shortchanged on military supplies. The administration raised public diplomacy funding for South Asia to $1.08 million, with another $200,000 for operations in India and Pakistan. The problem, however, was not the availability of funds but that propaganda could not paper over the contradictions in the administration's policies toward the region.[73]

Indeed, propaganda efforts that did not specifically relate to regional policies fared far better. Take the US pavilion at the Indian Industries Fair in New Delhi in 1955. Designed by John Vassos, the pavilion was a single-story modernist structure with a giant model of an atom on its roof. At 100,000 square feet, it was by far the largest pavilion in the fair. Despite its modern design and massive size, it was built using traditional Indian methods by Indian workers. The atom atop the structure, as well as the "atomics exhibition" inside, aimed to showcase

Eisenhower's "atoms for peace" policy, which promised nuclear technology for developing countries. The "atomics exhibition" included a thirty-foot-high, full-scale replica of the graphite reactor at Brookhaven, New York. To escort visitors, including such luminaries as Nehru and Khrushchev, the US embassy recruited sixty guides, all students of science outfitted in orange Brookhaven jumpsuits. The nuclear reactor, as well as the closed-circuit television studio, drew enormous crowds that left deeply impressed by American technological modernity.[74]

The pavilion in New Delhi provided the template for similar exhibitions in other parts of the Third World. In 1956, the Eisenhower administration participated in the Jeshyn International Fair in Kabul. The decision to set up a pavilion was made rather late, owing to the limited American interests in Afghanistan. Nevertheless, in the wake of the visit to Kabul by Khrushchev and Bulganin, Washington thought it imperative to mark its presence in the fair. The administration approached Buckminster Fuller, the architect famous for his geodesic domes. Realizing that Kabul was "the heart of the Heartland"—the geopolitician Halford Mackinder's term for Eurasia—Fuller agreed. With exactly three months to go, he took additional risk in insisting that Afghan laborers build the US pavilion. In the event, the translucent dome was up in time and gripped the imaginations of Afghan visitors. As *Time* breathlessly reported, "Every testimony was that this last-minute victory in the charm war was won by the dome, not by the merchandise inside."[75]

By contrast, covert efforts in the subcontinent proved rather more difficult to pull off. The CIA-funded Congress for Cultural Freedom (CCF) had a front organization known as the Indian Committee for Cultural Freedom (ICCF). The latter counted among its members such prominent Indian leaders as Jayaprakash Narayan and Minoo Masani, both erstwhile socialists and current critics of Nehru. Underscoring the importance that it attached to a leading nonaligned country like India, the CCF hosted its second conference in Bombay, putting up a stellar cast of foreign speakers—W. H. Auden and Stephen Spender, H. J.

Muller and Norman Thomas, among others—as well as inviting some seventy Indian delegates. Although the CIA connection was revealed only in the late 1960s, Nehru suspected that the Americans funded the ICCF. On more than one occasion, he singled it out as "an American organized committee trying to put across the American viewpoint."[76]

While the conference succeeded in riling up the Indian government, it did little to burnish the "free world's" credentials in India. American conservative James Burnham's *Partisan Review* piece on his trip to India for the conference sounded almost like a parody of late-nineteenth-century travelogues. Burnham's article was, of course, addressed to his readership: "We, whose culture is Anglo-Saxon as well as European." India, he pronounced, was beset with poverty—"stark, abject, disease and dirt-ridden, absolutely and unyieldingly wretched." The Indians were themselves to blame for their depraved state, which stemmed, above all, from their irrational religion. The Indians, Burnham confidently stated, "are quite capable of refusing to 'improve their standard of living' even when it is easily possible for them to do so." By slaughtering a chunk of its cattle and controlling the breeding of the rest, "India could have—Western reason can demonstrate—the most productive cattle and dairy industry in the world." Indians cows, alas, "are divine and they are therefore never to be slaughtered." Burnham's Anglo-Saxon orientalism contained more than a touch of old-fashioned racism: "Against the velvet blackness of the Indian context, the non-Indian is abstracted into a type....[B]y the last day of the Bombay Congress for Cultural Freedom only Max Yergan, the negro sociologist, was, thanks to dark skin, distinctive and distinguishable."[77]

From 1955, the CCF also funded an Indian journal of ideas, *Quest*. While unaware of its link to the CIA, the journal's Indian editors and contributors accepted foreign funding in order to avoid dependence on their government. The first editor of *Quest*, the poet Nissim Ezekiel, preferred a tilt to the West rather than to the Soviet Union. But he was not minded to follow any straightforward party line. In his inaugural editorial, Ezekiel insisted that the journal chose Western sponsorship in order to have the requisite freedom to criticize the government and mount an Indian project of "opposition to authority." In practice, however, *Quest's* elective affinity to American anticommunism continually hobbled the journal in the Indian context. The CCF, for its part, was unable to channel it in the desired directions and gave up on it within a few years.[78] Over the following decade, the United States would spread its cultural influence rather more successfully in the subcontinent not through high-cultural South Asian publications like *Quest* but through the emerging popular culture at home.

6

NEW FRONTIER IN SOUTH ASIA

A S HE STOOD ON THE STEPS of the Capitol to deliver his inaugural address on January 20, 1961, President John F. Kennedy
cut a striking contrast with his predecessor. Few Americans failed to
note the youth, energy, and activism of their new president against the
age, experience, and conservatism of Dwight Eisenhower. Kennedy's
speech played on these themes, claiming, "The torch has been passed
to a new generation of Americans."[1] Yet Kennedy's worldview was
not a stark departure from his predecessor's. Like Eisenhower, Kennedy saw the Cold War as the defining paradigm of world politics—a
long-term struggle that had to be waged on the political, ideological,
military, economic, scientific, and cultural fronts. If anything, with the
growing militancy of Mao Zedong's China, the challenge to American

preponderance posed by the Communist bloc seemed stronger and the need for the United States to stand firm ever more urgent.

The ideological matrix underpinning the new president's grand strategy had an impeccable pedigree, yoking notions of liberalism and providentialism to faith in the power of American ideals and modernization theory to transform the world in the United States' image. Kennedy was the most articulate exponent of an updated version of manifest destiny for the mid-twentieth century. As he said in his State of the Union address in January 1962, "People everywhere look to us," especially to "the splendor of our ideals." Indeed, "our Nation is commissioned by history either to be an observer of freedom's failure or the cause of its success."[2]

Yet the global context in which the United States would have to secure its primacy underwent far-reaching changes in the 1960s. First, as the decade progressed, the Cold War ceased to be a contest between two tightly organized alliances. On the one hand, the sharpening differences between the Soviet Union and China undid the idea of a monolithic Communist bloc under Moscow's leadership. On the other hand, the postwar recovery of Europe and the advent of leaders like Charles de Gaulle began to change the character, if not the nature, of the transatlantic alliance. Second, the acceleration of decolonization brought a multitude of new states into being and a host of challenges in their wake. The Third World at once became a new constellation in Cold War politics and an arena of superpower competition.

Third, the 1960s witnessed the early stirrings of what would later be called globalization. A confluence of forces in this decade made for growing interconnections between different parts of the world. For one thing, there was unprecedented technological development. The dangers of a thermonuclear apocalypse, the images of the Earth from space, the increasing affordability of air travel, and the explosion of satellite television all contributed to an emerging sense of what Marshall McLuhan termed the "global village." For another, the world economy was undergoing market integration of a kind not seen since the

1920s. This was particularly the case with capital markets, which were gradually unshackled starting in the late 1950s following the return of European currencies to full convertibility under the Bretton Woods system. The emergence of multinational corporations presaged new forms of economic globalization and challenges to the established order of nation-states. Finally, there was a curious similarity in forms of social conflicts within society—notwithstanding their vast differences and particularities. In particular, a generational discontent among the youth who came of age in the 1960s took the shape of an unwillingness to accept established authority in families, universities, and states. The Cold War became seen as a stultifying force that preserved these structures of authority and prevented meaningful change.[3]

Kennedy and his successor, Lyndon Johnson, held the reins of power in a period molded by these altering contours of the Cold War, decolonization, and incipient globalization. This necessitated significant departures from the policies of Eisenhower—especially in the context of South Asia. As the dissolution of European empires swelled the ranks of the Third World, the Kennedy administration believed that the locus of Cold War competition was swiftly changing. As Secretary of State Dean Rusk noted, the struggle against the Soviet Union was shifting from "the military problem in Western Europe to a genuine contest for the underdeveloped countries."[4] Unlike the previous administration, Kennedy's emphasized the importance of cultivating the neutralist or nonaligned countries.

Kennedy had indicated his broad attitude toward nonaligned states in his inaugural speech, when he said, "We shall not always expect to find them supporting our view." An early paper prepared by the State Department held—*pace* John Foster Dulles—that neutralism was "rather a political attitude than a moral conviction." These countries "cherish a spirit of militant anti-colonialism" coupled with "anti-Western and anti-capitalist" proclivities. All the same the United States had to engage them in order to forestall Soviet influence. This shift in policy did not, however, reflect the waning of older cultural assumptions. On the contrary, the new administration persisted with older forms of paternalism and superiority. Thus the neutralists were deemed susceptible to the lures of communism, owing to their "craving for status and material advancement." They were often "myopic, seeing issues through the haze of their own preoccupation and antipathies." They were "difficult to deal with," as their policies stemmed from "irrational attitudes and extremist tendencies."[5] Yet pragmatism demanded the United States set aside such irritants and expand its influence among the nonaligned countries. As Kennedy observed, "We cannot permit all those who call themselves neutrals to join the Communist bloc....[I]f we lose them, the balance of power could swing against us."[6]

India loomed large in the administration's thinking about the neutralists and the Third World. As senator, Kennedy had already championed economic aid to India. The appointment of high-profile figures with known sympathies for India signaled the direction in which his administration wished to move. Chester Bowles was appointed undersecretary of state, and Phillips Talbot, an academic with long-standing connections to India, as assistant secretary for the Near East and South Asia. Economist and close friend of the president John Kenneth Galbraith was sent as ambassador to India. The president himself spoke highly of Jawaharlal Nehru in public. But privately, he found the Indians—especially Nehru and his colleague V. K. Krishna Menon—rather difficult to deal with. As Robert Komer, a key aide to Kennedy on South Asia, recalled, "No Westerner who goes [to South Asia], unless he is a terrible romantic or a mystic ... ends up liking Indians better than the Pakistanis.... [I]t was almost despite our prejudices that we were going in that [India's] direction."[7]

India acquired prominence in Kennedy's grand strategy for yet another reason. The president and his aides were acutely concerned about "Red China," which they saw as a highly radical, ideological, and bellicose power. They regarded China as problematic because it could not only egg on the Soviet Union to confront the United States but also threaten the non-Communist states of Asia. Kennedy saw a democratic India as a political and ideological bulwark against Communist China. On the campaign trail, he had declared, "No struggle in the world deserves more time and attention…[than] the struggle between India and China for the economic and political leadership of the East.…We want India to win that race with Red China. We want India to be a free and thriving leader of a free and thriving Asia." In office, Kennedy made his thinking clear. "Despite the fact that the Pakistanis are our allies, we must recognize the importance of India. If the Indians joined the Chinese, we would have no free South Asia. Our aim is to make the sub-continent of Asia strong. Even under present Indian leadership, we can work with India."[8]

ECONOMIC AID WAS THE Kennedy administration's principal tool in reorienting the relationship with India. Even before being sworn in to office, Kennedy appointed a special task force to look at ways of assisting India's economic development. The task force was chaired by Walt Rostow—the high priest of modernization theory, advisor to Kennedy since 1957, and senior figure in the new administration. Rostow recommended $500 million in annual aid to India for the next five years and another $500 million every year in food assistance under the PL480 program. This coincided neatly with India's third five-year plan, unveiled in 1961. This ambitious plan envisaged a 30 percent increase in agricultural output, a 70 percent rise in industrial production, and a 30 percent growth in national income. This necessitated a huge increase in public and private investment. Of the 75 billion rupees of expenditure foreseen in the public sector, external aid would finance almost 30 percent ($4.6 billion)—and this did not include PL480 assistance. The task force's recommendation, then, would amount to over half of India's foreign aid requirement for the third plan. Kennedy endorsed the idea. The administration's first foreign aid budget allocated to India an unprecedented $500 million—a little over twice what was on offer to the rest of the Third World.[9] Further, at an Aid to India consortium convened by the World Bank in April 1961, the administration prevailed upon Britain, West Germany, and Japan to match the American commitment by coughing up $1 billion for the first two years of India's third plan.

This policy turn delighted the Indians. They were particularly pleased that repayments of US aid in foreign exchange had been reduced to the minimum and that India would have maximum leeway in deciding where to spend the monies allocated. Nehru wrote to Kennedy thanking him for the "generous approach to our problems and also for exercising your country's great influence on the other participants of the aid programme."[10] And the two leaders kept up a warm personal correspondence. Washington, too, was encouraged by India's stance on the two issues that concerned it the most on the grand strategic plane: China and the nonaligned group of countries.

Sino-Indian relations had been in free fall since 1959. When Kennedy's special envoy, Averell Harriman, visited India in late March 1961, he found Nehru receptive to Washington's views on China. "[Nehru] said he is greatly disturbed by Peking's aggressive attitude," reported Harriman, "and believes the danger to [the] world comes from Peking rather than Moscow." The prime minister added, "Chinese Communists were at [the] height of their aggressive intentions and the situation is dangerous."[11]

Equally significant was India's attitude toward the newly established Non-Aligned Movement. Nehru had in fact sought to scuttle the idea of a meeting of nonaligned countries. For one thing, he was wary of his peers among the nonaligned countries: Tito of Yugoslavia and Gamal Nasser of Egypt. And he found the leaders of the newly independent nations too radical and unpredictable for his tastes. For another, Nehru was all too aware of India's dependence on American and Western aid and had no desire for a contretemps such as the one over the Bandung conference. Tito and Nasser, however, forced his hand by publicly announcing a conference in Belgrade in September 1961. Nehru told Galbraith that he would attend but "without much enthusiasm" and hoped to ensure that the conference was "as sensible as possible." At the conference, Nehru considerably tamped down the militancy of his fellow heads of state. He would not support any declaration that took a stance on the German question. Nor would he support the demand for a clear deadline for winding up colonialism.[12] Washington was thrilled.

By the same token, Pakistan regarded this upturn in US-India relations with deep disquiet. In fact, Kennedy's statements about India on the campaign trail had worried the Pakistanis. General Ayub Khan and his colleagues had hoped that Richard Nixon, an established friend of Pakistan, would beat his young rival for the White House. Not only were these hopes dashed, but the new administration promptly proceeded to cozy up to India. Within weeks of Kennedy's inauguration, Ayub told the American ambassador that "he was frankly concerned that in pre-election speeches as well as in statements following assumption of office, administration leaders had on several occasions made warm statements concerning India and other neutrals and had not made such statements about Pakistan and other allies, except NATO."[13]

The Americans, for their part, worried about the Ayub regime's attempts to negotiate with China on the disputed boundary and to secure project aid from the Soviet Union. In his meeting with Harriman, Ayub insisted that while he had taken some steps to "normalize" Pakistan's relations with Beijing and Moscow, the "focal point of Pakistan's policy continued to be friendship with U.S." He then spoke at length "on [the] importance of [a] solution to [the] Kashmir problem and his belief that [the] US should do more to bring Nehru around to negotiation." When Vice President Lyndon Johnson visited Islamabad in May 1961, Ayub yet again pressed him to use America's growing leverage over India to push for a settlement of the Kashmir dispute. When Johnson replied that the United States had "little influence with Nehru on the question," Ayub tartly argued that "India's flexibility today was gone. With the pressure from the Chinese Communists, India relied even more heavily upon the United States. In fact, it had no alternative." Much to his chagrin, Johnson refused to budge. "He did not in fact think that Nehru would listen to us on the Kashmir question."[14]

The Pakistanis were equally annoyed by the Kennedy administration's apparent unwillingness to back their second five-year plan. The plan, covering 1960 to 1965, had been formulated with substantial input from American economists with the Harvard Advisory Group. It called for a total investment of about $5 billion, nearly $2.3 billion of which would have to come from foreign aid. Unlike India, Pakistan could not look to the Soviet Union for any serious assistance. But the Kennedy administration was prepared to commit no more than $150 million for the 1961–1962 financial year. What is more, it failed to secure any comparable commitment from the Aid to Pakistan consortium organized by the World Bank. The Pakistani foreign minister bluntly told the Americans that "as allies of the West they were entitled to more favorable consideration than neutrals such as India."[15] Not prepared to fork out larger sums, the administration invited Ayub to visit Washington that summer to assuage Pakistani pride.

India and Kashmir figured prominently in the talks between Kennedy and Ayub. Drawing out three maps, the Pakistani leader insisted that his country faced threats from the Soviet Union, Afghanistan, and, above all, India. Unless the Kashmir problem was resolved, Pakistan would remain imperiled. Kennedy observed, "The Indians are not going to march. They already had what they wanted in Kashmir." He added that he could "understand India's desire" to hold on to what it had in Kashmir as well as its need to position troops there "to keep out Pakistan, which had irredentist feeling." Dismayed, Ayub insisted that Kashmir was the test of India's willingness to coexist with Pakistan. Kennedy replied that it was not obvious how the United States could prevail upon Nehru. "We could not even bring Chiang Kai-shek, whom we had helped more than anyone, to do what we saw was in his own interest." Ayub refused to relent: "Nehru now had to come to the U.S. He had no maneuverability left...Why could the U.S. not see that?" Kennedy coolly responded that the United States was "not all that influential with

Nehru on Kashmir. It was a bone-deep issue." Nevertheless, he assured Ayub that when Nehru visited Washington later in the year, he would make "a major effort" on Kashmir. If the effort failed, parried Ayub, would the United States support Pakistan's attempt to raise the issue again at the United Nations? Kennedy agreed. Ayub also queried if the administration intended to provide military aid to India. In the event that it did, he warned, "the Pakistani people would force his country out of the pacts and alliances and everything." Kennedy assured him that no military aid was on offer to India. If a situation, "such as an impending war with China," led New Delhi to ask for arms aid, he would "talk with President Ayub first" and then decide how to proceed.[16]

Despite these difficult conversations, the Americans warmed up to Ayub. The Pakistani president also cut a wide swathe in Washington, DC's social circuit. By contrast, the much-anticipated visit by Nehru in November 1961 proved deeply disappointing. The Indian leader was well past his prime and tired throughout the visit. His conversations with Kennedy were shallow and meandering. Nehru came into his own only when Kennedy broached the subject of Kashmir. After giving a lengthy historical background to the dispute, Nehru replied that the only solution was to drop all territorial claims and settle on the status quo with minor adjustments to the cease-fire line. "Perhaps later," he added for good measure, "the two countries could have some form of confederation or something else." Not surprisingly, Kennedy felt that talking to Nehru was "like trying to grab something in your hand, only to have it turn out to be just fog." He would later describe Nehru's trip as "the worst head-of-state visit I have had."[17] Nevertheless, it confirmed the administration's views on the need to shore up India's position, to mollify Pakistan, and to avoid serious involvement in Kashmir.

TROUBLE, HOWEVER, WAS BREWING at the other end of the subcontinent. Afghanistan had not figured prominently in the administration's thinking when it entered office. During his visit to Washington in February 1961, Ambassador Henry Byroade urged the State Department to pledge support for Afghanistan's second five-year plan spanning the years 1961 to 1966. Over the past decade and more, US aid to the country had amounted to a paltry $182 million. In light of growing Soviet clout in Afghanistan, Byroade convinced the department to promise the Afghans approximately $82 million for the rest of the plan period—a sum that paled in comparison with what was on offer to India and Pakistan. This aid would go toward completing ongoing projects, such as the landing strip at Kandahar International Airport and the construction of the Herat airport, as well as to starting new ones, like the Kandahar-Kabul highway.[18]

By the time the administration's thinking on foreign aid crystallized, Afghanistan had sunk out of sight. The imprint of Rostow's ideas was evident in the State Department's position that the United States would "make long-term commitment [only to] those countries whose stage of development, planning and internal resources mobilization [were] sufficiently advanced" and that "promise self-sustained growth in foreseeable future." In consequence, the administration informed Byroade that it would not offer long-term commitment to Afghanistan's second plan. Indeed, he could convey "nothing of substance" to the Afghan government. This volte-face stunned the ambassador. It came as such "a great shock" that he cabled the State Department asking if the message had been "erroneously sent." He warned that the "application of pure economic theory" divorced from geopolitical realities would undermine the administration's policy of winning the support of neutral countries adjoining the Soviet Union.[19] Alas, some neutrals were more important than others.

Difficulties with aid apart, the Kennedy administration soon had a crisis on its hands. It stemmed from Afghanistan's continued refusal to accept the Durand Line and persistence with its claims to all Pashtun territory on the other side of the line. The demand for "Pashtunistan" had been central to Prime Minister Daoud's attempts at nation building as well as extracting support from the superpowers. Following Ayub Khan's coup and ascent to power in Pakistan, the problem had begun to simmer again. A Pashtun himself, Ayub claimed to know the "mind" of his adversaries and insisted that a tough approach would force the Afghans to beseech the Americans for support. Thus he publicly labeled Pashtunistan a "stunt" and berated the Afghan royal family and its minders.

Pakistani truculence prompted Daoud to send a large group of armed tribesmen across the Durand Line in 1960. The incursion resulted in heavy loss of personnel and face for Daoud. Worse, the Pakistanis used the opportunity to station their army and paramilitary forces in the tribal areas, bringing the region under military control as never before. The entire episode called into question Daoud's political standing. In an attempt to recover ground, he began stoking the resentment of the tribes against the Pakistani military presence. The Pakistanis responded forcefully, including with the use of airpower. Although the Americans had urged both sides to step back, the situation seemed poised to escalate.

Byroade feared that in the event of a conflict, the Afghans would look to the Soviet Union for assistance, while the Americans would be obliged to stand by the Pakistanis. He conceded that the history of American attempts at mediating between the two neighbors had "not been a happy one." Yet he felt that it was "difficult to sit idly by and face [the] prospect not only [of] loss of our considerable investment here but of this issue becoming [an] active additional trouble spot in world situation."[20]

Harriman met Daoud in Rome and expressed concern about the situation. The Afghan leader, in turn, complained about the Pakistanis' use of American weapons, including aircraft. Ayub was no more receptive to Harriman's message, insisting that the Afghans had mobilized their forces besides stirring up trouble across the Durand Line. In any case, Pakistan "had enough equipment of its own to deal with Afghanistan intrusions."[21]

In his discussions with Kennedy in Washington, Ayub observed that the Russians were constructing a network of roads in Afghanistan—one that would eventually allow them to build up to twelve army divisions and threaten Pakistan, if they so desired. The United States, he added, was "obligingly building lateral roads for [the Russians]." Kennedy felt overt Soviet aggression in the region was not the danger. Rather, he feared Pakistan might confront "the possibility of guerrilla warfare and Communist party control." Pakistan was capable of responding to border incidents and hitting back hard, replied Ayub. The United States should "tell the Afghans it would give aid when their actions justif[ied] it." When Kennedy observed that at least Afghanistan was not yet a Soviet satellite, Ayub retorted that this was thanks to Russian forbearance. The Afghan royal family was no longer an independent entity, though he felt the Soviets "did not yet have the Communist Party cells in Afghanistan to take over."[22]

Following his US trip and encouraged perhaps by Kennedy's noncommittal stance, Ayub decided to get tougher with the Afghans. Toward the end of August 1961, he closed down all Pakistani consulates in Afghanistan and asked the Afghans to follow suit in two weeks. Although the border was not officially closed, the Pakistanis clamped down on all transit routes. In response, Kabul went a step ahead and severed diplomatic relations. Back in Washington, Komer worried that the Russians might egg on the Afghans "to pour on some oil to raise tensions a little more" and that a "minor border war" was a possibility. Talbot flew to Kabul, and the State Department offered "good offices" to both sides—notwithstanding the fact that this would irk the Pakistanis.[23]

In discussions with the American ambassador, Ayub stood firm on his Afghan policy. While he would not reconsider his decision to close the consular posts, he was agreeable to the United States conveying to Afghanistan that he did not want a break in diplomatic ties or seek to choke all transit arrangements. With the Afghans, the Americans emphasized the importance of finding practical arrangements for transit via Pakistan. Much of Afghanistan's needs, including American materials, flowed along these routes. Meantime, they also expressed willingness to explore the possibility of opening up routes through Iran, even though these could not substitute for the Pakistan transit. Daoud took a rigid stance. He told Ambassador Byroade, "The Pakistanis think that if they are given free hand they can settle Pushtunistan [sic] problem by force. As sincere friend of US I wish tell you that if Pakistanis are proceeding on this basis this is greatest mistake you can imagine, and if they persevere in this policy it is certain to cause disaster for whole area." The threat of a turn toward the Soviets was not so veiled. Referring to Kennedy's statements on self-determination, he argued that the Pashtuns should have the chance to decide their fate. If they opted to go with Pakistan, the Afghan government would abide by their choice. The Americans, of course, had no desire to go down this rabbit hole.[24]

As both sides balanced on the brink of a conflict, Kennedy sent personal messages to Ayub and Afghan king Zahir Shah, appealing to them to ensure practical arrangements for transit between the two countries. In delivering the missive to the Afghan ruler, Byroade noted that Afghanistan could "turn to north for immediate relief and its northern neighbor will be only too pleased to exploit Pak-Afghan impasse." But such help would pave the way for eventual political domination. The American envoy emphasized the "unwisdom of over-dependence upon a ruthless neighbor whose historic designs on Afghanistan are now augmented by Communism's imperialistic philosophy." The shah heard him out before replying that Afghanistan would not surrender its independent policy under any circumstances. All the same, he felt that the "Pushtunistan policy was right one for Afghanistan to follow" and that "policies of Ayub [were] dangerous in the extreme." Ayub, for his part, persisted with his earlier stance. Pakistan would not permit the opening of Afghan consulates or trade agencies as these were "centers of subversive activities." It would consider special arrangements— if Afghanistan refrained from raking up the issue of Pashtunistan.[25]

In another attempt to break the impasse, Kennedy dispatched his ambassador in Canada, Livingston Merchant, to Kabul and Karachi. After three weeks of hectic shuttling and parleying, Merchant concluded that his mission had failed. It would be unwise to push Ayub any further, and the United States should leave Afghanistan to its own devices. Washington reluctantly concurred. In March 1962, a national intelligence estimate accurately concluded that the Soviet Union was "now virtually assured of having the dominant foreign influence on Afghanistan's future." However, Moscow might not want to "cash in on its investment at an early date." Besides, the Afghans would continue to look to America for some economic aid. So, the assessment concluded with an optimism belied by its analysis: "We are likely to have with us for a considerable future time an Afghanistan very like that we have known for the past few years."[26]

Another year passed before relations between Afghanistan and Pakistan began to limp toward normality. The trigger was Daoud's resignation and replacement with a more amenable prime minister. Soon after, the two sides met in Teheran and agreed to restore diplomatic ties and reopen their consulates. Both also exercised restraint along the Durand Line. Yet the shah insisted when he met Kennedy later in the year, "This does not mean that the basic problem has been solved." Pashtunistan, he maintained, was not "a question of territorial claims or expansionist policy, but a matter of giving moral support to a people to whom the Afghans are attached by both tradition and blood."[27] In any event, the problem lay down the road for Kennedy's successors to tackle.

MEANWHILE, THE ADMINISTRATION HAD its hands full with further crises on the subcontinent. Even as curtains fell on the Merchant mission to Afghanistan and Pakistan, another unexpected conflict flared up. On December 17, 1961, India invaded Portuguese Goa and swiftly took control of the enclave. Goa had briefly been an irritant in US-India relations during the Eisenhower administration, but the Nehru government had desisted from using force to resolve the problem despite Portugal's recalcitrance. At the Belgrade conference of nonaligned states, African nationalists pointedly criticized India for putting up with Portuguese imperialism and even questioned Nehru's commitment to the anticolonial movement. Clashes between Portuguese troops and Indian activists on the borders of Goa in late November handed the Nehru government a convenient pretext for using force majeure. Yet Nehru continued to weigh the costs of military action against the pursuit of a negotiated settlement with Lisbon.

From Washington's standpoint, the situation was tricky owing to Portugal's status as a North Atlantic Treaty Organization (NATO) ally. Then again, the administration did not wish to be seen as standing on the wrong side of the colonial question. Urged by Galbraith, the South Asia hands in the State Department argued that "maximum possible U.S. public support for ultimate freedom for Goa from Portuguese rule" must accompany requests to the Indian government to desist from using force. To be sure, Lisbon would resent such a statement, which would have wider repercussions in other parts of the Portuguese empire. Still, "the time [had] come to deal with this issue as a whole." However, Secretary of State Rusk was more mindful of NATO imperatives. Following a request for American support from Portugal, Rusk instructed that the Indian government be warned against the use of force, which the United States would oppose in the UN Security Council. Galbraith argued against "any suggestion that we are responsive to pressure by Portuguese" but pleaded with the Indians to refrain from ordering their troops into Goa.[28] His efforts led Nehru to delay the invasion by forty-eight hours, but eventually the Indians went ahead.

The Portuguese promptly asked the UN Security Council to convene an emergency session and discuss the invasion of Goa. On December 18, the US ambassador to the United Nations, Adlai Stevenson, tabled a draft resolution calling for an immediate cease-fire, the withdrawal of Indian troops, and resumption of bilateral negotiations. Rusk called the Indian ambassador, B. K. Nehru, and brusquely "deplore[d] the Indian action after all our efforts to prevent violence." He warned that this crisis would "undoubtedly put a strain on public attitudes [toward India] in [the United States]." He also asked Stevenson to convey the administration's views "very sharply to the Indians privately." "The Indian double standard," he bristled, "is becoming a triple standard." Stevenson overlooked the injunction to convey the message in private. When the Russians expectedly vetoed the resolution, he mounted the high horse. "If the United Nations is not to die as ignoble a death as the League of the Nations," he declared, "we cannot condone the use of force in this instance and thus pave the way for forceful solutions of other disputes."[29]

Stevenson's performance infuriated the Indians. Nehru wrote Kennedy a long, injured letter stating the case for military action in Goa. Kennedy took a pragmatic view of the matter, though he did use the opportunity to call out India for its hypocrisy. "The minister (preacher) has been caught coming out of the brothel," he told Ambassador Nehru, "and the people are clapping. And Mr. Ambassador, I wish to tell you that I am clapping with them."[30] In his reply to Nehru, Kennedy made the point more politely. As the son of Irish immigrants, he wrote that India had his "sympathy on the colonial aspects of this issue." His "major concern," however, was Goa's impact on American opinion. On the one hand, it was "a shock to the majority who have admired your country's ardent advocacy of peaceful methods, and a reinforcement to those who did not enjoy what they called 'irresponsible lectures.'" On the other, it would certainly complicate aid appropriations—"our most difficult political battle." All said, the president expressed his keenness to ensure good relations with India.[31]

Kennedy's concerns were not off the mark. Democratic senator from Missouri Stuart Symington launched a blistering attack on the administration's aid to India. The influential senator disliked Nehru and his policy of nonalignment. Many Americans viewed the Indian defense minister, Krishna Menon, as an ogre, but Symington particularly detested him. In May 1962, he convinced the senate to pass an amendment to the administration's foreign aid bill, slicing the package for India by 25 percent. "Where is the logic," he exclaimed, "in providing such multi-billion dollar assistance to a country whose Secretary of Defense constantly attacks us...and whose leaders constantly threaten with military aggression some of the most steadfast and loyal friends the United States has in the free world?"[32]

Just as the administration began vigorously lobbying against the budget cuts, India shot off a flamethrower by announcing that it was purchasing MiG fighter aircraft from the Soviet Union, a decision spurred by the American sale of F-104s to Pakistan following Ayub's visit. Yet Galbraith immediately voiced concern that such a move might strengthen the hands of India's critics in the senate. Kennedy asked him to convey privately to Nehru that the Indian decision would likely deliver a sharp blow to aid appropriations for India. Komer took a more relaxed view. "I don't think we should break our backs to forestall MIG purchase," he argued. For one thing, it would "encourage Delhi to take strong line against Chinese." For another, there was no danger that the Indians would look to the Soviets for all arms purchases. "Indians are too smart for this."[33]

Nevertheless, the State Department launched a major effort to persuade the British to offer their Lightning fighters to India as an alternative to the Soviet MiGs. The Indians would not bite as the MiGs were on offer for purchase in Indian rupees rather than foreign currency. They were impervious to American remonstrations that this was tantamount to military aid from Moscow. At the same time, the administration failed to convince the British government to offer India attractive terms—despite a lengthy series of exchanges between Kennedy and Prime Minister Harold Macmillan.[34] Eventually the Americans acquiesced in the purchase of the MiGs. More importantly, the administration managed to have the budget cuts restored.

The Indian annexation of Goa not only impinged on US aid discussions but also pushed to the fore the perennial problem of Kashmir.

No sooner had the Security Council been alerted to the situation in Goa than Ayub decided to raise the issue of Kashmir at the United Nations. The Americans, however, felt that "a tendentious debate in UN [would] move us away from Kashmir settlement." So they sought to head off a debate at the Security Council. Galbraith managed to nudge Nehru to express his willingness to move toward direct negotiations with Pakistan. The administration then appraised Ayub of this and asked him to "take full advantage of this welcome development." The Pakistani president, however, maintained that Goa had confirmed India's aggressive behavior and that Pakistan had no choice but to take Kashmir to the United Nations.[35]

Pakistan's stance forced the administration to reexamine its approach to South Asia. Komer of the National Security Council (NSC) argued, "If we must choose between these countries there is little question that India (because of its sheer size and resources) is where we must put our chief reliance." He felt that Ayub was pushing the Americans to support his "forward policies vis-à-vis India and Afghanistan... which runs contrary to our larger strategic interests in the area." The American interest in maintaining a strong and stable subcontinent necessitated the resolution of disputes such as Kashmir and Pashtunistan. If the United States wanted an early resolution of these disputes, it would have to push for "compromise solutions." This would entail "a new tack in our approach to Ayub." Before pledging more aid to Pakistan, insisted Komer, "we had better take a new look at our Pakistan relationship and ask whether we are giving too much and not getting enough in return."[36]

The South Asia Desk at the State Department sounded a different note. Admittedly, "India's weight in international affairs can do more to help us or harm us than can Pakistan's." Even so, choosing between the two countries would amount to "a failure of policy: we need both." As far as Pashtunistan was concerned, the United States, rather than attempting mediation, should "work toward the obsolescence of this problem through resolution of the associated transit trade issue." Kashmir was a rather more dangerous problem. But the regional specialists were skeptical of any American initiative: "No final political solution of the Kashmir dispute is presently possible or in view in the near future." The administration should, however, impress on both sides that their continuing rivalry was undermining US efforts to boost their economic development.[37]

Assistant Secretary of State Talbot, however, felt that the administration ought to push India and Pakistan to negotiate on Kashmir. At his suggestion, Kennedy agreed that they should propose a high-level mediator. The administration's choice, World Bank president Eugene Black, had successfully brokered a recent agreement between India and Pakistan on the sharing of Indus waters.[38] Ayub accepted the proposal but refused to withdraw Pakistan's reference to Kashmir at the United Nations. Nehru bluntly refused to accept mediation on Kashmir, though he invited Ayub to New Delhi for talks. The Pakistani president, in turn, insisted on preparatory meetings in advance of a summit. India agreed but demanded that Pakistan withdraw the matter from the United Nations. Faced with Ayub's determination to press ahead, the United States voted in support of Pakistan's position. As expected, the Soviets vetoed the resolution on Kashmir.

WHILE THE DEADLOCK ON Kashmir persisted, the boundary dispute between India and China was coming to a boil. In late 1961, India embarked on a "forward policy" of planting puny posts all across the frontier to assert its territorial claims and deter the Chinese from making deeper inroads into the contested areas. In turn, China decided to deploy its own troops to encircle Indian positions. Yet the Chinese were alert to the potential costs of a major offensive against Indian positions. Beijing instructed the People's Liberation Army (PLA) to avoid skirmishes or opening fire without permission from higher headquarters. While China had considerable military superiority over India, Mao Zedong thought that the PLA could not "blindly" take on the

Indian forces: "We must pay attention to the situation." The Chinese were already feeling "severely threatened on their southern border" by American involvement in Laos and Vietnam, concerns enhanced by the Kennedy administration's May 1962 decision to deploy US troops in Thailand. Chinese leaders also worried about their southeast coast. They believed that Chiang Kai-shek would try to take advantage of the mainland's economic problems and launch a military attack along with the United States.[39] So, Mao was cautious of using force against India.

Nevertheless, from May 1962 Chinese troops began periodically threatening Indian posts, though they always backed off without launching an attack. As tensions soared, the two sides sought to negotiate on the sidelines of the Geneva conference on Laos in which both India and China were participants. The breakdown of these talks led the Chinese to reconsider their options vis-à-vis India. By this time, Beijing had good reason to believe that a war against India would not draw in other powers. The Geneva agreement on the neutralization of Laos precluded a US-led or -backed attack on China via that country. This increased the possibility that a Sino-Indian war would remain a limited affair. More importantly, the United States had assured Beijing that it would not support an invasion of the mainland by Chiang Kai-shek.[40]

Since early 1962 Chiang had been contemplating major military action against the mainland, encouraged both by the acute economic crisis there and by the Sino-Soviet estrangement. In June he told the Americans that he had "a military machine capable of exploiting the deterioration of Communist control on the Mainland."[41] The Kennedy administration, however, felt that these arguments mirrored the debates preceding the Bay of Pigs fiasco and was loath to support any such misadventure by Chiang. Large-scale troop movements by the Chinese complicated the situation across the Taiwan Strait. To restrain both sides, Washington assured Beijing, via the Soviets and the British, that it would not support an attack on the mainland. Meanwhile, Zhou Enlai directed the Chinese ambassador in Warsaw, Wang Bingnan, to meet his US counterpart and probe America's stance.[42] On June 23, Wang met John Cabot and expressed Beijing's concerns about the US military buildup in South Vietnam and Thailand and, most importantly, about the Kuomintang's preparations for an invasion. Cabot emphatically stated that the United States "had no intention of committing or supporting aggression against his side anywhere."[43] A few days later, President Kennedy declared at a press conference that the United States opposed the use of force in the Taiwan Strait area. Wang later recalled that all this "had a great impact on policy decisions at home."[44] Indeed, the conjunction of failed negotiations and these international developments led Beijing to reassess its interest in seeking a peaceful resolution of the border crisis.

The Americans were, of course, unaware of the ramifications of their stance toward China. On the contrary, they were pondering the possibility of an Indian request for military aid in the event of an escalation along the border. As early as March 1962, there were straws in the wind. When Chester Bowles visited New Delhi, the Indian chief of the General Staff, Lieutenant General B. M. Kaul, asked him "bluntly in great confidence whether we would come to India's aid in [the] event [of] open ChiCom armed invasion." Kaul suggested that the two sides engage in "secret conversations" on contingency plans—even if these were "not fully sanctioned by Menon and/or Nehru." By mid-October 1961, just days before the Chinese attacked India, the State Department and the Pentagon were examining the feasibility of providing India transport, communication, and other military equipment—should New Delhi make such a request.[45]

By this time, Beijing had decided to launch a major attack all along the disputed frontier with India. The Chinese had sounded out the Russians and got a wink and a nod from Nikita Khrushchev. The Soviet leader also promised to place on hold the delivery of the MiG fighters to India.[46] On the morning of October 20, 1962, the Chinese offensive began. Just four days later the PLA was in effective control of all the territory Beijing claimed at the western end (Ladakh) of the boundary and had occupied the key town of Tawang in the east. Although the Sino-Indian conflict coincided with the Cuban Missile Crisis, the Kennedy administration remained responsive to India's needs.

On October 25, the Indian finance minister and the foreign secretary told Galbraith that a request for military assistance was "inevitable and imminent." The next afternoon, Ambassador Nehru formally handed to Kennedy a letter from his prime minister asking for American assistance in coping with the Chinese threat. The president not only assured him of "our full sympathy and support" but also agreed to make "no reference to arms or to aid" in deference to Indian sensibilities. Kennedy did indicate, however, that his administration would like to see Krishna Menon's departure from office.[47] Galbraith's energetic machinations helped secure this objective within a week. Thereafter, the Americans had no difficulty displaying semantic solicitude for Nehru's nonalignment, especially since it lay in tatters. In his meeting with Galbraith on October 29, Nehru "hoped that this did not mean a military alliance between the United States and India." "We insist on such thing," came the prompt reply.

Within four days of the Indian request, the first American planes carrying light weapons landed in Calcutta. Over the following days, no fewer than forty-one aircraft carrying over 40,000 tons of equipment touched down in India. Galbraith wrote to President Kennedy, "Past three weeks have brought great change here—no doubt the greatest change in public attitudes since World War II." This was a perceptive observation. Equally pointed were his remarks about India's leader. "Now nothing is so important to him," Galbraith noted, "than to maintain the semblance of this independence. His age no longer allows for readjustment. To a point we can, I feel, be generous on this."[48] Although cognizant of their growing leverage with India, the Americans failed to foresee the total collapse of Nehruvian nonalignment.

On November 16, the PLA launched the second phase of operations. While the Indian forces put up a staunch resistance in Ladakh sector in the north, those in the eastern sector along India's North East

Frontier Agency ignominiously collapsed, virtually without a fight. By the evening of November 19, the Indian army was helpless to withstand further onslaughts. In the west the Chinese seemed likely to advance to Leh; in the east they were poised to enter the plains of Assam. Nehru now approached the United States for air cover. Barely half a dozen senior officials knew of the terms the Indian request—none of the cabinet members learned of them until much later. Writing to President Kennedy, Nehru described the situation as "really desperate": "We have to have more comprehensive assistance if the Chinese are to be prevented from taking over the whole of Eastern India. Any delay in this assistance reaching us will result in nothing short of a catastrophe for our country." Nehru requested immediate dispatch of at least twelve squadrons of fighter aircraft and radar installations as well as American military personnel to man them. American planes flown by American pilots would "protect [Indian] cities and installations from Chinese attacks." What is more, Nehru also wanted them to "assist the Indian Air Force in air battles with the Chinese air force over Indian areas."[49]

Nehru's missive stunned the Americans. Rusk cabled Galbraith that it amounted to "a request for an active and practically speaking unlimited military partnership between the United States and India to take on [the] Chinese invasion [of] India." The administration was "not at all convinced" that the Indians were prepared to face up to realities. Nehru's request implied "not only a military alliance between India and the United States but complete commitment by us to a fighting war." Such a proposal, Rusk insisted, "cannot be reconciled with any further pretense of non-alignment." Nehru had to be "entirely clear" in his own mind before the Americans made up theirs.[50]

In the event, Nehru was spared the ignominy of having American fighters safeguard Indian territory. The following day, the Chinese announced a unilateral cease-fire and subsequent withdrawal of troops. While the immediate danger had receded, India was still reliant on American military assistance to hold its own against a renewed Chinese offensive.

Over the following months Washington and New Delhi wrangled over the amount of military aid. Secretary of Defense Robert McNamara forcefully argued that the Chinese threat to India was "essentially a small one." India needed no more than seventeen divisions comprising some 650,000 troops—as opposed to its plans for a buildup to 1.4 million men. The air threat to India was minimal: "The Indians could meet this air threat by themselves if they were not so inefficient." Still, the Americans agreed to commit along with Britain to provide air defense for Indian cities in the event of resumed hostilities, seeing this as "the least expensive way to reassure India of our continued interest in its defense." The Indians, however, harbored outsized hopes for $1.6 billion over three years, while the Americans believed that India needed no more than $300 million—including aid for defense production—over this same period. The administration was also eager to ensure that Britain picked up a portion of the tab. The problem was not merely financial, however. As McNamara put it, "There was also a serious political problem involved in the Indian military buildup as it bore on Kashmir."[51]

PAKISTAN HAD BEEN FOLLOWING the flow of American military assistance to India with mounting concern. Kennedy informed Ayub in late October 1962 of his decision to provide arms to India, though he hastened to assure the Pakistani leader that he would ensure these were not deployed against his country. Annoyed that he had not been consulted in advance, Ayub tartly replied, "The arms now being obtained by India from you for use against China will undoubtedly be used against us at the very first opportunity." The threat from India could only be removed "if there is a settlement of the question of Kashmir." The Americans thought that the Pakistanis had "whipped themselves into a near hysterical state," yet felt they owed Karachi no apology. They were, however, concerned about Pakistan's "flirtations with the Chinese communists."[52]

Once the scale of India's military requests became apparent, the Kennedy administration decided to step up on Kashmir; at the same time it would not cave in to maximalist demands from Pakistan. As Rusk briskly put it, "We are prepared to tell Nehru that if we give him major military aid he should agree to negotiate at a suitable point on Kashmir. Ayub cannot ask more of us, and we are unable to provide more."[53] The president sent Averell Harriman to the subcontinent to knock heads together. Ayub wanted to start with a joint statement from him and Nehru, explicitly stating their readiness to negotiate on Kashmir. He also pressed Harriman to use American leverage with India to obtain a settlement. Nehru initially demurred. The time was not propitious for such an attempt, he claimed, especially in terms of public opinion in India. But his final meeting with Harriman left no doubt about India's standing on the matter. Nehru said he was ready for talks but had a "very limited concept in mind such as adjustment [along the] cease-fire line." Galbraith said "this [was] not enough." Nehru had no choice but to agree to talks with "an open mind and without preconditions." Harriman was pleased to note that "Nehru had become clearer minded and more down to earth than he had been at earlier meetings."[54]

Yet in the subsequent negotiations the Indians held their own. Indian officials sought and obtained Nehru's approval for plans to partition Kashmir. These envisaged alterations to the cease-fire line that would be favorable to Pakistan. The Indians were clear that there could be no compromise on the valley, for the lines of communication to Ladakh passed through it. The opening round of talks in Rawalpindi on December 26 got off to an unpropitious start: Pakistan and China announced that they were set to sign a border agreement. India claimed the areas covered in the agreement as part of Kashmir. The discussions nevertheless went ahead, and the Indians made it amply clear that the question was not of transferring the valley to Pakistan but of drawing an international boundary through Kashmir.

Ahead of the second round in Delhi, American officials considered various possibilities, including "an undivided state of Jammu and

Kashmir jointly administered and jointly defended by India and Pakistan."[55] But the two sides themselves continued to fence over the parameters of an accord without placing anything concrete on the table. Meanwhile, State Department officials came up with a plan for partitioning the valley: transfer substantial territory in the northwest of the valley as well as the western portion of Jammu, while providing India a sliver of territory in the northern end of the valley to maintain a buffer between the valley and Ladakh. The free movement of peoples and jointly administered bureaucracies would supplement these territorial exchanges.[56] On hearing its outlines, the senior Indian negotiator immediately rebuffed the plan. Kennedy himself was skeptical. As he wrote to Macmillan, "Nehru is unlikely to settle Kashmir with too obvious a gun at his back." Yet, ahead of the third round of talks, Kennedy wrote directly to Nehru pointing out the advantages of a settlement on Kashmir for India's global role as well as its relations with the United States.[57] Although more forthcoming in this round of negotiations, the two sides made no headway.

"The odds are increasingly against an early Kashmir settlement," Komer informed the president, "but we must play out the hand."[58] To break the impasse, Washington and London joined forces to prepare a "guidance document" aimed at facilitating a settlement. The document maintained that relinquishing claims to the valley of Kashmir was impossible for both India and Pakistan. Hence, both must end up with a sizeable portion of it. Armed with the plan, Komer and Rostow traveled to the subcontinent in early April. The Anglo-American intervention boomeranged as the Indians saw it as a "full tilt on the side of Pakistan." Nehru let fly with Kennedy: "I am convinced that these ill-considered and ill-conceived initiatives, however well-intentioned they may be, have at least for the present made it impossible to reach any settlement on this rather involved and complicated question."[59] Following a visit to the subcontinent in early May, Rusk reluctantly concluded that it was "most unlikely that a Kashmir settlement can be negotiated which would not cause serious difficulties for both governments internally."[60]

The failure of the sixth and final round of talks in mid-May 1963 confirmed Rusk's pessimistic conclusion.

The Kennedy administration's decision to proceed with military aid for India despite the failure of the Kashmir negotiations deeply angered Pakistan. Ayub retaliated by not only expanding ties with China and the Soviet Union but also temporarily halting the expansion of American intelligence facilities in Pakistan. To arrest the slide, Undersecretary of State George Ball went to Pakistan for talks with Ayub in August 1963. The president was not optimistic about the prospects of the visit or indeed about the state of the relationship: "There wasn't much for Ball to say except to repeat our position. We weren't getting much from the Pakistani either. About all the alliance was worth to us were the intelligence facilities." At most Ball could convey the American distaste for the dalliance with China and point out that "if they don't play ball [on intelligence], we will give our aid to someone else."[61] Not only did Ball's trip prove unfruitful, but the Pakistanis soon after invited Chinese premier Zhou Enlai for a state visit.

The holes in the fabric of Kennedy's South Asia policy were evident. But it is not clear how he would have sought to mend them. Three months later, an assassin's bullet brought the president down.

FOR ALL THEIR DIFFERENCES in background, personality, and style, Lyndon Johnson's foreign policy essentially continued Kennedy's. The ideological assumptions, political objectives, range of instruments, and key personnel all remained intact. The larger context in which their policies played out was similar too. Both had to cope with the conjunction of a shifting Cold War constellation and the acceleration of decolonization, though the early glimmers of globalization were more discernable in the Johnson years and more influential in shaping his foreign economic policy. The latter was also inflected by Johnson's fierce commitment—unmatched by Kennedy—to domestic reform under the Great Society program.[62] Given his domestic priorities and his long years in the Senate, Johnson was also more mindful than Kennedy of carrying (or manipulating) congressional opinion on foreign initiatives.

The foreign policy team that Johnson inherited from Kennedy was unclear where the new president stood on South Asia. They recalled his tour of the region in 1961, when he had struck a balanced note in his assessments but clearly been more taken with Ayub than Nehru. When Ayub had visited the United States later in the year, Johnson went out of his way to put on a lavish barbeque at his Texas ranch. His subsequent note to Ayub was effusive: "It is seldom that I have been so very much impressed by a man." As Vice President Johnson played little role in the transformation of South Asia policy attempted by Kennedy and his team. Nor did he seem to grasp the impulses behind that effort. "Why is it," he asked an official, "that Jack Kennedy and you India lovers in the State Department are so Godammed [sic] ornery on my friend Ayub?" Not surprisingly, advocates of a tighter relationship with India, such as Komer, were concerned that Johnson might undo Kennedy's turn in South Asia policy and become "more pro-Pak."[63]

A couple of weeks after Johnson assumed office, National Security Advisor McGeorge Bundy and Komer urged the president to approve a five-year, $300 million program of military assistance to India. The proposal had originated with Chester Bowles, who had recently replaced Galbraith as ambassador in India. The collapse of the American plan to provide $500 million for a new steel plant at Bokaro in the Indian state of Bihar had partly spurred the idea. The plan had signaled an unprecedented willingness on the part of the United States to support the Indian program of state-led heavy industrialization. While Kennedy had staunchly supported the idea, the Congress had snuffed it out on ideological as well as financial grounds. By offering a military assistance program (MAP), Bowles hoped at once to take the sting out of the Bokaro fiasco and to obtain a set of assurances from India, including a commitment to limit both its military buildup vis-à-vis

Pakistan and military aid from the Soviet Union. In recommending the plan, Bundy and Komer pointed out, "We cannot afford to give Pakistan a veto on our Indian policy."[64]

Johnson not only declined to take an early decision but also proved impervious to Bowles's repeated pleas for action on the India front. At the same time, the president looked askance at Pakistan's attempts to sidle up to China. Speaking to Foreign Minister Zulfikar Ali Bhutto after Kennedy's funeral, Johnson pointedly referred to the Chinese premier's forthcoming visit to Pakistan. There would be a "serious public relations problem here," he warned Bhutto, "if Pakistan should build up its relations with the Communist Chinese." Pakistan could not afford to take the United States for granted: "The strongest men in Congress in favor of Pakistan are also the strongest against the Chinese Communists." Bhutto was "deeply upset" by this opening encounter.[65]

The question of military aid to India and Pakistan came up again in the wake of a mission to the subcontinent led by Joint Chiefs of Staff chairman General Maxwell Taylor. In his recommendations, Taylor endorsed the package advocated by Bowles for India and for the same reasons. To assuage Pakistan's concerns, he advised a similar five-year military assistance program. These ideas met with wide approval in the administration. The president, however, sought to move gradually. While open to "exploratory approaches" to both countries, he wanted them to know that there could be "no irrevocable five year MAP commitments." What the United States could offer each year would depend on Congress and on the performance of both countries, with the latter measured against clear expectations. India should commit to imposing "reasonable limits" on the diversion of foreign exchange from development to defense. Pakistan should live up to its alliance obligations on China and intelligence facilities.[66] This set the parameters and the tone for much of Johnson's South Asia policy. And they would be reinforced by the deepening involvement in Vietnam, the rising concerns about China's role in Southeast Asia, and the growing congressional pressures on foreign aid.

In March 1963, Johnson sent Phillips Talbot to Pakistan for some straight talk with Ayub. During their testy meeting, Talbot bluntly stated that the United States was "profoundly disturbed" by Pakistan's burgeoning ties with China. This turn in Pakistani policy would cause "at minimum confusion and doubt and at maximum much more serious problems." While the United States was trying to contain China in Southeast Asia, "Pak actions seem to enable them to make hay in South Asia." The United States "was disturbed that Pak actions [were] undermining our efforts." Ayub agreed that US-Pakistan relations had become "strained": "What could we [the United States] expect except that Pakistanis would be unhappy over US aid to India." He then held forth on India's military buildup and unwillingness to settle the Kashmir dispute, scoffing at Talbot's claim that US military aid to India was actually quite limited. As far as China was concerned, he insisted that Pakistan was pursuing "a very limited relationship." After the meeting, Talbot grimly concluded, "Our problems in Pakistan have not been resolved."[67]

Meanwhile, Johnson's advisors were pressing him to ignore Pakistani protests and move ahead with India. They could not "permit the tail to wag the dog," claimed Komer. As the Sino-Soviet split widened, he pointed out, the Soviets were going all out to woo India. Although the United States had invested $4.7 billion to date in India's economic development, its political-military policy had lagged behind. The timing was also critical given the possibility of a leadership succession in India as Nehru was aged and ailing. "If India falls apart we are the loser." Even if India reverted to a pro-Soviet nonaligned stance, "our policy in Asia will be compromised."[68]

Johnson would not be hustled, however. Following a visit to Washington in April 1964 by the Indian defense minister, Y. B. Chavan, the president gave a go-ahead for military aid. But India's hopes for a five-year program were disappointed, for Johnson approved only $50 million in military assistance for the financial year 1965. The administration also turned down India's requests for F-104 fighter air-craft, leading the Indians to place further orders for MiGs from Russia. Chavan's visit proved abortive in another way: Jawaharlal Nehru died on May 27, 1964.

The announcement of military assistance for India led to a chorus of ululations from the Pakistanis. Bhutto stated in the National Assembly that the United States had shown "utter disregard" for Pakistan and that the time had come "for Pakistan to undertake an appraisal of its foreign policy and review her political and military commitments." In an interview with a British tabloid the following day, Ayub observed, "Today American policy is based on opportunism and is devoid of moral quality. . . . [Pakistan] has been let down by politicians she regards as friends."[69] When Ayub sent a formal letter to Johnson griping about military aid to India, Johnson's bile rose. He curtly told the Pakistani ambassador that leaving the US-led alliances would not be in Karachi's interest, "but that would have to be Pakistan's decision." Much to the envoy's concern, the president gravely noted that "we were coming to the point at which we would all have to re-evaluate the condition of our relationship." Johnson also asked his own ambassador in Pakistan to convey to Ayub that "we Americans felt strongly about China; we were having all sorts of trouble with China in Southeast Asia right now." He was upset, too, about Pakistan's unsupportive stance on Vietnam, especially in light of a previous commitment by Ayub to consider sending some troops to the region. As for Pakistan's obsession with Kashmir, Johnson "didn't think that either side would settle." Given the different directions in which the United States and Pakistan were pulling, Johnson decided not to invite the Pakistani leader to visit before the American presidential elections in November: "He did not see much point in another session of unproductive argument with Ayub."[70]

In the aftermath of Johnson's electoral victory, American officials sought to pick up pieces with Pakistan. In early January 1965, Johnson agreed to extend an invitation to Ayub to visit the United States. The

State Department recommended using the visit to "halt the drift in our relations with Pakistan." Ayub needed reminding that if Pakistan sought to maintain its alliance with the United States, its relations with China could not "exceed the speed limits" set by Washington. The Pakistani president should have no doubt about the links between American aid and his alliance commitments. Buoyed by his own victory in Pakistan's presidential "election," Ayub readily concurred in "the urgent requirement for face-to-face meeting with President Johnson."[71]

The Pakistanis, however, proceeded to worsen the situation. Ahead of his trip to Washington Ayub undertook highly publicized visits to Moscow and Beijing. His embrace of the Chinese leadership, pledge of collaboration with China, and censure of America's involvement in Vietnam all galled the Johnson administration deeply. To the surprise and dismay of some of his advisors, Johnson was sufficiently piqued to withdraw the invitation to Ayub just nine days before he was due to arrive. In a gauche attempt to demonstrate evenhandedness on South Asia, Johnson also retracted an invitation for the new Indian prime minister, Lal Bahadur Shastri, to visit the United States.

Already struggling to step out of Nehru's shadow, Shastri was deeply hurt by such rough handling. He told Bowles that "he had been personally embarrassed before his country, his party and world"—especially at a time when India was "striving diligently to cooperate" with the United States on such controversial matters as the Vietnam War. Now his ability to pull India's weight in the Third World had been "greatly diminished." The "manner in which the invitation had been cancelled," he said, "indicated [a] deep psychological gap between India and the US which he was afraid could never be bridged." Bowles glumly characterized this the "most serious" situation he had ever encountered in dealing with India over many years.[72]

The *Economist* quipped that the United States had managed "the unusual diplomatic feat of giving offence to both [India and Pakistan] simultaneously." American officials thought otherwise, believing that both countries would now "reflect on the moral that Uncle Sam should not just be regarded as a cornucopia of goodies, regardless of what they do or say."[73]

THIS SMUG ASSUMPTION WAS put to the test almost immediately. In early April 1964, the Pakistanis undertook a military probe in the disputed areas of the Rann Kutch along India's western borders. The Indian government responded by pumping its forces into the area. Soon the two sides were embroiled in localized military action. By late April, the Americans worried that the fighting could escalate into all-out war between the two countries. The timing, of course, was most unfortunate. As South Asia analysts pointed out, "The fighting in Kutch...has propelled us once more into the center of a subcontinental dispute at a moment when our leverage in both countries is at a low point."[74] A particularly neuralgic aspect of the crisis was Pakistan's use of American tanks. The United States had not only assured India over the years that this would not happen but also forbidden India from deploying US-provided arms against Pakistan. The Indians were incensed on both counts. New Delhi demanded that the administration punish Pakistan by cutting off all aid forthwith. Washington had little option but to proscribe the use of American weapons by both sides. This, in turn, angered the Pakistanis. The administration's encouraging Britain to take the lead in brokering a cease-fire reflected the depths plumbed by American standing in the subcontinent.

Instead of getting a grip on the situation, Johnson chose to double down on his approach of being an equal opportunity offender in South Asia. In a bid to pressure both sides to step back from confrontation, he decided to tighten the flow of aid. The president insisted on clearing all aid decisions. He disallowed any advance aid programs to the two countries, even if it meant money appropriated by the Congress remained unspent.[75]

Given their concerns about China, the Americans were already keener to bring Pakistan to the heel. Komer had told Johnson that it was important to disabuse Ayub of the notion that he could "have his cake and eat it too." The United States had ploughed in some $3.2 billion in economic aid to Pakistan, not to mention an additional $1.5 billion for the Pakistani military. All this had evidently benefited Pakistan. Indeed, Komer had held, "Our dilemma is that U.S. economic aid is making Pakistan a real success story, so we hate to cut back for political reasons."[76] Now Johnson elected to move back a July 1965 meeting of the Aid to Pakistan consortium organized by the World Bank and expected to commit $500 million to Pakistan. The two-month postponement enraged the Pakistanis, especially since the consortium meeting for India had already taken place. "Anyone can see that this amounts to more than a mere delay," snapped Ayub to the American ambassador. The Pakistani president claimed that he had done his best to explain his "independent" foreign policy to the United States. "He did not see that there was much more he could try to do." Pakistan, he maintained, would have to "cut the coat according to the cloth."[77]

As American influence nose-dived, fighting broke out afresh in the subcontinent. In early August 1965 Pakistani irregulars began to infiltrate across the cease-fire line (CFL) in Kashmir. On August 13, Prime Minister Shastri approved military strikes on their bases across the CFL. Two weeks later, Pakistan responded to Indian moves by launching a full-scale assault on the southern town of Akhnur, aimed at sealing off Indian-held Kashmir. Faced with the grim prospect of losing the province, Shastri authorized a conventional attack across the international boundary in Punjab. India and Pakistan were now at war—the most serious conflict between the neighbors since late 1948.

On September 1, UN Secretary-General U Thant called for an immediate cease-fire and withdrawal of all troops behind the old CFL. Johnson instructed the American UN ambassador to immediately back U Thant's appeal. The administration knew that it faced a grave crisis in the subcontinent, but the president desisted from bringing direct pressure to bear on the combatants and chose instead to go down the UN route. No sooner had Indian tanks rolled across the international border on September 6 than Ayub met with the American ambassador and demanded that the United States come to Pakistan's assistance: "You have a bilateral obligation and we are going to demand fulfill-ment." Washington promptly turned down the request: "Neither we nor any other friends [of] both parties can assist in coping with this or other root causes of Indo-Pak tensions without immediate and re-spected cease-fire and withdrawal of forces [on] both sides." India re-ceived an identical message.[78]

Prominent voices in Congress called for an immediate cessation of all aid to the warring countries. Sensitivity to congressional opinion apart, the administration was anxious to avoid prolonging the war and secure an early cease-fire. "We are going to put all our chips behind U Thant," Johnson declared. So the administration decided to suspend military aid to both India and Pakistan. Komer advised Johnson that the move would "lead to howls from both, but it should also help bring home to them the consequences of their folly."[79]

The administration was divided, however, on how far it should go in managing the crisis. Secretary of State Rusk felt that prolonged war could lead to "collapse and communal chaos" in the subcontinent. This could have secondary effects "all along the Asian rim": in Iran, In-donesia, and Japan. Rusk wondered whether the United States could "maintain or even afford non-involvement." It might get both countries to agree to a cease-fire by promising "full support" for efforts to negoti-ate all outstanding disputes, including Kashmir. Komer and Bundy at the NSC, however, saw little point in going down this well-worn track and believed they should stick to backing UN efforts. The president agreed.[80]

They all conceded, however, the danger of Chinese involvement in the war. Early on, Beijing had issued statements affirming total support for Pakistan. On September 8, it issued a formal note to India alleging border violations, demanding withdrawal of its forces, and warning of dangerous consequences. Rusk was unsure how far the Chinese would go, but their intervention could "convert the Pakistan-India war into a Free World–Communist confrontation." Johnson told Ambassador Nehru that the possibility of Chinese entry into the war was "giving us grey hairs right now." But he was reluctant to warn them against it: "Stronger US public noises about the Chinese Communist threat might only provoke Peiping."[81]

On September 16, the Chinese handed a second note to India, demanding the demolition of certain military structures along the border within three days, failing which India would face "grave consequences." This sounded rather like an ultimatum of war.[82] The next day B. K. Nehru met with Rusk and conveyed a request for the United States to issue to formal warning to Beijing against intervention in the war, believing this would deter the Chinese. He also requested that the "US come to India's assistance if Chicoms attack," adding that "the nature of such assistance would be for US to decide." Rusk replied that a formal warning was a major decision—one that only the president could make. In a meeting that evening, Johnson directed the Departments of Defense and State to prepare contingency plans for his review— although "no preparatory military moves should now be made in the area."[83]

In the UN Security Council, the American ambassador warned the Chinese of the grim consequences that would follow from any attempt to exploit the India-Pakistan conflict. Finally, the administration turned the squeeze on Pakistan to accept the United Nations' terms for a cease-fire; the Indians were already agreeable. After some prevarication, Pakistan acquiesced on September 22.

In the aftermath of the 1965 war, Johnson was loath to expend his political capital on South Asia. As the United States was increasingly enmeshed in Vietnam, the president effectively adopted an attitude of "a plague on both your houses" toward India and Pakistan. Thus, when the Russians came forward to facilitate a postwar settlement by getting the two sides together in Tashkent, Johnson extended his support. Inasmuch as the Soviet Union wanted to tone down the India-Pakistan rivalry and keep the Chinese out the subcontinent, the United States was content to go along.

The depth of Johnson's disenchantment with the subcontinent became evident in his meeting with Ayub toward the end of 1965. Johnson plainly told Ayub that "we were not going to let Pakistan tell us how to handle India....Our Indian policy is our business." At the same time, if Pakistan wanted close ties with the United States, it could not have "a serious relationship" with China: "We could not live with that." Invoking an image that said much about his chastened view of the region, Johnson added, "We understood certain relationships just as a wife could understand a Saturday night fling by her husband so long as she was the wife."[84]

ON ONE ISSUE, THOUGH, President Johnson remained intensely—not to say excessively—involved in South Asia policy: food aid. Johnson's interest in this area reflected the changing economic context with which his foreign policy had to cope. In the first place, the balance-of-payments deficit that he inherited from Kennedy began galloping owing to a variety of factors, including the emerging transnational circuits of dollar flows. Since the dollar-gold link underpinned the financial order, there was a danger of not just a run on the greenback but the unraveling of the international monetary order. Johnson was disinclined, however, to take steps to rein in the deficit. For these would necessarily crimp the two central initiatives of his presidency: the Great Society program and the Vietnam War.[85] In this situation, scaling back on foreign aid became an ineluctable choice.

Food aid became a particularly fraught issue owing to a second consideration. Influential figures in the Johnson administration and beyond pictured a Malthusian specter haunting the world. Global demand for food would soon outstrip US capacity. In consequence, it was important to push recipient countries to introduce agricultural practices along American lines—especially the use of hybrid seeds, pesticides, and fertilizers. Johnson liked the idea of linking continued food aid to such reforms by the recipients. It struck him not only as a solution to several problems confronting US foreign policy but also as continuous with his ideas for reform at home. As Johnson told the Indian ambassador at the height of the 1965 war, "What I am doing in this country this year, I would like to do worldwide. My foreign policy is the Great Society."[86]

India became a proving ground for the efficacy of US food policy owing to the collapse of its third five-year plan under the combined weight of the war against China and subsequent rearmament. Sluggish industrial and agricultural growth during this period further increased the country's external dependence. In early 1964, soon after he took office, Johnson sent Secretary of Agriculture Orville Freeman to India. Meetings with political leaders, planners, and experts from the Ford and Rockefeller foundations convinced Freeman of the imperative of a "successful national food policy" in India. "We should have insisted," he lamented, "that she [India] invested more in the agricultural sector of her economy as a condition for our heavy PL-480 transfers. That's history."[87]

Johnson was determined not to repeat history. Instead the president embarked on a "short tether" policy of approving only limited shipments of food for short periods as a way of pressuring the Indians into undertaking American-style agricultural reforms. Described in India as a "ship to mouth" policy, it caused considerable anguish in the country—especially in the wake of successive monsoon failures in 1965 and 1966 that sent the food aid requirement skyrocketing from 4 million to 10 million tons a year. Johnson's advisors, too, were troubled by his determination to persist with this tough-minded policy in the face of possible famine. In September 1965, Bowles pointed out that "food shortage in India is likely to be serious to desperate in next 12 months." If the United States "failed [to] maintain shipments effects on

India and our position here would be drastic." Komer worried that if the "Indian public came to believe we were using food as an instrument of pressure, it would be a real setback to our influence."[88]

Freeman thought it "immoral not to do something" for hungry Indians. The president, he noted, was "willing to put in food and put in fertilizer, but he wanted the assurance of some results.... [I]f they [Indians] wanted to get the MiGs and the steel mills and get ready for war that was up to them, but he wasn't going to put any food for these purposes."[89] Freeman negotiated with his Indian counterpart, C. Subramaniam, on an agreement committing India to allocating $5 billion for agriculture during the fourth five-year plan (more than double the allocation in the previous plan). It also set benchmarks for fertilizer output, the use of high-yield varieties, and catering to foreign private investment in the production of fertilizer in India. Johnson kept a hawk's eye on India's efforts. The president's close interest on this issue surprised even the Indians. "That Subber Mainyam of yours," he told Ambassador Nehru, "he's a good feller."[90] Yet Johnson would not relax the short tether.

The Indians saw this not just as a well-meaning attempt to spur food production in India but also as an effort to line their country up behind the United States in such unpopular ventures as Vietnam. This view was not off the mark. Johnson had stated on several occasions that he wanted Shastri to mute the criticism on Vietnam as another quid pro quo for food. Shastri's successor, Indira Gandhi, had a sharper nose for the realpolitik at play. As she wrote a trusted advisor only days before becoming prime minister, "Brave words notwithstanding, there is anxiety to go to America, who will I have no doubt give PL 480 food aid and everything at a price. The manner of execution will be so deft and subtle that no one will realise it until it is too late and India's freedom of thought and action will have both been bartered away."[91]

In office, Prime Minister Gandhi had to reckon with the reality of India's perilous food crisis. During her visit to the United States in

March 1966, she went out of her way to be amenable. The two leaders, she observed, "had indeed found they had much in common." And their two countries could have "a good working partnership." What is more, the joint statement issued at the end of the visit stated that India understood the American position on Vietnam. Johnson, for his part, agreed to secure congressional support for food as well as for the World Bank's efforts to promote economic development in India.[92]

The World Bank, in fact, was contemplating farther-reaching reforms in the Indian economy. In late 1964, a Bank mission led by Bernard Bell undertook a searching survey of the state of the economy. The Bell mission identified a series of problems, many familiar but now acute: low agricultural productivity and inefficient public industries, excessive regulation and curbs on private investment, feeble exports and an overvalued currency. Bell's mammoth report, submitted in October 1965, recommended no fewer than sixteen major reforms, starting with a devaluation of the rupee.[93] Thereafter, the Bank leaned heavily on the Indian government to embark on liberalization of the economy.

In the aftermath of her trip to Washington, Indira Gandhi consulted a small group of economic advisors, all of whom supported the move.[94] On June 5, 1966, she announced a 35 percent devaluation of the rupee. The public responded to the decision virulently, charging the prime minister both with undermining India's economy and with selling out to the Americans. Senior members of the Congress party, who had been kept out of the loop, lashed out against her. Worse, the aid package expected by India (especially nonproject assistance to the tune of $1 billion) failed to materialize.[95] Prime Minister Gandhi quietly placed the rest of the reform package on hold. The new agricultural strategy—proclaimed the "Green Revolution"—did pay off. Between 1965 and 1972, the production of wheat in India doubled. Nevertheless, Johnson's rough tactics with food shipments during the drought of 1966 ensured that few Indians were willing to credit the United States with the turn toward food self-sufficiency.

The Johnson administration adopted a similar approach toward PL480 supplies to Pakistan, though the food situation in that country was never quite as bad as in India. Of greater concern to the Pakistanis was the cessation of military aid following the 1965 war. In April 1967, the United States announced a new arms policy for the subcontinent: a stop to all military aid to India and Pakistan, a ban on military sales (excepting spare parts for previously supplied equipment), and American intent to prevent third countries from supplying arms to either unless such sales helped stabilize or reduce their military expenditures. The Pakistanis promptly responded with a list of spare parts they wanted to buy. Thereafter, they sought to push the envelope with demands for ammunition as part of a larger sales package of around $10 million. By the end of the year, the Pakistanis were requesting the sale of at least two hundred tanks—their total requirement was five hundred—to replace the older Shermans. Following a meeting with Ayub, Johnson agreed to permit the sale of tanks from Italy and Turkey to Pakistan. He also directed his officials to consider whether the United States could directly replace the Shermans.[96]

Johnson's softening stance stemmed partly from a Russian announcement of military sales to Pakistan. Yet the administration's effort to introduce a modicum of flexibility into its arms policy toward South Asia ran into sand. The Germans refused to sell tanks directly to Pakistan; the Italians wanted a large order of 750 tanks at an exorbitant price; the deal negotiated between Pakistan and Iran did not make it past the Washington bureaucracy. In retaliation, the Pakistanis asked the Americans to shut down the base in Peshawar from which the Central Intelligence Agency undertook surveillance flights over the Soviet Union. By August 1968, the American ambassador in Pakistan, Benjamin Oehlert, was grimly warning the administration, "Our national interests in this country—indeed in this part of the world—have reached a crisis." The Soviet Union's growing clout in the subcontinent was evident. If Pakistan was forced to rely on Russia for arms, then "all of our other vital interests in this part of the world, including Iran,

Turkey and Saudi Arabia, are jeopardized." Oehlert believed that India and its supporters in the administration had thwarted the supply of tanks to Pakistan.[97]

A more important problem, albeit one to which the ambassador seemed purblind, was the state of Pakistan's economy. In the decade following Ayub's seizure of power in 1959, Pakistan had registered impressive economic growth: averaging 5.5 percent annual growth in gross national product (GNP) over the period. This performance was fueled by American economic aid as well as American expertise in the form of economists from Harvard's Development Advisory Service, who had been working in the country since 1954 and helped draw up its five-year plans. Unlike the Indians, the Pakistanis were more receptive to specific American ideas as well as their financial aid. Starting in 1959, government policy on agriculture made extensive use of market incentives. Pakistan also embraced the "Green Revolution" technologies faster than India and reaped their benefits earlier. Industrial policy aimed to spur private industries through low direct taxes, liberal depreciation allowances, generous subsidies for exports, and the absence of antimonopoly laws. By 1969, the share of industry had risen to 12 percent of GNP from almost zero at the time of partition.

These headline figures, however, masked serious problems in the economy. After the 1965 war, aid flows declined, and defense expenditures shot up. As prices, especially of food, began to rise, the weaknesses of the economic model came to the fore. In the first place, there was an extraordinary concentration of wealth in the hands of a few business groups: the planning commission unofficially put the figure at twenty-two. In a retrospective account written in 1970, the Harvard advisors quietly conceded that the policies they espoused had "also led to a highly concentrated pattern of industrial ownership."[98] The focus on growth without any consideration for equity had ensured that "social sectors have made little progress." Further, the pattern of growth was also skewed heavily in favor of West Pakistan and against East

Pakistan. On a range of issues from budget allocations and foreign exchange policy to industrial and agricultural policies, the government accorded favorable treatment to West Pakistan. Bengali economists from East Pakistan, who had worked in the planning commission, mounted a piercing critique of the development model as essentially a neocolonial one, with East Pakistan serving as an appendage to the economy of West Pakistan.

Even the much-vaunted program of rural development in the East Pakistani province of Comilla—modeled on the Community Development Program in India—failed to deliver on its early promise. Part of the problem was inadequate financing. But another part of the problem was that President Ayub Khan saw the project as a vehicle to buy the loyalties of an upwardly mobile rural class in East Pakistan and hence allowed political priorities to dictate its course. As a Bengali economist witheringly observed in 1968, "The programme to date is [nothing] more than a slightly more elaborate welfare or relief measure introduced into the rural areas, along with the slightly more sordid motive of winning the allegiance of [a] narrow class."[99]

In the event, a popular movement in both East and West Pakistan would overthrow Ayub Khan in early 1969 due in equal measure to his authoritarian politics and his attempt to operationalize the ideas of modernization theory. But as late as 1968, American advisors and scholars regarded him as the ideal type of an authoritarian modernizer—the kind that the Third World most needed. Harvard political scientist Samuel Huntington, for instance, lauded Ayub as a leader in the mold of "a Solon or Lycurgus, or 'Great Legislator' on the Platonic or Rousseauian model."[100]

Some senior officials in the Johnson administration also sought to revive the flagging alliance with Pakistan. In the waning days of the Johnson administration, Ambassador Oehlert reminded the president of his own words: "You were sick and tired of the India lovers in the State Department." He pleaded with Johnson "not to let them get away with it." Invoking the words of another leading Texan Democrat, John Nance Garner, Oehlert exhorted Johnson, "Let us strike a blow for freedom."[101] The sentiment was, in fact, more reminiscent of John Foster Dulles, architect of the alliance with Pakistan. But yet another stalwart of the Eisenhower years would undertake the rejuvenation of the alliance.

7

THE DANGEROUS DECADE

I N EARLY MAY 1971, the great gospel singer Mahalia Jackson undertook a ten-day concert tour of India. The highlight of her trip was a three-hour concert in New Delhi before a throng that cheered her to the echo and wanted her to go on. As a final encore, Jackson sang the anthem of the civil rights movement, "We Shall Overcome." In the audience that evening was Prime Minister Indira Gandhi, accompanied by the American ambassador to India and the Indian army chief. "I have been gospel singing for 42 years," said Jackson at the end of the performance, "but today I have very much for which to be thankful to God with great people like the Prime Minister sitting here."

Jackson's visit encapsulated the circuits of culture that connected the United States and the subcontinent. For starters there was music. Early in her life, Mahalia Jackson had resolved only to sing of the glory of God. Yet her music had a profound influence on the development of American jazz. Although jazz had arrived in the subcontinent decades earlier—especially via the city of Bombay—it acquired a devout following in the 1960s. EMI's records did rather well in India: "Haan Main American Jazz Kharidta Hun! [Yes, I buy American jazz!]," proclaimed an Indian figure clutching an LP in an advertisement.[1]

More important was the American government's role in promoting jazz in the subcontinent. From the late 1950s, successive administrations sought to use jazz as a vehicle for disseminating American influence in the Third World. As a popular art stemming from the world of African Americans, jazz seemed ideally suited both to revise notions of American racism in the decolonized countries and to showcase the vigor and creativity of American democracy.[2] American artists understood the political agenda behind these tours, though they embraced it only up to a point. Dizzy Gillespie, to take but one example, wrote to Dwight Eisenhower after a tour, "Our trip…proved conclusively that our interracial group was powerfully effective against Red propaganda. Jazz is our own American folk music that communicates with all peoples regardless of language or social barriers." Indeed, Gillespie sought to reach beyond the elite audiences that American embassies hoped to attract to such performances. Ahead of his concert in Karachi, Gillespie refused to start playing until the gates were opened to the "ragamuffin children": "They priced the ticket so high the people we were trying to gain friendship with couldn't make it." At the same time, Gillespie was no propagandist for the US government. "I sort of liked the idea of representing America," he later observed, "but I wasn't going to apologize for the racist policies of America."[3]

Yet American officials believed that jazz had a role to play in the contest for the hearts and minds of South Asians. When Jack Teagarden and his sextet toured India (and other parts of the subcontinent) in 1959, a senior officer of the US Information Service told them that "jazz was a great tool in helping save the country from the Reds."[4] The Golden Gate Quartet—a gospel group—toured India in 1962 and found the southern state of Kerala (which had elected the first Communist government in the country) on the itinerary. The group's reception there delighted State Department officials: "This is the *red state* of India—very excellent."[5]

The following year Duke Ellington toured Afghanistan, Pakistan, and India. In Kabul, no fewer than 5,000 people turned out for his performance at the Ghazi stadium. The man as much as his music enthralled the crowd. Faiz Khairzada, a young jazz aficionado, recalled chatting with Ellington after the concert about his dreams to make films in Afghanistan. "You make the movie, kid," said the Duke, "and I'll do the music for it." Ellington himself remembered "riding around all night" listening to music in Afghan cafés: "They have their own thing going on there and it's good."[6] In India, Ellington's band jammed with local musicians and left the jazz scene breathless. A leading newspaper, the *Indian Express*, put it well: "Duke Ellington's Orchestra played the poetry of jazz. We lost our hearts."[7]

In 1964 came the world's best-known jazz artist: Louis Armstrong. "Welcome Satchmo," screamed a large advertisement placed by H.M.V. in the *Times of India*. Armstrong was well known among English-speaking Indians: theaters in several cities had screened his movies, and just months before he landed in India, his single "Hello Dolly" had risen to the top of the billboard charts. Armstrong's visit coincided with that of the pope; yet the musician drew packed audiences everywhere.[8]

The conveyer belt of culture did not, however, run in one direction. The musical traditions of the subcontinent, especially India, also influenced American artists. When Dave Brubeck toured India in April 1958, he played an impromptu jam session alongside sitar player Abdul Halim Jaffar Khan. On returning to New York, he recorded the album *Jazz Impressions of Eurasia*, which included "Calcutta Blues," the first recorded attempt at incorporating Indian melodic and rhythmic elements into jazz. Duke Ellington's tour resulted in "Far East Suite," another piece of music that sought to come to terms with India. By this time, Indian music was beginning to gain traction in the United States, owing to the efforts of two young men of genius: Pandit Ravi Shankar and Ali Akbar Khan. Ravi Shankar's partnership with George Harrison would put Indian music squarely in the middle of 1960s counterculture. This cultural confluence spawned the remarkable genre of Indo-Jazz taken forward by such brilliant artists as John Coltrane and L. Subramaniam.[9]

Even more than its music, India's spiritualism drew a generation of Americans to the subcontinent. The beatniks set the trend early in the decade. In 1961, Allen Ginsberg met an Indian lady named Pupul Jayakar at the home of American photographer Dorothy Norman, both close friends of Indira Gandhi. Very like the transcendentalists of the previous century, Ginsberg, deeply anguished by the materialism and militarism of his country, looked to India as a source of spiritual renewal. "While you look to her to find answers," said Jayakar, when Ginsberg poured out his heart, "the young in India look to the west. What do you expect to find?" Ginsberg said he wanted to experience poverty, find a guru, and move closer to God. What is more, he wanted to experiment with drugs. "After all, God is very funny, and He might even accept drugs as a way to Him." Ginsberg implored her, "Can you help me find a gay guru?" Jayakar was utterly bemused: "An eccentric guru?"[10] This encounter, which paved the way for the "hippy trail," also foreshadowed the creative confusions that would mark American spiritual encounters with India.

The country did not disappoint Ginsberg, though war and the Cold War caught up with him there too. The coincidence of the Cuban Missile Crisis and the Sino-Indian War led him to outline a "Positive Program for Peaceful Progress"—an interesting example of the creativity unleashed by the conjuncture of the Cold War, globalization, and counterculture in that decade. Ginsberg's plan included allowing Communist China to join the United Nations and the Tibetans to present their case there, a "Telestar TV Debate with Khrushchev, Kennedy, Mao & Nehru at UN together translated into all languages," and, above all, "international legalization of kif, ganja, marijuana, cannabis, hashish, Bhang."[11]

The 1960s also witnessed a spurt of interest among Americans in "New Age" Hinduism, a trend strengthened by the amendment and liberalization of the Immigration Act in 1965. This led to a sizeable increase in the Indian population of the United States. Between 1871 and 1965, the United States had admitted just about 16,000 Indians. In the decade after 1965, over 96,000 Indians made their way into the country. The American census of 1980 reported 387,223 Indians. Much of the new wave of Hinduism aimed to cater to the needs of the growing Hindu population in the United States. But soon the gurus understood the opportunity and advantages afforded by branching out to Americans. The Hare Krishna movement, Maharishi Mahesh Yogi's Transcendental Meditation, Guru Maharaj's Divine Light Mission, and Osho Rajneesh's ashrams all started out on the West Coast of the United States and expanded rapidly—notwithstanding a backlash from Christian fundamentalist groups that decried the mushrooming of Hindu "cults."[12]

Music and religion were not divorced from the tumultuous politics of the decade. Indeed, these years saw the expansion and revival of older currents of influence between African Americans and India. Martin Luther King Jr. had first heard of Mohandas Gandhi in a speech by Mordecai Johnson, president of Howard University, in 1950. In the wake of the Montgomery boycott five years later, King cited Mahatma as the paramount influence on his thought and practice, including Gandhi's ideas as interpreted by an earlier generation of Americans such as Richard Gregg.

In 1959, King visited India, staying at various locations where Gandhi had lived and meeting many of his associates, from Jawaharlal Nehru onward. The similarities between caste in India and race in the United States were evident. During a visit to a school for the Dalit, or "untouchable," caste children in Kerala, King would later recall, he was introduced as a "fellow untouchable from the United States of America." Although not oblivious of the cruelty of the caste system, he concluded, "India appears to be integrating its untouchables faster than the United States in integrating its negro minority."[13] In any event, King believed that Gandhian nonviolence was the route for African Americans. An exchange reported in 1966 by famous singer and King associate Joan Baez, between her partner and their eleven-year-old daughter, nicely captures the impact of Gandhi's ideas on young Americans of the 1960s:

> "Did Gandhi have a penis?" she asked.
> "Yes," he answered.
> "Did he have a vagina too?"
> "No," said Ira. "He was a man, and men just have a penis."
> "Well," she said, pausing at the doorway, "it's just that he was so nice...I thought he might have had both."[14]

As the decade wore on, though, younger radical blacks denounced King's adoption of Gandhian methods. "Christian? Gandhian?" said Malcolm X, "I don't go for anything that's non-violent and turn-the-other-cheekish." Stokely Carmichael of Black Power declared, "I am not going to beg the white man for anything I deserve. I'm going to take it."[15] Although King deeply disapproved of their methods, Black Power in turn influenced a radical movement among India's Dalits in the early 1970s. The Dalit Panthers explicitly took their cue from African Americans. As a manifesto declared, "Even in America, a handful of reactionary whites are exploiting blacks. To meet the force of reaction and remove this exploitation, the Black Panther movement grew. From the Black Panthers, Black Power emerged....We claim a close relationship with this struggle."[16]

Indira Gandhi's presence at Mahalia Jackson's concert also affirmed old solidarities. Back in 1958, she had organized a Paul Robeson Day in support of the African American artist whose passport the US State

Department had revoked for his views on the Cold War. Jackson would recall the prime minister admiringly as "that busy woman with many things on her mind, many things to do!" Indeed Indira Gandhi had many things to do—not least keeping a weather eye on the crisis bubbling up in East Pakistan that would soon pit the United States against India.

WHEN RICHARD NIXON TOOK office in January 1969, he faced the challenge of renewing the United States' global preponderance. The changing dynamics of the Cold War, the rise of the Third World, and the acceleration of globalization had unmistakably worn down American hegemony as constructed in the wake of World War II. Over the following decade, Presidents Nixon, Gerald Ford, and Jimmy Carter would struggle to master these forces.[17]

The Nixon Doctrine called on America's allies in Europe and Asia to step up their contribution to regional security. This demand for burden sharing would not suffice to restore American hegemony. Pulling America out of the bog in Vietnam while preserving its reputation as a superpower necessitated a new triangular diplomacy. Nixon and National Security Advisor Henry Kissinger sought at once to establish new bases for the relationships with China and the Soviet Union and to get both Communist powers to exercise restraint. Carter would later seek to continue the détente with the Soviet Union while deepening ties with China. The draining war in Vietnam pushed American deficits deep into the red and forced the Nixon administration to break the dollar-gold link that underpinned the Bretton Woods order. The ensuing system of market-driven exchange rates led to an extraordinary spurt in capital movements and set the stage for financial globalization, with the dollar as the global reserve currency. The oil shocks that reverberated across the world after the Arab-Israeli War of 1973 simultaneously underlined and accentuated economic globalization.

The ensuing great inflation of the 1970s eroded the social compact in Western democracies and pushed them toward a neoliberal order that privileged markets over states and individuals over collectivities. At the same time, the economic challenges of the 1970s undermined Third World attempts to demand a new international economic order and forced them to accept the discipline of markets—now administered through the World Bank and the International Monetary Fund (IMF). More than merely an economic phenomenon, globalization also involved the increasing standardization and diffusion of cultural norms by transnational actors. While this was already evident in the countercultural movements of the 1960s, the next decade witnessed the rise to prominence of human rights as an alternative to older ideological polarities. While Nixon and Kissinger were loath to recognize the growing salience of human rights, Carter embraced them as part of his foreign policy.

These geopolitical, economic, and cultural changes bore heavily on American engagement in South Asia in the decade following Nixon's inauguration. As ever, policies reflected larger contextual considerations as well as the predilections of policymakers. The latter were not arbitrary but carried the traces of America's historical involvement with the region. No American president entered the White House with greater exposure to South Asia than Nixon. As vice president in the Eisenhower administration, he had been present at the creation of the US-Pakistan alliance. At the same time, he had imbibed that era's worst prejudices against India, biases reinforced by the politics of US foreign policy in 1960s. The pro-India leanings of the Democrats struck him as "a prime example of liberal soft-headedness."

Thus sneering references to Indians—as "a slippery, treacherous people," "devious," ruthlessly self-interested, and so forth—pepper the Nixon administration's records, whereas the Pakistanis and their military dictator are certified as "honorable." These characterizations were entirely continuous with images of Hindus and Muslims, Indians and Pakistanis purveyed over the past two centuries. The gendered language reserved for Indira Gandhi—"bitch" and "witch" were favored epithets—suggest a concern with masculinity stretching back at least to the late nineteenth century.

We can gauge the tenacity of this historical and cultural background from the fact that it was hardly confined to Nixon, Kissinger, and their coterie. It was equally influential in shaping the views, minus the profanity, of a figure like Daniel Patrick Moynihan: the Harvard professor, public intellectual, and member of the John F. Kennedy and Lyndon Johnson administrations, whom Nixon appointed as his ambassador to India in 1973. Moynihan wrote to Nixon that India's ingratitude for US economic aid flowed from the laws of karma: the giver should express gratitude, for he accumulates good karma. "This is not a professor's notion," he added. "It can be read in Kipling." Following an Indian nuclear test in 1974, Moynihan would write in his journal, "You have got to admire the chutzpah. A nation half in rags which cannot feed itself."[18] Later still, he would publicly state that India had nothing to export but communicable diseases—a remark straight out of Katherine Mayo's controversial yet best-selling *Mother India*.

The Nixon administration's engagement with South Asia began on a difficult note. Even before the inauguration, there was a crisis in Pakistan. Ayub Khan's decade-long dictatorship was faltering in the face of mass protests. As in other parts of the world in 1968, students were at the forefront of the protests in Pakistan. Indeed, Pakistani students explicitly took their cue from the protests elsewhere, including in the United States, an indication of manifold effects of the incipient globalization.[19] By March 1969, the protestors had forced Ayub to step down. The army chief, General Yahya Khan, took his place, promising a turn toward democracy. When Nixon entered office in January 1969, Kissinger recalled, "Our policy objective on the subcontinent was, quite simply, to avoid adding another complication to our agenda."[20]

Visiting India in the summer of 1969, Nixon reiterated to Indira Gandhi his commitment to India's economic development. "We will go to Mars together," he assured her.[21] From the Indian standpoint, the main sticking point was the possibility of a revivified military relationship between Pakistan and the United States.[22] Soon after assuming office, Nixon had ordered "a thorough review of our military supply policy in South Asia." Nixon and Kissinger looked askance at the Johnson administration's arms embargo: "The practical consequence was to injure Pakistan, since India received most of its arms either from Communist nations or from its own armories."[23] The president's next stop was Pakistan, where the question of military supply predictably cropped up. The Pakistanis insisted that they sought nothing more than a "minimum deterrent" against India. Kissinger replied, "We are looking at military supply policy and will attempt to be sympathetic."[24]

Yet Washington waited until October 1970 to formally announce a "onetime exception" to the arms embargo, which would allow Pakistan to procure nearly $50 million worth of replacement aircraft and some three hundred armed personnel carriers. The Indian reaction was predictably strong. "I do not say that you should not take decisions in your own national interests," said Indira Gandhi to Secretary of State William Rogers, "but I want to make you aware of our feelings." Even so, both sides refrained from pushing things to the breaking point. By early 1971, Kissinger observed, US-India relations "had achieved a state of exasperatedly strained cordiality, like a couple that can neither separate nor get along."[25] New Delhi regarded the decision as a continuation of American support for Pakistan since 1953. In fact, the decision was the outcome of a radical departure from the old strategy of enlisting Pakistan for anti-Communist alliances in Asia. The exception owed to a major American interest at stake: the opening to China.

From the outset, Nixon was candid, even with the Indians, about his desire for a new relationship with China. Yet the attempt to reach out to China was wrapped in secrecy. Nixon and Kissinger kept in the dark senior colleagues in the administration, particularly the much despised State Department, the US Congress, and America's closest allies. To explore China's willingness to recast its ties with the United States, Nixon almost simultaneously opened two parallel, secret channels of communication through Romania and Pakistan, though the latter was deemed more secure than former.

Meeting General Yahya alone on August 1, 1969, Nixon expressed interest in seeking an accommodation with China and asked him to pass this message to Beijing and use his influence to promote it. Yahya agreed but indicated that Pakistan expected a quid pro quo. A few weeks later, Kissinger told the Pakistanis that Yahya should communicate on this subject only through his ambassador in Washington, Agha Hilaly, who in turn should speak only to Kissinger. Almost three months passed before Yahya came back to Nixon, suggesting an approach to the highest level of the Chinese government and asking for "specific points of discussion."[26] Yahya kept up this dilatory style until the Americans agreed to sell arms to Pakistan. Thereafter, the China channel worked just fine.

Nixon asked Yahya to convey two points to the Chinese leadership. First, "we will make no condominium [with the Soviet Union] against China and we want them to know it." Second, Nixon was willing to send an envoy to Beijing "to establish links secretly."[27] During his visit to China in November 1970, Yahya conveyed Nixon's message to Zhou Enlai. After three days of deliberation, Zhou reverted to Yahya with a message for Nixon from Chairman Mao Zedong: "In order to discuss the subject of vacation of China's territory called Taiwan, a special envoy from President Nixon would be most welcome in Peking."[28] In response, the White House proposed that American and Chinese representatives meet at "an early convenient moment" to discuss the modalities of a higher-level meeting in Beijing. The latter "would not be limited only to the Taiwan question but would encompass other steps designed to improve relations and reduce tensions."[29] This message was passed to the Chinese on January 5, 1971. For the next three months, though, there was no word from Beijing. Meantime, a crisis erupted in East Pakistan.

The Bangladesh crisis of 1971 is usually understood as the product of long-standing differences—political, cultural, and economic—between the two wings of Pakistan. In fact, it stemmed from more immediate factors—especially the radicalization of the movement for autonomy in East Pakistan after Ayub's exit. The military regime had failed to anticipate the outcome of the general elections of 1970. The Awami League, led by Sheikh Mujibur Rahman, aka Mujib, took all seats but one in East Pakistan, securing an overall majority even though they had failed to win a single constituency in West Pakistan. Conversely, the Pakistan People's Party of Zulfikar Ali Bhutto emerged as the single-largest party in the western wing but did not win a single seat in the east. Yahya and his military colleagues were loath to hand over power to the Bengalis. Bhutto played along with them and ensured that the Awami League's rightful claim to office was thwarted.

Following a period of political negotiations and military buildup, the Pakistan army launched a massive operation aimed at snuffing out the Awami League and its bases of support. From the end of March 1971, Bengali refugees began to trickle into India. Within eight weeks this had turned into a flood, and by the end of the summer the Indians counted 10 million refugees in their territory. With India's assistance, surviving Awami League leaders—the Pakistanis captured Mujib—proclaimed a Provisional Government of Bangladesh. Remnants of Bengali units of the Pakistan army and paramilitary forces began to regroup and train in camps run by the Indians along the border with East Pakistan. A major conflict loomed in the subcontinent.

ON THE AFTERNOON OF March 26, Kissinger chaired the Washington Special Actions Group to consider the situation in East Pakistan. Expressing surprise at the breakdown of talks, he sought an assessment from the regional experts. Christopher Van Hollen of the State Department observed that the military would make an effort to prevent secession, but its ability "to maintain law and order in East Pakistan over the long run approaches zero." Kissinger said that he had spoken briefly to the president earlier that day: "He doesn't want to do anything. He doesn't want to be in the position where he can be accused of having encouraged the split-up of Pakistan. He does not favour a very active policy. This probably means that we would not undertake to warn Yahya against a civil war." The group concluded that the United States should "continue its policy of non-involvement."[30]

Meanwhile the US consul-general in Dhaka, Archer Blood, sent a series of cables, detailing the terror unleashed on the populace by the Pakistan army. Labeling the military action a "selective genocide," he questioned the "continued advisability of present USG [US Government] posture." "We should be expressing our shock at least privately to GOP [Government of Pakistan]," urged Blood. He followed up a week later with a collective message from American foreign service personnel in Dhaka. Titled "Dissent from U.S. Policy Toward East Pakistan," this cable argued that the current policy "serves neither our moral interests broadly defined nor our national interests narrowly defined." The administration, it claimed, "has evidenced what many will consider moral bankruptcy" in dealing with a conflict "in which unfortunately the overworked term genocide is applicable."[31]

Regional specialists in the State Department also advocated the "use of selective influence" by continuing support for certain development activities but holding off on programs "which would contribute directly to the prolongation of the civil war." This included placing on hold military supplies to Pakistan. An irate Kissinger regarded the State Department's stance as nothing less than a "preemption of Presidential prerogatives"—a move "heavily influenced by its traditional Indian bias." He insisted that "we must go to the President before we hold up any shipments. This would be the exact opposite of his policy.... The President thinks he has a special relationship with Yahya; he would be most reluctant to take him on."[32]

On May 2, Nixon scribbled a note: "*To all hands. Don't* squeeze Yahya at this time." He underlined the "don't" three times.[33] As earlier, Nixon's approach to China shaped his stance. In fact, just the day before he had received a message from the Chinese, expressing their willingness to "receive publicly in Peking" an envoy of Nixon or even the president himself. Nixon decided that Kissinger would undertake a secret trip to Beijing and lay the ground for a presidential visit. By early June 1971, the stage was set for Kissinger's momentous trip to China. In this context, Nixon and Kissinger understandably sought to place the South Asian crisis on the backburner. They believed that the United States needed just enough time to ensure the success of their opening to China. When Ambassador Joseph Farland observed that, in the long run, West Pakistan could not hold on to the eastern wing, Kissinger exclaimed, "All we need is six months."[34]

Nixon and Kissinger turned their attention to the country that could undo their best-laid plans: India. From April 1971, the United States had been picking up intelligence on India's support for the Bengali rebels. A report of Indian troop concentration along the eastern border with Pakistan alarmed Kissinger. He told Nixon that he had instructed the US ambassador to tell New Delhi that "we were strongly opposed to military action." Nixon replied, "If they go in there with military action, by God we will cut off economic aid.... [T]hey have got to know that if [sic] what is in jeopardy here is economic aid. That is what is in jeopardy." A couple of days later, Kissinger urged Nixon to write to Indira Gandhi and "bring pressure on her not to take military action." The Indians were "such bastards," "the most aggressive goddamn people around there." Nixon agreed that India deserved a "mass famine."[35]

On June 16, 1971, Indian foreign minister Swaran Singh reached Washington. Before Singh's meeting with the president, Kissinger told Nixon that they ought to give him a combination of sympathy and "great firmness": "I am just trying to keep them [the Indians] from attacking for 3 months." He asked Nixon to say that the United States would provide $60 million in refugee aid and that they were working with Yahya in their own way. "It's a little duplicitous," he conceded, "but these bastards understand that." Singh told Nixon that refugees were pouring into India "every second" and that the tally had touched the

6 million mark. India wanted conditions created in East Pakistan for the return of these refugees. Nixon assured him that he understood the need to tackle the "deeper causes" of the refugee problem. "One way the public pressure, another way the private, shall we say, persuasion," he observed.[36]

Days after Swaran Singh's visit, the *New York Times* reported that two Pakistani freighters were ready to sail from New York carrying military equipment for Pakistan. Follow-on reports indicated that a third ship was loading. Although the quantity of equipment was small, India responded sharply. The Indian government lodged a formal protest, urging the State Department to stop the shipments from reaching Pakistan. As the relationship spiraled downward, Kissinger set off for the subcontinent.

In his meetings with Indira Gandhi's powerful principal secretary, P. N. Haksar, Kissinger observed that a war with Pakistan would not be in India's interests: "China would certainly react and this would lead you to rely upon Soviet assistance. Such a development will cause complications for us in America." Haksar insisted, "We in India are not seeking the conflict. In fact, we wish to avoid the conflict. We want a peaceful solution." In the event of Chinese involvement, he added, "it is not unreasonable for us to expect and to hope that the United States would take a sympathetic attitude towards our country." When Haksar sought his views on China, Kissinger guardedly stated, "We are desirous of improving our relations. We think that we can now quickly move forward in this direction."[37]

Meeting with Pakistani officials in Rawalpindi, Kissinger stressed the need for Pakistan to "defuse the refugee issue so that it could be separated from the issue of the political structure of East Pakistan." Pakistan should "internationalize" its response to the refugee problem by inviting international observers. "Linking the two [issues]," he said, "will only prolong the current situation which could lead to war. War would be catastrophe." Kissinger urged Yahya to appoint a new civilian authority in East Pakistan in order to oversee a program for the return of refugees. Yahya agreed to consider these suggestions.[38] The next day, feigning an upset stomach, Kissinger took a secret flight to Beijing.

After Kissinger's trip to China, US policy began shifting from a disinclination to squeeze Yahya to an active tilt in favor of Pakistan. Nixon formally announced the opening to China and his forthcoming trip to Beijing on July 15. The next day the National Security Council convened to consider the South Asia crisis. The president said it was imperative that the Pakistanis not be embarrassed. The Indians would like nothing better than to use this opportunity to destroy Pakistan. Admitting that he had "a bias" on this issue, he insisted that the Indians would not get "a dime of aid, if they mess around in East Pakistan." The United States could not allow a war in South Asia in the next three to four months—until "we take this journey" to Beijing. When Nixon asked how the Chinese would respond in the event of an Indian attack on Pakistan, Kissinger said that "he thought the Chinese would come in." He concluded, "If there is an international war and China does get involved, everything we have done [with China] will go down the drain."[39]

So the administration had to serve India a stern warning against attacking Pakistan. Meeting Ambassador L. K. Jha on July 17, Kissinger warned that if war broke out between India and Pakistan and China became involved on Pakistan's side, "we would be unable to help you against China." It is not clear if he said explicitly that this applied only to a war begun by India.[40] The Indian government believed that Kissinger had stated that the United States "would not intervene in any conflict between India and Pakistan even if China did so."[41] In response, New Delhi concluded within weeks a treaty of peace and friendship with the Soviet Union, which included a clause calling for mutual consultations in the event of a threat to either party.

THE NIXON ADMINISTRATION'S STANCE on the Bangladesh crisis drew much popular censure in the United States. The countercultural currents of the previous decade seemed almost to have gathered in force to oppose Washington's handling of the humanitarian problem. Above all, the Concert for Bangladesh, conceived by famous Indian musician Pandit Ravi Shankar and his friend George Harrison, inscribed the crisis into the American imagination. The concert sought to bring together the brightest stars in the rock music firmament: John Lennon and Ringo Starr, Eric Clapton and Bob Dylan, Billy Preston and Leon Russell. Barring Lennon, the entire ensemble turned up to perform on August 1, 1971.[42]

The event's impact reverberated well beyond the venue. Apart from its attracting wide coverage in newsprint, images from the concert were broadcast by television channels across the world. A boxed three-record set was released soon after the concert and climbed to the top of the charts across the world. The photograph of an emaciated child sitting in front of an empty plate on the album cover became an iconic image of Bangladesh. The accompanying notes held the Pakistan Army responsible for "a deliberate reign of terror" and for perpetrating "undoubtedly the greatest atrocity since Hitler's extermination of the Jews."

Other iconic figures such as Joan Baez took up the cause of their own volition. In the last week of July, Baez performed at Stanford University before an audience of 12,000. At another huge concert at the University of Michigan, she sang the "Song for Bangladesh." Ginsberg took another trip to India in September 1971 and traveled out on Jessore Road from Calcutta to see the refugee camps near the East Pakistani border. On returning home, he wrote a poem, "September on Jessore Road," published in the *New York Times* on November 14, 1971. Ginsberg's poem, like the songs of Harrison and Baez, tugged at America's conscience. But the Nixon administration remained unmoved.

In early November 1971, Indira Gandhi visited Washington as the final stop on an international trip to drum up support for the Indian position on the crisis. Nixon hoped to buy time and deter India from embarking on war—at least until he had completed his own visit to Beijing. For Nixon and Kissinger believed that if they allowed India to humiliate Pakistan, their reputation in the eyes of China would suffer irreparable damage.

On the morning of November 4, Nixon and Indira Gandhi, flanked by Kissinger and Haksar, met in the Oval Office. The consequences of military action, Nixon warned, "were incalculably dangerous.... The American people would not understand if India were to initiate military action against Pakistan." Prime Minister Gandhi rehearsed the Indian position at some length: "It was no longer realistic to expect East and West Pakistan to remain together." When Nixon suggested withdrawing troops from the borders and observed that Yahya was prepared to do so, the prime minister did not respond, leaving Haksar to point out that militarily this was not feasible for India.[43]

Nixon and Kissinger met in the Oval Office the next morning to take stock of the previous day's discussion. Nixon remarked that Mrs. Gandhi was being "a bitch," but "we really slobbered over the old witch." To his aide Bob Haldeman, Nixon boasted, "You should have heard, Bob, the way we worked her around. I dropped stilettos all over her." In the next meeting later in the day, they decided, the president would play it "cool."[44] That afternoon, however, Indira Gandhi assumed her iciest air of aloofness. She made no reference at all to the subcontinental crisis; nor did she respond to Nixon's suggestion of the previous day. Instead, she took the initiative in quizzing Nixon about US foreign policy across the globe. Her attitude, Kissinger would later write, "brought out all of Nixon's latent insecurities." Indeed, Nixon would later tell Kissinger, "What I'm concerned about, I really worry about, is whether or not I was too easy on the goddamn woman when she was here.... She was playing us. And you know the cold way she was the next day.... [T]his woman suckered us."[45]

Soon after her visit to Washington, Prime Minister Gandhi decided to intervene militarily in East Pakistan. Her efforts to secure international support for the repatriation of refugees had failed to yield any tangible result. What is more, the Bengali rebels were turning restive and suspicious of Indian motives. As the Indian military began to push deeper into East Pakistan, Yahya and his colleagues started panicking. On December 3, Pakistani planes bombed airfields in western India. The third Indo-Pakistan war was formally underway.

"[THE] PAKISTAN THING MAKES your heart sick," said Nixon to Kissinger on learning of the war that same day. "For them to be so done by the Indians and after we have warned the bitch."[46] At a meeting later that day, Kissinger said, "I've been catching unshirted hell every half-hour from the President.... He wants to tilt towards Pakistan."[47] This desire stemmed from reputational concerns. Nixon and Kissinger believed that if they stood by while India cut Pakistan to size, the Chinese would regard the United States as an unreliable partner. The dismembering of Pakistan would lead "all other countries watching it ... [to conclude] that the friends of China and the United States have been clobbered by India and the Soviet Union."[48]

On the afternoon of December 6, 1971, Kissinger met Soviet counselor Yuli Vorontsov to convey a message to the Soviet general secretary, Leonid Brezhnev. Nixon was unable to understand how the Soviet Union sought a détente with the United States while "encouraging Indian military aggression against Pakistan." America and the Soviet Union, he warned, were "at a watershed in our relationship." If Moscow agreed to support a resolution for cease-fire and withdrawal, the United States would work with the Soviets on a political solution. Nixon followed up with a written message to Brezhnev the next day, claiming that the Soviet Union was backing India's quest to partition Pakistan. These actions ran counter to "recent encouraging trends" of cooperation between Washington and Moscow. It would be in everyone's interest "if the territorial integrity of Pakistan were restored and military action were brought to an end." Nixon asked Brezhnev to use his "great influence" on India toward these ends.[49]

On December 6, the Central Intelligence Agency (CIA) received intelligence from an Indian source that Prime Minister Gandhi had briefed her cabinet that day and emphasized that India had three aims in the war: quick liberation of Bangladesh, incorporation into India of the southern part of Azad Kashmir (Pakistan-administered Kashmir), and the destruction of Pakistan's military might so that it could never again challenge India.[50] Nixon and Kissinger seized upon this as firm evidence that India sought not only to liberate East Pakistan but thereafter to launch a major attack on West Pakistan as well. To begin with, Nixon decided to cut off economic aid to India, as he had threatened all along. After December 3, Nixon believed that India would be discredited in the eyes of its Democrat supporters for having started the war. Further, the White House sought to ensure the flow of arms into Pakistan. Since the United States had imposed an embargo, this had to be arranged through third parties. The Americans approached the shah of Iran the next day and encouraged him to transfer military equipment and munitions to Pakistan. Thereafter, the United States asked key Muslim countries—Jordan, Iran, Saudi Arabia, and Turkey—to supply weapons to Pakistan through an arms backchannel.

Nixon and Kissinger also sought to draw China into the fray. This would not only rattle New Delhi but also signal their own resolve and reliability to Beijing.[51] By the time the CIA's input came, Nixon was toying with the idea of getting the Chinese to intervene in the crisis. On the evening of December 6, he felt "strongly that we should do it." Nixon told Kissinger, "I think we've got to tell them [the Chinese] that some movement on their part we think toward the Indian border could be very significant." He felt that they should also let the Chinese know about their communications with the Russians: "Damnit, I am convinced that if the Chinese start moving the Indians will be petrified. They will be petrified."[52]

On December 10 Kissinger met with the Chinese UN representative, Huang Hua, and conveyed a message from Nixon that "if the People's Republic were to consider the situation on the Indian subcontinent a threat to its security, and if it took measures to protect its security, the US would oppose the efforts of others to interfere with the People's Republic." The "immediate objective" must be to prevent India from attacking West Pakistan. If nothing was done to stop this, "East Pakistan [would] become a Bhutan and West Pakistan [would] become a Nepal. And India with Soviet help would be free to turn its energies elsewhere."[53] Huang's response was blandly diplomatic. He agreed to convey Nixon's message to Premier Zhou Enlai.[54]

By the time Kissinger met Huang, the White House had set in motion two other, most consequential decisions. The first was to raise the pressure on the Soviet Union to lean on India. The second was to "convince the Indians the thing is going to escalate. And to convince the Russians that they are going to pay an enormous price." Apart from getting the Chinese to move, the Americans could "take an aircraft carrier from Vietnam into the Bay of Bengal. . . . We just say we're moving them in, in order to evacuate American civilians." "I'd do it immediately," said Nixon. "I wouldn't wait 24 hours." Pakistan, Nixon felt, was "going to lose anyway. At least we make an effort, and there is a chance to save it."[55] On December 10, Nixon instructed the chief of naval operations, Admiral Elmo Zumwalt, to assemble an impressive naval task force and move it off the coast of South Vietnam into the Malacca Strait and onward to the Bay of Bengal. Task Group 74 included the largest aircraft carrier in the navy, the USS *Enterprise*.

The war, meanwhile, was going India's way. Indian forces had made rapid thrusts into East Pakistan. Yet to this point they had only worked to secure as much territory as possible. Dhaka had not been even a gleam in eye of Indian military planners. The threat of an American intervention, as well as Moscow's nervous reaction to it, however, convinced New Delhi that it could only attain its political aims by a decisive military victory involving the capture of Dhaka and the surrender of Pakistani forces. So Indian forces began to converge on Dhaka from three directions.

Meanwhile, Nixon and Kissinger anxiously awaited Beijing's response to their request. "I'm pretty sure," said Kissinger, "the Chinese are going to do something and I think that we'll soon see."[56] On the morning of December 12, they received word that the Chinese wanted urgently to meet. Huang Hua read out a message from Beijing. China, having "carefully studied the options" put forth by Kissinger, felt that the Security Council should reconvene and push for a resolution calling for cease-fire and mutual withdrawals. There was not a word about moving against India.[57] Four days later, the Indian army took an unconditional surrender from the Pakistanis in Dhaka, now the capital of independent Bangladesh.

In the face of this massive failure of crisis management, Nixon and Kissinger deluded themselves that they had pulled off a victory. "Congratulations, Mr. President," replied Kissinger. "You have saved W. Pakistan."[58] In fact, there was little evidence that India ever wanted to turn on West Pakistan. They had used a flawed and incomplete piece of intelligence to deceive their colleagues as well as themselves. When the dust settled on the crisis, it was clear that US policy toward South Asia had suffered an enormous setback.

THE 1971 CRISIS WAS an important point of inflection in the United States' economic engagement with South Asia. As soon as war broke out, the Nixon administration turned off all economic aid to India, including nearly $87 million in the pipeline. In the frosty aftermath of the conflict, the Indians were not minded to ask for money. On the contrary, in May 1972 the Indian government asked that all Americans working on economic aid in India depart within a month. When Ambassador Kenneth Keating, his term over, made a farewell call on Prime Minister Gandhi later that summer, she brusquely told him, "It doesn't matter to us in the least what the US does about debt relief or aid. India will survive and progress with or without help from the US."[59]

In fact, the economic relationship between the two countries was set to change even before the Bangladesh crisis. The economic corollary to the Nixon Doctrine was a trimming of the American foreign aid program by turning away from bilateral, project-based aid and technical assistance and toward regulating multilateral financial flows to developing countries. India would, of course, be the centerpiece of these reforms. The Indian government, too, was keen on changing the terms of its economic ties with the United States. While New Delhi wanted continued food aid under PL480 and nonproject financial assistance, it now sought greater access to American markets for its exports. Thus, when Nixon visited India in 1969, Indian officials told their American counterparts of the need to "increase [the] commercial content of the relationship." Admittedly, the limitations on trade stemmed from "some Indian weaknesses [as well as] some US policies." Yet a change in "US attitudes," they pointed out, would be "valuable."[60] As a first step toward reorienting economic ties, the two sides agreed to reduce the US Agency for International Development's footprint in India.

In the wake of the 1971 crisis, the desire on both sides to overhaul the economic relationship intensified even as their ability to work together toward this end diminished. Two major problems proved tricky to tackle. The first was the repayment of American loans by India even as aid came to halt. This implied a net outflow of dollars from India and the need to schedule these payments in ways that did not excessively crimp Indian imports. The second problem was the enormous rupee balance accumulated by the United States through PL480 assistance. The program allowed recipient countries to pay in their own currency as opposed to dollars. Given the scale and length of PL480 assistance for India, the United States had accumulated over $3 billion worth of rupees—some 40 percent of the total currency in circulation. Indians worried about both the potential leverage that the United States held over the Indian economy and the inflationary consequences of expending this huge sum in rupees.

Another sotto voce concern among Indian policymakers was the use of these monies to bankroll CIA activities in India. Following the disclosure in 1966 that the Congress for Cultural Freedom, a famous anti-Communist advocacy group, and its affiliate in India were front organizations for the CIA, the Indian government began discerning an "American hand" all over the country. The 1971 crisis and especially the assassination of Chile's Salvador Allende accentuated these concerns. An increasingly unpopular prime minister also found hitting out against alleged American subversion handy.[61] And no amount of American assurances could assuage the Indian concerns. Keating's successor as American ambassador, Daniel Patrick Moynihan, felt that the United States "must pull the C.I.A. out of India. It is a devastating liability while it remains.... Unquestionably we would get better and cheaper information. The alternative is to remain on the front page of the Indian press for yet another decade, with a quarter of the charges true and three quarters believed to be true."[62]

Moynihan's tilt against the CIA was a nonstarter, but he did deal successfully with the whopping sum in rupees held by the United States. Moynihan argued that a generous settlement would "bring off a symbolic rapprochement with India" at "near zero cost to the administration." "The word generous is a bit deceptive," he insisted. "This is, after all, Monopoly money."[63] In February 1974, following protracted discussions, India and the United States inked an agreement. About a third of the rupee balances (750 billion rupees) would go to covering the costs of the US embassy in India over the next two decades. Washington would "grant" the remainder (166.4 billion rupees) to the Indian government for developmental activities, especially agriculture. Moynihan not only presented the Indian government with a check for 166.4 billion rupees but also wrote to *The Guinness Book of World Records* to record this as the largest ever payment by check.

The Indian efforts to expand trade with the United States, however, failed to make headway. Indian ministers and officials frequently pointed out the need to move from aid to trade. Speaking to a group of American businessmen in 1973, the new Indian ambassador to Washington, T. N. Kaul, made a pitch for doubling Indian exports to the United States in the next year or two. Kaul also pressed Kissinger to help "substitute trade for aid," which needed "some encouragement" from the administration to American businesses.[64] Moynihan's efforts to revive the long-dead negotiations on a treaty of friendship, commerce, and navigation also met with an unenthusiastic reception in Washington. Meanwhile the gales of globalization buffeted the Indian economy, pushing it in a direction that met with American approval.

The international oil crisis of 1973 hit India hard, triggering rampant inflation and a rapid slide in balance of payments. At its height from mid-1973 to September 1974, inflation in India rose at an annual rate of about 33 percent. In response, the government began cutting expenditures and tightening monetary policy. In July 1974, Indira Gandhi introduced an extremely tough package of anti-inflationary fiscal, monetary, and income-policy measures. Further, the prime minister swallowed her pride and approached the IMF for assistance. The $925 million financed largely from the IMF's low-conditionality facilities, which didn't demand much by way of structural reforms from recipients, helped stabilize the current balance-of-payments account. The IMF loan was, of course, contingent on American approval and marked another turning point in India's economic engagement with the United States.

Even as US policy toward India limped along, New Delhi stunned the world by conducting an underground nuclear test on May 18, 1974. The Indian nuclear program began with the establishment of an Atomic Energy Commission in April 1948. Prime Minister Nehru's enthusiasm for the program stemmed primarily from its technological potential and possible benefits for India's development. At the same time, Nehru knew that the line dividing a nuclear research program and a weapons program was rather thin. Although strongly opposed to the possession and use of nuclear weapons, he left the door ajar for India to go down this route, if necessary, in the future. The Indian nuclear program depended naturally on the sharing of technology and expertise by scientifically advanced countries. The first research reactor in India came from Canada, while the United States helped construct and provided nuclear fuel for the first nuclear power plant in Tarapur.

In the aftermath of the 1962 Sino-Indian War, the Indian government grew concerned about the growing Chinese nuclear weapons program. In the mid-1960s, India even sought a multilateral nuclear guarantee from the existing nuclear weapons states. When this effort failed, India refused to accede to the 1968 Treaty on the Non-Proliferation of Nuclear Weapons on the grounds that it discriminated against the nuclear have-nots.

The United States had kept a keen eye on India's civilian nuclear program, especially after its refusal to join the Non-Proliferation Treaty in 1968. Over the years, the United States had explicitly dissuaded India from going nuclear. In November 1970, the Nixon administration had handed an aide memoire to India claiming that any use of American nuclear materials for a test would contravene the terms under which these were made available to India. Yet, as late as January 1974, the embassy in India had held that there was "no evidence to confirm an Indian decision to explode a nuclear device or to manufacture nuclear weapons or delivery systems." Indeed, "Indian preoccupation with economic malaise tends to militate against an early decision to exercise nuclear options."[65] The Indian test therefore came as a surprise to the Nixon administration.

Domestic political considerations—not least the economic crisis and the resultant slide in the prime minister's standing—certainly influenced the timing of the test, officially called a "peaceful nuclear explosion." Yet the decision to test dated back to around September 1972. The reasoning for it remains a matter of scholarly debate, but the Nixon administration's sending the USS *Enterprise* to the Bay of Bengal in the final stages of the 1971 war was no doubt a factor. In an October 1972 *Foreign Affairs* essay, Indira Gandhi pointedly criticized "the dispatch of the warship *Enterprise* to support a ruthless military dictatorship and to intimidate a democracy."[66] In any event, the challenge for American policymakers was not to divine the causes of the decision but to deal with its consequences.

The State Department's first instinct was to condemn the test as a breach of the global nonproliferation order. However, Secretary of State Kissinger—then traveling in the Middle East—ordered a "low-key" statement. Kissinger felt that the deed was done: "The challenge is no longer keeping India from going nuclear; it is stabilizing a new nuclear 'power' within the international framework and trying to dissuade others from following suit." A CIA assessment after the test supported this approach, concluding, "India is considering military applications of its nuclear capability and possible sources of delivery systems but has not yet firmly committed itself to a weapons program."[67] The Indians too struck a conciliatory note with the Americans. Meeting Moynihan a month after the test, Indira Gandhi stated that India was prepared to join a comprehensive nuclear-test-ban treaty "which brought everybody in and was not discriminatory." India worried that countries with nuclear weapons such as China and France had already stayed out of the Non-Proliferation Treaty. Once such a treaty was in place, India would support a treaty for international regulation and supervision of peaceful nuclear explosions. "The responsibility for moving in this direction," she maintained, "was with other nuclear countries which have stockpiles of weapons."[68]

The nonproliferation lobby in Washington, however, circled the wagons against India. If one of the poorest countries in the world got away with testing a nuclear device, then others would soon follow suit. Citing Canada's decision to sever nuclear ties with India owing to its use of plutonium produced in a Canadian reactor, the lobby called on the Nixon administration to punish New Delhi. The nonproliferation lobby's influence on Democrats led to a curious reversal of roles. Hitherto, the strongest supporters of India had been in the Democratic Party. Following the nuclear test, however, many Democrats turned more censorious of India, while Republicans became more supportive.

In late October 1974, Kissinger visited the subcontinent. Ahead of his trip, he sounded out the Indian ambassador in Washington about his thoughts on the nuclear issue. "We recognize India as a nuclear power," he said, "and would like to deal with you as such." The United States acknowledged that India had "nuclear weapons capability" but did not want to "split hairs or argue" about whether New Delhi planned to weaponize it. His main concern was to prevent other countries such as Pakistan from developing nuclear weapons. "It may be advisable for India and the U.S.," he went on, "either bilaterally or jointly with other nuclear powers, to agree that they will not transfer nuclear explosive technology to non-nuclear countries or other nuclear technology except under strict safeguards." Kaul replied, "If there was a consensus among the nuclear powers, then we might consider joining such a consensus."[69] As before, the Indians insisted that any measure to bring them into the nonproliferation regime apply to all existing nuclear powers.

By the time Kissinger visited the subcontinent, Nixon had resigned in the shadow of Watergate. Gerald Ford, however, persisted with his overall approach to foreign policy, including toward South Asia. Thus, in his private meeting with Indira Gandhi, Kissinger frankly told her "that their nuclear explosion was a bomb no matter how India described it; that her undertaking not to produce nuclear weapons did not mean the next government would not do so; and that we were not interested in recriminations but in how to prevent further proliferation." When the prime minister asked for specific proposals, Kissinger asked Moynihan to follow up.[70]

In subsequent meetings, Moynihan and his successor, William Saxby, conveyed a series of steps that India could adopt to prevent further proliferation: "no [peaceful nuclear explosion (PNE)] assistance to other states, [International Atomic Energy Agency (IAEA)] safeguards over nuclear supply, restraint in supply of sensitive materials and technology, and physical protection of nuclear materials and facilities." The Indians "informally indicated that they would not export nuclear explosive technology" but were unwilling to engage in discussions on extending IAEA safeguards to other Indian facilities and coordinating nonproliferation policies with other nuclear suppliers.[71]

Meanwhile, the United States was working to plug holes in the nonproliferation regime. In August 1974, the Zangger Committee, comprising twenty states committed to coordinating export restrictions on key nuclear materials and technology, agreed with the IAEA to establish a "trigger list" of items that would not be supplied to nonnuclear weapon states. In April 1975, Kissinger convened a secret meeting in London of a nonproliferation cartel that would later become the Nuclear Suppliers Group. He sought and obtained additional agreements by nuclear technology suppliers to demand stronger safeguards from the countries to which they exported. To prevent countries from emulating the Indian example, they also placed an extensive list of equipment and items essential for a nuclear device under multilateral controls.[72]

As the administration's efforts rumbled on, the Congress began to take a tougher line. The nonproliferation lobby brought into its crosshairs the nuclear power plant at Tarapur, which showcased nuclear cooperation between America and India. Under a thirty-year commercial contract, the United States supplied enriched uranium for the plant. In turn, India agreed to bilateral and IAEA inspections and safeguards to prevent diversion of nuclear materials for other purposes. Prior to the Indian nuclear test, the US government routinely approved fuel exports for Tarapur. Thereafter, though, fuel shipments came under the spotlight.

IN 1976, DEMOCRATIC PRESIDENTIAL candidate Jimmy Carter was already castigating the Ford administration for a flaccid nonproliferation policy—especially toward India. On the campaign trail Carter also presented a tougher approach to nonproliferation as an important component of his foreign policy. Carter's interest in this area stemmed from his experience as an engineer on a nuclear submarine. Days after moving into the White House, he ordered a major review of nonproliferation policy.

The other innovation in Carter's foreign policy—attention to human rights—also threatened to place the United States on a collision course with India. In June 1975, Indira Gandhi had invoked the emergency powers of the constitution to effectively shut down Indian democracy. American friends of India sharply criticized this bout of authoritarianism, which included mass incarceration of opposition leaders and dissidents. The Ford administration, however, chose to maintain a studied distance from developments within India. A week before Carter's inauguration, Prime Minister Gandhi lifted the emergency and announced elections in March 1977. At the polls, she suffered a humiliating defeat, and a coalition of parties opposed to her formed a new government. The man who took over as prime minister, Morarji Desai, was a veteran congressman. An experienced administrator, Desai cut a curmudgeonly figure. In his penchant for moralizing, though, the new Indian prime minister more than matched the new American president. Not surprisingly the two men got along well and kept a courteous correspondence.

Ahead of Carter's visit to India in January 1978, Secretary of State Cyrus Vance pointed out two major political objectives for the United States. The first was for the president to "consolidate [his] personal relationship of mutual trust and confidence with Prime Minister Desai, without arousing excessive Indian expectations." This should lead to an affirmation of the "congruence of U.S. and Indian national values and concern for democratic process and human rights." The second objective was to "lay the groundwork for acceptance of full-scope safeguards," to avert further nuclear testing by India, and to secure Indian support for a comprehensive test ban. To convince the Indians about adopting full-scope safeguards, which would bring maximum transparency to their nuclear program, the president should make clear that pending nonproliferation legislation in Congress would render impossible any further "interim" shipments of nuclear fuel—unless India moved to embrace safeguards.[73]

Carter accomplished the first part of his agenda in India easily. He and Desai issued the "Delhi Declaration," avowing common values and objectives. The second objective proved less tractable. Desai bristled at hearing that India would only receive nuclear fuel if it accepted full-scope safeguards, a policy that he viewed as an encroachment on Indian sovereignty. Carter noted that Desai was "quite adamant and said that only after all nations quit producing weapons, including ourselves and the Soviets, could India accept such restrictions or inspections."[74] In short, the Indian position had toughened under the new government.

Soon after, the US Congress passed the Nuclear Non-Proliferation Act of 1978—the centerpiece of the administration's nuclear policy. The act mandated that the United States could export sensitive nuclear materials, including enriched uranium, only to countries that placed all their nuclear facilities under IAEA safeguards. Countries like India, which had hitherto refused to accept full-scope safeguards, had a year and a half to fall into line. Those that did not would be unable to import nuclear materials from the United States, whatever the prior contractual arrangements. In other words, the Americans had enacted a law demanding what the Indians had already refused.

Visiting Washington in April 1979, Indian foreign minister Atal Behari Vajpayee made clear that New Delhi would not embrace safeguards. It was prepared to turn to others for fuel after 1980 and to proceed with reprocessing of plutonium. In his meeting with Vajpayee, Carter displayed more than a hint of impatience. "We do not seek to impose our will on other countries," he said. Yet US law would govern US policy. "India will have to decide how it wants to proceed," he continued, "whether it wishes to go into plutonium reprocessing or even peaceful nuclear explosions." India had to realize, however, that "if there is no agreement on safeguards, further cooperation on Tarapur would be impossible."[75]

Carter's testiness also reflected other concerns bubbling up in his administration about its policy toward South Asia. Economic relations with India had hit a new low under the Desai government. Although the United States remained India's largest trading partner, the volume of trade was measly. Nor was India at all attractive to American businesses as a destination for investment. For all its pro-business rhetoric, the Desai government had begun to put into effect policies designed by the previous government to exercise close control over foreign capital in India. It enforced the Foreign Exchange Regulation Act, which placed a ceiling of 40 percent foreign ownership in Indian enterprise and required existing owners to reduce their equity holdings to that limit, with unprecedented vigor. This led to the departure from India of two American giants: Coca-Cola and IBM. And it left a hefty dent in US business interest in India.

Washington also had deep concerns about the regional implications of India's nuclear status, especially, the prospect of Pakistan acquiring the bomb.

THE YEAR 1971 ALSO marked the beginning of Pakistan's nuclear program. On August 1, the country's first nuclear reactor—provided by Canada under an agreement negotiated in 1965—went live. Although the reactor produced significant amounts of plutonium-239 in its spent fuel rods, Pakistan required a reprocessing plant to extract it. Only an established nuclear power could provide such a plant. France had offered one for $300 million—a price the Pakistanis deemed prohibitive. In the wake of the disastrous defeat in 1971, however, no price seemed too heavy to ensure Pakistan's security against India.

On January 20, 1972, President Zulfikar Ali Bhutto convened a secret meeting in Multan of the country's senior nuclear scientists. Vowing to restore the pride of Pakistan, Bhutto bluntly asked the gathering, "Can you give it [nuclear weapons capability] to me?" When a young scientist answered in the affirmative, Bhutto shot back, "But how long will it take to build a bomb?" Perhaps five years came the answer. "Three years," said Bhutto emphatically. "I want it in three."[76]

Procuring a plutonium reprocessing plant, however, proved a longer and more arduous task. When India tested its nuclear device in 1974, the Pakistanis were still negotiating with the French.

Pakistan's reaction to the test was naturally sharp. As the US ambassador in Islamabad put it, the Indian nuclear test "has created profound shock in Pakistan, has greatly exacerbated chronic feelings of insecurity, and has led to all-out GoP [Government of Pakistan] efforts to seek urgent security guarantees and arms aid from major powers." To bolster Pakistan's confidence, the Ford administration decided in February 1975, following a visit by Bhutto, to lift the embargo on weapons transfers, albeit only on a cash basis. Although the embargo was removed for both Pakistan and India, New Delhi promptly protested the move. Washington's subsequent decision to sell A-7 fighter planes to Pakistan elicited a sharper reaction from India. In light of the Indian nuclear test, though, the Americans were in no mood to mollify New Delhi.

Sales of conventional weaponry apart, the Ford administration hoped to dissuade the Pakistanis from going down the nuclear path. Despite Bhutto's assurances that he did not want to develop nuclear weapons, the Americans remained unconvinced. Ford wrote to Bhutto expressing his "deep personal concern" and asking the Pakistani leader to "give serious consideration to foregoing present plans to acquire reprocessing and heavy water facilities until your future nuclear program is sufficiently developed."[77] But the Pakistanis were not exploring only the plutonium route to a bomb.

As early as 1971, Bhutto had heard from a young Pakistani metallurgist working in the Netherlands about a new method to enrich uranium using centrifuges—an alternate route to obtaining fissile material for a nuclear device. Abdul Qadeer Khan worked for the large Dutch engineering firm FDO, a major subcontractor for the European Uranium Enrichment Company. Khan was part of an effort to build an advanced ultracentrifuge uranium enrichment plant for European nuclear power programs. After the Indians tested in 1974, Khan wrote yet again to Bhutto offering his services. To his surprise, he received a reply asking him to return to Pakistan. Over the next months, Khan meticulously copied the blueprints and technical data for a prototype centrifuge recently designed by German scientists—a theft facilitated by his additional role as technical translator and typist. Meeting Bhutto in early 1975, Khan made an impassioned pitch for centrifugal enrichment of uranium as a faster and cheaper alternative to the plutonium route along which Pakistan's nuclear program was plodding. Taken in, Bhutto authorized the establishment of a centrifuge enrichment laboratory at Kahuta near Islamabad. With his blessings, Khan mounted a massive clandestine operation to source components and materials from abroad for constructing the centrifuges. In the summer of 1976, Bhutto prevailed upon the Chinese to provide the designs and technology necessary to fashion a bomb out of the fissile materials.[78]

By this time, Khan was on the CIA's radar. When he failed to return from his vacation in Pakistan, the Dutch authorities had tipped off the CIA. The latter's subsequent report indicated the establishment of a laboratory in Kahuta. But not until the end of 1977 did the CIA learn that the laboratory was a uranium enrichment facility. Soon American satellites provided images of a vast complex in Kahuta. These, along with reports of large imports of centrifuge-related technology, put the Carter administration on Pakistan's case.[79]

During the first half of Carter's tenure, the United States seemed at loggerheads with Pakistan. Ahead of Carter's inauguration, Bhutto too announced general elections in March 1977. At the patently rigged polls, the ruling Pakistan People's Party received an extraordinary majority of the vote, winning no fewer than 82 percent of the seats in the National Assembly. The opposition took to the streets, and soon Pakistani cities and towns were awash with protests. In a bid to outflank the opposition, Bhutto announced a policy of Islamization, promising the introduction of sharia within six months. But the protests rolled on relentlessly. A beleaguered Bhutto began to speak of an international conspiracy to unseat his government led by the "superpower" that had

lost the Vietnam War. The Carter administration's decision to proscribe tear gas exports to Pakistan on human rights grounds strengthened Bhutto's suspicions. These gained further currency when Carter
suspended the sale of A-7 fighters approved by his predecessor. On July
5, 1977, a military coup led by General Mohammed Zia ul-Haq—an
officer the Pakistani president had promoted to army chief over six senior generals—ousted Bhutto.[80]

Zia not only imposed martial law in the country but also arrested
and tried Bhutto on charges of murder and "other high crimes." In
March 1978 the Lahore High Court found Bhutto guilty and sen-
tenced him to death. The impending judicial execution of the former
president led to pleas of clemency from several world leaders, including
Carter. But Zia refused to budge. The Supreme Court heard an appeal
toward the end of the trial, with Bhutto presenting a remarkable case
in his own defense. In February 1979, the Court upheld the guilty verdict by a single vote. Carter weighed in with another personal appeal
for clemency. The US Congress adopted a resolution calling on Zia to
pardon Bhutto. But the Pakistani dictator was unmoved. On April 4,
1979, Zulfikar Ali Bhutto, the mercurial leader who gave Pakistan its
first genuinely democratic constitution, was executed.

By that time, the Carter administration knew enough about Pakistan's uranium enrichment program. In March 1979, Deputy Secretary
of State Warren Christopher had warned Zia that unless the United
States received credible assurances that Pakistan was not building a
bomb, President Carter would have to suspend all aid, as required under the Symington Amendment to the Foreign Assistance Act of 1961.
Zia immediately assured Christopher that the Pakistani program was
"entirely peaceful," but he would neither rule out a peaceful nuclear explosion nor accept international safeguards. The Carter administration
rejected such "assurances" and cut off economic aid to Pakistan.[81]

In the summer of 1979, the Carter administration reluctantly concluded that it had "reached a dead end" in its nonproliferation efforts
in South Asia: "We face the certain prospect of two nuclear states in

this troubled area." Washington now toyed with the idea of playing the "honest broker" by getting the Pakistanis to forswear a PNE, the Indians to give a formal commitment to Pakistan that they would not develop nuclear weapons, and the Chinese to provide assurances to India that they would not deploy their nuclear assets against India.[82] This ludicrously hopeful attempt fell through the cracks of the Washington bureaucracy. Meeting Chinese leader Deng Xiaoping in January 1980, US Defense Secretary Harold Brown said that the United States was still opposed to the Pakistani nuclear program, "but we will now set that aside for the time being" and resume aid to Pakistan.[83] This dramatic volte-face in Carter's policy stemmed from developments in the region. Just days earlier the Soviet Union had intervened militarily in Afghanistan.

8

SOWING IN THE WIND

T HE ROOTS OF THE Soviet intervention in Afghanistan stretched back to the latter's domestic politics in the 1960s. When Prime Minister Sardar Mohammed Daoud stepped down in March 1963, the king had embarked on an "experiment with democracy" to at once bolster his position and forestall Daoud's making another bid for power. This allegedly democratic interlude threw up a succession of fractious and apolitical parliaments that left the executive's power untouched. This period, however, witnessed the rise of three opposition groups that would transform the politics of Afghanistan over the following decade.[1]

The Communist group had two rival factions, both owing allegiance to the Soviet Union and led by Soviet-trained men. Parcham (Banner), led by Babrak Karmal, consisted of mostly of Kabul-based

Dari-speaking Afghans and sought a bourgeois revolution that would overthrow the monarchy and prepare the ground for a second, proletarian revolution. Khalq (Masses), led by Noor Mohammed Taraki and his deputy Hafizullah Amin, drew on rural, Pashto-speaking Afghans and aimed directly at proletarian revolution on the Bolshevik model. Neither group ever attracted more than a few hundred core workers. An attempt in the mid-1960s to unite as the People's Democratic Party of Afghanistan (PDPA) unraveled owing to Karmal's old links with Daoud.

The second group comprised Islamist organizations, many of whose leaders were educated in Egypt and influenced by the Muslim Brotherhood. Alarmed by the growth of the Communist factions and Soviet influence in Afghanistan, they formed the Jamiat-i-Islami Afghanistan (Islamic Society of Afghanistan) in the mid-1960s. The Jamiat was the cradle of future leaders of the Islamist resistance to the Soviet occupation of the country: Burhanuddin Rabbani, the ethnic Tajik who led the Jamiat; Rabbani's young protégé and another Tajik, Ahmad Shah Massoud; and Abdul Rasul Sayyaf and Gulbuddin Hekmatyar, ethnic Pashtuns who would go on to form their own outfits.

The third group was essentially an informal patronage network centered on Daoud. Devoid of any ideology, it sought to undermine the king, the executive, and the parliament and so enable Daoud's return to power. In July 1973, it pulled off a bloodless coup against the monarch and proclaimed Afghanistan a republic. On seizing power Daoud promptly suspended the constitution and all political activity. In a bid to secure his base, he initially harked back to his pet themes: Afghan neutrality with a tilt toward the Soviet Union and the demand for Pashtun self-determination on either side of the Durand Line with Pakistan. The Parchamis supported Daoud's coup, and many of them also joined the new regime.

Daoud fell into the familiar mold of authoritarian modernizers. Assisted by the Parchamis, he set off a violent campaign against the "reactionary" Islamists. Following a failed coup attempt in December 1973, the main Islamist leaders fled to Pakistan. Their calls for a popular jihad against the Daoud regime went mostly unheeded, even as government forces slaughtered some six hundred of their followers. In Pakistan, they found Zulfikar Ali Bhutto's government willing to support their cause. Not only was the Pakistani prime minister riled by Daoud's claims concerning "Pashtunistan," but he also found himself combating an insurgency in Baluchistan buttressed, he believed, by Afghan support. Aided by the Pakistani military and intelligence, the Islamists got down to waging a protracted insurgency against the Afghan government. Their efforts received a fillip with the advent of Mohammed Zia ul-Haq and his Islamist policies.[2]

Meanwhile, Daoud sought to reduce his dependence on Parcham and the Soviet Union. Thus, he began playing down the problems with Pakistan and reaching out to Iran, Saudi Arabia, and Egypt—all key US allies in the Middle East. In mid-1976, Daoud send his brother and foreign minister, Mohammed Naim, to Washington. Naim told Secretary of State Henry Kissinger that contrary to popular perception, the Daoud government was not pro-Communist. Afghanistan had turned to Moscow owing to America's reluctance to assist in the early years. Now the regime felt the weight of Soviet money, expertise, arms, and officers in the country: "The security situation vis-à-vis our Soviet neighbor is becoming more and more undesirable." Daoud sought overt American friendship and assistance. "It should be seen by everyone," insisted Naim. The Gerald Ford administration was unwilling to commit specific economic aid. Kissinger, however, offered secret sharing of intelligence on Soviet activities in Afghanistan.[3]

Moscow followed this turn in Afghan policy with chagrin. In April 1977, Soviet leader Leonid Brezhnev asked Daoud to remove all non-Soviet foreign experts in Afghanistan. The Russians also encouraged the two Communist factions to come together under the PDPA and mount a concerted opposition to Daoud's regime. When Daoud cracked down on the PDPA, its sympathizers in the military carried out a coup on April 27, 1978, killing Daoud and his family. Moscow may have known of, but was not involved in, the coup. The new PDPA regime—with Taraki as president, Karmal as vice president, and Amin as first deputy prime minister—declared Afghanistan a democratic republic with fraternal ties to the Soviet Union. Moscow immediately recognized the regime and funneled considerable economic and military aid to Afghanistan. By the end of 1978, some 4,000 Soviet civilian and military advisors were assisting the PDPA regime in various spheres and at all levels.[4]

Factional fights soon broke out within the regime. Khalq ran rings around Parcham, dispatching Karmal and his senior advisors abroad as ambassadors and subsequently dismissing them. Taraki sought to force-march Afghanistan toward socialist modernity, promoting literacy for boys and girls, increasing women's rights, and striking at many aspects of traditional Afghan society. These progressive measures accompanied establishment of a Stalinist secret police that killed and incarcerated thousands of regime opponents. The backlash was not late in the coming. In March 1979, a motley group of Islamist insurgents, townspeople, and defectors from the Afghan army garrison at Herat turned on the Soviet advisors, killing over a dozen of them. The Russians, in turn, undertook a bombing campaign on behalf of the regime, killing several thousand Afghans and leveling large parts of the city. A similar Islamist-inspired military revolt at the other end of country in Jalalabad drew another bloody response from the regime. Soon the Taraki government faced a full-scale civil war. The Afghan army was hemorrhaging due to defections as well as losses inflicted by the insurgents. Even as its grip on the countryside slipped, the regime was up against underground cells operating in Kabul.

While Taraki continually pressed Moscow for more troops, the Soviets sought to avoid an overt military intervention. Instead they urged him to soften his stance toward the Islamists and work with local religious notables. Taraki was unwilling to countenance such advice. In another bloody twist to the story, Taraki was arrested and executed by his deputy Amin in September 1979. His removal put the Soviets off balance. Not only had Amin snubbed Moscow, but he was a rather more difficult customer to deal with. The Soviets believed that he would fail to get a grip on the rapidly deteriorating situation and turn to the United States. So they began preparing quietly to intervene and replace Amin with Karmal.

Writing to Brezhnev in early December 1979, KGB chief Yuri Andropov warned of the risk of Amin's "political reorientation to the West." He was keeping his contacts with American officials under wraps and had also "promised tribal leaders to distance himself from the Soviet Union." Andropov argued that Moscow could ill afford to lose "the domestic achievements of the Afghan revolution." That would sow the seeds of Islamism in Soviet Central Asia. Nor could it risk a "turn to the West." On December 8, Brezhnev gave the go-ahead for a Parcham takeover and military intervention in support of Karmal's regime. On December 24, Soviet aircraft began flying troops into Afghanistan. Three days later, Amin was killed. By the morning of December 28, the Soviets had taken effective control of Kabul and other major cities of Afghanistan.[5]

THE UNITED STATES TOO had been following the chronic instability in Afghanistan with some concern. The Jimmy Carter administration took a measured view of Daoud's deposition in 1978. Secretary of State Cyrus Vance was open to engaging the new regime, while his officials pushed to continue providing small doses of economic aid to ensure that Taraki did not end up in the Soviets' lap. National Security Advisor Zbigniew Brzezinski was more skeptical. In the event, Carter decided to recognize the regime and send Adolph Dubs as ambassador to Kabul. By the end of the year, it was clear that Taraki could not be kept from embracing the Soviets. Worse, in February 1979, Dubs was kidnapped by an extremist group and killed in a botched rescue operation. The Americans were irate. They thought "the Afghan officials, advised by Soviets, were too peremptory in their showdown with weapons and probably caused the death of our ambassador."[6] The Carter administration terminated all aid to Afghanistan.

In early March, the Central Intelligence Agency (CIA) noted that Islamist insurgents had achieved striking successes against the regime and proposed a range of covert actions to assist them—perhaps in concert with Pakistan and Saudi Arabia. Both countries had already expressed their concerns to Americans about the situation in Afghanistan. The president himself observed, "The Soviets are getting in more difficulty in Afghanistan." While the idea of "sucking the Soviets into a Vietnamese quagmire" appealed, senior State Department officials were unsure of the Islamists' ability to undertake a sustained insurgency and concerned about the likely Soviet retaliation against Pakistan. A special coordination committee of the National Security Council met on April 6 to consider an array of covert options, ranging from small-scale propaganda to arming and training the Afghan fighters. The consensus favored an active role limited to nonlethal assistance channeled through Pakistan.[7]

The CIA continued to brief the president on the situation in Afghanistan in April and May 1979. Brzezinski warned Carter that "if the Soviets came to dominate Afghanistan, they could promote a separate Baluchistan, which would give them access to the Indian Ocean while dismembering Pakistan and Iran." The national security advisor wanted to up the ante. He felt that Moscow was on the horns of a dilemma: whether to abandon Afghanistan or occupy the country at the risk of sinking into a bog. American policy must accentuate the predicament. In recommending increased support for the Afghan Islamist fighters to Carter, he observed that "this aid was going to induce a Soviet military intervention." On July 3, 1979, Carter signed off on covert assistance to the Afghan mujahedeen in the form of cash or non-military supplies given either directly or through third countries. The half a million dollars that the administration forked out disappeared in a flash. Soon Zia and other Pakistani officials were pressing the United States for arms and equipment for the Afghan insurgents.[8]

As the Soviet intervention unfolded in the last week of December, Brzezinski sent a memo to Carter that set the tone for the administration's response. The Soviet invasion of Afghanistan posed "an extremely grave challenge" for the United States. In conjunction with the Iranian crisis, which had led to the overthrow of America's stalwart ally, the shah, "it could produce Soviet presence right down on the edge of the Arabian and Oman gulfs." While Afghanistan "could become a Soviet Vietnam," Washington could not afford to be complacent, lest it invite domestic attacks and risk its reputation with allies. "It is essential," Brzezinski wrote, "that Afghanistani [sic] resistance continues." This meant sending rebels more money and arms as well as some technical advice. To make the above possible," he continued, "we must both reassure Pakistan and encourage it to help the rebels. This will require a review of our policy toward Pakistan, more guarantees to it, more arms aid." Besides, the United States must coordinate its assistance to the Afghan rebels with China and the Islamic countries. "Our ultimate goal," Brzezinski wrote in another memo, "is the withdrawal of Soviet troops from Afghanistan....Even if this is not attainable, we should make Soviet involvement as costly as possible."[9]

Carter agreed. The Soviets' intervention was a "radical departure" from the restraint they had exercised since the invasion of Czechoslovakia in 1968. It also marked a sharp departure from his own previous attempts to keep ties with Moscow on an even keel. Carter was "determined to make this action as politically costly as possible." Apart from condemning it publicly, he wrote, "I also sent on the Hot Line the sharpest message I have ever sent to Brezhnev, telling him that the invasion of Afghanistan would seriously and adversely affect the relationship between our two countries."[10] He then followed this up by imposing a range of sanctions on the Soviet Union and subsequently boycotting the 1980 Moscow Olympics.

The Pakistanis were initially conflicted about how to respond to the Soviet intervention. A minority of Zia's advisors felt that their country was too weak to take on the Soviet Union in Pakistan's own neck of the woods. Others argued that Kabul was too unimportant to be Moscow's real objective and speculated that the Soviets aimed to create a launch pad for further incursions into Pakistan, Iran, or perhaps the Arabian Sea. In any event, fighting the Russians inside Afghanistan was better than adopting a defensive posture. While the risks were real, Pakistan could count on political support against Moscow from most countries at the United Nations. Furthermore, the Soviet invasion presented an opportunity as well as a threat. Indeed, in Zia's reading the former outweighed the latter. Here was a chance to enable the Islamist groups he had backed to become the internationally recognized and supported Afghan opposition. This would at once advance his own Islamist agenda and ensure a pliable Afghanistan in the future. So Zia eventually decided that Pakistan would publicly oppose the Soviet intervention, take in refugees fleeing Afghanistan, and provide covert support to Afghan insurgents while publicly disavowing any involvement.

Following a telephone conversation with Zia, Carter convened a meeting on January 4 to discuss aid to Pakistan and the Afghans. The president preferred to "send them the kind of weapons they could use in the mountains in a portable condition.... We need to get as many other nations as possible to join us in a consortium so that Paks [sic] won't be directly seen as dependent or subservient to us." The State Department proposed asking Congress for $150 million in aid and credits for Pakistan, consideration of debt relief, and a waiver of the legislation proscribing economic and military aid owing to Pakistan's nuclear program. In this context the Americans told the Chinese that they were going soft on Pakistan's nuclear activities. Meeting an envoy of Zia soon after, Carter offered a two-year economic and military aid package worth $400 million, though he turned down a Pakistani request for advanced F-16 fighter planes. The Pakistanis well understood their massively enhanced bargaining power with the United States. Speaking to journalists on January 18, Zia dismissed the American offer as "peanuts": "Pakistan will not buy its security for $400 million." American assistance had to be commensurate with the risks that Pakistan would run. Carter was initially put off: "Suits me fine," he confided to his diary. All the same, the administration sought to smooth things over with the Pakistanis.[11]

Brzezinski and Deputy Secretary of State Warren Christopher flew to Islamabad. Ahead of their meeting with Zia, Carter had declared in his State of the Union address that the United States would help "Pakistan resist any outside aggression." But Zia sought a similar assurance vis-à-vis India. Not only were the Americans unwilling to comply, but their enhanced aid package of $500 million fell short of Pakistani expectations. Indeed, much to the administration's discomfort, the Pakistanis publicly declared their disinterest in any aid package of this size. Eventually, the administration agreed to drop plans to extend aid and instead offered a generous debt rescheduling package. On covert assistance, though, there was a meeting of minds. Brzezinski secured Zia's assent for a large-scale effort to arm and support the Afghan fighters. What is more, at his next stop in Riyadh, he convinced the Saudis to match America's contribution to covert war dollar for dollar.[12]

By the summer of 1980, the covert program had expanded dramatically to include "all manner of weapons and military support" for the mujahideen. A couple months later, Brzezinski grumbled to the CIA that the administration was not providing enough weapons to the insurgents and wanted everything sent that the Pakistanis were willing to receive.[13] To ensure deniability, the CIA procured used Soviet weaponry from Africa and the Middle East and passed them on to Pakistan. The Pakistanis, however, set the terms of engagement. The CIA would hand over all cash and materiel to Pakistan's Inter-Services

Intelligence (ISI), which in turn would disburse them to the Afghans. The CIA would not interact directly with the fighters. The ISI also chose which Afghan groups to patronize, its favorites being the Islamist outfits headquartered in Peshawar.

The Pakistanis also benefited from China's interest in keeping the Soviets at bay in Afghanistan. Very like the Pakistanis, the Chinese believed that Afghanistan was a mere staging ground for a larger southward drive to Pakistan and Iran or at least to the port of Gwadar on the coast of Balochistan. Beijing deemed not allowing the Soviets to move beyond Afghanistan vital. The Chinese outlined their objectives and policy in Afghanistan to the Americans: unconditional withdrawal of Soviet troops, restoration of Afghan sovereignty, and aid to the mujahideen resisting the Russians. By February 1980, the Chinese had begun funneling money via Pakistan to arm the rebels. Almost three hundred Chinese military advisors stationed along the Afghanistan-Pakistan border trained and guided the mujahideen. Soon Chinese small arms and ammunition became a major source of supply for the resistance.[14]

In October 1980, Carter invited Zia to Washington. The American president found that he "liked Zia very much. He's calm. I think very courageous. Intelligent."[15] This was high praise indeed for a man whose human rights record might have arched a presidential eyebrow just a few years back. Now, overruling the State Department's recommendation, Carter offered to sell F-16s to Pakistan. Zia waved the proposal aside, saying the decision could wait until Carter was free of the burdens of the presidential campaign. In fact, the Pakistanis had already concluded that Carter was unlikely to get reelected. And they looked forward to working with Ronald Reagan.

THIS PROVED A SHREWD assessment. Just three weeks into Reagan's presidency, the State Department made a strong case for aid to Pakistan, "a front line state under heavy Soviet pressure." The memorandum argued that Pakistan's "national integrity [and] its anti-Soviet posture are critical to our larger interests in the region....Our credibility, four-teen months after the Soviet invasion, is low, but Pakistani expectations of the new administration are high....We do not have much latitude for delay since the atmosphere could quickly sour."[16] The Reagan admin-istration swiftly pulled its act together and prepared a five-year, $3.2 billion package, which included forty F-16s, in concessional financing. In Islamabad, the American ambassador worked on Zia to ensure that he would not spurn this substantially larger offer. Even so, Zia refused to bite unless the United States addressed Pakistan's other concerns.

The most important of these was, of course, the nuclear program. State Department analysts had pointed out that "Pakistan will not give up this program." It had become too closely identified with Pakistani nationalism for any government to forsake—not least a military regime. While there was "a slight possibility" that Pakistan might be dissuaded from testing, this would be "difficult to accomplish."[17] When Foreign Minister Agha Shahi visited Washington in April 1981, Secretary of State Alexander Haig described the Pakistani program as "a private matter." It need not become a centerpiece of US-Pakistan relations. Pa-kistan's testing a nuclear device would hamper the administration's ef-forts to provide economic and military aid. The subtext was that things would be fine as long as Pakistan refrained from exploding a device. The other issue on which Pakistan sought and obtained assurances was continuation of the modus operandi for cooperation between the CIA and the ISI in assisting the mujahideen.[18]

The covert cooperation tightened under the Reagan. During the first three years of the administration (1981–1983), funding remained at about $60 million a year, matched by the Saudis. By early 1982, in re-sponse to requests from officials on the ground, CIA director William Casey sought at least another $20 million a year. When he met Zia in April, the Pakistani dictator gave him the works. Pointing to a map of the region with a large red triangle pinned atop Afghanistan, Zia underlined the Soviet threat to the Persian Gulf. The United States, he intoned, had a "moral duty" to draw a line in the sand. The objective in

Afghanistan, said Zia, should be "to keep the pot boiling but not boil over." When Casey agreed on the need to up the ante, Zia asked for better antiaircraft weaponry: "The Pathans [Pashtun Mujahideen] are great fighters but shit-scared when it comes to airpower."[19]

The Pakistani nuclear program nevertheless continued to raise the hackles of the American nonproliferation lobby. The Reagan administration grew concerned that mounting evidence of Abdul Qadeer Khan's clandestine purchases and of Chinese cooperation could give Congress a convenient pretext to turn off aid to Pakistan. To check the situation, Reagan sent a personal letter to Zia via General Vernon Walters, erstwhile deputy director of the CIA.

In their meeting on July 4, 1982, Walters told Zia that Washington had "incontrovertible" intelligence that Pakistani representatives had "transferred designs and specifications for nuclear weapons components to purchasing agents in several countries for the purpose of having these nuclear weapons components fabricated for Pakistan." US law, he continued, mandated that the administration inform the Congress. Zia flatly denied everything. "Pakistan did not have a weapons development program....He could not believe that such designs could have been submitted to foreign purchasing or manufacturing agents without his knowing it and he had no knowledge of any such weapons development programs....He could give his word of honor as a soldier that they would not develop, much less explode a nuclear weapon or device." Walters concluded, "Either he really does not know or he is the most superb and patriotic liar I have ever met." In another meeting the next day, Zia accepted American intelligence as accurate but claimed that Pakistan was not involved and that the evidence pointing to that was fabricated. He hoped Pakistan would have a chance to defend its case. Zia's statement, as Walters cattily put it, amounted to saying, "It did not happen, but you can be sure it won't happen again."[20] This was enough for the Reagan administration to tell the Congress with a straight face that Pakistan was not pursuing nuclear weapons.

Yet evidence of the Pakistani program continued to pile up. In October 1982, Walters returned to Islamabad with drawings of Chinese-influenced nuclear weapons designs picked up by the Americans. Zia categorically denied any Pakistani activity toward weapons development. Pakistan was "not, repeat not, engaged even in a research program in the nuclear weapons field." He had looked into the previous allegations and found nothing to corroborate American claims. If there were genuine evidence of wrongdoing by any Pakistani individual, Zia would "hang that chap upside down." He would do nothing to jeopardize American aid to Pakistan. Walters ended the conversation by hoping that "no further blips would show up on our radar."[21]

Ahead of Zia's visit to Washington in November 1982, Secretary of State George Shultz wrote to President Reagan that the administration's South Asia policy was "threatened by Pakistan's nuclear weapons program." Despite Zia's repeated claims that Pakistan was not developing a bomb, "there is overwhelming evidence that Zia has been breaking his assurances to us." The State Department was "absolutely confident" that its intelligence was "genuine and accurate." Indeed, it had recently located a potential nuclear test site in Pakistan. Nevertheless, the administration had to be "mindful of the essential role that Pakistan plays in support of the Afghan resistance." Since opposing the Soviets in Afghanistan was the lynchpin of the US commitment to countering Soviet military thrusts globally, "Pakistan bears directly on U.S. global, as well as regional, interests." Shultz laid out three options. Tell Zia that if Pakistan continued its quest for nuclear weapons, the administration would cut military and economic aid, that the Congress would move to thwart aid, or that these efforts would "seriously jeopardize our security relations."[22]

Given this assessment of Pakistan's centrality to US global strategy, the administration unsurprisingly plumped for the last and least controversial option. "We got along fine," noted Reagan. "He's a good man....Gave me his word they were not building an atomic or nuclear bomb."[23] Yet again this sufficed for his administration to carry on with its mendacity to the Congress.

OVER THE FOLLOWING MONTHS, the Reagan administration moved toward a marked escalation of its support for the Afghan resistance. In mid-1983, the American ambassador in Pakistan called for a review of US policy toward Afghanistan. "There is a good chance," he wrote to Shultz, "that our current set of policies will not take us where we want to go—bringing about the complete withdrawal of Soviet troops." The Russians could "afford to take casualties at the present rate interminably." The United States had not yet shown that it could "increase the costs they have to pay." The mujahideen, he argued, "may have fought the Soviets to a stalemate in Afghanistan, but over the long run the decisive factor will be Soviets' staying power and limited mujahideen resources."[24]

In the past three years, the mujahideen had indeed held their own against the Soviet forces. The rapid dissolution of the Afghan army after the invasion enormously complicated Soviet attempts to bring the insurgency to heel. Equally problematic was the Afghan peasantry's willingness to assist the insurgents with supplies and information. The Pakistan-based Islamist outfits had managed to co-opt many local commanders fighting the regime in various provinces of Afghanistan. Although not enthusiastic about the Islamists' ideology, commanders like Ahmad Massoud in the Panjshir Valley wanted access to the weaponry and supplies at the disposal of the mujahideen. The Islamists also benefited from the immense pool of indoctrinated volunteers in the rapidly mushrooming madrasas and Afghan refugee camps in Pakistan.

The mujahideen were a fractious lot, however. To keep them from fissuring, the ISI designated six major Afghan groups as recipients of money and materiel. Yet the split between Burhanuddin Rabbani's Jamiat-i-Islami and Gulbuddin Hekmatyar's Hizb-i-Islami (Islamic Party) proved particularly tricky for the Pakistanis to manage.

Eventually, a combination of pressure from Zia and money from the Saudis ensured a working truce. At the same time, the Pakistanis did not want the Afghans to create a unified entity owing to concern about its potential influence and independence. Thus, the ISI made short work of an August 1981 attempt by five of the parties (all close to the Jamiat) to form an umbrella organization. In time, the Saudis insisted that a seventh group represent their interests. The Ittehad-i-Islami (Islamic Union) was led by Abdul Rasul Sayyaf, who had embraced Wahhabi Islam during his years in Cairo and was funded by a young Saudi billionaire named Osama bin Laden. The CIA referred to the leaders of these groups as the Seven Dwarves.[25]

Back in Washington, the CIA's director made a forceful pitch for raising the stakes. An archetypal Christian cold warrior, Casey believed that the Soviets could be not just contained but defeated in Afghanistan—with momentous consequences for the larger struggle against communism. "Here is the beauty of the Afghan operation," he told his colleagues. "Usually it looks like the big bad Americans are beating up on the natives. Afghanistan is just the reverse. The Russians are beating up on the little guys. We don't make it our war. The Mujahedin [sic] have all the motivation they need. All we had to do is give them help, only more of it."[26]

In January 1984, Casey briefed Reagan and the National Security Council. To date, the mujahideen had killed or wounded some 17,000 Soviet soldiers and destroyed about 2,750 Soviet tanks and 8,000 other vehicles. The Soviets had also lost 350 to 400 aircraft. The mujahideen controlled nearly two-thirds of the Afghan territory. The war had already cost the Soviets $12 billion in direct expenses. The United States had achieved all this at a price of just $200 million, with the Saudis throwing in an equal amount.[27] Casey's drive to raise more money for the mujahideen received supported from an unexpected quarter. Representative Charlie Wilson of Texas was a senior Democrat on the House Appropriations Committee. Wilson's fondness for booze, drugs, and sex sat oddly with his zeal to support the Islamists rebels.

All the same, he pushed the Congress to increase covert funding by $40 million. Simultaneously, Casey traveled to Riyadh and convinced the Saudis to raise their contribution. In October 1984, both sides agreed to commit $250 million each for the next year.[28]

In March 1985, President Reagan issued National Security Decision Directive 166 on American objectives and strategy in Afghanistan. "The ultimate goal of our policy," the document stated, "is the removal of Soviet forces from Afghanistan and the restoration of its independent status." Over the next five years, the United States would pursue a series of "interim objectives": demonstrate to the Soviets that their strategy is not working, deny Afghanistan as a base for the Soviets to move into the Persian Gulf, foster Soviet diplomatic isolation in the Third World and among the Islamic countries, and prevent the defeat of the Afghan resistance. In pursuit of these medium- and long-term objectives, the United States would have to "improve the military effectiveness of the Afghan resistance in order to keep the trends in the war unfavorable to the Soviet Union." Affirming Pakistan's pivotal role, the directive said that Washington would have to "maintain good relations with Pakistan.... [S]uch relations are essential to the program. This will include responding to Pakistani security requirements arising from their support to the resistance."[29]

The massive expansion of the covert assistance program also encouraged Zia to adopt a more aggressive posture toward the Soviet Union. Convinced the Soviets posed no serious threat to Pakistan, he asked the CIA for detailed maps and imagery of the areas along the northern border of Afghanistan with Soviet Central Asia. Although the CIA initially hesitated, Zia began sending small teams of mujahideen to carry out attacks and sabotage inside Soviet territory.[30] This turn in Pakistani policy coincided with the rise to power of Mikhail Gorbachev in Moscow.

Gorbachev's initial instinct was to adopt a tougher policy both in the war and in diplomatic dealings with Washington and Islamabad. At the same time, he asked the general staff to prepare a plan for a gradual withdrawal of Soviet forces from Afghanistan starting in mid-1986. In October 1985, Gorbachev bluntly told Afghan president Babrak Karmal, "We'll help you, but only with arms, not with troops. And if you want to survive you'll have to broaden the base of the regime, forget socialism, make a deal with the truly influential forces, including the Mujahedin commanders and leaders of now hostile organizations."[31] Gorbachev hoped both to ensure that the Soviets were not bled white in Afghanistan and to create sufficient military pressure for a diplomatic settlement that would leave in place a friendly regime in Afghanistan.

In pursuit of this strategy, the Soviets ratcheted up their military operations in Afghanistan. Special forces units, helicopter gunships, intense bombing, and indiscriminate sowing of landmines followed in quick order. Moscow also sternly warned Islamabad to desist from instigating attacks on Soviet territory. The mujahideen staved off major Soviet offensives in the Kunar and Panjshir Valleys and in Paktia and Heart provinces. But they were beginning to feel the heat.

The Soviet escalation touched off an intense debate in the Reagan administration about providing Stinger antiaircraft missiles to the mujahideen. The Pakistanis had been demanding better antiaircraft weapons for a while. But the balance of opinion in Washington was against such a move. Apart from concerns about Soviet reaction, both the Joint Chiefs of Staff and the CIA worried that this cutting-edge military technology would end up in the wrong hands. In December 1985, senior Pentagon officials suggested providing Stingers to the Afghan fighters. Secretary of State Shultz also came out in support of this step. When Casey visited Pakistan in February 1986, Zia insisted, "This is the time to increase the pressure." The same month the administration decided, in principle, to approve the provision of Stingers. By September, the mujahideen were deploying them in combat.[32]

A few months later, the CIA also passed on to the Afghans a night-vision device to go with the Stingers. Against these weapons, the Soviets' aircraft proved helpless. The skyrocketing cost of deploying airpower forced the Kremlin to change tack and focus on ground operations. In so doing, it played into the strengths of the mujahideen. Apart from giving the insurgents an operational edge, the Stingers also raised their morale and provided good propaganda material.

The Afghan jihad was also awash with funds. In 1987, the United States shoveled $630 million into the covert program. The Saudis matched it dollar for dollar. Bin Laden and his associates channeled more holy warriors from Arab lands to the camps in Pakistan. In fact, the Americans looked to raise an "international brigade" of jihadists on the lines of the international antifascist brigade in the Spanish Civil War, but it did not work out as planned. Even so, the Afghan war had become a proving ground for Islamist radicalism. Zia added his own plans to mix. As early as 1980, he had met the leader of Jamaat-i-Islami Pakistan, Maulana Abdul Bari, and broached the idea recruiting Kashmiris from the Indian and Pakistani sides for a covert war against India. They could divert some of the arms and money provided by the Americans to an insurgency in Kashmir. The maulana blanched at the suggestion, expressing concern about the Americans. "But how can the Americans stop us from waging jihad in Kashmir," asked Zia, "when they themselves are waging jihad in Afghanistan?" By mid-1983, the ISI had set up camps in Pakistan to train the Kashmiris recruited by the Jamaat.[33] "We expected post-Soviet Afghanistan to be ugly," recalled then deputy CIA director Robert Gates in 1996, "but never considered that it would become a haven for terrorists operating worldwide."[34] The worst was yet to come.

THE ENORMOUS INCREASE IN covert funding for Pakistan led the Reagan administration to redouble its efforts to ensure that the Pakistani nuclear program stayed under the radar. But the Pakistanis would not oblige. In June 1984, US Customs agents detained three Pakistani nationals at the Houston airport when they tried to export a box of krytrons, high-speed switches that were a crucial component of the trigger mechanism in a nuclear bomb. The men neither had an export license nor a good explanation for the krytrons' intended use. The incident suggested that the Pakistanis were in the last stage of nuclear development. Asked for an explanation, Zia disavowed any knowledge of the men. The administration, for its part, ensured that the case was "sandbagged."[35]

The nonproliferation hawks in the Congress struck back by threatening to tighten the law. The existing law proscribed aid to countries that possessed a "nuclear device." This enabled the administration to absolve the Pakistanis, knowing full well that they were continually sourcing components for a device and assiduously working toward one. The administration, however, maneuvered a lighter amendment through the Congress that required the president to certify annually that Pakistan had no "nuclear device." The Pressler Amendment of 1985 did not set an onerous requirement for the administration to meet. But Pakistan continued to make things difficult.

Just months after passage of the Pressler Amendment, American intelligence sources claimed, "Pakistan produced an atomic weapon in early October [1985] with onsite Chinese assistance." The Americans knew that the Kahuta plant could produce enough fissile material for several bombs. Nevertheless, it was "our assessment that Pakistan does not possess a device."[36] Still, ahead of Pakistani Prime Minister Muhammad Khan Junejo's trip to Washington in July 1986, the accumulating evidence of his country's drive toward nuclear weapons worried the administration. "Our problem," Reagan confided to his diary, "has to do with the evidence that Pakistan is on the way to having a nuc. bomb in spite of a pledge to us that they wouldn't." Reagan explained to Junejo that he had to certify Pakistan's nonnuclear status to Congress every year in order to secure aid for the war in Afghanistan. Junejo said that "he had no knowledge of that [a nuclear program] but he would get into it & pledged to me they would keep their agreement." Reagan laconically noted, "I believed him."[37]

The potential dangers of such implicit faith became apparent when Pakistan and India lurched toward a crisis later that year. Since an Israeli strike on an Iraqi nuclear reactor in June 1981, Zia had worried about the prospect of an Indian or a joint Indo-Israeli strike on the nuclear facility in Kahuta. When Walters met him in October 1982, Zia claimed to have "recently received serious intimations on joint Indian-Israeli action against Pakistan."[38] The administration assessed that "at some point India or Israel may decide to launch a preventive strike at Pak nuclear facilities, but we have no indications that military action is likely in the near term."[39] In August 1984, the CIA reported that it had lost track of two Indian strike aircraft squadrons based in Punjab. The White House surmised that "India is building up militarily on the Pak. border. Their concern is whether Pakistan is developing nuclear weapons."[40] Panicked into action, the Reagan administration sent a stiff warning to New Delhi. Although the Pakistanis believed that the Indians had blinked in the face of this warning,[41] no evidence suggests that India had planned an air strike. More accurate was the Reagan administration's intelligence in late 1982, indicating that India was considering another nuclear test,[42] though the Indian prime minister eventually dropped the idea. Nevertheless, the Reagan administration understood the regional risks it was running in turning a blind eye toward the Pakistani nuclear program.

In the 1986–1987 winter, Prime Minister Rajiv Gandhi authorized the Indian army to conduct Exercise Brasstacks, a major air-land maneuver in the western deserts to simulate a war against Pakistan. Apart from testing the newly mechanized formations of the Indian army, Brasstacks was apparently intended to convey a deterrent threat to Pakistan for its efforts to stoke insurgency in Punjab. By some accounts, it even sought to provoke a clash. In any event, it sufficiently alarmed the Pakistanis, who responded with their own buildup.

The Americans thought that India "underestimated the degree to which Brasstacks would be seen as saber-rattling and thus would prompt reaction and counter-reaction."[43] As the two militaries stood ready for conflict—not only near the exercise area but also along the southern approaches to Kashmir—the Americans realized the gravity of the situation and leaned on both sides to pull back from the brink. Of equal concern to the Reagan administration was an interview given by Abdul Qadeer Khan to a senior Indian journalist, boasting that Pakistan had a bomb. Though perhaps a veiled nuclear threat to India, the statement cast doubt on the administration's assurances about the Pakistani program. Worse, the *Observer* in London carried the story on the very day that Reagan was to deliver his annual statement to Congress on nonproliferation. The president proceeded to do just that, even though the administration was left red in the face.

The Reagan administration was determined not to allow Congress to stanch the flow of aid to Pakistan. When the National Security Planning Group met in March 1987, the president was convinced that Pakistan was "necessary to our help of the Mujaheddin [*sic*].... We must & will continue to give aid to the freedom fighters."[44] Reagan's National Security Decision Directive 210 of May 1987 yet again affirmed, "Pakistan remains the key to our ability to implement a policy of opposition to Soviet aggression in Afghanistan. Critical to Pakistan's ability and willingness to play this role is Islamabad's confidence in our support.... Any lessening in our commitment could add to pressures on Pakistan and cripple our broader policy objectives regarding Afghanistan." Continued economic and military assistance to Pakistan "will require effective management of Congressional concerns, inter alia, about the Pakistan nuclear program."[45] There could be no clearer statement of the administration's intent to shield the Pakistani program.

Washington focused on the payoff in Afghanistan. By late 1986, Gorbachev recognized that his strategy had failed to deliver. "Of course we could leave Afghanistan quickly," he conceded. But to do so would deal a blow to Soviet standing among revolutionary movements worldwide. And the prospect of a Soviet withdrawal without assured stability in Afghanistan made regional powers like India deeply uneasy. Besides, how could the Kremlin explain the costs of the war to the

Soviet people? Yet Gorbachev understood that persisting with the occupation would put at risk his program of domestic reform and his efforts to reduce tensions with the United States.[46]

As a first step toward a phased pullout, Moscow replaced Afghan president Babrak Karmal with the head of the Afghan secret police, Mohammad Najibullah, and instructed him to start a process of "national reconciliation." The UN-supported negotiations between Moscow and Islamabad in Geneva gathered momentum. Gorbachev failed to secure American and Pakistani assurances of noninterference in Afghanistan after the Soviet withdrawal. Zia told Reagan that he would sign an agreement to that effect but had no intention of abiding by it. When Reagan warned him that this would amount to lying, Zia quipped, "We've been denying our activities there for eight years. Muslims have the right to lie in a good cause."[47] In the event, Gorbachev went ahead and signed the Geneva Accords of April 1988, promising to pull out troops by February 1989.[48] Just over three months later, Zia died in a mysterious plane crash. By the time the last Red Army soldiers departed from Afghanistan the next year, Pakistan had a new prime minister, Benazir Bhutto, and the United States had a new president, George H. W. Bush.

In the decade following the Soviet invasion of Afghanistan, the US relationship with India underwent a paradoxical change. On the one hand, the tremendous expansion in American aid to Pakistan for services rendered in Afghanistan met with New Delhi's deep disapproval. On the other hand, India's aspirations for economic transformation at home, as well as its realization of the dramatic change in the Cold War under Reagan and Gorbachev, led to a change in India's bilateral relations. While the intensification of Indo-US disagreement over Pakistan was predictable at the outset, the changing character of the two nations' ties proved both surprising and enduring.

The victory of Indira Gandhi in the Indian general elections of mid-January 1980 did not portend well for Washington's relationship with New Delhi. The upswing in ties under Morarji Desai was not expected to continue under his successor. "Mrs. Gandhi is winning in India," Carter noted in his diary. "I'll try to be friends with her, but I think she's inclined toward the Soviets."[49] American diplomats in the region were equally skeptical, underlining the gulf between "US global and Indian regional preoccupations and the impediments posed by [the two countries'] differing historical experiences."[50] The weary realism of officials in the State Department reflected the accuracy of this analysis. "US-India relations," wrote Assistant Secretary of State Harold Saunders to Warren Christopher, "do not prosper in a Cold War environment when the natural inclination of the Indian leadership to tilt toward the Soviet Union more is offensive to us and injurious to our interests." This situation was "compounded by Mrs. Gandhi's return to power with her long held suspicions of US policies and motives." Quoting the great British climber Leigh Mallory, who famously said he wanted to scale Everest because it was there, Saunders added, "We want satisfactory relations with India because 'it is there': 650 million strong with considerable military power, relative stability under democratic institutions, and a substantial industrial and resource base... remarkably resilient to radical movements or encroachment by any big power—ourselves, the Chinese or the Soviets."[51]

Indira Gandhi's concern stemmed from the possibility of the United States offering massive military aid to Pakistan, including F-16s. In April 1981, she sent two senior and trusted advisors to dissuade the Reagan administration from providing such advanced systems to Pakistan, which she claimed would upset the strategic balance in the subcontinent. The Americans maintained that "a strengthened Pakistan, in close relationship with the USA, poses no threat to India, and indeed should contribute to the overall stability of the subcontinent." When they formally announced the F-16s deal in June 1981, the Indian government responded with a familiar blast of complaint and criticism that American policy was spurring an arms race in South Asia. Washington responded coldly, "Our aid to Pakistan is not aimed at India. The USA is not fuelling an arms race."[52] This set the tone for periodic wrangling for the remainder of the decade.

Conventional weapons aside, the Indians also worried about the United States' willingness to overlook Pakistan's patent attempts to ac-quire a nuclear device. Thus when Congressman Stephen Solarz visited India in May 1986, he asked Prime Minister Rajiv Gandhi if a congres-sional stipulation, forbidding Pakistan from using the arms provided it against India, would assuage New Delhi's concerns. The prime minister observed that most arms provided to Pakistan were, in fact, deployed close to its borders with India. In any case, if Washington wanted to help Pakistan deter Soviet or Afghan aggression, "why provide Paki-stan with Harpoon missiles which is mounted on naval vessels? Why provide Pakistan with the latest advanced tanks which cannot be used in mountainous terrain on the Afghan-Pak border?" Turning to nu-clear weapons, Gandhi added that "he had it from 'some high source in the United States' that Pakistan had made significant progress towards making their own nuclear weapons and that the [US government] has not been able to prevent this despite all the assurances which Pakistan has given."[53] The Indians further resented the United States' seeking to push them to engage in a nuclear dialog with Pakistan—apparently along the lines of that between the superpowers—while taking scant notice of an elaborate proposal by India for moving toward global dis-armament. Spurned by the nuclear powers, Prime Minister Gandhi gave the go-ahead to his scientists to move ahead with the weaponiza-tion of Indian nuclear capability.

The Americans, for their part, frowned on India's stance on Af-ghanistan. When the Soviets invaded in 1979, New Delhi housed an unstable, short-lived government. Prime Minister Chaudhary Cha-ran Singh told the Soviet ambassador that the military intervention was unacceptable to India, especially since it targeted a neighbor and a nonaligned country. Urging Moscow to pull out of Afghanistan as soon as possible, he also stated that India would espouse this stance in the United Nations. The Indian government issued a statement regretting the Soviet intervention and seeking the withdrawal of Soviet troops.

Indira Gandhi changed this policy soon after she took over. While she too deemed the Soviet intervention in India's neighborhood highly undesirable, she refrained from publicly voicing her disapproval and privately tried to persuade Moscow to make a planned exit and Kabul to wean itself of Soviet military support. In June 1980, Indian foreign minister Narasimha Rao met his Soviet counterpart, Andrei Gromyko and urged Moscow to pull out and leave in place a multilateral security arrangement that would ensure Kabul maintained its traditional policy of neutrality. The unfolding US policy of providing covert assistance to Islamist groups via Pakistan and concern about growing Pakistani and Islamist influence in the Afghan countryside shaped Indira Gandhi's stance.[54] India's decision to abstain from a UN General Assembly resolution condemning the invasion of Afghanistan drew much opprobrium from its friends in the Third World. But the prime minister broadly stuck to her approach. When she traveled to Moscow in October 1982, Leonid Brezhnev told her, "I want to get out of Afghanistan. Madam, you know that region well! Show me a way to get out of Afghanistan." Mrs. Gandhi paused and replied, "Mr. general secretary, it is a good idea to withdraw your forces from Afghanistan. The way out is the same as the way in."[55]

When Rajiv Gandhi visited Washington in July 1985, he sought to assure Reagan that India shared American concerns about Afghanistan. "He made it plain to me," Reagan noted, "that while he wants to maintain friendly relations with the Soviet U., at the same time however he says India does not want Soviet U. to have a foothold anywhere in S. Asia."[56] Reagan and Shultz asked him to persuade the Soviets to agree to an early withdrawal from Afghanistan. Soon after, Gandhi sent the Indian foreign secretary to Moscow, but there was no appreciable shift in the Indian position.

During Rajiv Gandhi's second visit to the United States in October 1987, the Americans yet again pressed him to work on the Russians. The Indian government authorized contacts with some mujahideen groups in Pakistan, as well as with the erstwhile king and the Najibullah government, to find a way of overcoming the diplomatic impasse. In February 1988, Rajiv Gandhi told the Americans that the "bottom line" for India was to avoid Afghanistan's becoming a fundamentalist state. "Iran is already fundamentalist. If Afghanistan should go the same way, then the pressure on Pakistan to follow suit would be great and then we would have fundamentalism on our border." At the same time, he added, "we also don't want the Soviets on our border."[57]

Rajiv Gandhi emphasized this point with the Soviets as well—albeit in a different key. As he told Gorbachev, "If Afghanistan becomes a fundamentalist country or if the Americans have a strong influence there, like in Pakistan, Afghanistan will not be a truly independent country, and this will create problems for us." His efforts to persuade Gorbachev to insist that a complete halt to external meddling accompany a Soviet withdrawal went nowhere. Gorbachev told Najibullah, "The Indians are concerned that a normalization of the situation in Afghanistan will result in Pakistan directing its subversive activities against India....But this position takes only India's interest into account 100 percent while the interests of Afghanistan and the Soviet Union are a mere 20 percent."[58]

When Najibullah came to New Delhi in April 1988, the Americans worried that India would undermine the Geneva Accords. Ronen Sen of the Prime Minister's Office assured Ambassador John Gunther Dean that "India had no special affection for Najibullah or the PDPA." New Delhi's concern was Pakistan's desire to project Gulbuddin Hekmatyar as the leader of the Islamist front in Peshawar. Hekmatyar, Sen noted, was "a fundamentalist...a zealot who would ruthlessly impose his brand of fundamentalist Islam on Afghanistan should he gain power." India had been "less concerned when Rabbani led the alliance, considering him to be more educated and thoughtful." Unfortunately, as a Tajik, Rabbani did not have a tribal base among the Pashtuns. The American claims that "Hekmatyar's brand of fundamentalism was significantly different from that of the radical regime in Iran" cut no ice with India. In conferring with Najibullah, New Delhi was only interested in exploring alternatives to extremists like Hekmatyar, "such as a coalition of technocrats and moderates of different backgrounds." Instead of cutting India out of the peace settlement in Afghanistan, Sen added, Pakistan should confer with India. "India and Pakistan were both unavoidably part of the Afghan equation."[59] In a subsequent meeting with the American ambassador, Rajiv Gandhi reiterated that India could "live with any kind of a government in Kabul which is not run by extreme Islamic fundamentalists."[60] However, Pakistan and the United States were determined to accord no say to New Delhi in the endgame in Afghanistan. And the Indian effort fell through the trapdoor of history.

Notwithstanding these grave differences, there were green shoots in the bilateral relationship between the United States and India. Just over a year into the Reagan presidency, Indira Gandhi decided to accept an invitation to visit Washington. The two leaders met in October 1981 at a summit on global economic issues held in Cancun, Mexico. Their two countries were formally on opposite sides of the divide. The United States pushed for greater private-sector participation and higher reliance on international financial markets for developing countries, while the Third World called for concessions on debt and better trade terms from the developed countries. In fact, India's position on these issues was subtly shifting away from the Third World consensus of the previous decade due to internal as well as external considerations.

In the wake of the economic crunch triggered by the global oil crisis of 1973, Indian officials had grown skeptical of adhering to Third World positions at the cost of India's own economic interests. As a policy-planning document noted, "It is not clear what, if anything, we have gained from going along with the consensus in the non-aligned and developing countries forum."[61] A second spike in oil prices following the

Iranian Revolution in 1979 accentuated these concerns. During Indira Gandhi's final term in office, India geared its economic diplomacy toward securing its interests and bridging the divide between the First and Third Worlds on economic issues. Thus, at the Cancun Summit, Mrs. Gandhi observed, "We are not wedded to certain phrases....We are more interested in the results and substance....We are not suppliants, nor are we confrontationists. It is our experience that the interests of the developed and developing countries are so intertwined that we can all survive in harmony only in conditions of true interdependence."[62]

This change in India's position also reflected the evolving economic policies at home. On returning to power, Indira Gandhi confounded her critics by adopting a pro-business attitude entirely at odds with her policies of the early 1970s.[63] From 1980 onward, her economic policy focused on raising the profitability of industrial and commercial establishments by easing restrictions on capacity expansion, removing price controls, and reducing corporate taxes. The public-sector enterprises, too, were urged to shed their flab and get competitive. Another important development during this period was the liberalization of electronics imports, particularly of computers. This provided the basis for the subsequent expansion of the telecommunications and software industries in India.[64] At the same time, Mrs. Gandhi had no desire for full-scale liberalization and sought to manage external economic pressures to allow a gradual relaxing of the state's grip on the Indian economy.

The conjunction between internal and external imperatives was evident in India's approaching the International Monetary Fund (IMF) for assistance in November 1980. The combination of a severe drought, a sharp surge in oil prices, and the overall weakness of the global economy had led to a drastic slide in the balance of payments and a spike in inflation. The Indian government realized that the solution lay in overhauling and dramatically improving the efficiency of the public investment program. As part of its sixth five-year plan (1981–1986), New Delhi would undertake a major macroeconomic adjustment program supported by a $5.8 billion loan from the IMF under its Extended

Fund Facility, on top of World Bank funds to the tune of $2 billion a year.

The Indian government also preemptively signaled to the IMF that it was willing to take tough measures to mobilize domestic resources and cut back on expenditures. In the budget of 1981, Indira Gandhi's government increased indirect taxes sharply and later allowed a steep increase in administered prices of domestic crude oil, kerosene, electricity, and fertilizer. Although the opposition criticized these measures as anti-poor and as caving to international pressure, Mrs. Gandhi passed them off as voluntarily government efforts to stave off a massive recession.[65]

Although some IMF officials were pleased with India's readiness to adopt a stabilization and liberalization package, the Indian loan request was controversial. The United States, in particular, was not convinced that India needed to tap the IMF. Rather, Washington believed that India should borrow from financial markets to cover its needs. The US Treasury secretary and the IMF's American executive director criticized the proposal. It seemed as though the United States would vote against the loan and probably carry some of its allies along. In the event, Mrs. Gandhi and Ronald Reagan met on the sidelines in Cancun and got on well. At the Indian prime minister's request, the United States softened its position and abstained from voting on the loan at the IMF meeting a few weeks later. Critics of India in the US Congress attacked the abstention, claiming that New Delhi should have been forced to cancel a $3 billion purchase of Mirage fighters from France. Called to testify on the Hill, the IMF's American executive director insisted that military spending was a sovereign decision out of IMF purview.[66] The American vote in the IMF suggested a thaw in the United States' relationship with India, importantly enabled by New Delhi's changing economic policies and orientation toward the international economy.

In keeping with the improved mood music, Indira Gandhi agreed to seek a compromise solution on a more nettlesome issue: fuel for the Tarapur reactor. Under American law, the United States could not continue to supply fuel to Tarapur beyond 1982. Since March 1981, the two sides had conducted three rounds of talks. Although the Indians found the Reagan administration less focused on nonproliferation, the negotiations failed to make much headway. Even as Indian officials prepared for a showdown with the Americans, Mrs. Gandhi changed tack. Instead of breaking with the United States yet again on nuclear matters, she sought to use the Tarapur imbroglio to improve ties with Washington. Ruling out unilateral action, she informed a parliamentary committee that the government would take a decision based on "the national interest and overall bilateral relations with the U.S." Over the following months, the two sides hammered out a solution with which both could live. India agreed to extend safeguards—not in perpetuity but until 1993, when the original supply contract would have expired. Further, they settled on France as the alternate supplier for Tarapur.[67]

Indira Gandhi unveiled her new priorities vis-à-vis the United States during her visit to Washington in July 1982. As during her first prime ministerial trip in 1967, she struck a friendly note and impressed her interlocutors with her willingness to do business. More importantly, the prime minister and President Reagan launched an initiative for scientific and technological cooperation—a partnership on which India was keen to build. This nexus between India's internal transformation and its ties with the United States deepened under her successor and son, Rajiv Gandhi.

In one of his earliest speeches in office, Rajiv Gandhi declared his intention to "build for an India of the twenty-first century." At the core of his notion of modernization was the need to embrace high technology, particularly information technology, to transform India's economy and society. Access to cutting-edge technology was contingent on cultivating ties with the United States: the other superpower had little to offer India in the domain of high technology. It also called for increased trade with the outside world: "Exports must become a major focus of Indian industry. A rapidly growing modernizing economy will need a growing volume of imports and an expanding flow of technology. We can only pay for the inflow if we can pay more than what we are doing now."[68]

A month after Rajiv Gandhi's assumption of office, New Delhi and Washington concluded a memorandum of understanding (MOU) on technology transfer. The MOU was formally signed in May 1985 ahead of Gandhi's first visit to the United States. The young Indian prime minister made a considerable impression in Washington. "The general tone and atmospherics," senior officials noted, "was exceptionally good." Geopolitical issues apart, Gandhi made clear that his priorities were acquiring technology and opening up commerce. The prime minister told the Americans that he would move swiftly to address their concerns on "no nuclear end use"—an essential assurance for the administration to implement export license procedures in accordance with the technology-transfer MOU. "You do not have to worry," Gandhi told Commerce Secretary Malcolm Baldrige, "we will have a tight clamp on that." In turn, Baldrige told Gandhi that India's requests for export licenses would be processed "expeditiously" and that India would be treated "similar to a free world country." Gandhi and Baldrige also discussed US commercial bids to secure contracts in India, including those by Control Data and Harris for computers, General Electric for gas turbines, and Boeing for aircraft. The Indian prime minister also met with Defense Secretary Caspar Weinberger. They agreed that "development of an arms sales relationship would be a step-by-step confidence building process."[69] In his speech at the banquet hosted by Reagan, Rajiv Gandhi underlined his view of America's importance to his country: "India today is poised for greater growth.... [W]e must necessarily acquire the most advanced knowledge wherever it is generated."[70]

Over the following months, India pressed hard for outcomes in these domains. But the Indians had not reckoned on the Washington bureaucracy. Almost a year on, State Department officials complained, "Indian expectations about the Memorandum of Understanding are unrealistic." While they had provided "some important items," there were still "long delays on both commerce and munitions cases." Nevertheless, they realized that "Rajiv continue[d] to view high technology as crucial to the relationship" and that progress on this front was essential to maintaining the momentum generated by his visit. The "most important" pending request for technology transfer, one to which "Rajiv personally attache[d] great importance," was the Cray XMP-24 supercomputer.[71]

India sought this cutting-edge computer for enhanced tracking of global weather patterns to aid its agriculture. But the Cray XMP-24 could also assist with development of nuclear weapons and ballistic missiles, cryptography, and conventional military applications. In the protracted debate within the administration, the Departments of State and Commerce came out in support of this technology transfer, while the Departments of Defense and Energy and the National Security Agency were opposed. "An unstated, but nonetheless real, factor," recalled an American official, "was the preference among some Defense Department officials for Pakistan and a related reluctance to expand security relations with India."[72]

In March 1987, the Reagan administration finally arrived at a compromise solution. Instead of the Cray XMP-24, the United States offered the Cray XMP-14, which, the Americans told the Indian government, was sufficient for the "meteorological calculations which India [sought] to perform." The Indian junior minister for external affairs quipped that India-US relations were like the titles of two Dickens novels: *Great Expectations* and *Hard Times*. The Americans, however, bluntly informed the Indian foreign minister that India was "in a position now to take a giant step into the technological big leagues by obtaining a supercomputer. India should consider whether it wants to enjoy these benefits now or wait, perhaps for some years."[73] India went for the XMP-14.

Military technology too was on the Indian wish list. Even before Rajiv Gandhi's visit in 1985, the two sides had begun exploring possible technical cooperation in the development of India's own next-generation fighter aircraft: the Light Combat Aircraft (LCA). In late 1985, the Indians lit upon the GE 404 engine—used in the F-18—to power the LCA. The Reagan administration was open to the idea in principle. Yet Washington moved so slowly on the technical approvals that Ambassador Dean despaired of US-India relations: "Once again hopes were aroused here only to succumb to the usual disappointments.... To the Indians it will appear that no matter how sincere our intentions when face to face, we cannot deliver in a timely fashion."[74]

At the same time, Washington was not shy of using its newfound relationship with India to push American commercial interests. In July 1984, Boeing had received a letter of intent from Indian Airlines on the purchase of the company's 757 aircraft for the Indian fleet. The following year, India reopened the contract and accepted bids from Europe's Airbus as well. Following hectic lobbying by Boeing, Vice President George H. W. Bush wrote directly to Prime Minister Rajiv Gandhi, "The United States Government attaches great importance to this opportunity for Boeing." The Indian government, he hoped, would give "serious consideration to this latest proposal from Boeing and...evaluate it with the same attention as was afforded Airbus Industrie."[75]

In a bid to step on the gas pedal, Rajiv Gandhi visited Washington yet again in October 1987. Ahead of his trip, State Department officials patronizingly observed, "While Rajiv Gandhi has not fulfilled the promise both we and the Indian people saw in him two years ago, he apparently still favors economic liberalization and improved relations with the U.S." The Reagan administration sought to use this visit to announce a "substantial expansion" of two-way trade, including with the establishment of a bilateral trade-promotion group chaired by the private sector with government representation.[76]

American officials noted, "The President and the Prime Minister demonstrated excellent rapport on bilateral relations." In New York, Rajiv Gandhi had breakfast with senior American businessmen at a meeting sponsored by the Indo-US Joint Business Council. Unlike his grandfather, he did not find this gathering of American capital around a table repellent. The CEOs told Gandhi about both "their interest in doing business in India and their frustration at licensing, bidding and other difficulties they encounter despite a liberalized economy." He listened intently while they "specifically mentioned intellectual property (patent) protection, arbitrary export requirements and other problems for U.S. investors." In meetings with American officials, Gandhi agreed that both sides should ask their private sectors for recommendations to improve trade and investment. He also pledged Indian cooperation in the ongoing Uruguay Round of the General Agreement on Tariffs and Trade and promised to "stand firm against pressures for increased protection."[77]

In mid-1988, Rajiv Gandhi looked back with a measure of satisfaction on India's relations with the United States. "We have come a very long way," he told Ambassador Dean, "in a very short period of time." The two sides were able to talk to each other not just on technology cooperation but in all areas. "There is no more schism between us," he added. The two countries had "learned to avoid confrontation and we can certainly continue to make a lot more progress."[78] The internal deliberations of the Indian government echoed these thoughts. An assessment of US-India relations prepared by the Indian foreign office in early 1989 noted that bilateral trade had risen from $1.5 billion in 1977 to $5.5 billion in 1988. Since signing the technology-transfer MOU, India had imported high technology worth $1 billion from the United States. To be sure, "US foreign and strategic objectives have often militated against India's security concerns in South Asia." Still, "Indian and American perceptions of some international issues and political traditions provide for a mutually beneficial relationship."[79]

Nevertheless, Washington's Pakistan policy continued to cast a baleful shadow on its ties with India. In December 1987, India found itself tagged with Pakistan in a curious and unprecedented manner. In response to increasing reports of Islamabad's covert pursuit of the bomb, Senator John Glenn and others tried to block the administration's six-year $4 billion package for Pakistan. In response, a Senate appropriations subcommittee placed on hold all aid to India until aid to Pakistan was restored. Ronen Sen told Dean that the "linkage" between India and aid to Pakistan would have a "deleterious effect." The prime minister, he said, was hopeful that "humpty dumpty [could] be put together again." Sen bluntly pointed out that this move had given a handle to the opposition to attack the prime minister for his bold attempt at reorienting the relationship with the United States.[80] Rajiv Gandhi was indeed on the back foot at home. Mired in allegations of corruption over a defense deal, his government looked increasingly inward. Days after the fall of the Berlin Wall in November 1989, Rajiv Gandhi lost the general elections.

9

IN THE UNIPOLAR WORLD

T HE CRUMBLING, STARTING IN 1989, of Communist regimes in central and eastern Europe marked the beginning of the end of the Cold War. Two years later the Soviet Union had disappeared from the map. The United States now stood as the sole superpower on the world stage, with no competitors in sight. Charles Krauthammer aptly declared it the "unipolar moment." The American victory was not just political and strategic but also ideological and economic. In the summer of 1989, Francis Fukuyama wrote a famous essay claiming "an unabashed victory of economic and political liberalism." Fukuyama argued, "What we may be witnessing is not just the end of the Cold War, or the passing of a particular period of post-war history, but the end of history as such: that is, the end point of mankind's ideological evolution and universalization of Western liberal democracy as the final form of human government."[1] Indeed, a wave of democratization, the opening up of hitherto controlled economies, and a massive surge in globalization accompanied the end of the Cold War.

The Defense Policy Guidelines (DPG) drafted under President George H. W. Bush sounded the keynote of American strategy after the end of the Cold War. "Our strategy," a leaked draft of the document noted, "must now refocus on precluding the emergence of any potential global competitor." Hence, there would be neither major retrenchment of American forces nor any winding down of its alliance systems. What is more, "because we no longer face either a global threat or a hostile non-democratic power dominating a region critical to our interests, we have the opportunity to meet threats at lower levels." Hence the United States should seek to pacify regional rivalries, check the emergence of regional hegemons, and prevent the spread of nuclear and missile technology. Managing regional instability in ways that promoted "the spread of democratic forms of government and free and open economic systems" formed yet another overarching objective.[2]

The Bill Clinton administration adhered to every tenet of primacy identified in the DPG and added some more. In a major speech in September 1993, National Security Advisor Anthony Lake observed that a defining "feature of this era is that we are its dominant power." Not only did Washington possess unmatched economic and military power, but "America's core concepts—democracy and market economics—[were] more broadly accepted than ever." In these circumstances, "the successor to a doctrine of containment must be a strategy of enlargement— enlargement of the world's free community of market democracy." The United States should promote markets and globalization, employ military and political power to isolate aggressive regimes, prevent the spread of nuclear weapons, advance human rights, and address humanitarian crises.[3]

What implications did the US post–Cold War strategy have for South Asia? The DPG sought to prioritize regional and nonproliferation goals. As the document asserted, "We will seek to prevent further development of a nuclear arms race on the Indian subcontinent." Toward this end the United States would work toward getting "India and Pakistan to adhere to the Nuclear Non-Proliferation Treaty and to place their nuclear energy facilities under International Atomic Energy Agency safeguards." Further, the United States "should discourage Indian hegemonic aspirations over the other states in South Asia and on the Indian Ocean." As far as Pakistan went, "a constructive U.S.-Pakistan military relationship will be an important element in our strategy to promote stable conditions in Southwest Asia and Central Asia. We should therefore endeavor to rebuild our relationship given acceptable resolution of our nuclear concerns."[4]

This suggested that the United States would be on a collision course with both India and Pakistan. Indeed, during the first decade after the Cold War, US strategy directly targeted their nuclear programs. The end of the Cold War also posed major conundrums for Pakistani and Indian foreign policies. Islamabad had always worried that US aid would cease once the war in Afghanistan was won. With the collapse of the Soviet Union, Pakistan's value to the United States was not clear. The collapse of the Soviet Union also came as a shock to India, though under Rajiv Gandhi Indian policy had started to move closer to that of the United States. By early 1992, Prime Minister Narasimha Rao had fashioned a "new look" policy, which acknowledged that developing good relations with the United States was the highest priority. Without giving up on India's fundamental interests, such as its strategic capabilities, New Delhi sought to expand economic and technological relations and defense cooperation to the extent possible.[5]

Another momentous development complemented political acknowledgment of American unipolarity and enabled an eventual transformation in US-India relations. This was Rao's decision to embark on major economic reforms in July 1991. The dismantling of the so-called License-Permit-Quota Raj and the subsequent embrace of globalization once again made India a potentially attractive partner for the United States. The advent of the unipolar moment allowed American policymakers to realize the vision of a global capitalist order under US leadership—a vision interrupted by the Cold War and the pursuit of autonomous economic development by countries like India. New Delhi's turn toward the United States and the global economic order underpinned by American hegemony, therefore, had a graceful symmetry.

These changes did not occur in a trice, however. Indeed, even as the Cold War wound down, the challenge for US policy in the region came from the most familiar corner: Kashmir.

THE CONJUNCTION OF LONG-STANDING subcontinental problems with the global events of 1989 set off the Kashmir crisis of 1990.[6] Since the India-Pakistan War of 1971, Kashmir had receded into the background. Although that conflict did not concern Kashmir, India ensured that the Shimla Agreement of 1972 placed the onus of resolving the dispute over that territory on the two neighbors and effectively ruled out any role for external actors. Over the following years, New Delhi also attempted to tighten its political grip on Kashmir by co-opting the stalwart Kashmiri leader Sheikh Abdullah. Things did not work out as planned. In power, the sheikh proved a doughty defender of Kashmir's autonomy and resisted New Delhi's attempts to undermine it. After his death in September 1982, his son Farooq Abdullah took over as chief minister. Farooq lurched between confrontation and cooperation with New Delhi, resulting first in his dismissal from office and then an alliance with the ruling Indian National Congress for the Kashmir elections of 1987.

Meanwhile, Pakistan was biding its time. As early as 1980, Mohammed Zia ul-Haq had joined forces with the Jamaat-i-Islami to recruit young Kashmiris from India for a covert war. The American-supported Afghan jihad provided the organizational model, the financial resources, and the political cover for a future campaign in Kashmir. The dismissal of Farooq Abdullah gave a fillip to these efforts by galvanizing the small Islamist groups in the Kashmir Valley. These outfits also took their ideological cue from the Islamist revolts in Iran and Afghanistan. The Islamic Students League, for instance, designed a flag depicting a globe, topped by a Kalashnikov rifle with a flag on its bayonet carrying a verse from the Koran and the phrase "Muslims of the world, unite."[7]

Ahead of the state elections in March 1987, a dozen Islamist parties that had hitherto lacked electoral clout banded together to form the avowedly pro-Pakistan Muslim United Front, which appeared to strike a chord with young Kashmiri Muslims in the valley but did poorly at the polls. The coalition led by Abdullah won a sweeping victory amid allegations of widespread rigging. As political unrest began to bubble up in the valley, the Inter-Services Intelligence (ISI) reached out to the Jammu and Kashmir Liberation Front (JKLF), a nationalist outfit that had long sought to wage an armed struggle for Kashmir's independence but had slipped into hibernation in exile. Although the JKLF lacked the Jamaat's Islamist credentials, the ISI saw it as more capable of recruiting youngsters for an insurgency against India. In early 1988, the first lot of Kashmiris from India trained under the ISI's supervision.

By the summer of 1988, the JKLF had kicked off a campaign of bombing and terror in the valley. Its insurgency unfolded against the wider backdrop of the collapse of communism in eastern Europe and the onset of the First Palestinian Intifada. The group's highest-profile success was the December 1989 kidnapping of the daughter of Indian home minister Mufti Mohammed Sayeed. As Sayeed was a Kashmiri politician, Prime Minister Vishwanath Pratap Singh had intended his appointment to this senior cabinet position as an olive branch to his people. Instead, the kidnapping and subsequent release of the mufti's daughter touched off a huge wave of popular protest against India and accelerated the insurgency by drawing many more recruits. The ISI responded by massively scaling up its involvement in the insurgency.

In early 1990, New Delhi accused Pakistan of arming and training Kashmiri militants to wage a covert war against India. Islamabad shot back that it was merely providing diplomatic and moral support for "freedom fighters" in Kashmir. The Pakistan army also undertook a large-scale military exercise close to the border with India. Very like India's Exercise Brasstacks, Zarb-i-Momin aimed at once to test Pakistan's conventional military capabilities and to warn India against flexing its muscles in response to the escalating insurgency in Kashmir. Pakistani Prime Minister Benazir Bhutto had been in power for just about a year and had limited say on strategic matters. After conferring with the army chief and the president of Pakistan, Bhutto sent a senior diplomat, Sahabzada Yaqub Khan, to convey a tough message to India. In his meetings with the Indian foreign minister and prime minister, Yaqub spoke bluntly of Pakistan's stance on Kashmir and elliptically about "clouds roaring with thunder" and "lightning in the skies."[8]

The Indians were unsure if this was a veiled nuclear threat, but they took it seriously. Prime Minister Singh made clear that "India would have to review its peaceful nuclear policy if Pakistan employed its nuclear power for military purposes." Indian intelligence suggested that Pakistan was planning a surprise attack in northern Punjab to sever the lines of communications on the Indian side and a declaration of independence by Kashmiri insurgents that would provide a pretext for the Pakistan army to attack the valley. In consequence, some Indian army formations were mobilized. On March 13, 1990, Bhutto added fat to the fire when she traveled to Pakistani Kashmir and vowed a "thousand-year war" in support of the insurgents. While she may have been angling to shore up her domestic standing, the Indians took her statement gravely. Prime Minister Singh responded in Parliament, "I warn them that those who talk about 1,000 years of war should examine whether they will last 1,000 hours of war." Warning the Pakistanis that "such a misadventure would not be without cost," he exhorted Indians to be "psychologically prepared for war."[9]

This slide toward conflict in the subcontinent alarmed the George H. W. Bush administration. Already in January 1990, it had sent a senior State Department official to India and Pakistan to confer on the situation in Kashmir. The ensuing military moves and political warn-ings led the Central Intelligence Agency (CIA) to worry about the prospect of war and the shadow of nuclear weapons. In early April, Islamabad complained to Washington that Indian forces had moved into offensive positions. Although the American ambassadors in both countries confirmed that this was not true, the State Department pub-licly warned, "There is a growing risk of miscalculation which could lead events to spin dangerously out of control." Since the CIA remained concerned about the potential for nuclear weapon use in the event of war, the Bush administration decided in mid-May to send Deputy Na-tional Security Advisor Robert Gates to South Asia.[10]

Arriving in Islamabad on May 20, Gates met with the Pakistani president and army chief—Bhutto was out of the country. Gates warned the Pakistanis that a war would not remain confined to Kash-mir. The Americans had war-gamed every scenario and were sure that Pakistan would end up losing. What is more, in the event of war, Islam-abad could expect no support or assistance from Washington. Gates urged Pakistan to refrain from supporting terrorism in Kashmir, tone down its rhetoric, and work toward confidence-building measures with India. The United States would help such a process by techni-cally verifying that both sides had pulled back their troops. In New Delhi, Gates relayed a similar message, telling the Indians to back away from the brink and adding that the Pakistanis would shut the terrorist training camps. Although the Pakistanis had held out no such specific assurances, Gates believed they would fall in line with the American warning. The Indians, however, refused to initiate talks until Pakistan turned off its support for the insurgents.[11]

Nevertheless, in the wake of the Gates mission, both coun-tries took unilateral steps to defuse the crisis. India withdrew its ar-mored formations to their peacetime locations and proposed several confidence-building measures. Pakistan too agreed to retract its forces and commence an expansive dialog through the two sides' foreign sec-retaries. Throughout the crisis, the Bush administration refrained from taking any position on Kashmir and maintained that the two sides must discuss the matter bilaterally. This appeared to fit snugly with India's position on this thorny issue. Subsequently, however, American officials indicated to their Indian counterparts that they might be willing to facilitate a solution by acting as a conduit for an exchange of suggestions by the two countries. They also indicated that while they might not favor a plebiscite, Kashmir remained disputed territory and Pakistan's claims could not be altogether ignored.[12]

Both the Bush and the Clinton administrations also took India to task for its violations of human rights in Kashmir. The State Department's annual reports on human rights discussed a range of abuses by Indian security forces: torture of prisoners, mass shootings of demonstrators, large-scale detentions without trial, rapes, and extrajudicial killings. The 1991 report stated that Kashmir barely had a functioning legal system and that no terrorist detainees had yet been tried for their crimes. The 1993 report went further in observing that the legal protection provided to Indian security forces in Kashmir created a climate of impunity: "There is no evidence that any member of the security forces has been punished for an incident of custodial death or custodial torture in Jammu & Kashmir." Although India had its fair share of critics in the US Congress, the Bush and Clinton administrations refrained from administering anything more than a rap on the knuckles.[13]

The fallout of the 1990 crisis was altogether more serious for Pakistan, for it focused the Bush administration's attention on Pakistan's nuclear program. In the wake of the Gates mission, US intelligence agencies unanimously told the president that Pakistan had a bomb. After shuffling his feet for a while, Bush gave in and refused to certify Islamabad's nonnuclear status to the Congress. His national security advisor recalled that the president was "genuinely sad" about cutting Pakistan off.[14] But with Soviet troops out of Afghanistan, there was little strategic rationale for continuing to reward its recalcitrance.

Washington's decision came as a thunderclap to Islamabad. The country was already in political turmoil owing to the president's dismissal of Bhutto on charges of corruption. Now the American economic and military aid of $564 million for 1991 was frozen. At the time, Pakistan was the third-largest beneficiary of American aid after Israel and Egypt. The cessation of almost $300 million in arms and equipment every year particularly stung the Pakistani military. All technology transfer stopped in its tracks, including the seventy-one F-16s for which Pakistan had paid $658 million. The economic impact was less immediate as Pakistan already had $1 billion worth of aid in the pipeline, which would continue to flow. And Islamabad hoped that the embargo on aid would lift before long.

The new Pakistani prime minister, Nawaz Sharif, also went public with the Pakistani nuclear program. In a well-publicized tour of the Kahuta complex, he told an assembled group of scientists, "We salute the dedication of Dr. A. Q. Khan (a national hero) and all his team members for giving a sense of pride to our nation." Pakistan's foreign secretary told the *Washington Post* that the country had the components to assemble "at least one device."[15] By flaunting their nuclear capability, the Pakistanis evidently hoped to convince Washington to drop the sticks and return to carrots.

Pakistan similarly brazened out the Bush administration's efforts to tackle it on support for terrorism. In May 1992, Secretary of State James Baker wrote directly to Sharif, "We have information indicating that ISI and others intend to continue to provide material support to groups that have engaged in terrorism." While he appreciated the earlier promises that Pakistan would "take steps to distance itself from terrorist activities against India," US law obliged the administration to impose "an onerous package of sanctions" on states sponsoring terrorism. The administration called on Pakistan to eschew its support for terrorism. Delivering the missive, the American ambassador added that the ISI and the army were "supporting Kashmiri and Sikh militants who carry out acts of terrorism....We're talking about direct, covert Government of Pakistan support." In subsequent internal discussions, the ISI director-general argued, "We have been covering our tracks so far and will cover them even better in the future. These are empty threats." He insisted that the CIA needed the ISI. Sharif stressed the importance of talking nicely to the Americans while "doing whatever you have to do." The key requirement was to step up contacts with the American media and Congress to deal with allegations of terrorism.[16]

President Bush's surprise defeat in the elections later that year gave Islamabad a reprieve. The first months of the Clinton administration coincided with a furious tussle in Pakistan between the president and the prime minister—a contest that ended with the army forcing Sharif to step down and the return to power of Bhutto. The Clinton administration's policy was "maintaining support for Pakistan as a quasi-democratic, relatively pro-Western Islamic state."[17] While Washington continued to look askance at Pakistan's support for the Kashmir insurgency, it chose not to bring matters to a head. This enabled Pakistan both to deepen its support for the insurgency and to edge out relatively secular, nationalist groups like the JKLF and replace them with staunchly Islamist outfits floated by the ISI, like the Hizbul Mujahideen and the Lashkar-e-Taiba.

Early Clinton administration statements on Kashmir irked the Indian government. In testimony before the House Subcommittee on Asian and Pacific Affairs, John Malott of the State Department's newly created Bureau of South Asia Affairs said that the United States was "neither accepting nor rejecting a plebiscite." Although he added that Kashmir was "a zero sum situation" and that "the most valuable role we can sometimes play is to remain silent," New Delhi thought he was hinting at a change in policy under the new administration. Robin Raphel, assistant secretary of state for South Asia, compounded Indian concerns by saying that the United States regarded "the whole of Kashmir as disputed territory, the status of which needs to be resolved." She went on to add, "We do not recognize the instrument of accession as meaning that Kashmir is forever an integral part of India." While the substance of her remarks marked no departure from the previous American stance, her comments about the instrument of accession revived Indian anxieties about US partiality for Pakistan on Kashmir. Washington's insouciance about New Delhi's concerns allowed this issue to fester. Eventually, during Benazir Bhutto's visit in April 1995, President Clinton declared in a joint press conference, "A mediator can only mediate if those who are being mediated want it."[18]

CLINTON'S SOUTH ASIA POLICY went substantially further than that of his predecessor in one area: nonproliferation. The administration's oft-stated objective was to "cap, rollback and eliminate" the Indian and Pakistani nuclear weapons programs. In August 1993, senior officials told the visiting Indian foreign secretary that they would like India to cap its nuclear technology and testing programs, cut its production of fissile material, and place its nuclear facilities under comprehensive safeguards and monitoring arrangements. They also wanted India to pull back from its missile development and testing programs. While they realized that India would not sign the Non-Proliferation Treaty (NPT), they expected her not to stand in the way of its indefinite and unmodified extension.[19] But New Delhi was not inclined to fall in line with any of these requirements, which ran counter to India's own aspirations for a seat at the high table of global politics.

By the spring of 1994, Washington sought to convince Islamabad to announce a freeze in the production of fissile material and to open up the Kahuta facility to international inspections. As a reward for good behavior, the United States would offer a "Pressler relief"—a limited waiver of the sanctions that would allow Pakistan to receive the F-16s that were gathering dust at a US Air Force base in Arizona. In discussions with the Americans, Prime Minister Bhutto observed that international inspections were too heavy a price. The army chief dismissed the suggestion that the F-16s were a concession: "We will *choke* on your carrots!"[20]

Over the next year and a half, New Delhi veered toward conducting a nuclear test. A confluence of events heightened its concerns and shaped Indian policy: the indefinite extension of the NPT in May 1995, nuclear tests by China and France soon after the NPT conference, revelation of China's provision of M-11 missiles to Pakistan, and the passage of the Brown Amendment allowing for release of Islamabad's F-16s. There were domestic considerations besides. The Indian military-scientific and strategic communities pressed the government to allow a test before international negotiations for the Comprehensive Nuclear-Test-Ban Treaty (CTBT) acquired momentum. In the fall of 1995, Prime Minister Rao approved preparations for a test.

On December 15, 1995, the *New York Times* carried a front-page story that US satellites had detected heightened activity at the Pokhran test site, indicating that India might be preparing to test a nuclear device. The American ambassador, Frank Wisner, called on Rao's principal secretary and showed him a satellite image. He warned that a test would boomerang on India, leading to the imposition of a full dose of sanctions. When Clinton called Rao and reinforced the message, the prime minister only said that India would not act irresponsibly.[21] Rao pulled out of the tests all the same.

The entire episode, especially the news stories, dented the Indian government's domestic standing. More importantly, it touched off a debate on whether and under what circumstances India should consider joining the CTBT. Clinton's decision to sign the CTBT in September 1996 fanned these intense public discussions in India. In his second term in office, Clinton made the CTBT a priority for his efforts in South Asia. By mid-1997, the administration had embarked on an effort to convince India to sign the treaty, hoping Pakistan would follow suit. The weak and unstable coalition government in New Delhi during this period went along with an American request for a nuclear dialog without committing to any proposal.

In March 1998, an alliance led by the Hindu nationalist Bharatiya Janata Party (BJP) came to power. Prime Minister Atal Behari Vajpayee was arguably India's most seasoned politician. As foreign minister in the Morarji Desai government, Vajpayee had dealt with the Jimmy

Carter administration on India's nuclear program and had advocated rapprochement with the United States. His party too had well-defined views on nuclear policy and had pledged in its election manifesto to conduct tests. In office, Vajpayee moved quietly but decisively to assert India's status as a nuclear power.

The Indian nuclear tests of May 11 and 13, 1998, took Washington by surprise. Although the BJP's stance on nuclear matters was well known, the Clinton administration had believed that the Vajpayee government would not actually go down that route. A CIA assessment prepared in April 1998 argued, "Several constraints will temper its ability to act on its rhetoric.... The BJP faces pressure in international forums—such as the United Nations and the Conference on Disarmament—to make Indian policy conform to international conventions on proliferation issues." New Delhi also hoped to bid for permanent membership on the UN Security Council. BJP leaders had "in private conversations with US officials...stress[ed] 'continuity' on issues of importance to the West."[22] Indeed, even the Indian defense minister, George Fernandes, had assured visiting American officials that the government would not test. To be fair, Fernandes himself had not been in the loop. Furthermore, learning from the aborted attempt of 1995 the Indian agencies resorted to elaborate secrecy and deception to evade American eyes in the skies. However, the underlying problem was that CIA analysts expected Indian politicians to behave as American politicians did. "We did not sufficiently accept," conceded the CIA's director, "that Indian politicians might do what they had openly promised."[23]

Clinton was irate. "We're going to come down on those guys like a ton of bricks," he told his aides.[24] His administration trained a full battery of sanctions on India, halting defense sales and export licenses for munitions, denying government credit as well as loans from American banks, stopping loan guarantees and credits for American exports to India, and withdrawing US support for loans and assistance from international financial institutions, including the World Bank and the International Monetary Fund. Washington also coordinated with many governments and international bodies to issue statements condemning the Indian tests.

The administration mounted an equally urgent effort to dissuade Islamabad from following suit. When Pakistan conducted five nuclear tests on May 27, the Clinton administration slapped sanctions on Islamabad as well. Speaking at a press conference on June 3, Clinton called both sets of tests "self-defeating, wasteful and dangerous." The president, however, came down harder on India, accusing the BJP government of betraying Gandhi's ideals of nonviolence. As Clinton recalled, he was "deeply concerned" about the Indian test, "not only because I considered it so dangerous, but also because it set back my policy of improving Indo-U.S. relations and made it harder for me to secure Senate ratification of the Comprehensive Test Ban Treaty."[25]

IMMEDIATELY AFTER THE INDIAN tests, Vajpayee wrote to Clinton emphasizing the security challenges India faced from two of its neighbors: China, "an overt nuclear weapons state on our borders, a state which committed armed aggression against India in 1961," and Pakistan, "a covert nuclear weapons state" that had thrice attacked India and continued to sponsor terrorism in Kashmir. Much to New Delhi's consternation, the administration promptly leaked the letter to the American press. Worse, when Clinton visited Beijing days later, the United States and China issued a joint statement, decrying the Indian and Pakistani tests as "a source of deep and lasting concern," promising "close coordination" to prevent an arms race in South Asia, and expressing their willingness to help India and Pakistan "resolve peacefully the difficult and long-standing differences between them, including the issue of Kashmir."[26]

The joint statement was apt to rekindle New Delhi's concerns about US-China collusion against India—concerns that went all the way back to 1971. Nevertheless, the Vajpayee government persisted in its efforts to mend fences with Washington. Immediate as well as long-term concerns drove Indian policy. At the strategic level, Vajpayee wanted to bring about a fundamental change in India's relations with the United States. In the unipolar context, India as a large democracy and growing economy was well placed to forge close ties with the United States and so accelerate its own economic growth and pursue its international ambitions. The latter included securing international acceptance of its status as a nuclear weapons power. A more immediate concern was getting Washington to relax the sanctions on India. The American sanctions had come at a time when the 1997 Asian financial crisis was already buffeting the Indian economy, and their continuation could inflict significant pain.

Ironically, this conjuncture highlighted India's tightening embrace of globalization as well as the United States' interest in her emergence as a liberal and open market economy. From this stemmed Clinton's avowed desire to improve ties with New Delhi. Indeed, he saw India as a poster child for the age of globalization. As Deputy Secretary of State Strobe Talbott recalled, the president would "often cite India—with its resilient democracy, its vibrant high-tech sector, its liberal reforms that had begun to revitalize a statist and sclerotic economy, and its huge consumer market—as a natural beneficiary of globalization and therefore potentially a much more important partner for the United States."[27]

Early on, the Clinton administration conveyed to Indian officials that New Delhi should remain committed to economic liberalization and privatization. The United States was interested in the Indian market as well as in opportunities to invest in India.[28] India featured prominently in the administration's "Big Emerging Markets" initiative. In January 1995, Commerce Secretary Ron Brown led a "presidential business development mission" to India. As the CEO of General Electric put it, "India was desperate for liquidity and needed technology. If two-way trade could be improved, we all stood to benefit." In 1997, the United States and India signed an agreement that removed tariffs and barriers to trade in all services relating to information technology.

Indian industry was initially keen to maintain tariffs on computer hardware in order to nurture that sector's growth. But the Clinton administration convinced New Delhi that India should play to its strengths in software development and related services.[29]

Meanwhile, American investment banks had already entered Indian capital markets. In January 1994, Morgan Stanley became the first US-based bank to launch a fifteen-year equity mutual fund in India. The fund aimed to raise 3 billion rupees but ended up raising 10 billion. Soon American and other foreign institutional investors began warming up to Indian equity markets. Foreign direct investment from the United States was slower in the coming. The Clinton administration energetically pushed Enron's $3 billion investment in a gas-fired power plant in Dabhol in western India. The project eventually became mired in disputes over cost escalation and sank owing to the corruption scandal that enveloped Enron.

Despite growing bilateral economic ties and India's accession to the World Trade Organization in 1995, Washington and New Delhi sparred over economic issues. Back in 1989, the Bush administration had placed India on the "Super 301" watch list—a reference to paragraph 301 of the Omnibus Trade Competitiveness Act of 1998, which required the president to take retaliatory steps against countries that restricted US commerce. Washington had cited three specific complaints against India: its foreign investment policy, which restricted foreign equity participation to 40 percent; the nationalization of its insurance market and denial of access to American companies; and its policy on intellectual property rights, which limited patents to five years and hurt American pharmaceutical companies' business prospects in India.

New Delhi initially refused to talk to the Americans about these issues. In late 1992, India changed tack and told US Trade Representative Carla Hill that "the very process of economic reforms and liberalization in India could get stymied if the US assumed a confrontationist, all-or-nothing posture *vis-à-vis* India."[30] Subsequent Indian reforms assuaged American concerns on the first two issues, though intellectual property rights remained a continuing point of friction. Against this backdrop, New Delhi wanted to ensure that the sanctions imposed after the nuclear tests did not corrode the economic ties so carefully built up over the past few years.

On May 27, 1998, Vajpayee formally stated in the Indian parliament, "India is now a nuclear-weapon state. This is a reality that cannot be denied." The prime minister reiterated that India would observe "a voluntary moratorium and refrain from conducting underground nuclear test explosions." The government, he added, had "also indicated willingness to move towards a *de jure* formalisation of this declaration."[31] In other words, now that India had demonstrated nuclear weapons capability, it was open to joining the CTBT. Two weeks later, Vajpayee's trusted advisor and later foreign minister, Jaswant Singh, met Talbott in Washington. India, he said, was ready to "find a modus vivendi with the U.S. and with the global nuclear order." It was prepared to participate in a number of arms control agreements, so long as they did not require India either to renounce what it had done or what might be imperative for its security in the future. India was already de facto adhering to the CTBT. In exchange for the removal of sanctions, Jaswant Singh said, India might take the next step: "de jure formalization of our position and acceptance of the letter of the treaty."[32]

The Clinton administration was willing to lift sanctions if India met a series of conditions. First, it had to sign the CTBT. Second, it must freeze the production of fissile material and cooperate in negotiating a permanent ban on production. Third, it had to embrace a "strategic restraint regime." This would limit the types of ballistic missiles that India possessed to the two it already had. Further, India would agree not to deploy these missiles close to the border with Pakistan and to neither mount warheads on the missiles nor store them nearby. Fourth, India must adopt stringent, "world-class" controls on exports of strategic materials and technology. Finally, India must resume dialog with Pakistan "to address the root causes of tension between them, including Kashmir." The Americans thought these proposals reasonable inasmuch as they did not require India to forsake its nuclear weapons and sign the NPT. But the Indians bristled at the notion that they had to meet "benchmarks" laid down by the United States.[33]

Strobe Talbott and Jaswant Singh negotiated on these issues in several rounds over many months. While the Vajpayee government hoped to use this dialog as a strategic opening to the United States, it refused to sign anything on the dotted line, including the CTBT. By constantly invoking the domestic pressures facing Vajpayee's minority government, the Indians tactfully deflected American demands. Ultimately, the US Senate's refusal in October 1999 to ratify the CTBT would put paid to the Clinton administration's efforts. In the meantime, a major crisis flared up in the subcontinent.

Since the onset of the insurgency in the late 1980s, the Line of Control (LoC) between India and Pakistan in Kashmir had turned into a war zone. The Pakistan army's attempts to help terrorists cross the LoC under covering fire came up against the Indian army's determination to thwart the infiltration. The exchange of small arms and artillery fire was routine. Both sides deployed hundreds of thousands of troops along and athwart the LoC in Kashmir. In the wake of the nuclear tests, the LoC turned more active than ever. At the same time, the prime ministers of India and Pakistan began attempting a rapprochement. Vajpayee traveled to Lahore by bus in early 1999 for a meeting with Sharif. This bold move led to the Lahore Declaration in which both sides committed to nuclear confidence-building measures as well as dialog on all outstanding disputes, including Kashmir. The bonhomie generated by the summit proved short-lived, however.

In the 1998–1999 winter, Pakistani forces crept across the northern portion of the LoC and occupied Indian army positions in the Kargil area. Hitherto, both sides had vacated high-altitude posts in winter to avoid unnecessary casualties owing to weather and returned to them in spring. By preemptively occupying these posts, the Pakistan army sought to gain a commanding position overlooking the key Indian lines of communication in northern Kashmir and to credibly threaten

Indian control of them. A secondary objective was to give a boost to the insurgency in Kashmir and set the stage for international intervention on the Kashmir dispute. The new Pakistan army chief, General Pervez Musharraf, conceived the operation. It was (and remains) unclear to what extent Nawaz Sharif knew about and approved these plans.

Despite some intelligence suggesting large-scale Pakistani infiltration into Kashmir, the Indian government had not taken much notice. In the wake of the Lahore summit, New Delhi believed that relations with Pakistan were on the mend. The Pakistani action thus caught the Indians by surprise in both military and political terms. New Delhi initially underestimated the scale of the Pakistani action, but soon it began reinforcing the Kargil area with additional troops and undertaking systematic, if costly, operations to expel the Pakistanis. From the outset, Prime Minister Vajpayee was clear that the operations, including the use of air power, should be restricted to the Indian side of the LoC. Nevertheless, Indian army formations were also mobilized to the international border with Pakistan.

The Pakistanis hotly denied any involvement of their forces in Kargil, claiming that Kashmiri insurgents had undertaken the infiltration. But with increasing evidence of Pakistani involvement, they found few takers for their version. The Pakistanis shot down a couple of Indian air force helicopters close to the LoC and pushed their own troops close to the borders. By May 1998, a conventional, if geographically limited, war was underway in South Asia. And the situation brimmed with the risk of further escalation.

Washington watched the conflict with mounting alarm. The Clinton administration feared that India would strike across the LoC. Such a move could have incalculable consequences, including the involvement of third countries: China and the Arab states on Pakistan's side; Russia and Israel on India's. It could also lead to an all-out war with the danger of a nuclear exchange. "The nuclear scenario," noted Bruce Riedel of the National Security Council, "was obviously very much on our minds."[34] Having been caught out by the Indian nuclear tests, the administration—including the president—had worried about the prospect of a nuclear war in the subcontinent. To head off this possibility, Washington swung into action in May 1998.

American officials began meeting regularly with the Pakistani and Indian ambassadors. Secretary of State Madeleine Albright called Nawaz Sharif and Jaswant Singh, while General Antony Zinni, commander in chief of CENTCOM, spoke with Musharraf. In these private conversations, the Americans stuck to the same line: Pakistan had provoked the crisis and must withdraw its forces behind the LoC. To the Indians, they also urged restraint so as not to widen the conflict. The Talbott-Singh channel also came in handy during the crisis. The Indians were at once surprised and relieved that the United States was not tilting toward Pakistan.

When the private messages to the Pakistanis failed to make an impact, the administration went public with the information that Pakistani soldiers were involved in the operation and called on Islamabad to respect the LoC. In late June 1999 Clinton spoke to Sharif and Vajpayee and sent them letters as well. He also sent Zinni to warn Sharif and Musharraf that India would cross the LoC if Pakistan did not reel in its troops. The Pakistanis professed to be unfazed. So Washington sought to raise the pressure another notch by holding up a $100 million loan that Islamabad urgently needed.

Yet, by the end of the month, the fighting had intensified. As casualties rose on both sides, the temptation to escalate seemed difficult to resist. American intelligence assessments suggested that full-scale war could become a real possibility. On July 2, however, Nawaz Sharif pleaded with Clinton to come up with a plan to stop the fighting and prepare the ground for an American-mediated settlement of the Kashmir dispute. Sharif expressed his readiness to travel to Washington to discuss such a settlement. Clinton told Sharif that he was welcome provided he understood two things. First, he had to agree to withdraw his troops back across the LoC. Second, Clinton would not agree to intervene in the Kashmir dispute, "especially under circumstances that appeared to reward Pakistan's wrongful incursion."[35] In another call with Sharif the following day, Clinton held to this line. Sharif did not accept these conditions: he merely said he was on his way. Nevertheless, Clinton called Vajpayee and apprised of him of the conversation.

On July 3, as Sharif flew to Washington, American intelligence found evidence that the Pakistanis were preparing their nuclear arsenal for possible deployment. Clinton's officials, Talbott recalled, had "a sense of vast and unprecedented peril." Memories of the Cuban Missile Crisis came flooding back.[36] Ahead of the meeting with Sharif, National Security Advisor Sandy Berger told the president that the objective was to induce a Pakistani withdrawal but also to help Sharif stay in power. The fact that the prime minister was coming to Washington with his family suggested that he was unsure of his position at home. Talbott added that Clinton must also bear in mind Indian sensitivities. The United States seemed poised to clear decades of mistrust in New Delhi about the American attitude toward Pakistan.

In their meeting on July 4, Clinton emphasized that a Pakistani withdrawal could not be linked to an American diplomatic intervention in Kashmir. Sharif insisted that Pakistan would withdraw its forces provided India committed to settling Kashmir within a specific time frame. "If I were the Indian prime minister," Clinton shot back, "I'd never do that." In any case, he was unwilling to go down this route. The president warned Sharif of the dangers of sleepwalking into a major war: "I genuinely believe you could get into a nuclear war by accident." In their one-on-one session, Clinton warned that the Pakistani moves to prepare nuclear-armed missiles for deployment could lead to catastrophe. Eventually, Clinton persuaded Sharif to issue a statement about restoring the status quo on the LoC. At Sharif's insistence, Clinton added a line saying that following restoration of the sanctity of the LoC, he would take a personal interest in encouraging a speedy resumption of the dialog agreed to in Lahore.[37]

By July 26, the last of the Pakistani intruders had pulled back behind the LoC.

Although sincere in his assurances to Sharif, Clinton was unable to deliver. In October 1999, General Musharraf deposed Sharif following a gauche attempt to forestall a coup. US-Pakistan relations sank to a new low. So frayed were their ties that the following year Palestinian leader Yasser Arafat offer to intercede on Musharraf's behalf with Clinton.[38]

By contrast, US relations with India broke through to previously untouched heights of trust and goodwill. Clinton was now raring to undertake his long-planned visit to the subcontinent. At the end of October 1999, he waived many of the sanctions against India while retaining them on Pakistan. The administration sought to demonstrate that it wished to deepen relations with democratic, though nuclear-armed, India while going slow with Pakistan's military dictator. American businesses, eager to partake of the Indian growth story, supported Clinton's move to reduce sanctions on India. Equally important was the political activism of the Indian American community. Their contributions had already led to a massive increase in the size of the bipartisan Indian caucus in the US Congress. This enabled them to ensure congressional backing for the differential approach that the Clinton administration sought to adopt toward India and Pakistan.[39]

The ideological underpinnings of the opening to India were evident when Clinton wrote to Vajpayee, "As leaders of the world's two largest democracies you and I have a special responsibility to demonstrate that democracy provides the best foundation not only for domestic prosperity and stability but for cooperation and harmony among democratic nations." Vajpayee enthusiastically responded that India and the United States were "natural allies."[40] In India, Clinton received a rapturous reception. Indian parliamentarians all but mobbed him after his address. Vajpayee rose to the occasion by quoting Walt Whitman's "Passage to India." Clinton and Vajpayee signed a "Vision for the 21st Century," affirming their desire to create a "closer and qualitatively new relationship" while minimizing the persistent differences over India's nuclear weapons.

Stopping in Islamabad for a few hours on his way home, Clinton wagged a disapproving finger in a televised address. Acknowledging Pakistan's role in the opening to China and the winning of the Afghan war, he said the United States and Pakistan were in a new, globalizing world. "The political situation, the economic situation, the tensions in this region"—all were "holding Pakistan back from achieving its full potential in the global economy." Advising Pakistan to give democracy and dialog with India a chance, he added, "We cannot and will not mediate or resolve the dispute in Kashmir." At the same time, he pointedly added, "no grievance, no cause, no system of beliefs can ever justify the deliberate killing of innocents." In fact, on the day Clinton landed in India, a group of militants from Hizbul Mujahideen and Lashkar-e-Taiba had massacred thirty-five Sikhs in a village in South Kashmir. But the president apparently worried about not just Kashmir but the globalization of terrorism emanating from Pakistan and Afghanistan.

SINCE THE LATE 1980s, Afghanistan had become the cauldron for a witches' brew of extremism and terrorism. In the aftermath of the Soviet withdrawal, the United States had no definite policy toward Kabul. The Bush administration hoped that Pakistan could manage the jockeying for power in post-Soviet Afghanistan. The Americans realized that the Islamists were likely to prevail in this struggle but hoped that past support would render the new regime reasonably well disposed toward the United States. Among the many mujahideen leaders, two emerged as the main contenders to supplant Mohammad Najibullah: Gulbuddin Hekmatyar, the Pashtun leader and favorite of the ISI; and Ahmad Shah Massoud, the Tajik leader who had maintained an arm's-length relationship with the Pakistanis and the Peshawar cliques.

With the Soviets out of the way, the ISI convinced the mujahideen to switch from guerilla tactics to conventional operations, and together they planned a major assault on the city of Jalalabad in eastern Afghanistan. But the Najibullah regime proved no pushover. A combination of

Pakistani overconfidence, mujahideen infighting, and overall lack of coherence and direction led to considerable losses for the attacking forces. Thereafter Moscow began supplying the besieged city, enabling the regime to hold its own. By late April 1989, the mujahideen offensive had ground to a halt. The ensuing bitter recriminations further fractured relations between the various Islamist groups.

Among the outfits battered in the abortive assault was the Arab contingent led by the Saudi Osama bin Laden. In the aftermath of Jalalabad, bin Laden shifted focus to the Middle East. Initially, he sought to work with the Saudis and even attempted to foment a jihad against the socialist government of South Yemen. However, the American presence in Saudi Arabia during the Gulf War led bin Laden to turn his gaze on the United States and its Saudi collaborators. After falling out with his compatriots, bin Laden decamped to Sudan, where an Islamist government was in power. By April 1996, he was back in Afghanistan.

Meanwhile, the Pakistanis struggled to corral their fractious Islamist allies in Afghanistan. The mujahideen would countenance no suggestion of working with other groups to form an interim government in Kabul. Patrons in Pakistan bolstered their intransigence. As the senior Pakistani diplomat dealing with the mujahideen ruefully recalled, "The army and the ISI were inclined to favor those who showed capacity to be ruthless rather than those wanting to be part of a future dispensation through maneuver and compromise."[41] Soon after the collapse of the Soviet Union, Najibullah presented himself to the Americans as a bulwark against radical Islamism and sought their support. The failure of this attempt convinced him to step down. But Massoud and Hekmatyar remained at loggerheads. Despite the ISI's support for the latter, Massoud upstaged his rival, and his forces took over Kabul in April 1992.

Over the next two years, the Islamist militias fought each other for the control of Kabul and other cities. Alliances congealed and dissolved, leaving thousands dead and wrecking Afghanistan's primitive infrastructure and struggling economy. As the civil war continued, the binding ties of Islam gave way to ethnic divisions. The Tajik-dominated government led by Burhanuddin Rabbani and Massoud held the areas around Kabul and the Panjshir Valley. In Herat and western Afghanistan, Ismail Khan held sway, while the Uzbek warlord Rashid Dostum and the Hazaras, respectively, controlled northern and central Afghanistan. A council of mujahideen commanders based in Peshawar held the three eastern Pashtun provinces bordering Pakistan. Hekmatyar's influence was confined to a small area south and east of Kabul. Unlike other parts of Afghanistan, the south, especially areas around Kandahar, did not fall under sway of any ethnic warlord. And from there rose the Taliban.

The inhabitants of the south were predominantly from the Durrani clan of the Pashtuns. Compared to the Ghilzai Pashtuns of eastern Afghanistan, the Durranis had received much less money and materiel from the ISI during the war against the Soviets. Although the term "Taliban," meaning "Islamic students," came into currency only around 1994, they were active in and around Kandahar in the later stages of the Afghan jihad. Most of them had studied in the madrasas of Pakistan before returning to take up arms against the Russians. From the outset, these Pashtun youngsters in southern Afghanistan saw themselves as devout and disciplined in contrast with the apathetic and rapacious mujahideen. The local populace and militias turned to the courts run by these men to settle their disputes under Islamic law. Many of the Taliban returned to their villages after the Soviets departed, but the anarchical situation in Kandahar and its environs brought them back into the fray. The Taliban once again began running courts and prisons, adjudicating disputes over property, and enforcing a local system of tariffs. Starting out with a consultative leadership structure, the Taliban over time came to be dominated by the reclusive Mullah Mohammed Omar.[42]

By 1994, the Pakistani government was deeply uneasy about the situation in Afghanistan. The Pakistanis held that they had a right to control Afghanistan as well as an interest in doing so. In their view, their efforts during the anti-Soviet jihad had entitled them to a "friendly government" in Kabul, under which Afghanistan would provide "strategic depth" to Pakistan in its rivalry with India. Islamabad invoked these euphemisms to rationalize its quest for dominance in Afghanistan, but Pakistan's reach seemed to exceed its grasp. During Benazir Bhutto's second term as prime minister, economic considerations overlaid this strategic calculus. Following the collapse of the Soviet Union, Islamabad wished to promote trade and commercial ties with the Central Asian republics. The shortest route ran from Peshawar to Kabul and thence north to Uzbekistan. But the incessant fighting around Kabul rendered using this route impossible. The alternative was to clear a route from Quetta to Kandahar and Herat and on to Turkmenistan.

With Bhutto's approval, her Pashtun interior minister, Naseerullah Babar, tapped the Taliban to provide security for convoys along this route. In October 1994, the Taliban demonstrated their value by making short work of a garrison in Spin Baldak controlled by Hekmatyar's forces. Buoyed by Pakistani arms and advisors, they swiftly moved on Kandahar. Pakistan rejoiced at the victory, with Babar proudly confiding to journalists that the Taliban were "our boys."[43] The fall of Kandahar to a group of relatively unknown fighters, however, shook the Afghan warlords as well as the country's neighbors.

Assisted by Pakistan, the Taliban juggernaut remorselessly rolled on. Within three months of the fall of Kandahar, they controlled twelve of the country's thirty-one provinces and stood at the outskirts of Herat and Kabul. In early September 1995, the predominantly Shiite province of Herat fell to the Taliban, forcing Ismail Khan to flee. The Taliban's siege of Kabul over the next ten months led to a curious concatenation of forces, including the return to Kabul of Hekmatyar in order to protect the Rabbani government. In the fall of 1996, the Taliban and their advisors changed their strategy. They followed a surprise offensive on Jalalabad on August 25 with lightning strikes on the provinces to the east of Kabul. On the evening of November 26, 1996, the Taliban entered Kabul as Massoud's forces withdrew to the Panjshir

Valley. In a display of ruthless brutality, they captured Najibullah from the UN compound, castrated and shot him, and strung his body up in a prominent Kabul square. Now only northern Afghanistan remained out of their control. There a loose coalition of warlords, including Massoud and Dostum, known as the Northern Alliance, had the support of Iran, Russia, and India—all of which wished to keep the Taliban at bay. In turn, Pakistan and Saudi Arabia stepped up their support to the Taliban.

The Taliban's brand of Islamic fundamentalism differed from that of the Afghan Islamists. The latter, inspired by the ideas of the Muslim Brotherhood in Egypt and the Jamaat-i-Islami in Pakistan, sought to adopt a Leninist model of party organization in order to create an internationalist Islamic state capable of coping with the challenges of modernity. Thus, while they sought to establish a modern version of a pure Islamic society, the Islamists were relatively open to ideas about an Islamic economy and social justice, as well as women's education and participation in the community.[44]

The Taliban, however, claimed allegiance to the Deoband tradition. A branch of Sunni Hanafi Islam, it began in British India as a revivalist yet also forward-looking movement that emphasized learning and spiritual experience and espoused a limited role for women and intolerance of Shiites. The ulema of the Deoband seminary were prominent in public debates over the position and role of Muslims in colonial India, and their ideas had touched Afghanistan by the late nineteenth century.[45] But the Deoband tradition did not acquire prominence among Afghans until the 1980s, when children of Afghan refugees began to attend the madrasas run by the Jamiat-Ulema-i-Islam (JUI) of Pakistan. Although the JUI had been around since the creation of Pakistan, it had never matched the prominence of its rival, the Jamaat-i-Islami. That changed with the advent of the Taliban. No sooner had the Taliban taken Kabul than they imposed the strictest form of Islamic rule, banning women from schools and work and forcing them to wear top-to-toe veils; forbidding television, sport, music, and dance; meting out to offenders the crudest forms of punishment; and grimly threatening the Shiites and other minorities.

The Clinton administration kept a weather eye on the rise of the Taliban. In December 1994, intelligence sources told the Americans that the ISI was "deeply involved in the Taleban [sic] take over in Kandahar and Qalat." After the fall of Herat, Pakistan denied playing a major role in the Taliban offensive. The Pakistani foreign secretary told US Assistant Secretary Robin Raphel, "Pakistan has significant contact with and gave some support to the Taliban," but claimed the latter needed little assistance as they enjoyed "widespread material support throughout the Pashtun areas of Afghanistan."[46]

In this early period, Washington politically supported the Taliban, regarding it as an anti-Shiite, anti-Iran, and pro-Western outfit. Secretary of State Warren Christopher noted that Islamabad had been "supporting the Taliban and attempting to forge a military and political alliance among the Kabul regime's opponents." Yet, he maintained, "Pakistan has been no more interventionist than other players"—Iran, Russia, and India. Indeed, "we share Pakistan's goal of a stable legitimate central government not beholden to foreign powers." The administration worried only that Pakistan might not be able to deliver on this objective.[47]

Strategic considerations apart, the United States was also eager to tap into Central Asia's massive hydrocarbon resources. The Union Oil Company of California was heavily lobbying Washington to work with the Taliban to stabilize Afghanistan and so ensure the flow of Central Asian oil through a pipeline in Afghanistan and Pakistan into the Indian Ocean. Visiting Kabul, Kandahar, and Mazar-i-Sharif in April 1996, Raphel stated, "I am here to urge the Afghans themselves to get together and talk. We are also concerned that economic opportunities here will be missed, if political stability cannot be restored."[48]

However, the Taliban's utter disregard for human rights, especially its crackdown on women, complicated the Clinton administration's efforts to work with them. Washington initially maintained a studied silence on the Taliban's actions in Herat and other places. But after the capture of Kabul, the administration found itself under intense pressure from feminist groups in the United States. Ahead of the presidential election in November 1996, Bill Clinton wanted to ensure the women's vote—especially in light of the Monica Lewinsky scandal. So when the Taliban first reached out to the United States, the administration took a careful stance. The Taliban representative said that "they [thought] highly of the U.S., appreciate[d] U.S. help during the jihad against the Soviets, and want[ed] good relations with U.S." Before "publicly opening" relations with the United States, they wanted to establish diplomatic ties with Islamic countries such as Saudi Arabia and the United Arab Emirates—not least to avoid giving the impression that they were "an anti-Shia tool of the U.S." The American official replied, "The U.S. wants to be in touch with Taliban and work with them." He urged the Taliban to reach out to "all Afghan religious and ethnic groups," including Dostum and Massoud, to build a durable peace. He added that the United States was "deeply concerned" about the Taliban's view on such issues as "due process and respect of basic human rights, especially relating to women." The Taliban's assurance on these issues was essential to ensure the flow of international aid for the reconstruction of Afghanistan.[49]

Of greater concern to Washington were reports of bin Laden's return to Afghanistan in 1996. In the wake of the bombing of the Khobar Towers in Saudi Arabia, the Americans began to fix their sights on bin Laden. Mullah Omar had granted shelter to him on customary and religious grounds, while also taking Saudi advice to ensure that the guest cooled his heels. But bin Laden proved irrepressible. In August 1996, he published in a London-based Arabic newspaper his "Declaration of War Against the Americans Occupying the Land of the Two Holy Places."[50] In a meeting with a senior Taliban official, the American ambassador to Pakistan mentioned reports about bin Laden's presence near Jalalabad. The Taliban official blandly replied, "I assure you he is not in the areas controlled by the Taliban administration. This [keeping him out] is an objective of our movement."[51]

A few weeks later, when the Americans brought this up with Mullah Mohammed Rabbani, foreign minister of the Taliban regime, the latter admitted that bin Laden was living in the Jalalabad area "as a guest, a refugee...Like an Afghan refugee in the United States." When told that bin Laden was implicated in terrorist attacks on Saudi Arabia and known to be plotting against America and that his presence would tarnish the international image of the regime, Rabbani observed, "In this part of the world there is a law that when someone seeks refuge he should be granted asylum. But if there are people who carry out terrorist activities then you can point these out. We have our senses and will not permit anyone to carry out these filthy activities."[52]

By this time, American intelligence had also picked up the presence in eastern Afghanistan of a training camp for Harkat-ul-Ansar (HUA), "an Islamist extremist organization that Pakistan support[ed] in its proxy war against Indian forces in Kashmir." The HUA was on the CIA's radar owing to the kidnapping of American tourists in the Kashmir Valley. The Pakistanis claimed that Indian intelligence had orchestrated the kidnapping in order to discredit the insurgency in Kashmir. Raphel, however, dismissed these accusations as "not credible." The Americans subsequently interrogated a senior HUA militant captured by Indian forces and learned that the hostages had been put to death. Furthermore, HUA was reportedly reaching out to bin Laden for financial assistance.[53]

As the pieces started to fall into place, it seemed that the Pakistan-backed Kashmiri terrorists who were reaching out to bin Laden were also training in camps not far from his location in territory controlled by the Pakistan-supported Taliban regime. Not surprisingly, the Americans raised the HUA camps with the Taliban. Senior Taliban leaders blithely replied that they had not set up the camps: "They had been established during the [Afghan] jihad [and] Kashmiris had been trained there." Nevertheless, the Taliban was shutting down the camps.[54] Despite knowing this was not true, the Americans refrained from pressing the Taliban on this issue.

Washington's reluctance stemmed from a desire to find a modus vivendi with the Taliban that would also advance core American interests. Following three trips to Afghanistan, American officials in Pakistan reported in early 1997 that the Taliban had brought peace and stability to the areas under their control. Shops were full and the markets humming with activity. "In short," they argued, "life is not so bad and the people of Kandahar would be crazy not to prefer Taliban theocracy to factional warfare." To be sure, the Taliban did not care much for human, women's, or minority rights. Yet, the officials cabled to Raphel, "in the past few weeks Mullah Omar has tried to create a kinder, gentler Taliban occupation."[55]

In any case, the officials argued, "not to engage the Taliban would be a mistake." It would leave them "only more isolated, possibly more dangerous, and certainly more susceptible to those wishing to direct Taliban energies outside Afghanistan." All-out engagement was not an option either. Not only could it fail, but if it succeeded, it could leave the United States "closely associated with a regime we find repugnant." Washington should steer the middle course of "limited engagement to try and 'moderate and modernize' the Taliban." Apart from keeping up public criticism of the regime's actions, Washington should also lean on the new Pakistani prime minister, Nawaz Sharif. In particular, the United States should "make an all-out effort to press the Taliban to expel Bin Laden from their territory.... The 'carrot' for the Taliban would be some badly-needed international acceptance and good will."

The Taliban, however, refused to give up bin Laden. Nor did they take American advice to negotiate a settlement with Massoud and Dostum. In April 1998, President Clinton sent his UN ambassador, Bill Richardson, to confer with the Taliban regime in Kabul. Mullah

Rabbani insisted that the Taliban would soon control all of Afghanistan. As for bin Laden, Rabbani repeated that he was their guest and they would monitor his activity themselves.[56] On August 7, 1998, two trucks loaded with explosives rammed into the American embassies in Nairobi, Kenya, and Dar-es-Salaam, Tanzania. The Nairobi bombing killed 213, including 12 Americans, and left 4,500 wounded. The toll in Dar-es-Salaam was eleven dead and eighty-five injured—all Africans. The trail led back to bin Laden. On August 20, Clinton responded with cruise missile strikes on a training camp in eastern Afghanistan that bin Laden was expected to visit. He turned out to be elsewhere, but the strike ended up killing Kashmiri militants from Harkat ul Mujahideen (HUM)—as the HUA had called itself since the imposition of US sanctions on it in 1997—as well as their ISI trainers.

Mullah Omar lashed out at the United States, vowing, "We will never hand over Bin Laden to anyone and protect him with our blood at all cost." The Americans, for their part, sought to raise the diplomatic pressure on the Taliban regime by leaning on Saudi Arabia and Pakistan. While the Saudis were cooperative, noted Ambassador William Milam in Islamabad, "there is little evidence that GOP has done anything substantial" with regard to putting pressure on the Taliban." He suggested that Washington should convey to Islamabad that bin Laden's continued presence in Afghanistan could "complicate U.S-Pakistani relations." When Nawaz Sharif visited Washington in November 1998, Secretary of State Madeleine Albright impressed upon him the importance of getting bin Laden out of Afghanistan.[57] In his meeting with Clinton, Sharif said that the United States should follow up on the Richardson visit: "I urge you to have some direct contact with [the]Taliban."[58] After subsequent meetings in Islamabad, Milam concluded that Pakistan was "not disposed to be especially helpful" in getting bin Laden.[59]

The Clinton administration now began to toughen its approach toward Pakistan as well as Afghanistan. Meeting with Pakistani foreign minister Sartaj Aziz in early January 1999, Milam emphasized two points. First, Pakistan should reconsider its support for the Taliban. "Have four years of all-out support for the Taliban improved Pakistan's position?" he asked. Second—the "most critical point"—Pakistan should use its influence with the Taliban to get bin Laden extradited to a country where he could be brought to justice. Aziz listened intently but declined to say much. At the end of May 1999, Milam warned a Taliban representative of the consequences of sheltering bin Laden. The Taliban official claimed that in response to American pressure, they had removed bin Laden's communication gear. Miffed, he had moved out of the Taliban-controlled area. Indeed they had "no idea where Bin Ladin now was." The official added that bin Laden was "a bomb" to them. If they overtly expelled him, the Afghan people would rise up against the regime. Hence, they had sought quietly to convince him to leave.[60]

When Nawaz Sharif returned to Washington at the height of the Kargil crisis, Clinton lambasted him about Afghanistan. Pakistan was the main sponsor of the Taliban, which in turn allowed bin Laden to run a global terror network from its territory. Although the United States had repeatedly sought Sharif's aid in getting bin Laden, he had never helped; instead the ISI worked with the Taliban and bin Laden to foment terrorism. Clinton threatened to issue a statement mentioning Pakistan's role in supporting terrorism in Afghanistan as well as in India.[61]

Kashmiri terrorists' hijacking of Air India Flight 814 from Kathmandu dramatically highlighted this nexus of terrorism in South Asia. They took the plane to Kandahar, and the Indian government found itself compelled to negotiate with a shadowy group of terrorists, with the Taliban acting as intermediaries and the Pakistanis hovering in the background. In order to secure the release of the hostages, the Indian government had to hand over HUM leader Maulana Masood Azhar, who was imprisoned in India. The ISI immediately escorted

Azhar to Pakistan, where he raised funds to set up another outfit, the Jaish-e-Mohammed. These developments alarmed American officials. Bruce Riedel felt the hijacking was "an unmistakable wake up call": an act of terror "linked directly to the Taliban backed by al Qaeda, the Kashmiris, and the ISI."[62] Nine months on, bin Laden paid down his debt to Mullah Omar by orchestrating the assassination of Ahmad Shah Massoud on September 9. Two days later, he attacked America.

10

THE NEW CENTURY

THE TERRORIST ATTACKS OF September 11, 2001, were seen not only as a challenge to American primacy but also as a dramatic rupture in the course of world history since the end of the Cold War. The rise of global terrorism had apparently punctured complacent notions about the "end of history" in ideological terms and irenic notions about globalization. President George W. Bush's muscular and reckless response was also regarded as a sharp departure from the foreign policy of his predecessors.[1] With the benefit of hindsight, both sets of judgments seem dubious. Far from being disrupted, globalization surged in the immediate aftermath of 2001. The global movement of goods, services, and, above all, money reached altogether new heights. The global financial crisis of 2008 eventually derailed the juggernaut. The ensuing decade saw a noticeable reduction in globalization, especially in cross-border financial transactions. The prolonged economic slow-down and stagnation also led to a backlash against pro-globalization policies in the United States and western Europe, with consequences that are still playing out.

The emergence of Al Qaeda and other terrorist groups with a global reach hardly challenged American hegemony. The United States remained without any peer competitor. In the wake of the global finan-cial crisis, the United States experienced a relative decline in economic power in comparison with other large emerging economies, especially China. More importantly, from late 2010 China adopted an assertive foreign policy aimed partly at the United States' dominant position in maritime Asia.

The trajectory of US foreign policy after 9/11 did not change as sharply from the immediate past as then anticipated. To be sure, the United States attacked Afghanistan and Iraq and launched a seemingly interminable "global war on terror." But these wars also flowed from the logic of American hegemony in a unipolar context and cannot be simplistically attributed to predilections of the neoconservatives in the Bush administration.[2] Indeed, under President George W. Bush the grammar of American primacy remained the same—even if the accent had changed. In a 2002 speech at West Point, he asserted, "America has, and intends to keep, military strengths beyond challenge—thereby making the destabilizing arms races of other eras pointless, and lim-iting rivalries to trade and peace." The National Security Strategy of 2002 clearly set the ideological tone of his administration, noting that the Cold War "ended with decisive victory for the forces of freedom—and a single sustainable model for national success: freedom, democ-racy, and free enterprise." Unlike his predecessors, President Bush asserted America's right to act unilaterally. But this did not mark a vast departure from the past: US foreign policy had always had a strong unilateralist streak.[3]

The essential continuity in the longer arc of post–Cold War Amer-ican hegemony was evident under President Barack Obama. Obama took office intending to wind down the wars in Iraq and Afghanistan and promising a change from Bush's approach to the war on terror. But extricating the United States from these conflicts without damaging its global standing proved rather more challenging. What is more, the Obama administration's interventions in Libya and Syria aimed as much at regime change on questionable premises as anything attempted by his predecessor. Notwithstanding the obvious differences in personal style, Obama was no more hesitant than Bush to cast aside the niceties of international law in pursuing the war on terror.

Nor did his view of American primacy yield anything to his predecessors. The United States, he repeatedly stated, was the "indispensable nation," and its hegemony benefited the world as well as America. The challenge for Obama was to sustain American primacy against the backdrop of the global financial crisis and the weakening of the American economy. As one presidential aide wrote, "Obama believes American is an indispensable nation, but one that must be careful in its ambitions. His policies at home and abroad have been about renewing and sustaining American power.... The defining element of Obama's grand strategy is that it reflects the totality of American interests—foreign and domestic—to project global leadership in an era of seemingly infinite demands and finite resources."[4]

US grand strategy during the Bill Clinton presidency and the Bush and Obama presidencies differed most saliently in their approaches to China. The Clinton administration encouraged and facilitated the integration of China into the global economic order. This accorded with the overall strategy of promoting market economies. In the afterglow of the victory over the Soviet Union, the Clinton administration did not believe that China's economic growth would result in an increase in its military capabilities and an expansion of its strategic goals. The administration hoped instead that economic liberalization would lead to a gradual move toward liberal political norms. Further, it hoped that embedding China in the global order would "socialize" Beijing into a "responsible stakeholder" in the liberal international order led by

America. The Bush administration, by contrast, saw China as a potential challenger on the horizon and sought to head off such a possibility. Given the interdependence between the American and Chinese economies, limiting China's access to American and Western markets was no longer possible. Instead, the Bush administration sought to create countervailing partnerships with important countries in China's periphery by propelling their growth.[5] The Obama administration built on and extended this strategy for dealing with an emerging China.

During the Bush and Obama years, South Asian countries were prominent both in the war on terror and in the efforts to cope with China's rise: Pakistan and Afghanistan in the former and India in the latter. A region that some had regarded as peripheral thus became a key site for the exercise of American hegemony in the opening decades of the twenty-first century.

Soon after the Cold War ended, India's external orientation simultaneously underwent two major shifts that set the stage for a strategic redefinition of its ties with the United States. With the collapse of the Soviet Union, India's older framework of nonalignment was no longer useful. In acknowledging American primacy, New Delhi merely recognized the realities of the post–Cold War world. More significant was India's decision to liberalize its economy and embrace globalization. Yet its determination to pursue strategic autonomy—especially in the domain of nuclear weapons—had hobbled US-India relations, despite deepening political and economic ties.

However, the upswing in US-Indian ties over the next decade and a half did not stem just from the removal of this thorny issue. Nor did it owe to their commonly held concerns about the implications of China's rise for the balance of power in Asia. Rather, it occurred because a dramatic change in historically ingrained cultural perceptions crucially complemented a growing strategic and economic convergence. And globalization was a key vector of change in this dimension too.

In the first place, the extraordinary rise in immigration to the United States from India spurred this remarkable cultural shift. Starting from the mid-1990s, there was a noticeable spike in numbers, with an annual average of 65,000 new entrants from India during the 2001–2010 period. In the ensuing years, the annual numbers would exceed 120,000. The boom in information technology and the reorganization of global value chains facilitated this spurt in immigration. Both their educational and social attainments and the high-skilled visa regime (H1-B) under which they came to the United States ensured that Indian immigrants were far ahead of other immigrant communities in terms of family and per capita income. Their extraordinary successes as entrepreneurs in Silicon Valley and the quintessentially American motel industry recast the image of Indians as achievers in the American mold.[6] But this wave of Indian immigrants also benefited from America's own turn toward multiculturalism and diversity over the past decade.

Indians' designation as a "model minority" became something of a cliché invoked by American leaders across the political spectrum. Speaking at the 2002 convention of motel owners—almost all Indians—former vice president Al Gore said, "You are part of this economy, integral to the health of the US, accounting for $40 billion in commerce each year.... It won't be long before you are known as people and families who are deeply, passionately, knowledgeably involved in making our beloved United States of America what it should be." Two years later, Newt Gingrich told a similar convention, "You are what the American dream is all about.... You will make America a better country for us and our kids and grandkids."[7]

Equally swift was the change in Indian elites' cultural attitudes toward America. Education in America served as a cultural conveyor belt for Indian elites. At the turn of the century, the percentage of Indian business, scientific, bureaucratic, and political elites educated in the United States comfortably outstripped those who had studied elsewhere, including Britain, the favored destination until a couple decades earlier.[8]

Globalization also enabled the diffusion in India of American pop-ular and consumer culture to a hitherto unprecedented degree. For much of the twentieth century, American popular music, especially jazz and rock, had a cult following in India. With the advent of transna-tional satellite television in 1991, American pop found a massive new audience. MTV came to India in 1994 as MTV Asia and soon turned into MTV India. In terms of content, too, the channel switched to a creative mix of Western and Indian cinema music. The VJs typically spoke a mix of English and Hindi sprinkled liberally with American-isms.[9] As music went digital in the Internet age, young Indians kept up effortlessly with the latest trends on the American scene. Possessing Jimi Hendrix or Duke Ellington LPs was no longer a status symbol in certain enclaves of elite India as in earlier decades.

American consumer culture had failed to make inroads until the onset of liberalization and adoption of globalization in India. Although some iconic American brands like Coca-Cola had been around until the 1970s (when it was forced to leave), Indians had little appetite for American-style consumerism. For one thing, the Indian state closely regulated the production and import of consumer goods, which, in any case, only a tiny section of the population could access. For another, the Indian elite—especially the political and the bureaucratic—took pride in a culture of conspicuous nonconsumption. For a third, Indian companies competing with American brands often emphasized their ability to cater better to local tastes. Consider this advertisement for Sonex Jeans from the 1990s:

Questioner (Male): Your favourite game is Baseball or Cricket?
Respondent (Male): Cricket.
Questioner: How do you spell 'colour'?
Respondent: C-O-L-O-U-R.
Questioner: Not C-O-L-O-R?
Respondent: Of course not.
Questioner: Do you celebrate Halloween or Holi?

Respondent: Holi.

Questioner: Then, why do you wear jeans with an American label?

Announcer: Sonex Jeans, not made in America, thankfully.[10]

All this changed swiftly as India opened its doors to American multinational corporations along with their consultants and advertising agencies.

Take the case of McDonald's. Prior to opening its first outlets in India in 1996, the Chicago-based company undertook a careful four-year study of the market and its potential customers. Although McDonald's had adapted itself to local tastes in many countries, India presented a particularly difficult problem owing to the fact that many Indian Hindus would not eat beef, while Indian Muslims would not touch pork. The company began by serving lamb burgers. When this effort failed, McDonald's India quickly shifted to chicken and potato patties with the option of a jumbo-sized "Maharaja Mac." In a bow to the cultural sensibilities of the average customer, outlets also maintained an open, visible kitchen with clearly demarcated areas of vegetarian and non-vegetarian food preparation. The advertising strategy also emphasized that despite its glittering stores, McDonald's was an affordable option for most middle-class Indians. Indeed, the company premised its pricing strategy on high volume with low per-unit cost. All this enabled McDonald's to expand enormously in India—notwithstanding opposition from certain quarters.[11] KFC took the McDonald's example a step further by opting not to serve chicken in certain predominantly (and stridently) vegetarian cities, such as Ahmedabad in western India.

The adaptation of American brands to Indian sensibilities occurred in other domains of consumption too. Nike decided to target cricketers—an entirely new market for the company. Its Indian advertising agency, JW Thompson, came up with an enormously successful commercial for the 2007 Cricket World Cup. Unlike its competitors, which went for cricket celebrity endorsements of their brands, Nike's advertisement went for the everyday player of cricket in India. As traffic comes to a halt on a busy street, a raucous game of cricket breaks out—showcasing the atypical ways in which the game is played all across the country. The voiceover says, "Wherever, whenever, however, Indian cricketers 'Just Do It.'" The appeal to the cricketer in every potential customer worked exceedingly well for Nike, especially in the context of the Indian team's debacle in the world cup.[12]

In the first decade of the new century, the American "market empire" had finally arrived in the subcontinent. As elsewhere, its ability to shape consumer sensibilities in its own mold depended to a considerable extent on its dexterity in adapting to underlying local tastes and preferences. And, as elsewhere, consumer culture helped buttress American hegemony in this part of the world.[13] Awareness of this churning background of economic, technological, demographic, and cultural change is crucial in understanding the course of American policy in South Asia over the past two decades.

DURING GEORGE W. BUSH's first months in office, his team focused on neither Afghanistan nor Pakistan. Richard Clarke, White House counterterrorism specialist, urged National Security Advisor Condoleezza Rice to conduct an urgent review of Al Qaeda's activities. "We would make a major error," he wrote, "if we underestimated the challenge al Qida [sic] poses."[14] The Bush administration did review policy toward Islamabad in the summer of 2001, but it examined the risks of nuclear proliferation from Pakistan rather than terrorism.[15] The attacks of September 11, 2001, forced a dramatic shift in US policy toward Afghanistan and Pakistan.

Coincidentally, the head of the Pakistani Inter-Services Intelligence (ISI), Lieutenant General Mahmud Ahmed, was in Washington, DC, on the day of the attacks. President Pervez Musharraf had sent him a couple days earlier to persuade the Bush administration to engage with the Taliban. On September 12, the State Department summoned Mahmud for a meeting with Deputy Secretary of State Richard Armitage. "Pakistan faces a stark choice," said Armitage sternly. "Either it is with us or it is not; this was a black-and-white choice with no grey." The evidence pointed toward bin Laden, and Bush would go after the Taliban. Armitage added for good measure that Pakistan had "no maneuvering room."[16]

The following day, Ambassador Wendy Chamberlin conveyed to Musharraf a list of demands. These included logistical support; access to ports, airbases, and military facilities in Pakistan; intelligence sharing; use of Pakistani airspace; and interdiction of fuel and all supplies to the Taliban regime. After an hour of pressing, he agreed to these terms. Musharraf insisted, however, that India should play no part in the war on Afghanistan nor have any say in the government that replaced the Taliban. Further, while Pakistan would assist in capturing Al Qaeda operatives who came into the country, its own nationals—that is, terrorists operating against India—would be off-limits to the United States.[17] Having committed to the Americans, Musharraf then proceeded to sell the agreement to his corps commanders, arguing that he was extricating Pakistan from a "critical situation." But Musharraf also realized that becoming a frontline ally in another American war would have its own rewards. "We should offer up help," he told his close advisors with considerable prescience, "and mark my words, we will receive a clean bill of health."[18] Musharraf sent the ISI chief to persuade Mullah Omar to hand over bin Laden in the interest of saving his regime. The Taliban supreme commander was unyielding in his refusal.

As his administration began planning for the war, President Bush rejected any strategy based on a large American ground presence. Instead, he wanted the Afghans to take the lead in the ground campaign, supported by American intelligence, Special Forces, and air power.[19] The Bush administration saw the war in Afghanistan not just as an attempt to root out Al Qaeda and the Taliban but as a shot across the bow directed at other regimes that supported terrorists. As Defense Secretary Donald Rumsfeld grandiosely put it, "If the war does not significantly change the world's political map, the U.S. will not achieve its aim." Hence, American strategy would entail a swift entry into and exit from Afghanistan. The United States, Rumsfeld emphasized, "should not agonize over post-Taliban arrangements" and "should not commit to any post-Taliban military involvement."[20]

On October 7, 2001, the United States kicked off Operation Enduring Freedom. The initial strategy aimed to foster Pashtun resistance to the Taliban in southern Afghanistan in order to avoid depending on the Northern Alliance. But there were no credible candidates to lead a Pashtun uprising, especially after the Taliban murdered a former mujahideen commander, Abdul Haq, who had returned to southern Afghanistan. Others, like the Pashtun politician Hamid Karzai, were feeling their way through Pashtun lands without much success. After three weeks of futile bombing, the United States decided to switch its strategy and support the Northern Alliance, insisting that the latter declare their willingness to enter a political process that would reflect the interests of all ethnic groups in the country.

The new approach succeeded beyond expectations. On November 10, Mazar-i-Sharif, the Taliban stronghold in the north, fell. Aided by American Green Berets and greenbacks, the Northern Alliance galloped to Kabul. Mullah Omar pulled out of Kandahar on December 7 and made his way to the border with Pakistan. Bin Laden and as many as 2000 Al Qaeda fighters moved to the caves of Tora Bora. Although the United States embarked on an enormous bombing campaign, it was unable to persuade the Northern Alliance fighters to flush out Al Qaeda. By the time the complex of caves and tunnels was cleared on December 17, bin Laden was safely inside Pakistan.

The speed with which the Taliban's defenses crumbled surprised the Pakistanis. The ISI had told Musharraf that, owing to America's reluctance to commit its ground forces, the Taliban would hold on until the spring of 2002. So even as Musharraf burnished his credentials with the Americans by sacking three senior-most generals with known Islamist sympathies, he quietly authorized the continued supply of fuel and other essentials to southern Afghanistan via Baluchistan. ISI operatives and officers from Pakistan's Frontier Corps actively helped the Taliban plan its resistance in the south. Once the Americans decided to work with the Northern Alliance, the Pakistanis stepped up their covert assistance to the Taliban regime. Musharraf also wrote a long letter to Bush, stating that Pakistan would not accept a Northern Alliance government in Kabul and demanding adequate Pashtun representation in any future dispensation. When tens of thousands of Taliban fighters began crossing the border into Pakistan, ISI personnel and Frontier Corps guards guided them to camps in Baluchistan. And there Omar began rebuilding the Taliban.[21]

In the following months and years, Pakistan would continue its Janus-faced policy toward the American "war on terror." Musharraf and the ISI helped the Americans nab several key Al Qaeda operatives, including the mastermind of the 9/11 attacks, Khalid Sheikh Mohammed. These arrests and operations usually occurred before meetings with senior American officials. At the same time, Musharraf denied the presence of bin Laden on Pakistani soil and actively helped the Taliban leadership and rank and file regroup inside Pakistan. Attempts by some radical jihadi outfits to assassinate Musharraf ended up bolstering his standing with America.

At home, too, Musharraf proved adept at playing his opponents. When mainstream religious parties, including the Jamaat-i-Islami and the Jamiat-Ulema-i-Islam, protested the war in Afghanistan and Pakistan's alliance with America, Musharraf initially cracked down on them. Soon he moved to co-opt them by allowing the formation of the Muttahida Majlis-e-Amal (MMA, United Council of Action) ahead of the provincial elections of 2002. The MMA, dubbed the "Military-Mullah Alliance" by cynics, came to power in the two provinces adjoining Afghanistan.[22] The Taliban now enjoyed the patronage of the local governments as well as the Pakistani state.

Even as the war in Afghanistan was underway, Pakistan became embroiled in another major crisis with India. On December 13, 2001, five terrorists armed with assault rifles, grenades, and plastic explosives used a fake pass to enter the Indian parliament and attempted to storm the building. One attacker blew himself up at an entrance to the chamber; four others died in the ensuing firefight with security forces. The next day, Foreign Minister Jaswant Singh met with the Pakistani high commissioner in New Delhi, claiming that India had enough "technical evidence" of the involvement of the Islamic militant group Lashkar-e-Taiba (LeT) and presenting a set of demands to the Pakistani government. At a press conference that evening, he made these public. New Delhi wanted Islamabad to close the offices of the LeT and Jaish-e-Mohammed (JeM), a jihadi organization in Kashmir, to arrest their leaders, and to freeze their financial assets. When the Pakistanis refused to heed these demands, India mobilized its Indian army—including the strike corps—to the borders with Pakistan. The Pakistanis responded with a countermobilization.

In the immediate aftermath of the attack, the Bush administration decided on a strategy of engagement with Pakistan and India. The strategy called for back-to-back visits to the region by senior officials in order to draw down tensions and postpone decisions to launch hostilities. Secretary of State Colin Powell observed, "We had something like a roster for who would go down there." As Indian and Pakistani armed forces converged, the Americans grew increasingly worried. By December 25, 2001, the Central Intelligence Agency (CIA) had concluded that an invasion of Pakistani territory by Indian forces could escalate into a nuclear conflict. As concerns about Indian military action rose, President Bush called Musharraf and Indian Prime Minister Atal Behari Vajpayee and counseled patience and restraint.

The Americans also began to ratchet up pressure on the Pakistani government. Colin Powell spoke by telephone to Musharraf several times, urging him to blacklist certain terrorist groups operating in Kashmir. The Bush administration also placed the LeT and JeM on the State Department's list of designated foreign terrorist organizations, pointing the way forward for Pakistan. The United States discerned an opportunity to prod Pakistan in the desired direction when it learned that Musharraf intended to deliver a major speech in January 2002. Washington provided detailed suggestions to the Pakistani president on the content of the speech. The Americans reckoned that any positive gesture by Musharraf would draw the sting from the crisis. The implementation of any step by Islamabad would take time, and New Delhi would find it difficult to embark on a military campaign in the interim.

In a televised address to the people of Pakistan, Musharraf announced a ban on six militant outfits, including the LeT and JeM, and vowed to bring to justice those guilty of perpetrating terror. But he categorically refused to concede India's demand for extradition of twenty terror suspects: "There is no question of entertaining the Indian demand." Nevertheless, Musharraf allowed the LeT to continue operating under a new name in the guise of an Islamic charity. The Pakistani courts soon ordered the release of the commander of the JeM. Most importantly, insurgents began trickling into Indian Kashmir with the onset of spring. New Delhi quietly conveyed to US officials in New Delhi that another major terrorist attack would invite a strong military riposte from India.

The next attack was not long in coming. On May 14, 2002, three terrorists dressed in army fatigues stormed an Indian army camp near the city of Jammu. The attackers killed thirty-four and injured another fifty, before being shot down themselves. Many of the victims were the wives and children of Indian soldiers. The attack resulted in a groundswell of outrage. The Indian army chief publicly stated, "Time for action has come." Speaking in parliament a day after the attack, Prime Minister Vajpayee declared, "What has happened is very heinous, and we will have to counter it."

Immediately after the Jammu attack, President Bush spoke to Prime Minister Vajpayee. The latter bluntly informed him, "India will take appropriate action." The US State Department yet again launched a major diplomatic effort to prevent hostilities in the subcontinent. Powell believed that the Americans had some room for maneuver: India's military options were risky, and the Indian political leadership might balk at the prospect of a ruinous war. Powell also asked Musharraf to stop issuing threats that he could not possibly implement.

On June 1, Colin Powell publicly criticized Pakistan's reluctance to live up to its promises. "We were receiving assurances from President Musharraf that infiltration across the LoC would be ended," he noted. "But unfortunately we can still see evidence that it is continuing." The United States was "pressing President Musharraf very hard to cease all infiltration activities...and we are asking India to show restraint until we can determine whether or not infiltration activity has ceased." But Powell tacitly conceded the limits of American leverage with Pakistan when he observed that if Islamabad shifted its forces from the Afghanistan border, "that would take away from our campaign against Al Qaeda and remaining Taliban forces in western Pakistan....So we're trying to avoid that."

On June 6, 2002, US Deputy Secretary of State Richard Armitage left for the subcontinent. He met and conferred with Musharraf for nearly two hours. The Pakistani president insisted that "nothing is happening" across the Line of Control—a careful present-tense formulation. He also claimed there were no training camps for militants on Pakistani soil. Armitage presented evidence to the contrary and pressed for assurances about ceasing infiltration. According to one account, "Armitage believes that he elicited, confirmed and reconfirmed Musharraf's pledge to make cessation permanent." Another account has Armitage admitting that a permanent solution to the problem was "a bridge too far." On balance, it appears that the commitment Armitage cajoled out of Musharraf was tentative. The US official, however, felt that this was sufficient for his purposes. This was understandable, for the Bush administration's primary interest lay in averting a war in the subcontinent.

In New Delhi the next day, Armitage met the top Indian leadership, including Jaswant Singh and Vajpayee. In their discussions, he emphasized both the solemnity of Musharraf's pledge to curb cross-border infiltration and his own faith in the Pakistani leader's sincerity. The Indians came away with the impression that Musharraf had made a serious commitment, if not a guarantee. Emerging from his final meeting with the Indian prime minister, Armitage told the press that there was a "commitment to the United States by Musharraf to end permanently, cross-border, cross-LoC infiltration." In turn, Armitage asked India to adopt "reciprocal, de-escalatory steps" to defuse the crisis.

Within three days of Armitage's visit, India took a series of steps to reduce tensions. By mid-July the crisis had passed. In October 2002, India finally pulled back its troops from the forward locations, so ending the ten-month stand-off. Over the following year, the Bush administration encouraged India and Pakistan to take steps to reduce tensions along the LoC. In early 2004, Vajpayee and Musharraf agreed on a cease-fire.

As New Delhi and Islamabad moved toward this agreement, the Bush administration designated Islamabad a "Major Non-NATO Ally" and announced a $700 million aid package for 2004—over half of it for the military, with a paltry $19 million earmarked for "improving democratic participation." The Pakistanis binged on military purchases over the next couple of years, acquiring weapons and systems worth $9.8 billion. In all, between 2002 and 2007, the Bush administration gave Pakistan $3.5 billion in aid and $3.6 billion in payments for use of its facilities and services; it further wrote off debt to the tune of $3 billion.[23]

More importantly, the Americans offered Musharraf a graceful exit from Pakistan's clandestine nuclear activity. By early 2003, the CIA had uncovered Abdul Qadeer Khan's proliferation efforts as far afield as North Korea and Iran, the Middle East and South Africa. In a briefing to President Bush, a CIA official quipped, "With the information we've just gotten our hands on—soup to nuts—about uranium enrichment and nuclear weapons design, we could make CIA its own nuclear state." Because "Musharraf had heroically stepped up in the aftermath of 9/11," CIA director George Tenet met with the Pakistani leader one on one on September 24, 2003. "A. Q. Khan is betraying your country," said Tenet. "He has stolen some of your nation's most sensitive secrets and sold them to highest bidders.... We know this, because we stole them from him."[24] Musharraf took the cue. He immediately placed Khan under house arrest and got him to confess on national television that he had overstepped his bounds. Following Musharraf's exit in 2007, Khan would publicly insist that the Pakistan government had authorized everything he had done. But Musharraf had ensured that Pakistan got its "clean bill of health."

INDIA LOOKED ASKANCE AT these developments, wondering whether Washington had relapsed into its old habit of coddling Pakistan to further its geopolitical interests. In the aftermath of the India-Pakistan crisis, however, the George W. Bush administration embarked on a remarkable strategic initiative with India. While this built on the turnaround in US-India relations during the final years of the Clinton presidency, Bush's approach signaled a dramatic shift. India's unlikely success as the largest democracy and potential as a major emerging economy that embraced globalization had attracted Clinton. While Bush shared his predecessor's enthusiasm for Indian democracy, his administration saw the country through the strategic lens of preserving American hegemony from potential challenge by a rising China.

This was evident even before Bush assumed office. In a widely noted essay in *Foreign Affairs* during the 2000 presidential campaign, Condoleezza Rice wrote, "China's success in controlling the balance of power depends in large part on America's reaction to the challenge. The United States...should pay closer attention to India's role in the regional balance. There is a strong tendency conceptually to connect India with Pakistan and to think only of Kashmir or the nuclear competition between the two states. But India is an element in China's calculation, and it should be in America's, too. India is not a great power yet, but it has the potential to emerge as one." The 2002 National Security

Strategy similarly stated of the two countries, "We share an interest ... in creating a strategically stable Asia. Differences remain including India's nuclear and missile programs and the pace of India's economic reforms. But while in the past these concerns may have dominated our thinking about India, today we start with a view of India as a growing world power with which we have common strategic interests."[25]

Three considerations flowed from these premises. First, it was in the United States' strategic interest to enable India's rise as a major power—even if India was unwilling to join US-led alliances. Second, this would require Washington to take a considered view of India's nuclear program. Third, the United States should attempt a "de-hyphenation" of its relations with India and Pakistan. The Bush administration demonstrated it willingness to go down this route with a dramatic offer of full civil nuclear cooperation with India.

Since the Indian test of 1974, the United States had sought to curb India's nuclear program. The Nuclear Suppliers Group (NSG) was formed during the Gerald Ford administration to control and regulate nuclear commerce with India and other potential proliferators. The Jimmy Carter administration had used the 1978 Nuclear Non-Proliferation Act to halt fuel supplies, begun under a bilateral 1963 agreement, to the Tarapur reactor. Successive Indian governments had deeply resented this retrospective application of US law to overrule contractual obligations. And the protracted negotiations over fuel for Tarapur had vitiated US-India relations. So when, in late 2004, the Indian foreign secretary broached with Rice the idea of a bilateral energy dialog that could also address the lingering issue of allowing India to reprocess nuclear fuel from Tarapur, he was surprised to find the administration willing to go much further. Discussions progressed during Rice's visit to New Delhi in March 2005. The following month, a team of Indian negotiators led by the foreign minister landed in Washington.

American officials made clear that they wanted an agreement that would enable civilian nuclear commerce with India, despite its possession of a nuclear arsenal and its unwillingness to join the

Non-Proliferation Treaty. Although this was a stark departure from US policy to date, the road ahead was strewn with hurdles, the most arduous at this stage being the American requirement that India separate its "civilian" and "military" nuclear facilities and place the former under full-scope international safeguards. Deeply suspicious of American intentions, the Indian nuclear establishment, especially the scientific bureaucracy, only came around following assurance that India would draw up the separation plan and timeline in their entirety.[26]

On July 18, 2005, President Bush and Prime Minister Manmohan Singh released a joint statement announcing that the United States would "work to achieve full civil nuclear energy cooperation with India." While the need to promote nuclear energy and help India achieve energy security explained this shift in policy, the Bush administration had made clear the strategic rationale: "to help India become a major world power in the twenty-first century."[27] Concluding such an agreement, however, took over three years of intense negotiations and domestic political management by both sides.

The first step was to get the US Congress to pass legislation exempting India from certain provisions of the Atomic Energy Act of 1954. The nonproliferation lobby naturally got its act together to kill this legislation, especially in the Democrat-controlled House of Representatives. After passage of the Hyde Act, the United States and India had to negotiate an agreement under Section 123 of the 1954 act. The so-called 123 Agreement entailed resolving serious differences over such issues as India's desire for assured fuel supplies for the lifetime of the reactor (a legacy of Tarapur), termination of cooperation if India tested again, and provision of reprocessing and enrichment technology to India. At one point, President Bush interceded to break the deadlock.

The 123 Agreement nevertheless came under attack from both ends of the political spectrum in India. The leftist parties—allies in the coalition government led by Prime Minister Singh—targeted the government for having compromised India's strategic autonomy and turned the country into a "subordinate ally" of the United States. The Bharatiya Janata Party (BJP), despite its role in reorienting US-India nuclear relations, criticized the government for negotiating a weak agreement. The Singh government eventually had to face down a no-confidence motion in the parliament.

Thereafter India negotiated an agreement on safeguards with the International Atomic Energy Agency. The final step was getting a waiver for India from the NSG. Here, considerable US pressure on member states minded to oppose this move supplemented an intense diplomatic effort by India. On September 6, 2008, the NSG approved a "clean" exemption for India: no reference to testing, no discriminatory provisions, and no periodic review of India's nuclear record. As the then Indian foreign secretary observed, it was "a tribute to U.S. power and persuasion."[28]

The Bush administration thought it had "successfully delinked" its policies toward India and Pakistan. But it worried that "Pakistan and Afghanistan were tied together more than ever as the problem of cross-border terrorism deepened."[29] Indeed, by 2006 the situation along the Afghan-Pakistan border was clearly coming to a boil. American unwillingness to commit significant resources to this theater after 2001 complemented Pakistan's continued support for the Taliban. As the Taliban regrouped in safe havens in Pakistan and began intensifying their attacks inside Afghanistan, the relationship between the Afghan government led by Hamid Karzai and Pakistan deteriorated sharply. Karzai repeatedly raised the issue of Taliban camps and safe havens in Pakistan with the Americans, but to no avail. As a senior CIA official put it, "We had no illusions about what was happening but we had no capacity either.... The ISI was the only girl at the dance."[30]

The problem, however, was not only the presence of the Taliban in the Pakistani provinces adjoining Afghanistan. It was also the extraordinary cocktail of terrorist groups in the Federally Administered Tribal Areas (FATA) adjoining the North-West Frontier Province (NWFP). The Pashtun-populated FATA had an anomalous political and legal status within Pakistan and was run by a bureaucratic-military administration that went back to the British Raj. Bin Laden sought refuge there after fleeing Afghanistan. In FATA, as in the neighboring provinces, Al Qaeda and its affiliates could draw on social networks dating back to the Afghan jihad and on patronage from local tribes, notables, and religious establishments.

Apart from foreign terrorists embedded in local tribes, FATA had visiting jihadis from Punjabi outfits such as the Lashkar-e-Taiba and Jaish-e-Mohammed. In the wake of Musharraf's announcement of a clampdown on these groups, some of their cadres had temporarily relocated to FATA. Fighters from the Haqqani network, led by veteran Afghan jihadist and Taliban ally Jalaluddin Haqqani, operated on either side of the border between Loya Paktia and FATA. Gulbuddin Hekmatyar returned from Iran and settled down in the NWFP. While no longer a formidable figure, Hekmatyar nevertheless struck up a working relationship with the Taliban and Al Qaeda. This profusion of terrorist outfits created a network that drew on pooled logistics and services to fuse and advance their varied objectives in Afghanistan, India, and beyond.[31]

But it also led to blowback on Pakistan. Under American pressure, Musharraf sought to move against Al Qaeda in FATA. But this set off a tribal Pashtun uprising against the Pakistani state. The tribal fighters soon came together to form the Tehreek-i-Taliban Pakistan. The Pakistan Taliban embarked on a vicious campaign of insurgency and terror against the Pakistani state and people. Musharraf's attempts at alternately crushing and cutting a deal with the Pakistan Taliban further emboldened them. By 2007, Musharraf was losing his touch. His sacking of the chief justice of the Pakistani Supreme Court in March 2007 triggered widespread protests led by lawyers. Equally ham-handed was his handling of the occupation of Islamabad's Red Mosque by extremists. The latter's crackdown on "prostitution," including the detention of Chinese masseuses, forced Musharraf to send the army to flush out the militants in July 2007—an operation that killed hundreds and wounded many more. As his political standing rapidly slid, Musharraf yet again imposed martial law in November 2007.

The Bush administration had been keeping a wary eye on the developments in Pakistan. Apart from the growing political unrest, it also worried about the escalation in terrorist attacks within Pakistan. The combination there of assorted jihadi groups and nuclear weapons was the stuff of post-9/11 nightmares. A US offer to help secure the Pakistani nuclear arsenals aroused Pakistani suspicions. Islamabad nevertheless pocketed tens of million dollars to shore up its own systems. As the political crisis deepened in the spring and summer of 2007, the Bush administration attempted to bail out Musharraf. At his request, the Americans sought to forge a power-sharing arrangement with the exiled Benazir Bhutto. Given the gulf between them, this was a long shot, but finally a deal was announced on October 4. Two weeks later Bhutto returned to Pakistan.

Musharraf's imposition of martial law threatened to undercut the slender chance of his political survival. Bush was emphatic that the United States ought not to push him under. Despite his ideological predilection for democracy and against dictators, the president worried about the wider consequences of Musharraf's departure. "I don't want anyone pulling the rug out from under him," he told Rice. Vice President Dick Cheney added that Musharraf was essential for the war on terror. "But he's got no credibility left with the Pakistani people," said Rice. Bush insisted, however, that he would personally counsel Musharraf.[32] Meanwhile, Musharraf's old nemesis, Nawaz Sharif, also returned to Pakistan from his exile in Saudi Arabia. Faced with an unmanageable situation, Musharraf shed his uniform, lifted the emergency, and became civilian president of Pakistan. He lasted all of eight months.

In the meantime, the intricate circuit of terrorism in Pakistan set off a series of attacks across the region. On December 27, 2007, the Pakistan Taliban assassinated Benazir Bhutto in a suicide bombing. On July 7, 2008, the Haqqani group struck the Indian embassy in Kabul, leaving forty-one people dead. Five days later, the deputy director of the CIA traveled to Pakistan and presented evidence of ISI's complicity with the Haqqanis and other groups in FATA.[33] But the Pakistani leadership vehemently denied it. On November 26, ten terrorists of the Lashkar-e-Taiba came ashore in the Indian city of Mumbai on a fishing vessel and executed multiple attacks. They virtually held the city under siege for sixty hours and riveted the attention of the global media. They killed 164 people, including 6 Americans, and left over 350 injured. The audacity and sophistication of the attack marked it out from other acts of terrorism since 9/11.

When the ordeal ended, the Indian forces had captured one Pakistani terrorist alive. They pieced together an elaborate conspiracy planned over two years with considerable support from the ISI. This provoked a public clamor in India for retaliation against Pakistan. In its final days in office, the Bush administration scrambled to prevent another conflict in the subcontinent. Washington was particularly concerned that an Indian attack would lead the Pakistanis to switch their forces from the western borders with Afghanistan to the eastern ones with India. So, while Washington offered to cooperate in the investigation, American officials took the line that they were unsure whether the higher command of the ISI and the Pakistan army had known of the attack. In any event, New Delhi desisted from military strikes on Pakistan.

THE MUMBAI ATTACKS ALSO posed the first foreign policy crisis for the incoming Obama administration. Not surprisingly, President Obama ordered a strategic review of policy toward Afghanistan and Pakistan soon after his inauguration in January 2009. The review concluded that both Al Qaeda and the Taliban had staged remarkable comebacks. Attacks on US, North Atlantic Treaty Organization, and Afghan forces were steadily increasing in frequency and lethality. The situation in Pakistan was even grimmer. The country with the fastest-growing nuclear arsenal in the world was host to a mind-boggling collection of terrorist organizations and in the midst of a virtual civil war. Pakistan's relations with India remained tense. Another Mumbai-like attack would invite certain retaliation from India with the attendant risks of escalation all the way to nuclear war.[34]

The administration debated at length about the scale of American commitment to the two countries. The president had come to office vowing to get America out of Iraq and focus on Afghanistan. But Obama also sought to avoid any open-ended obligation, especially in the context of the financial crisis of 2008. The United States had 50,000 troops in Afghanistan, and the military commander wanted to add 30,000 more. Eventually the White House and the military settled on another 17,000 troops with an additional 4,000 trainers.[35] In an address to the nation on March 27, Obama outlined his new strategy for Afghanistan and Pakistan. The president said he had "a clear and focused goal: to disrupt, dismantle and defeat al Qaeda in Pakistan and Afghanistan." Announcing the increase in troops to fight the Taliban in eastern and southern Afghanistan, he also called on Congress to pass the Kerry-Lugar Bill, which would provide Pakistan with $1.5 billion a year for the next five years.

The escalation of fighting that summer yet again brought to the fore the issue of American military commitment to Afghanistan. The military wanted Obama to consider three options: send 10,000 trainers, or 40,000 troops, or even 85,000 troops. On November 25, 2009, Obama announced that he would send 30,000 more troops but would start withdrawing them from July 2011, when a transition to Afghan forces would start. In military terms, Obama agreed to a counterinsurgency strategy of "clear, hold, build and transfer," though he also embarked on a counterterrorism strategy involving the use of Special Forces and drones against targets inside Pakistan. Obama did not originate the use of drones, but he employed them rather more extensively than Bush.

Soon Obama grew disenchanted with the counterinsurgency campaign in Afghanistan. At bottom, his administration was never clear about its objective there: Did it aim merely to prevent the return of Taliban or to undertake a more extensive nation-building effort? In practice the military did a bit of both, but the president increasingly veered toward the option of stopping the Taliban surge, hunting down Al Qaeda, and bringing the troops back home. The successful killing of Osama bin Laden in a Special Forces raid in May 2011 underlined the appeal of a narrower military strategy. A year later, Obama claimed during a visit to Afghanistan, "The goal I set—to defeat Al Qaeda, and deny it a chance to rebuild—is now within our reach."[36]

This masked a range of problems undermining the US attempt to stabilize Afghanistan. For one thing, Obama's relations with Afghan president Karzai were rocky from the start. Obama minced few words in criticizing the corruption of the Karzai government and family. Karzai, for his part, believed that Washington wanted to get rid of him. The manner in which the Obama administration handled the Afghan presidential elections of 2009 lent some credence to his fears. Personalities and paranoia aside, there was a structural problem. Although installed in power by the Americans, Karzai knew that in order to cement his standing among his own people, he needed to demonstrate his independence from time to time—particularly when it came to condemning American military actions for causing civilian casualties. Washington, however, saw this as yet another instance of Karzai's ingratitude. By mid-2012, relations had worsened to the extent that Karzai refused to sign a strategic partnership agreement with the United States. The agreement, which would provide a framework for cooperation after withdrawal of US troops in 2014, was eventually concluded by Karzai's successor, Ashraf Ghani.

The second factor undermining US strategy was Washington's relationship with Pakistan. Despite increased aid under the Kerry-Lugar Bill, US-Pakistan ties had nose-dived over the years. The American operation to execute bin Laden in his safe house in Abbottabad stunned the Pakistanis. The revelation that bin Laden had been living within walking distance of the Pakistan Military Academy left Islamabad's claims of injured innocence in tatters. A couple months later, following an attack by the Haqqani group on the US embassy in Kabul, Chairman of the Joint Chiefs of Staff Admiral Mike Mullen told the Senate Armed Services Committee, "With ISI support, Haqqani operatives planned and conducted that truck bomb attack, as well as the assault on our embassy." They were also behind a string of other attacks in Afghanistan. The Haqqani network, he said, "acts as a veritable arm of Pakistan's Inter-Services Intelligence agency."[37]

This was the most forthright attempt to turn the spotlight on Pakistan's continued support for terrorism. Thereafter the Pakistanis quietly acquiesced in an enlarged program of drone strikes. But this scarcely sufficed to rake out the labyrinth of terrorism inside Pakistan. Worse, the attacks killed many Pakistani civilians and stoked popular anger against America. In the last years of the Obama administration, the United States threatened to withhold aid to Pakistan on the grounds that Islamabad was not doing enough. But Washington itself could do no more.

The Obama administration's efforts to reach out to the Afghan Taliban were no more successful. Contacts with senior Taliban representatives began early on but quickly came to nothing. For one thing, the Pakistanis were determined to thwart any independent contact between the United States and Taliban. For another, whether the United States and the Taliban could find common ground also acceptable to the elected government in Kabul was unclear. In any case, so long as the Taliban's sanctuaries in Pakistan remained intact, the United States could not bring enough military pressure to bear to force them to the negotiating table. Finally, the death of Mullah Omar plunged the Taliban into an internecine power struggle. The American assassination in a drone strike of Omar's successor, Mullah Akhtar Muhammad Mansur, further complicated Washington's quest for an opening to the Taliban.

By the time Obama left office, American officials were engaged with Pakistan and China in an attempt to bring the Taliban and Afghan officials together for a political dialog. Meanwhile, the Islamic State was beginning to register its presence in Afghanistan. This prompted a reassessment of American military commitment beyond 2016. Eventually Obama agreed to leave behind 10,000 troops to support the Ghani government and the Afghan security forces. America's long engagement with the subcontinent was set to continue under the next president.

THE CHALLENGE OF DEALING with a rising China was evident to the Obama administration from the outset. The global financial crisis cast into relief China's burgeoning economic power, especially since its accession to the World Trade Organization in 2001. The United States not only had to deal with China as an economic competitor and potential regional challenger in Asia but also needed its cooperation in tackling a range of multilateral problems, from global economic coordination to climate change. The administration realized that it must shape America's relationship with China such that it maximized the chance of China's rise becoming a stabilizing and constructive phenomenon rather than a threat to peace and equilibrium. The evolving strategy toward China had three components: first, welcoming China's emergence and accepting its legitimate and enhanced role in global affairs; second, ensuring that this rise conformed to the international norms and standards set by the United States; and third, fashioning the Asia-Pacific security environment to ensure that China did not challenge the status quo. The last entailed reviving America's traditional alliances with Japan, South Korea, and Australia, as well as developing new strategic partnerships with countries such as India.[38]

In practice, the Obama administration found balancing these components tricky. In the initial months, it emphasized the first strand of the policy in the hope that it would help secure the second. But this raised doubts about the administration's seriousness in backing its old allies and cultivating new ones. For instance, the joint statement issued during Obama's visit to China in November 2009 said, "The two sides…support the improvement and growth of relations between India and Pakistan. The two sides are ready to strengthen communication, dialogue and cooperation on issues related to South Asia and work together to promote peace, stability and development in that region."[39] The Indians read this as indicative of the Obama administration's willingness to work with China in getting India and Pakistan to recommence the diplomatic process suspended after the Mumbai attacks of 2008. Prime Minister Manmohan Singh pointedly objected to the language of the joint statement when he met with President Obama just a week later. More generally, the Indian government wondered whether the United States sought to establish a "G2" relationship with China—which would unavoidably downgrade India's interests.

By late 2010, China's willingness to adopt a more assertive stance on a wider range of issues than ever before was gradually becoming clear. The sweeping claims advanced by Beijing in the South China Sea particularly rattled many American allies in the Asia-Pacific. The administration now began to focus on a systematic effort to convince China and US allies of its commitment to upholding the status quo in the Asia-Pacific region. Writing in *Foreign Policy* in October 2011, Secretary of State Hillary Clinton outlined the administration's keenness, after a decade of wars in South Asia and the Middle East, to "pivot" or "rebalance" toward the Asia-Pacific. "One of the most important tasks of American statecraft over the next decade," she wrote, "will be to lock in a substantially increased investment—diplomatic, economic, strategic and otherwise—in the Asia Pacific region." The region itself—also dubbed the "Indo-Pacific"—was now expansively defined as "stretching from the Indian subcontinent to the western shores of the Americas" and spanning the Indian and the Pacific Oceans.[40]

The new policy toward Asia had several strands. On the diplomatic front, the United States embarked on a sustained effort to engage its old allies and potential partners to support the rebalancing toward Asia. On the military front, the United States would deploy more troops and naval forces in the Asia-Pacific. At that point, the American fleet was divided equally between the Pacific and the Atlantic. The rebalancing aimed to deploy 60 percent of US naval forces in the Pacific, leaving 40 percent in the Atlantic.[41] On the economic front, the administration gave a major push to negotiations for the Trans-Pacific Partnership (TPP) with twelve countries in the Asia-Pacific. More ambitious than a regular free trade agreement, the TPP would include provisions for protecting intellectual property, creating investor-friendly regulatory frameworks, ensuring that state-owned companies "compete fairly" with private companies, and establishing tighter environmental and la-bor standards. The provisions of the TPP at once targeted China and strove to restore American economic competitiveness in some of the most dynamic economies of the region.

The Obama administration accorded India a significant role in its efforts at pivoting toward Asia. Of the administration's desire for a strategic partnership with India, Clinton wrote, "The United States is making a strategic bet on India's future—that India's greater role on the world stage will enhance peace and security, that opening India's markets to the world will pave the way to greater regional and global prosperity, that Indian advances in science and technology will improve lives and advance human knowledge everywhere, and that India's vi-brant, pluralistic democracy will produce measurable results and im-provements for its citizens and inspire others to follow a similar path of openness and tolerance."[42] Her statement eloquently acknowledged the strategic, economic, ideological, and cultural forces that had led the United States to forge a new relationship with India. Yet, as Clinton conceded, differences between the two sides lingered.

For one thing, India hesitated to sign the "foundational" defense agreements on sharing logistics and communications that the United States deemed imperative to tighten their military ties. For another, the

United States felt that its companies had not reaped the commercial benefits of the civilian nuclear deal with India owing to the latter's restrictive laws on the liability of companies supplying nuclear materials. For a third, India looked askance at the ongoing TPP negotiations. Although the partnership mainly targeted China, it also left out India, owing to concerns about New Delhi's "obstructive" behavior in trade negotiations at the World Trade Organization. If the TPP came into force, then India would encounter a series of nontariff barriers in its economic relations with key Asian-Pacific economies. More generally, it proved difficult to fully harmonize India's avowed desire for strategic autonomy with American plans for a close security relationship.

The emergence in May 2014 of a strong BJP government led by Prime Minister Narendra Modi set the stage for removing many of these irritants. Concerned about the widening power gap between India and China, the Modi government decided to tilt heavily toward the United States. New Delhi amended its nuclear liability laws and announced its desire to purchase six nuclear reactors from GE and Westinghouse. It also signed a foundational logistics support agreement, as long desired by the Pentagon. The United States, in turn, designated India a "major defense partner" eligible for technology transfer on a par with its "closest allies and partners."

Most importantly, India and the United States issued in January 2015 a joint strategic vision statement on Indian Ocean and Asia-Pacific security. Although the document did not specifically mention China, it referred to the South China Sea and the need to avoid using force in settling territorial disputes. A series of regular exchanges, including trilateral ones with Japan, and military exercises, as well as a substantial increase in defense purchases by India, followed. Yet India refrained from undertaking a closer operational partnership. As the senior White House official dealing with South Asia later put it, "From the American vantage point, it is a strange partnership indeed in which India expects to receive some of our most sensitive military technologies, but resists engaging in basic joint naval patrols, or reacts with deep suspicion to cooperative defense activities."[43] All the same, by the time Barack Obama left the White House, he could take deserved satisfaction in having pulled India closer to the United States than at any point in history.

CONCLUSION

SEVEN MONTHS after his swearing in as the forty-fifth president of the United States, Donald Trump outlined his administration's strategy toward Afghanistan and the rest of South Asia. On the campaign trail and earlier, Trump had castigated Barack Obama's commitment to Afghanistan as wasteful and pointless. But now the president announced that he had changed his mind. A hasty withdrawal would have grim consequences. Afghanistan and Pakistan were home to the "highest concentration" of terrorist groups in any region of the world. "The threat is worse," he continued, "because Pakistan and India are two nuclear-armed states whose tense relations threaten to spiral into conflict." The United States had a vital interest in denying terrorists their safe havens as well as preventing them from acquiring nuclear weapons and materials. These assumptions were, of course, entirely continuous with those of his predecessors.

With his usual penchant for hyperbole, however, Trump announced that US strategy would "change dramatically." The United States would adopt an integrated approach combining diplomatic, economic, and military power. It would not indulge in nation building and would instead focus on "killing terrorists." Negotiations with elements of the Taliban could only follow an "effective military effort." Unlike his predecessor he would neither announce a timeline for withdrawal nor quibble with American generals about troop numbers. Further, he pointedly stated that the United States had been "paying Pakistan billions and billions of dollars at the same time they are housing the very terrorists that we are fighting. But that will have to change, and that will change immediately."

In the most significant departure from past policy, Trump went on to accord India a critical role in the United States' Afghanistan-Pakistan strategy. Even as he acknowledged India's contributions (to the tune of $3 billion) to the reconstruction and development of Afghanistan, he wanted India to do more: "India makes billions of dollars in trade with the United States, and we want them to help us more with Afghanistan, especially in the area of economic assistance and development." The strategic partnership with India, Trump announced, would now encompass South Asia as well as the Indo-Pacific.[1]

The governments of Afghanistan and India welcomed the speech—especially the determination to crack down on Pakistan's Janus-faced approach to terrorist outfits in its territory. At the same time, New Delhi was skeptical about whether the Trump administration would indeed manage to hold Pakistan accountable. For starters, the president's speech suggested that he sought a greater Indian footprint in Afghanistan but was also mindful of the security competition between India and Pakistan. Would he be prepared, then, to disregard Pakistan's concerns about the Indian presence in Afghanistan and allow India to increase its footprint there? Second, would the new policy be viable at a time when the

United States continued to rely on Pakistan for its logistical route into Afghanistan and when the Trump administration's antagonistic stance toward Iran precluded an alternative? Third, was isolating Pakistan a realistic possibility in the context of its deepening links with China? Finally, could the mercurial president be expected to hold any line in the medium term? The terms on which he sought India's cooperation indicated a desire to obtain quid for the quo—India doing more to help the United States in Afghanistan because it enjoyed a favorable trade balance with America. This did not comport with the evolving pattern of US-India strategic partnership premised on the idea that assisting India's economic development was in the United States' long-term strategic interests, irrespective of whether there was any short-term gain for America.

The administration's approach to China also concerned New Delhi. After mounting a swinging attack on China's trade policies during the campaign, Trump appeared to have modulated his views considerably. He had walked back from key elements of his predecessor's "rebalancing" strategy, questioning the value of alliances with Japan and South Korea and withdrawing from the Trans-Pacific Partnership. On the military side, likewise, it was unclear if Trump would persist with naval operations that challenged Beijing's attempts at changing the status quo in the disputed parts of the South China Sea. Underlying all this was the question of whether Trump and the nationalist revival he represented might lead the United States to turn its back on the liberal international order that the United States had constructed and led since World War II. This prospect understandably concerned India, both as a prime beneficiary of US-led globalization after the Cold War and as a strategic competitor with China.

This history of American involvement in South Asia suggests that the personalities, inclinations, and choices of presidents matter. But they matter less than we think, when we consider the longer sweep of history. People, as Karl Marx famously said, make their own history but not in circumstances of their own choosing—rather in circumstances "given and transmitted from the past."

Despite decades of engagement and enormous expenditure of resources and effort, the United States has yet to establish a stable hegemony in South Asia in which consent is easily won and coercion largely unnecessary. This owes partly to shortsighted American policies and choices that have had longer-term consequences: witness the military alliance with Pakistan in the 1950s or the support for Islamists in the 1980s. Indeed, it is difficult to think of any American president who has shown a consistently sure touch in his dealings with India, Pakistan, or Afghanistan. But the challenges in crafting a stable hegemony also stem from problems endemic to the region: deep-seated conflicts of identity, power balances, antagonistic political cultures, flawed institutional structures, and the absence of any impulse toward regional economic integration. The continuity of many of the problems in South Asia suggests that they are rather difficult to resolve: the United States will have to manage or endure them. Donald Trump is unlikely to be the last American president to grapple with them.

As the long history covered in this book suggests, the subcontinent has always been a useful vantage point from which to view the transformation of the United States from "colony to superpower." And it will remain so. The remarkable rise of American power is one of the central developments of modern world history. I have argued that we cannot understand the character and workings of this power solely by focusing on the core terrain in which it operated. Rather the regions of the margin and the periphery provide an oblique yet indispensable view of American power, perhaps none more so than South Asia.

From the young republic's search for a foothold in the commercial world dominated by older European empires to the dawn of the American century and the end of the Cold war, South Asia has featured significantly in the arc of American ascendency. The pursuit of power—economic, political, and military—has naturally figured prominently in US foreign relations with South Asia. The world's leading capitalist country has, of course, sought opportunities to open up the region's massive markets. But it also has, over long periods, allowed and indeed helped these countries to build state-led and relatively closed economies—all in the wider interest of upholding capitalism as a global system. Economic and political interests have thus been entwined in unpredictable ways. US strategic interests have further complicated the quest for power: recall the laments of successive presidents about economic aid to Pakistan.

These interests have also been refracted through the prisms of ideology and culture. Since the birth of the republic, the United States has melded a religious belief in itself as a divinely chosen land and people with a political belief in itself as the herald of liberty for the rest of the world. This ideology has shaped American views of and policies toward South Asia, as evident in the notion of manifest destiny in the 1840s and President George W. Bush's 2006 declaration that "the survival of liberty in our land depends on the success of liberty in other lands." It would be erroneous to dismiss this ideology simply as a mask for power. It has, on the one hand, licensed soaring ambition and lofty rhetoric unmatched by practice or policy. On the other hand, it has prompted serious attempts by generations of Americans— from missionaries to development experts, advocates of temperance to family-planning workers—to improve the lives of the peoples of South Asia.

These efforts delivered much less than their advocates had hoped in part because of the cultural attitudes that framed them. From the earliest encounters with the subcontinent, ideas about religion and race instilled in Americans a profound sense of difference and cultural superiority. As we have seen, American views about the subcontinent's religion and practices were not monolithic: many Americans took care to distinguish between degenerate Hinduism and vigorous Islam, while a few hailed the former as the summit of mystical religious thought. Still, these early impressions were reinforced over decades and persisted for much longer. What is more, they influenced American views of political developments, such as the emergence of the new states of Pakistan and India, and the crafting of US policy toward them.

Ideas of race, too, were neither static nor undifferentiated. Yet their persistence over a long period, especially in the form of hierarchical and paternalistic attitudes, is remarkable. Even those who opposed racism or the workings of American power in the region subscribed to these attitudes. It is tempting to suggest that American policies and efforts might have been more effective had those implementing them refrained from patronizing the region and claiming to know its interests better than the people living there. But, in practice, the hold of hierarchical thinking has proved difficult to shake.

This story of US involvement also opens up an important window onto the history of modern South Asia. Historians of the region have seldom looked beyond colonization and its discontents. Yet, as this book has shown, encounters with America were a crucial aspect of South Asians' encounters with modernity. This was evident in the early sites of connection in the nineteenth century and acquired enormous significance thereafter. American missionaries and agronomists, engineers and soldiers, businessmen and architects, artists and advertisers opened up unexampled vistas of modernity to the peoples of South Asia.

The brush with American modernity also meant coming up against American power. By the early 1940s it was clear that British rule or influence in the subcontinent could only persist if the United States allowed it to. A decade on, the United States had swept Britain aside and become the predominant external player in the region. American political, strategic, and economic interests and policies deeply influenced the trajectory of postcolonial South Asia. At crucial junctures, such as the Bangladesh crisis of 1971, the destiny of nations and peoples turned on the policies and choices of American leaders. A region once deemed peripheral to US global interests is now the site of the most prolonged application of American military power in the republic's history. The tension between Washington's strategic interests and its ideological stances has also shaped the politics of the region. Despite its avowals of liberty and democracy, the United States has willingly propped up military dictators and authoritarian rulers in Pakistan and Afghanistan. The real and perceived American meddling in these countries' politics has long been a source of anger. It is ironic, but not surprising, that today the peoples of certain parts of the region (especially India) are among those who view America most favorably, while those of other parts (Pakistan and parts of Afghanistan) are among those who take the dimmest view of the United States in global surveys of attitude.

The entanglement of the United States and South Asia has long played out against the wider backdrop of global history. When Walt Whitman composed "Passage to India" in 1870, the Suez Canal and the Union Pacific Railroad had just been completed, while the Atlantic Cable had been laid some years earlier. The poem begins with an homage to the "great achievements of the present...the strong light works of engineers." Its theme, baldly put, is that knowledge leads inexorably to faith. The "passage" refers, in the first instance, to the actual, physical passage enabled by these technological advances and the consequent shrinking of the globe. These ostensibly scientific endeavors, Whitman suggests, are working to realize "God's purpose": "the lands to be welded together." In so doing, the "passage" becomes one to "primal thought" embodied in the Hindu scriptures and thus ends being a "Passage to more than India."

Whitman's first vision of an American passage to India turned out to be accurate. Successive waves of globalization since he wrote have pulled the United States to South Asia and welded these lands together. In a prosaic sense, at least, Whitman's second vision has also been realized. The United States' engagement with the subcontinent has been shaped by "more than India," by other great powers that loomed large in Asia: Britain, Japan, the Soviet Union, and most recently China. The shifting contours of globalization and the rise of China as a global power will almost certainly shape the future course of US engagement with South Asia. And so, as Americans chart their passage in the years ahead, they would do well to remember Whitman's invocations of the region's "fierce enigmas" and "strangling problems."

ACKNOWLEDGMENTS

THIS BOOK has been several years in the making, and I have accumulated many debts along the way. I would like to thank the staff at the following archives and libraries: Nehru Memorial Museum & Library, National Archives of India, and Centre for Policy Research, New Delhi; National Archives and Records Administration, College Park; National Security Archive (George Washington University) and Library of Congress, Washington, DC; John F. Kennedy Presidential Library, Boston; Jimmy Carter Presidential Library, Atlanta; Ford Foundation Archives, New York; Van Pelt Library (University of Pennsylvania), Philadelphia; Sterling Memorial Library (Yale University), New Haven, Connecticut; British Library, London; The National Archives, Kew. This book is a work of synthesis as well as original research, so I am extremely grateful to all the scholars on whose work I have drawn.

Sandeep Bhardwaj provided indispensable research assistance as well as a patient sounding board for my arguments. The ideas in this book have been topics of discussion over the years with a large community of friends and colleagues. I am especially grateful to Aditya Balasubramanian, Rudra Chaudhuri, David Engerman, Devesh Kapur, Sunil Khilnani, Tanvi Madan, David Malone, Ambassador Shivshankar Menon, C. Raja Mohan, Anit Mukherjee, Rohan Mukherjee, Partha Mukhopadhyay, Karthik Nachiappan, Vipin Narang, Mahesh Rangarajan, Ambassador Shyam Saran, Pranay Sharma, Paul Staniland, and Zorawar Daulet Singh. I owe a great deal to Yamini Aiyar and other colleagues at the Centre for Policy Research. Notwithstanding my move to Mumbai, they have remained my constant interlocutors. I have been fortunate to continue working with Pratap Bhanu Mehta—now at Ashoka University. I am particularly grateful to Rudrangshu Mukherjee for inviting me to be a visiting professor at Ashoka.

Ramachandra Guha generously read the manuscript, and, as always, his perceptive comments and suggestions on style and substance improved it considerably. I am also grateful to my agent, Gill Coleridge, for her patience with this long-gestating manuscript and her sagacious advice throughout. It has been a privilege to work yet again with Lara Heimert at Basic Books. I am most grateful to Dan Gerstle for his incredibly helpful edits and suggestions on the manuscript. Jennifer Kelland did a terrific job of copyediting the text. Michelle Welsh-Horst and Alia Massoud managed everything with their customary efficiency.

Writing a book is inevitably an imposition on one's family—this one has been more so than the others. I owe more than I can say to my wife, Pritha, and our children, Kavya and Dhruv. Their fortitude, support, and love were crucial in enabling me to complete this book. My parents, Geetha and K. S. Raghavan, and my mother-in-law, Sukanya Venkatachalam, provided much-needed help at a critical stage in the writing of this book. One of the joys of researching this book was the opportunity to spend more time with the American side of my family. My sister Arunpriya and her husband, Balaji Radhakrishnan, provided my first personal introduction to the country, and I continue to learn about it from their daughters, Prerna and Pranaya. In New York, Vinaya Sampath and Sridev Raghavan were ever-welcoming hosts, and their children, Ankur and Akansha, cheerfully kept me company.

This book is in many ways the culmination of my research over the past fifteen years on the international history of modern South Asia. Years ago, Professor Sir Lawrence Freedman not only taught me the history of American foreign policy and supervised my first forays into research but also provided a model for combining historical scholarship with commentary on contemporary international affairs. Although I have consistently failed to live up to Lawry's standards in either domain, this book is for him—as a mark of my lasting gratitude, affection, and esteem.

NOTES

Introduction

1. "Statement by President on Death of Taliban Leader Mansur," The White House: President Barack Obama, May 23, 2016. Accessed online at https://obama whitehouse.archives.gov/the-press-office/2016/05/23/statement-president -death-taliban-leader-mansur.

2. Bob Woodward, *Obama's Wars* (New York: Simon & Schuster, 2010), 3–8.

3. Ashley J. Tellis and Jeff Eggers, *US Policy in Afghanistan: Changing Strategies, Preserving Gains* (Washington, DC: Carnegie Endowment for International Peace, May 2017), 5–8.

4. Carlotta Gall and Ruhullal Khapalwak, "Taliban Leader Feared Pakistan Before He Was Killed," *New York Times*, August 9, 2017. Accessed online at https://www.nytimes.com/2017/08/09/world/asia/taliban-leader -feared-pakistan-before-he-was-killed.html. For an earlier report that indicated sharing of intelligence by Pakistan, see Mark Landler and Matthew Rosenberg, "US Strike on Taliban Leader Is Seen as a Message to Pakistan," *New York Times*, May 23, 2016. Accessed online at https://www

.nytimes.com/2016/05/24/us/politics/afghanistan-pakistan-taliban-leader
.html?rref=collection%2Fbyline%2Fmujib-mashal.

5. Harlan's own account is in Josiah Harlan, *A Memoir of India and Avghanistaun* (Philadelphia: J. Dobson, 1842). For a superb biography, see Ben Macintyre, *Josiah the Great: The True Story of the Man Who Would be King* (London: Harper Press, 2004).

6. Brian Rouleau, *With Sails Whitening Every Sea: Mariners and the Making of an American Maritime Empire* (Ithaca, NY: Cornell University Press, 2014).

7. Macintyre, *Josiah the Great*, Kindle loc. 351, 368, 4077. For an excellent treatment of this vision, see Peter S. Onuf, *Jefferson's Empire: The Language of American Nationhood* (Charlottesville: University of Virginia Press, 2000).

8. Marjorie Jewett Bell (ed.), *An American Engineer in Afghanistan: From the Letters and Notes of A. C. Jewett* (Minneapolis: University of Minnesota Press, 1948), 114, 309, 317–18.

9. Rajiv Chandrasekaran, *Little America: The War Within the War for Afghanistan* (London: Bloomsbury, 2012), 301–3.

10. Robert J. McMahon, *The Cold War on the Periphery: The United States, India and Pakistan* (New York: Columbia University Press, 1994); Paul McGarr, *The Cold War in South Asia: Britain, the United States and the Indian Subcontinent, 1945–1965* (Cambridge: Cambridge University Press, 2013); Dennis Kux, *India and the United States: Estranged Democracies* (Washington, DC: National Defense University Press, 1991); Dennis Kux, *The United States and Pakistan, 1947–2000: Disenchanted Allies* (Washington, DC: Woodrow Wilson Center, 2000); Rudra Chaudhuri, *Forged in Crisis: India and the United States Since 1947* (New Delhi: HarperCollins, 2014); Dennis Merrill, *Bread and the Ballot: The United States and India's Economic Development, 1947–1963* (Chapel Hill: University of North Carolina Press, 1992); Corinna R. Unger, *Entwicklungspfade in Indien: Eine internationale Geschichte, 1947–1980* (Göttingen: Wallstein, 2015); Andrew Rotter, *Comrades at Odds: The United States and India, 1947–1964* (Ithaca, NY: Cornell University Press, 2000); Nico Slate, *Colored Cosmopolitanism: The Shared Struggle for Freedom in the United States and India* (Cambridge, MA: Harvard University Press, 2012).

11. Preeminently in the work of Sanjay Subrahmanyam. From a prodigious body of writings, see his *Explorations in Connected Histories: Mughals and Franks* (New Delhi: Oxford University Press, 2005) and *Three Ways to Be Alien: Travails and Encounters in the Early Modern World* (New Delhi: Permanent Black, 2012).

12. For a rare exception, see Kris Manjapra, *The Age of Entanglement: German and Indian Intellectuals Across Empire* (Cambridge, MA: Harvard University Press, 2014).

13. "Most Dangerous Place," *The Hindu*, March 11, 2000; "Remarks by the President on New Strategy on Afghanistan and Pakistan," The White House: President Barack

Obama, March 27, 2009. Accessed online at https://obamawhitehouse.archives
.gov/the-press-office/remarks-president-a-new-strategy-afghanistan-and-pakistan.

14. Anders Stephanson, *Manifest Destiny: American Expansion and the Empire of Right* (New York: Hill & Wang, 1995).

Chapter 1: Fortune, Fantasy, and Faith

1. Cited in Susan S. Bean, *Yankee India: American Commercial and Cultural Encounters with India in the Age of Sail, 1784–1860* (Salem, MA: Peabody Essex Museum, 2001), 33.
2. Bean, *Yankee India*, 33.
3. Holden Furber, "The Beginnings of American Trade with India, 1784–1812," *New England Quarterly* 11, no. 2 (1938): 235–37; G. Bhagat, *Americans in India, 1784–1860* (New York: New York University Press, 1970), 5–6.
4. Gauri Viswanathan, "Yale College and the Culture of British Imperialism," *Yale Journal of Criticism* 7, no. 1 (1994): 1–30.
5. Bean, *Yankee India*, 29.
6. Robert Middlekauff, *The Glorious Cause: The American Revolution, 1763–1789* (New York: Oxford University Press, 1982), 219–39.
7. George C. Herring, *From Colony to Superpower: U.S. Foreign Relations Since 1776* (New York: Oxford University Press, 2008), 34–38.
8. Bhagat, *Americans in India*, 8–15 (quote on 15).
9. Cited in Furber, "Beginnings of American Trade," 239.
10. Cited in Amales Tripathi, *Trade and Finance in the Bengal Presidency* (Calcutta: Oxford University Press, 1979), 30.
11. Seward W. Livermore, "Early Commercial and Consular Relations with the East Indies," *Pacific Historical Review* 15, no. 1 (1946): 32–35; Bhagat, *Americans in India*, 86.
12. Joy to Thomas Jefferson, January 20, 1793, in Holden Furber, "The Letters of Benjamin Joy, First American Consul in India," *Indian Archives* 4, no. 2 (1950): 220–21.
13. Herring, *From Colony to Superpower*, 56–70 (quotation on 69).
14. Cited in Livermore, "Early Commercial and Consular Relations," 35.
15. Joy to Edmund Randolph, November 24, 1974; J. H. Harrington to Joy, April 21, 1974, in Furber, "Letters of Benjamin Joy," 222, 225.
16. Joy to Randolph, November 24, 1794, in Furber, "Letters of Benjamin Joy," 222–23. On the tangled sovereignty of the East India Company, see Jon Wilson, *India Conquered: Britain's Raj and the Chaos of Empire* (London: Simon & Schuster, 2016), chap. 7.
17. Joy to Randolph, November 24, 1794, in Furber, "Letters of Benjamin Joy," 223–24.
18. Livermore, "Early Commercial and Consular Relations," 36–37 (quote on 36); Bhagat, *Americans in India*, 89–98.

19. Data from Furber, "Beginnings of American Trade," 258; *American State Papers: Commerce and Navigation* (Washington, 1832), 1:346–47, 512; quote from Bhagat, *Americans in India*, 43–44.

20. Cited in Bhagat, *Americans in India*, 29–31.

21. Cited in Furber, "Beginnings of American Trade," 249, 261.

22. Furber, "Beginnings of American Trade," 265.

23. Bhagat, *Americans in India*, 33–34, 66–67.

24. Herring, *From Colony to Superpower*, 115–21.

25. Cited in Bean, *Yankee India*, 126.

26. Cited in Bhagat, *Americans in India*, 45–46.

27. Cited in Bhagat, *Americans in India*, 47; Bean, *Yankee India*, 127.

28. Cited in Gordon Wood, *Empire of Liberty: A History of the Early Republic, 1789–1815* (New York: Oxford University Press, 2009), 706. The "communications revolution" is the central theme of Daniel Walker Howe, *What Hath God Wrought: The Transformation of America, 1815–1848* (New York: Oxford University Press, 2007).

29. Bean, *Yankee India*, 175–80, 211–13.

30. Bhagat, *Americans in India*, 108.

31. David G. Dickason, "The Nineteenth-Century Indo-American Ice Trade: An Hyperborean Epic," *Modern Asian Studies* 25, no. 1 (1991): 53–89.

32. Cited in Dickason, "The Nineteenth-Century Indo-American Ice Trade," 71–72.

33. There is a large literature on the mutiny. The best single study remains Rudrangshu Mukherjee, *Awadh in Revolt, 1857–58: A Study of Popular Resistance*, 1st paperback ed. (New Delhi: Permanent Black, 2002).

34. Cited in Bhagat, *Americans in India*, 109, 111. On the Panic of 1857, see Charles W. Calomiris and Larry Schweikart, "The Panic of 1857: Origins, Transmission and Containment," *Journal of Economic History* 51, no. 4 (1991): 807–34.

35. The literature on the American Civil War is enormous. The best single study is James McPherson, *Battle Cry of Freedom: The Civil War Era* (New York: Oxford University Press, 1988).

36. C. A. Bayly, *The Birth of the Modern World, 1780–1914* (Oxford: Blackwell, 2004), 161; Jurgen Osterhammel, *The Transformation of the World: A Global History of the Nineteenth Century* (Princeton, NJ: Princeton University Press, 2014), 514–71.

37. For a fine, recent account of the political economy of American slavery, see Walter Johnson, *River of Dark Dreams: Slavery and Empire in Cotton Kingdom* (Cambridge, MA: Harvard University Press, 2013).

38. Sven Beckert, *Empire of Cotton: A Global History* (New York: Knopf, 2014), 105–26 (quotation on 122).

39. Beckert, *Empire of Cotton*, 126–27.

40. Henry Piddington, *Memoir on the Proposed Improvements in Indian Cotton, Addressed to the Right Hon. Lord Auckland, Governor General of India* (Calcutta: W. Rushton & Co., 1840), 8.

41. Cited in Beckert, *Empire of Cotton*, 126–27, 131.

42. Peter Harnetty, "The Imperialism of Free Trade: Lancashire, India, and the Cotton Supply Question, 1861–1865," *Journal of British Studies* 6, no. 1 (1966): 70–96. Also see Peter Harnetty, *Imperialism and Free Trade: Lancashire and India in the Mid-Nineteenth Century* (Manchester, UK: Manchester University Press, 1972).

43. Cited in Beckert, *Empire of Cotton*, 254.

44. Cited in Beckert, *Empire of Cotton*, 255–56.

45. Bayly, *Birth of the Modern World*, 161–62; Beckert, *Empire of Cotton*, 292.

46. Journal of the *Ruby*, in Bean, *Yankee India*, 49, 51.

47. Journal of the *Tartar*, in Bean, *Yankee India*, 156.

48. Journal of the *Belisarius*, in Bean, *Yankee India*, 93–95.

49. Journal of the *Derby*, in Bean, *Yankee India*, 112.

50. Journal of the *Rockall*, in Bean, *Yankee India*, 239.

51. Journal of the *Belisarius*, in Bean, *Yankee India*, 98; Journal of the *Tartar*, in Bean, *Yankee India*, 160; Journal of the *Rockall*, in Bean, *Yankee India*, 245.

52. Journal of the *Belisarius*, in Bean, *Yankee India*, 96.

53. Journal of the *Belisarius*, in Bean, *Yankee India*, 96–97; Journal of the *Rockall*, in Bean, *Yankee India*, 262.

54. Journal of the *Tartar*, in Bean, *Yankee India*, 152, 160; Journal of the *Derby*, in Bean, *Yankee India*, 114.

55. For an excellent social history of the "dubash" during these years, see C. A. Bayly, *Empire and Information: Intelligence Gathering and Social Communication in India* (Cambridge, MA: Cambridge University Press, 1996).

56. Cited in Bean, *Yankee India*, 38; Journal of the *Belisarius*, in Bean, *Yankee India*, 96; cited in Bhagat, *Americans in India*, 121.

57. Journal of the *Ruby*, in Bean, *Yankee India*, 51; Journal of the *Derby*, in Bean, *Yankee India*, 111–12.

58. Cited in Bean, *Yankee India*, 74.

59. Omkar Goswami, *Goras and Desis: Managing Agencies and the Making of Corporate India* (Gurgaon: Penguin Random House India, 2016); Dickason, "The Nineteenth-Century Indo-American Ice Trade," 72; Bean, *Yankee India*, 164, 215–20.

60. Thomas Metcalf, *Ideologies of the Raj* (Cambridge, MA: Cambridge University Press, 1995); Uday S. Mehta, *Liberalism and Empire: A Study in Nineteenth Century British Liberal Thought* (Chicago: Chicago University Press, 1999).

61. The best treatment is Stephanson, *Manifest Destiny*.

62. For an excellent account of this overland expansion, see Bruce Cummings, *Dominion from Sea to Sea: Pacific Ascendancy and American Power* (New Haven, CT: Yale University Press, 2009).

63. Cited in Stephanson, *Manifest Destiny*, 42 (emphasis in original).

64. Journals of the *Belisarius* and the *Derby*, in Bean, *Yankee India*, 101, 103, 114.

65. Journal of the *Tartar*, in Bean, *Yankee India*, 145–46, 167.

66. Henry Field James, *Abolitionism Unveiled; or, Its Origin, Progress, and Pernicious Tendency Fully Developed* (Cincinnati, OH: E. Morgan, 1856), 228.

67. George Francis Train, *An American Merchant in Europe, Asia, and Australia* (New York: G. P. Putnam & Co., 1857), 268, 349, cited in Elizabeth Kelly Gray, "Whisper to Him the Word 'India': Trans-Atlantic Critics and American Slavery, 1830–1860," *Journal of the Early Republic* 28, no. 3 (2008): 392.

68. Stephanson, *Manifest Destiny*, 55.

69. Bayard Taylor, *A Visit to India, China, and Japan, in the Year 1853* (New York: G. P. Putnam & Co., 1855), 60–61, 268–73.

70. Journal of the *Rockall*, in Bean, *Yankee India*, 255.

71. Train, *An American Merchant in Europe, Asia, and Australia*, 212, 254. For a similar critique of British hypocrisy, see Karl Marx, "The Duchess of Sutherland and Slavery," *People's Paper*, No. 45 (March 12, 1853). Accessed online at https://www.marxists.org/archive/marx/works/1853/03/12.htm.

72. Robert B. Minturn Jr., *From New York to Delhi, by Way of Rio de Janeiro, Australia and China* (New York: D. Appleton & Co., 1859), 118, 190.

73. Mather was also instrumental in persuading Elihu Yale, erstwhile governor of Madras, to provide an endowment to the college in New Haven.

74. Journal of the *Derby*, in Bean, *Yankee India*, 117; Journal of the *Belisarius*, in Bean, *Yankee India*, 98.

75. Journal of the *Derby*, in Bean, *Yankee India*, 115; Journal of the *Tartar*, in Bean, *Yankee India*, 153.

76. For useful historical treatments, see Lata Mani, *Contentious Traditions: The Debate on Sati in Colonial India* (Berkeley: University of California Press, 1998); Kim Wagner, *Banditry and the British in Early Nineteenth Century India* (New Delhi: Primus Books, 2014).

77. Jeffrey H. Richards, "Sati in Philadelphia: The Widow(s) of Malabar," *American Literature* 80, no. 4 (2008): 647–75.

78. Mark Twain, *Following the Equator* (New York: Harper and Brothers, 1899), 2:98.

79. Report of November 28, 1789, in Bean, *Yankee India*, 41–43.

80. Journal of the *Tartar*, in Bean, *Yankee India*, 164–67.

81. Journal of the *Rockall*, in Bean, *Yankee India*, 246, 258; Journal of the *Tartar*, in Bean, *Yankee India*, 162.

82. Cited in Kenneth Latourette, *Missions and the American Mind* (Indianapolis: National Foundation Press, 1949), 28.

83. Emily Conroy-Krutz, *Christian Imperialism: Converting the World in the Early American Republic* (Ithaca, NY: Cornell University Press, 2015).

84. Rosalind O'Hanlon, *Caste, Conflict and Ideology: Mahatma Jotirao Phule and Low Caste Protest in Nineteenth-Century Western India* (Cambridge: Cambridge University Press, 1995), 50, 66, 111–12.

85. Rupa Viswanath, *The Pariah Problem: Caste, Religion and the Social in Modern India* (New York: Columbia University Press, 2014).

86. Sushil Madhava Pathak, *American Missionaries and Hinduism: A Study of Their Contacts from 1813 to 1910* (Delhi: Munshiram Manoharlal, 1967), 27–76; Milton Sangma, *History of American Baptist Mission in North-East India 1836–1950*, vol. 1 (Delhi: Mittal Publications, 1992).

87. Cited in Bean, *Yankee India*, 132, 170.

88. *Memoirs of Mrs. Harriett Newell* (Edinburgh: Ogle, Alardice & Thompson, 1817), 156–57, 160.

89. Nott cited in Pathak, *American Missionaries and Hinduism*, 80; John C. Lowrie, *Two Years in Upper India* (New York: Robert Carter and Brothers, 1850), 33.

90. Journal of the *Rockall*, in Bean, *Yankee India*, 263.

91. Taylor, *A Visit to India, China, and Japan*, 244.

92. Cited in Bhagat, *Americans in India*, 123.

93. Cited in C. A. Bayly, *Recovering Liberties: Indian Thought in the Age of Liberalism and Empire* (Cambridge, MA: Cambridge University Press, 2012), 50. The best introduction to Roy is Bruce Robertson, *Raja Rammohan Ray: The Father of Modern India* (Delhi: Oxford University Press, 1995).

94. Spencer Lavan, *Unitarians and India: A Study in Encounter and Response* (Boston: Skinner House, 1977).

95. R. K. Gupta, *The Great Encounter: A Study of Indo-American Literature and Cultural Relations* (New Delhi: Abhinav Publications, 1986), 94–96; Aakash Singh Rathore and Rimina Mohapatra, *Hegel's India: A Reinterpretation with Texts* (New Delhi: Oxford University Press, 2017).

96. Arthur Christy, *The Orient in American Transcendentalism* (New York: Columbia University Press, 1932); Carl T. Jackson, *The Oriental Religions and American Thought: Nineteenth-Century Explorations* (Westport, CT: Greenwood Press, 1981); Dale Rieppe, *The Philosophy of India and Its Impact on American Thought* (Springfield, IL: Charles C. Thomas, 1970).

97. Henry David Thoreau, *Walden and Civil Disobedience* (New York: Barnes & Nobles Classics, 2005), 9, 233.

98. Reproduced in Bean, *Yankee India*, 78.

Chapter 2: Under American Eyes

1. *Advocate of India*, January 28, 1896, Mark Twain Papers, Bancroft Library, University of California, Berkeley. I am grateful to Ramachandra Guha for sharing this material with me.

2. Mark Twain, *The Autobiography of Mark Twain* (Berkeley: University of California Press, 2013), 2:176.

3. Cited in Gupta, *Great Encounter*, 127.

4. Mark Twain, *Following the Equator: A Journey Around the World* (New York and London: Harper & Brothers,1899), 16.

5. A. B. Paine (ed.), *Mark Twain's Notebook* (New York: Harper, 1935), 281.

6. Twain, *Following the Equator*, 112.

7. Twain, *Following the Equator*, 348, 460, 399, 626.

8. Mark Twain, *Tales, Speeches, Essays and Sketches* (New York: Penguin, 2005), 268–69.

9. Jackson Lears, *Rebirth of a Nation: The Making of Modern America, 1877–1920* (New York: HarperCollins, 2009).

10. Bradford Perkins, *The Great Rapprochement: England and the United States, 1895–1914* (New York: Athenaeum, 1968).

11. Reginal Horsman, *Race and Manifest Destiny: The Origins of American Racial Anglo-Saxonism* (Cambridge, MA: Harvard University Press, 1981).

12. For a perceptive theoretical treatment, see Jayanta Sengupta, "Through Albion's Looking Glass? Constructions of India in American Travel Writing, c. 1850–1910," in Bharati Ray (ed.), *Different Types of History* (New Delhi: Pearson Longman, 2009), 333–58.

13. Richard H. Immerman, *Empire for Liberty: A History of American Imperialism from Benjamin Franklin to Paul Wolfowitz* (Princeton, NJ: Princeton University Press), 98–127.

14. William Seward, *Travels Around the World* (New York: D. Appleton & Company, 1873), 506–9, 464.

15. Cited in Sengupta, "Through Albion's Looking Glass?" 345.

16. Cited in David H. Burton, "Theodore Roosevelt: Confident Imperialist," *Review of Politics* 23, no. 3 (1961): 358n9, 360.

17. Ramachandra Guha, "The Two Phases of American Environmentalism: A Critical History," in Stephen Marglin and Frederique Apfel-Marglin (eds.), *Decolonizing Knowledge: From Development to Dialogue* (Oxford, UK: Clarendon Press, 1996).

18. David Gilmour, *The Long Recessional: The Imperial Life of Rudyard Kipling* (New York: FSG, 2002), 101, 125–16, 128.

19. Cited in Sydney Brooks, "American Opinion and British Rule in India" *North American Review* (December 1909): 774–75.

20. Cited in Burton, "Theodore Roosevelt," 356n1.

21. Andrew Carnegie, "The Opportunity of the United States," *North American Review* (May 1902): 606–12.

22. William Jennings Bryan, "British Rule in India," *India* (July 20, 1906).

23. Cited in Brooks, "American Opinion and British Rule in India," 775.

24. Andrew Preston, *Sword of the Spirit, Shield of Faith: Religion in American War and Diplomacy* (New York: Knopf, 2012), 177–79.

25. Cited in Lears, *Rebirth of a Nation*, 34.

26. Emily Rosenberg, *Spreading the American Dream: American Economic and Cultural Expansion, 1890–1945* (New York: Hill & Wang, 1982), 28–32; Preston, *Sword of the Spirit*, 184–85; Ian Tyrell, *Reforming the World: The Creation of America's Moral Empire* (Princeton, NJ: Princeton University Press, 2010).

27. Tyrell, *Reforming the World*, 56–57, 64.

28. Cited in Gupta, *Great Encounter*, 117.

29. Mary Louise Burke, *Swami Vivekananda in America: New Discoveries* (Calcutta: Advaita Ashrama, 1966).

30. "Religion Not the Crying Need of India," September 20, 1893, in Swami Vivekananda, *Complete Works of Swami Vivekananda* (Calcutta: Advaita Ashrama, 1970–73), Kindle loc. 2530.

31. "Christianity in India," Detroit, March 11, 1894, *Complete Works of Swami Vivekananda*, Kindle loc. 53755.

32. Cited in Earl Robert Schmidt, "American Relations with South Asia 1900–1940" (PhD thesis, University of Pennsylvania, 1955), 198.

33. Tyrell, *Reforming the World*, 92–93.

34. Sherwood Eddy, *India Awakening* (New York: Missionary Education Movement of the United States and Canada, 1911).

35. Cited in Schmidt, "American Relations with South Asia," 199.

36. Pathak, *American Missionaries and Hinduism*, 128.

37. Cited in Tyrell, *Reforming the World*, 183–84.

38. Schmidt, "American Relations with South Asia," 82, 133.

39. Pathak, *American Missionaries and Hinduism*, 170–71.

40. This and the following five paragraphs draw on D. Spencer Hatch, *Up from Poverty in Rural India* (Bombay: Oxford University Press, 1938) (emphasis in original).

41. Harold Isaacs, *Scratches on Our Minds: American Images of China and India* (New York: J. Day Co., 1958), 261–62.

42. Cited in Rotter, *Comrades at Odds*, 229.

43. David Omissi, *The Sepoy and the Raj: The Indian Army, 1860–1940* (London: Palgrave Macmillan, 1940); Isaacs, *Scratches on Our Minds*, 277.

44. Sanjoy Chakravorty, Devesh Kapur, and Nirvikar Singh, *The Other One Percent: Indians in America* (New York: Oxford University Press, 2017), 6.

45. Gary Hess, "The Forgotten Asian Americans: The East Indian Community in the United States," *Pacific Historical Review* 43, no. 4 (1974): 579–81.

46. Gary Hess, "'The Hindu' in America: Immigration and Naturalization Policies and India, 1917–1946," *Pacific Historical Review* 38, no. 1 (1969): 61–62.

47. Cited in Chakravorthy, Kapur, and Singh, *The Other One Percent*, 9–10.

48. Cited in Hess, "'The Hindu' in America," 63–64.

49. Maia Ramnath, *Haj to Utopia: How the Ghadar Movement Charted Global Radicalism and Attempted to Overthrow the British Empire* (Berkeley: University of California Press, 2011), 28–30.

50. Har Dayal, "India in America," *Modern Review* (July 1911): 1–11.

51. Cited in Hess, "The Forgotten Asian Americans," 585–86.

52. Don K. Dignan, "The Hindu Conspiracy in Anglo-American Relations During World War I," *Pacific Historical Review* 40, no. 1 (1971): 57–76; Hugh Johnston, "The Surveillance of Indian Nationalists in North America, 1908–1918," *BC Studies* 78 (1988): 3–27.

53. For an excellent, recent treatment, Seema Sohi, *Echoes of Mutiny: Race, Surveillance and Indian Anticolonialism in North America* (New Delhi: Oxford University Press, 2014). Also see Joan Jensen, "The 'Hindu Conspiracy': A Reassessment," *Pacific Historical Review* 48, no. 1 (1979): 65–83.

54. Lala Lajpat Rai, *The United States of America: A Hindu's Impressions and a Study* (Calcutta: R. Chatterjee, 1916).

55. Journal entry cited in Naeem Gul Rathore, "Indian Nationalist Agitation in the United States: A Study of Lala Lajpat Rai and the India Home Rule League of America 1914–20" (PhD thesis, Columbia University, 1965), 73.

56. Cited in Erez Manela, *The Wilsonian Moment: Self-Determination and the International Origins of Anticolonial Nationalism* (New York: Oxford University Press, 2007), 92.

57. Stephen Hay, "Rabindranath Tagore in America," *American Quarterly* 14, no. 3 (1962): 439–63.

58. Manela, *The Wilsonian Moment*, 96–97, 174–75.

59. Message to America, April 5, 1930, in *Collected Works of Mahatma Gandhi*, electronic book (New Delhi, Publications Division, Government of India, 1999), 49:13.

60. Cited in Manoranjan Jha, *Civil Disobedience and After: The American Reaction to Political Developments in India During 1930–1935* (Delhi: Meenakshi Prakashan, 1973), 114–15.

61. Jha, *Civil Disobedience and After*, 71–73.

62. Tyrell, *Reforming the World*, 216.

63. Asha Sharma, *An American in Khadi: The Definitive Biography of Satyananda Stokes* (New Delhi: Penguin, 1999); Kenton J. Clymer, "Samuel Evans Stokes, Mahatma Gandhi, and Indian Nationalism," *Pacific Historical Review* 29, no. 1 (1990): 51–76.

64. The best treatment of Gandhi's engagement with Thoreau is Anthony J. Parel, *Pax Gandhiana: The Political Philosophy of Mahatma Gandhi* (New York: Oxford University Press, 2016), chap. 9.

65. For a superb account, see Joseph Kip Kosek, *Acts of Conscience: Christian Nonviolence and Modern American Democracy* (New York: Columbia University Press, 2009) (Muste quoted at Kindle loc. 182).

66. Paul E. Teed, "Interfaith Encounter and Religious Pluralism: J. T. Sunderland's Mission to Brahmo Samajes of India, 1895–96," *American Studies* 50, no. 1 (2009): 51–69.

67. Lavan, *Unitarians and India*, 181–88.

68. Cited in Harnam Singh, *The Indian National Movement and American Opinion* (New Delhi: Rama Krishna & Sons, 1962), 189.

69. Cited in Singh, *The Indian National Movement*, 169–70.

70. Alan Raucher, "American Anti-Imperialists and the Pro-India Movement, 1900–1932," *Pacific Historical Review* 43, no. 1 (1974): 101–2.

71. Kosek, *Acts of Conscience*, chap. 3.

72. Cited in Lloyd Rudolph, "Gandhi in the Mind of America," in Sulochana Raghavan Glazer and Nathan Glazer (eds.), *Conflicting Images: India and the United States* (Glendale, MD: Riverdale Company, 1990), 155.

73. Reinhold Niebuhr, *Moral Man and Immoral Society: A Study in Ethics and Politics* (New York: Charles Scribner's Sons, 1932); Jawaharlal Nehru, *An Autobiography* (London: John Lane, 1936; reprint New Delhi: Penguin, 2004), 558–60.

74. Slate, *Colored Cosmopolitanism*, 44–47, 73.

75. Mrinalini Sinha, *Specters of Mother India: The Global Restructuring of an Empire* (Durham, NC: Duke University Press, 2007).

Chapter 3: Fighting for Freedom

1. Cited in Srinath Raghavan, *India's War: World War II and the Making of Modern South Asia* (New York: Basic Books, 2016), 47.

2. Cited in John A. Thompson, *A Sense of Power: The Roots of America's Global Role* (Ithaca, NY: Cornell University Press, 2015), 183.

3. Cited in Thompson, *A Sense of Power*, 142, 146.

4. The classic account is William Appleman Williams, *The Tragedy of American Diplomacy*, 50th anniversary ed. (New York: W. W. Norton, 2009). For a later and incisive analysis, see Rosenberg, *Spreading the American Dream*.

5. Cited in Patrick Hearden, *Architects of Globalism: Building a New World Order During World War II* (Fayetteville: University of Arkansas Press, 2002), 14–16. Also see Frank Ninkovich, *The Global Republic: America's Inadvertent Rise to World Power* (Chicago: University of Chicago Press, 2014), 160–68.

6. Cited in Hearden, *Architects of Globalism*, 41.

7. Robert Skidelsky, *John Maynard Keynes: Fighting for Freedom, 1937–1946* (New York: Viking, 2000), 99–133.

8. Hearden, *Architects of Globalism*, 29–33, 42–43.

9. Cited in Niall Ferguson, *Colossus: The Rise and Fall of the American Empire* (London: Penguin Books, 2005), 67.

10. Cited in Lloyd C. Gardner, "How We 'Lost' Vietnam, 1940–54," in David Ryan and Victor Pungong (eds.), *The United States and Decolonization: Power and*

Freedom (London: Palgrave Macmillan, 2000), 129. Also see Michael Hunt, "Conclusions: The Decolonization Puzzle in US Policy—Promise Versus Performance," in Ryan and Pungong, *The United States and Decolonization*, 207–29.

11. Cited in Peter D. Garlock, "The United States and the Indian Crisis, 1941–1943: The Limits of Anti-colonialism" (PhD thesis, Yale University, 1973), 14.

12. The classic study is William Roger Louis, *Imperialism at Bay, 1941–1945: The United States and the Decolonization of the British Empire* (Oxford, UK: Clarendon Press, 1977).

13. Quoted in Warren F. Kimball, *The Juggler: Franklin Roosevelt as Wartime Statesman* (Princeton, NJ: Princeton University Press, 1994), 14.

14. Cited in Kenton J. Clymer, *Quest for Freedom: The United States and India's Independence* (New York: Columbia University Press, 1995), 14–19.

15. British aide memoire, April 17, 1941; Hull to Halifax, May 28, 1941; press release, July 21, 1941, in *Foreign Relations of the United States* (hereafter *FRUS*), 1941, 3:170–74.

16. Memo on "India and the Lend Lease Act," May 14, 1941, File no. 2, Roosevelt Library Papers, Nehru Memorial Museum & Library (hereafter NMML).

17. Memorandum by Hull, May 7, 1941, *FRUS* 1941, 3:178.

18. Louis, *Imperialism at Bay*.

19. Raghavan, *India's War*, 216.

20. Interview with Evelyn Wrench, December 1941, in *Collected Works of Mahatma Gandhi*, 81:348.

21. Cited in Clymer, *Quest for Freedom*, 35.

22. Memorandum by Murray, November 7, 1941; Welles to Hull, November 15, 1941, *FRUS* 1941, 3:184–87.

23. Clymer, *Quest for Freedom*, 44.

24. Winston Churchill, *Hinge of Fate* (London: Cassell, 1951), 209; Churchill to Attlee, January 7, 1942, in N. Mansergh, E. W. R. Lumby, and P. Moon (eds.), *Transfer of Power: 1942–47* (London: Her Majesty's Stationery Office, 1970–1983), 1:14.

25. Memorandum by Berle, February 17, 1942, *FRUS* 1942, 602–4.

26. Long to Welles, February 25, 1942, *FRUS* 1942, 606.

27. Kamaladevi Chattopadhyay, *Inner Recesses Outer Spaces: Memoirs*, 2nd ed. (New Delhi: Niyogi Books, 2014), 238–39.

28. Cited in Clymer, *Quest for Freedom*, 45 (emphasis in original).

29. Roosevelt to Churchill (draft), February 25, 1942, in Warren Kimball (ed.), *Churchill and Roosevelt: The Complete Correspondence* (Princeton, NJ: Princeton University Press, 1984), 1:400–1.

30. Message to Winant, February 25, 1942, *FRUS* 1942, 604.

31. Amery to Linlithgow, March 10, 1942, in Mansergh et al., *Transfer of Power* 1: 396–97, 404.

32. *FRUS* 1942, 613, 617.

33. R. J. Moore, *Churchill, Cripps and India, 1939–1945* (Oxford, UK: Clarendon Press, 1979); Sarvepalli Gopal, *Jawaharlal Nehru: A Biography* (London: Jonathan Cape, 1975), 1:279–87.

34. Johnson to Roosevelt, April 11, 1942, *FRUS* 1942, 631–32.

35. Roosevelt to Churchill, April 11, 1942; Churchill to Roosevelt, April 12, 1942, *FRUS* 1942, 633–35.

36. Nehru to Roosevelt, in Sarvepalli Gopal (ed.), *Selected Works of Jawaharlal Nehru*, First Series (New Delhi: Jawaharlal Nehru Memorial Fund, 1979), 12:212–13.

37. Cited in Clymer, *Quest for Freedom*, 82.

38. Slate, *Colored Cosmopolitanism*, 127–33.

39. John Paton Davies, *China Hand: An Autobiography* (Philadelphia: University of Pennsylvania Press, 2012), 55–91.

40. Cited in Garlock, "The United States and the Indian Crisis," 192.

41. Louis Fischer, "Why Cripps Failed," *The Nation* (September 19 and 26, 1942); Edgar Snow, "Must Britain Give Up India?," *Saturday Evening Post* (September 12, 1942).

42. Garlock, "The United States and the Indian Crisis," 217–19.

43. Cited in Clymer, *Quest for Freedom*, 87–88.

44. Gandhi to Roosevelt, July 1, 1942, File No. 12, Roosevelt Library Papers, NMML.

45. Fischer telegram and letter to Roosevelt, August 5 and 7, 1942, File No. 12, Roosevelt Library Papers, NMML.

46. Cited in Hearden, *Architects of Globalism*, 95–96.

47. Garlock, "The United States and the Indian Crisis," 256–57.

48. Memorandum by Hull, August 15, 1942, File No. 12, Roosevelt Library Papers, NMML.

49. Cited in Kameshwar C. Wali, *Chandra: A Biography of S. Chandrasekhar* (Chicago: University of Chicago Press, 1990), 191.

50. Slate, *Colored Cosmopolitanism*, 144.

51. Garlock, "The United States and the Indian Crisis," 279–80, 316–21.

52. Garlock, "The United States and the Indian Crisis," 311–12; Clymer, *Quest for Freedom*, 101.

53. Cited in Garlock, "The United States and the Indian Crisis," 275, 291.

54. Louis, *Imperialism at Bay*, 199–200.

55. Clymer, *Quest for Freedom*, 70–71.

56. Christopher Thorne, *Allies of a Kind: The United States, Britain, and the War Against Japan, 1941–1945* (Oxford: Oxford University Press, 1978), 246–47.

57. Hull to Winant (for Phillips), November 20, 1942, *FRUS* 1942, 746–48.

58. Phillips to Hull, February 10, 1943, *FRUS* 1943, 187.

59. Phillips to Roosevelt, February 11, 1943, *FRUS 1943*, 190 (emphasis in original).
60. Hull to Phillips, February 17, 1943, *FRUS 1943*, 195.
61. Phillips to Hull and Roosevelt, February 18 and 19, 1943, *FRUS 1943*, 195–97.
62. Memorandum of conversation by Hull, February 20, 1943; Phillips to Roosevelt, February 23, 1943, *FRUS 1943*, 199–203.
63. Phillips to Roosevelt, March 3, 1943, *FRUS 1943*, 205–7.
64. Phillips to Roosevelt, April 19, 1943, *FRUS 1943*, 217–19.
65. Cited in Gary Hess, *America Encounters India* (Baltimore: Johns Hopkins Press, 1971), 106.
66. Clymer, *Quest for Freedom*, 162–64; Hearden, *Architects of Globalism*, 97.
67. Johannes Voigt, *India in the Second World War* (New Delhi: Arnold Heinemann, 1987), 98–99.
68. These negotiations can be followed in *FRUS 1941*, 192–99 (emphasis in original).
69. Voigt, *India in the Second World War*, 99.
70. Merrell to Hull, January 5, 1943; Phillips to Roosevelt, January 14, 1943, *FRUS 1943*, 248–49.
71. Memorandum by Hawkins, January 25, 1943; memorandum by Oakes, February 24, 1943, *FRUS 1943*, 250–51, 254.
72. Memoranda by Acheson, March 4 and 30, 1943, *FRUS 1943*, 258–59, 261–62.
73. Agent-general of India to State Department (enclosing memorandum), December 4, 1944, *FRUS 1944*, 275–77.
74. These discussions can be followed in *FRUS 1944*, 277–81.
75. D. A. Kearns-Preston, "The Importance and Future of Trade Between India and the United States," in A. N. Agarwala (ed.), *Position and Prospects of India's Foreign Trade: A Survey by Trade Commissioners* (London: Arthur Probsthain, 1947), 240–64.
76. Report of the American Technical Mission to India, WO 32/10269, The National Archives (hereafter TNA), London.
77. Cited in James M. Ehrman, "Ways of War and the American Experience in the China-Burma-India Theater, 1942–1945" (PhD thesis, Kansas State University, 2006), 49.
78. Cited in Garlock, "The United States and the Indian Crisis," 183.
79. Raghavan, *India's War*, 338–55.
80. On the background to this crisis, see S. L. N. Simha, *History of the Reserve Bank of India, 1935–1951* (Bombay: Reserve Bank of India, 1970), 337–40.
81. Merrell to Hull, June 13, 1943, *FRUS 1943*, 271.
82. Memorandum by Livesey, August 27, 1943; Halifax to Henry Morgenthau, November 9, 1943, *FRUS 1943*, 277–78, 281–82.
83. Memorandum of telephone conversation, January 8, 1944; memorandum of conversation by Oakes, January 26, 1944; memorandum of conversation by Allen, February 11, 1944, *FRUS 1944*, 248–49, 250–53, 257–58.

84. These discussions can be followed in *FRUS 1944*, 259–69.

85. Cited in Clymer, *Quest for Freedom*, 184–86.

86. Phillips to Roosevelt, September 9, 1943, *FRUS 1943*, 330–31.

87. M. S. Venkataramani, *Bengal Famine of 1943: The American Response* (Delhi: Vikas Publishing House, 1973), 40–59.

88. Churchill to Roosevelt, April 29, 1944; Draft Telegram from Roosevelt to Churchill, May 31, 1944, *FRUS 1944*, 271–73.

89. Cited in Venkataramani, *Bengal Famine of 1943*, 63, 73.

90. Charles F. Romanus and Riley Sunderland, *United States Army in Word War II, China-Burma-India Theatre: Stillwell's Mission to China* (Washington, DC: Center of Military History, United States Army, 1987), 151.

91. Exchanges between Delhi and London over Chinese troops in Ramgarh can be followed in WO 106/3547, TNA.

92. Theodore H. White (ed.), *The Stilwell Papers* (New York: Shocken Books, 1972), 161, 163.

93. Romanus and Sunderland, *Stilwell's Mission*, 270–71.

94. Barbara Tuchman, *Sand Against the Wind: Stilwell and the American Experience in China, 1911–45* (New York: Macmillan, 1970), 356.

95. Romanus and Sunderland, *Stilwell's Mission*, 359.

96. Memorandum by Davies, October 21, 1943, cited in Voigt, *India in the Second World War*, 222; Merrell to Hull, October 23, 1943, *FRUS China 1943*, 879–80.

97. Thorne, *Allies of a Kind*, 337.

98. Memorandum by Davies, December 1943, *FRUS China 1943*, 188–89.

99. Note of January 1943 in Davies, *China Hand*, 88–90.

100. White, *Stilwell Papers*, 277–78.

101. Tuchman, *Stilwell*, 431.

102. Eric D. Pullin, "'Noise and Flutter': American Propaganda Strategy and Operations in India During World War II," *Diplomatic History* 34, no. 2 (2010): 286–92.

103. Sarah Ellen Graham, "American Propaganda, the Anglo-American Alliance, and the 'Delicate Question' of Indian Self-Determination," *Diplomatic History* 33, no. 2 (2008): 249.

104. Pullin, "'Noise and Flutter,'" 294–95; Graham, "American Propaganda," 251.

105. Graham, "American Propaganda," 236.

106. Slate, *Colored Cosmopolitanism*, 152–55.

107. Cited in Gerald Horne, *The End of Empires: African Americans and India* (Philadelphia: Temple University Press, 2008), 163.

108. Frank Moraes, *Witness to an Era: India 1920 to the Present Day* (Delhi: Vikas Publishing House, 1973), 110–11.

109. Yasmin Khan, *The Raj at War: A People's History of India's Second World War* (London: Random House, 2015), 147–48.

110. P. N. Chopra and S. R. Bakshi (eds.), *Quit India Movement: British Secret Documents* (New Delhi: Interprint, 1986), 398–401.

111. Joan V. Bondurant, *Sketches of India with Forty Photographic Illustrations* (Ann Arbor, MI: Craft Press, 1946); Joan V. Bondurant, *Conquest of Violence: The Gandhian Philosophy of Conflict* (Princeton, NJ: Princeton University Press, 1956).

112. Cited in Clymer, *Quest for Freedom*, 190.

113. Vijayalakshmi Pandit, *The Scope of Happiness: A Personal Memoir* (New Delhi: Harper Collins, 1979), 186–92.

114. Cited in Clymer, *Quest for Freedom*, 214–15.

115. Louis, *Imperialism at Bay*, 459–64.

116. The best account is Robert Hildebrand, *Dumbarton Oaks: The Origins of the United Nations and the Search for Postwar Security* (Chapel Hill: University of North Carolina Press, 1990).

117. Statement to the press, April 17, 1945, *Collected Works of Mahatma Gandhi*, 86: 188–90.

118. Marika Sherwood, "India at the Founding of the United Nations," *International Studies* 33, no. 4 (1996): 408–12.

119. Manu Bhagavan, *The Peacemakers: India and the Quest for One World* (New Delhi: HarperCollins, 2012), 54.

120. On the longer background to India's participation in the conference, see Aditya Balasubramanian and Srinath Raghavan, "Present at the Creation: India, the Global Economy and the Bretton Woods Conference," *Journal of World History* 29, no. 1 (2018): 65–94.

121. Commission I, Committee 1, Second Meeting, July 4, 1944, in Kurt Schuler and Andrew Rosenberg (eds.), *The Bretton Woods Transcripts* (New York: Center for Financial Stability, 2012), 321–24.

122. Commission I, Third Meeting, July 10, 1944, *Bretton Woods Transcripts*, 70–73.

123. Cited in Hearden, *Architects of Globalism*, 315.

Chapter 4: Between East and West Asia

1. Cited in Rotter, *Comrades at Odds*, 15–16.

2. This paragraph and the next draw on Melvyn P. Leffler, *A Preponderance of Power: National Security, the Truman Administration, and the Cold War* (Stanford, CA: Stanford University Press, 1992); Thomas J. McCormick, *America's Half-Century: United States Foreign Policy in the Cold War and After*, 2nd ed. (Baltimore: Johns Hopkins University Press, 1995); Fred L. Block, *The Origins of International Economic Disorder: A Study of the United States International Monetary Policy from World War 2 to the Present* (Berkeley: University of California Press, 1977); Richard N. Gardner, *Sterling-Dollar Diplomacy: The Origins and Prospects of Our International*

Economic Order (New York: Oxford University Press, 1956); Barry Eichengreen, *Globalizing Capital: A History of the International Monetary System*, 2nd ed. (Princeton, NJ: Princeton University Press, 2008).

3. On these transitions, see Christopher Bayly and Tim Harper, *Forgotten Wars: The End of Britain's Asian Empire* (London: Allen Lane, 2007); Ronald H. Spector, *In the Ruins of Empire: The Japanese Surrender and the Battle for Postwar Asia* (New York: Random House, 2007); Robert J. McMahon, *Colonialism and Cold War: The United States and the Struggle for Indonesia Independence 1945–49* (New York: Cornell University Press, 1981).

4. John Darwin, *Britain and Decolonisation: The Retreat from Empire in the Post-war World* (Basingstoke, UK: Palgrave Macmillan, 1988); R. J. Moore, *Escape from Empire: The Attlee Government and the Indian Problem* (Oxford, UK: Clarendon Press, 1983).

5. Cited in McMahon, *Cold War on the Periphery*, 13.

6. Cited in McMahon, *Cold War on the Periphery*, 13, 15.

7. McMahon, *Cold War on the Periphery*, 18.

8. Cited in Kux, *Disenchanted Allies*, 20.

9. Margaret Bourke-White, *Halfway to Freedom: A Report on the New India* (New York: Simon & Schuster, 1949), 92–93.

10. Note, September 5, 1946, in Sarvepalli Gopal (ed.), *Selected Works of Jawaharlal Nehru* (New Dehi: Jawaharlal Nehru Memorial Fund, 1984), 2nd ser., vol. 1, 438–42 (hereafter *SWJN*).

11. Nehru to Stafford Cripps, December 17, 1948, cited in Judith Brown, *Nehru: A Political Life* (New Delhi: Oxford University Press, 2003), 213.

12. Khurshid to Jinnah, October 12, 1947, in Z. H Zaidi (ed.), *Jinnah Papers* (Islamabad: Quaid-i-Azam Papers Project, Culture Division, Government of Pakistan, 1993), 9:246–52.

13. Defence Committee of the Cabinet Meeting, October 26, 1947, F200/246, Mountbatten Papers, British Library, London.

14. Srinath Raghavan, *War and Peace in Modern India: A Strategic History of the Nehru Years* (London: Palgrave Macmillan, 2010), 107–24.

15. Memorandum of conversation by Thurston, January 10, 1948, *FRUS 1948*, pt. 1, doc. 215.

16. Aiyaz Husain, *Mapping the End of Empire: American and British Strategic Visions in the Postwar World* (Cambridge, MA: Harvard University Press, 2014), 1–104.

17. C. Dasgupta, *War and Diplomacy in Kashmir, 1947–48* (London: Sage, 2002), chap. 10.

18. Marshall to Austin, February 20, 1948, *FRUS 1948*, pt. 1, doc. 235.

19. Nehru to Vijayalakshmi, February 16, 1948, *SWJN SS* 5, 218.

20. Josef Korbel, *Danger in Kashmir*, rev. ed. (Princeton, NJ: Princeton University Press, 1966), chap. 6.

21. Marshall to Bevin, October 20, 1948; memorandum by Huddle, November 1, 1948; *FRUS* 1948, pt. 1, docs. 347, 354.

22. Raghavan, *War and Peace in Modern India*, 143–46.

23. Henderson to Acheson, August 15, 1949, *FRUS* 1949, doc. 1205.

24. Cited in McMahon, *Cold War on the Periphery*, 50–51.

25. Nehru note, September 15, 1951, Subject File 56, Vijayalakshmi Pandit Papers, NMML.

26. Anton Harder, "Not at the Cost of China: New Evidence Regarding the US Proposals to Nehru for Joining the Security Council," Cold War International History Working Paper 76, March 2015; McMahon, *Cold War on the Periphery*, 59.

27. Hughes to Harding, July 18 and 21, 1921; Harding to Amanullah, July 29, 1921, *FRUS* 1921, 258–61.

28. Cited in Jeffrey John Roberts, "Afghanistan and Western Policy: 1929–1956" (PhD thesis, Ohio State University, 1990), 328–29.

29. Roberts, "Afghanistan and Western Policy," 330–31.

30. Roberts, "Afghanistan and Western Policy," 352n37.

31. Amin Saikal, *Modern Afghanistan: A History of Struggle and Survival* (London: I. B. Taurus, 2006), 120. For a more detailed account, see Elisabeth Leake, *The Defiant Border: The Afghan-Pakistan Borderlands in the Era of Decolonization, 1936–1965* (Cambridge: Cambridge University Press, 2017), 104–48.

32. Memoranda of conversations, November 19 and December 8, 1948, *FRUS* 1948, pt. 1, docs. 395, 396.

33. Memorandum by McGhee, January 24, 1950; Acheson to embassies in Afghanistan and Pakistan, November 2, 1950, *FRUS* 1950, docs. 815, 821.

34. Acheson to embassy in Pakistan, November 28, 1950, *FRUS* 1950, doc. 823.

35. Memoranda of conversations, January 22 and March 12, 1951; Warren to Acheson, April 12, 1951; Acheson to embassy in Afghanistan, September 27, 1951, *FRUS* 1951, docs. 302, 314, 320, 355.

36. Acheson to embassy in India, July 24, 1951, *FRUS* 1951, doc. 176.

37. Letter to chief ministers, August 1, 1951, *SWJN SS* 16, pt. 2, 691–93.

38. Cited in McMahon, *Cold War on the Periphery*, 129.

39. Cited in Chaudhuri, *Forged in Crisis*, 52–53.

40. Acheson to Nehru, July 17, 1950, *FRUS* 1950, doc. 309.

41. Acheson to Nehru, July 25, 1950, *FRUS* 1950, doc. 351.

42. Cited in Gopal, *Nehru*, 2:103–4.

43. Entry of August 18, 1951, Dairy 32, K. P. S. Menon Papers, NMML.

44. Cited in Matthew Jones, *After Hiroshima: The United States, Race and Nuclear Weapons in Asia* (Cambridge: Cambridge University Press, 2010), 121.

45. Cited in Sunil Khilnani, "Making Asia: India, China and the Struggle for an Idea" (Jawaharlal Nehru Memorial Lecture, London, 2012), 7. I am grateful to Professor Khilnani for a copy of this text.

46. Nehru's note on conversation with Henderson, September 15, 1951, Subject File 56, Vijayalakshmi Pandit Papers, NMML.

47. Cited in Jones, *After Hiroshima*, 122.

48. Cited in McMahon, *Cold War on the Periphery*, 133.

49. Anita Inder Singh, *The Limits of British Influence: South Asia and the Anglo-American Relationship, 1947–56* (New York: St. Martin's Press, 1993), 94–98.

50. Warren to Acheson, May 15, 1951; Acheson to Warren, May 24, 1951, *FRUS 1951*, vol. 6, pt. 2, docs. 491, 492.

51. Memorandum of conversation by McGhee, October 18, 1951, *FRUS 1951*, doc. 497.

52. Kearns-Preston, "The Importance and Future of Trade Between India and the United States," 261. The author dealt with India in the US Department of Commerce.

53. Cited in McCormick, *America's Half-Century*, 52.

54. For a retrospective overview, see Gerald M. Meir and Dudley Seers (eds.), *Pioneers in Development* (Washington, DC: World Bank, 1984).

55. Sylvia Maxfield and James H. Nolt, "Protectionism and Internationalization of Capital: U.S. Sponsorship of Import Substitution Industrialization in the Philippines, Turkey and Argentina," *International Studies Quarterly* 34, no. 1 (1990): 49–81.

56. *Commercial America* 45 (1947).

57. Gilles Boquerat, *No Strings Attached: India's Policies and Foreign Aid, 1947–1966* (New Delhi: Manohar, 2003), 22–23.

58. Nehru to Wilcox, *SWJN*, vol. 2, 589–90.

59. Cited in Merrill, *Bread and the Ballot*, 26.

60. Cited in Boquerat, *No Strings Attached*, 104.

61. Extract from Bulletin 227, November 7, 1949, *FRUS 1949*, vol. 1, doc. 234.

62. Boquerat, *No Strings Attached*, 157–58.

63. Note to foreign secretary, August 12, 1948, *SWJN SS*, vol. 7, 627–30.

64. Cited in Boquerat, *No Strings Attached*, 112.

65. Cited in Rotter, *Comrades at Odds*, 112.

66. Stephen Springarn to Clifford, May 6, 1949, cited in S. C. Mudumbai, *United States Foreign Policy Towards India, 1947–1954* (Delhi: Manohar, 1980), 94.

67. Report and Recommendations on Loan Application of India, August 16, 1949, doc 2, World Bank Archives.

68. Cited in Merrill, *Bread and the Ballot*, 25.

69. Cited in Merrill, *Bread and the Ballot*, 26–27.

70. McMahon, *Cold War on the Periphery*, 48, 34; Merrill, *Bread and the Ballot*, 29.

71. Grady to Marshall, July 11, 1947, *FRUS 1947*, vol. 3, doc. 105.

72. Acting secretary of state to Pakistani ambassador, *FRUS 1947*, doc. 117.

73. McMahon, *Cold War on the Periphery*, 92–94.

74. Merrill, *Bread and the Ballot*, 63–65.

75. Rotter, *Comrades at Odds*, 97–105.
76. Nehru to Pandit, April 11, 1951, *SWJN SS* 16, pt. 1, 72–73.
77. Merrill, *Bread and the Ballot*, 50–53, 77–79.
78. Letter to Abram Chayes cited in Howard B. Schaffer, *Chester Bowles: New Dealer in the Cold War* (New Delhi: Prentice Hall, 1994), 71 (emphasis in original).
79. Cited in Merrill, *Bread and the Ballot*, 85.
80. Boquerat, *No Strings Attached*, 148–50.
81. Cited in Merrill, *Bread and the Ballot*, 84.
82. Cited in Odd Arne Westad, *The Global Cold War: Third World Interventions and the Making of Our Times* (Cambridge: Cambridge University Press, 2005), 25.
83. George Rosen, *Western Economists and Eastern Societies: Agents of Change in South Asia, 1950–1970* (Delhi: Oxford University Press, 1985), 8–13 (emphasis in original).
84. Ensminger Oral History Papers, Ford Foundation Archives, New York.
85. For fine recent studies of Meyer and community development, see Daniel Immerwahr, *Thinking Small: The United States and the Lure of Community Development* (Cambridge, MA: Harvard University Press, 2013); Nicole Sackley, "Village Models: Etawah, India, and the Making and Remaking of Development in the Early Cold War," *Diplomatic History* 37 (2013): 749–78.
86. Albert Meyer, *Pilot Project India: The Story of Rural Development at Etawah, Uttar Pradesh* (Berkeley: University of California Press, 1958), 20–22, 31.
87. Immerwahr, *Thinking Small*, 72–75.
88. This paragraph and the next draw on John Clark, *Hunza: The Lost Kingdom of Himalayas* (New York: Funk & Wagnalls, 1956).
89. Cited in Melvyn Leffler, "The Emergence of an American Grand Strategy, 1945–1952," in Odd Arne Westad and Melvyn Leffler (eds.), *The Cambridge History of the Cold War* (Cambridge: Cambridge University Press, 2010), 1:88.
90. Cited in Rotter, *Comrades at Odds*, 236–37.
91. Cited in McMahon, *Cold War on the Periphery*, 45, 62.
92. Cited in Rotter, *Comrades at Odds*, 87–88.
93. Cited in McMahon, *Cold War on the Periphery*, 56.
94. Jones, *After Hiroshima*, 39–41.
95. Cited in Rotter, *Comrades at Odds*, 168.
96. Cited in Jones, *After Hiroshima*, 44.
97. Cited in Slate, *Colored Cosmopolitanism*, 173, 175.
98. South Asian Regional Conference, February 26 to March 2, 1951, *FRUS* 1951, vol. 6, pt. 2, doc. 105.
99. Memorandum by Shepard Jones, July 31, 1951, *FRUS* 1951, doc. 480.
100. Note by Nehru, September 15, 1951, Subject File 56, Vijayalakshmi Pandit Papers, NMML.
101. Bowles to Acheson, December 6, 1951, *FRUS* 1951, vol. 6, pt. 2, doc. 489.

Chapter 5: Allies and Aid

1. Entry of January 22, 1952, in Robert Ferrell (ed.), *The Eisenhower Diaries* (New York: Norton, 1981), 210. Also see John Lewis Gaddis, *Strategies of Containment* (New York: Oxford University Press, 1982).

2. Cited in Robert. J. McMahon, "US National Security Policy from Eisenhower to Kennedy," in Westad and Leffler, *The Cambridge History of the Cold War*, 1:289.

3. Cited in McMahon, "US National Security Policy," 301.

4. Cited in McGarr, *Cold War in South Asia*, 56.

5. Cited in Jones, *After Hiroshima*, 124–25.

6. Preston, *Sword of the Spirit*, 384–410, 450–64.

7. Dulles to State Department, May 26, 1953, *FRUS 1952–1954*, vol. 9, pt. 1, doc. 49.

8. Cited in McMahon, *Cold War on the Periphery*, 157.

9. Byroade to Dulles, March 25, 1953; Dulles to Eisenhower, April 30, 1953, *FRUS 1952–1954*, vol. 11, pt. 2, docs. 1134, 1136.

10. Dulles to State Department, May 26, 1953, *FRUS 1952–1954*, vol. 9, pt. 1, doc. 49.

11. Memorandum of conversation between Dulles and Ayub, May 23, 1953, *FRUS 1952–1954*, vol. 9, pt. 1, doc. 46.

12. Ayesha Jalal, *The State of Martial Rule: The Origins of Pakistan's Political Economy of Defence* (Cambridge: Cambridge University Press, 1990).

13. Memorandum of the National Security Council (NSC) discussion, June 1, 1953, *FRUS 1952–1954*, vol. 9, pt. 1, doc. 137.

14. Cited in Kux, *Disenchanted Allies*, 72.

15. McMahon, *Cold War on the Periphery*, 166–68.

16. Memorandum of conversation by Hildreth, December 7, 1953, *FRUS 1952–1954*, vol. 11, pt. 1, doc. 1143.

17. Singh, *Limits of British Influence*, 123–36; McMahon, *Cold War on the Periphery*, 167, 169–70.

18. Cited in Kux, *Disenchanted Allies*, 58–59.

19. Cited in McMahon, *Cold War on the Periphery*, 171.

20. Memorandum by Dulles, January 5, 1954, *FRUS 1952–1954*, vol. 11, pt. 1, doc. 1147.

21. Nehru to Mohammed Ali, November 10, 1953; Nehru to Panikkar, November 12, 1953, *SWJN SS*, vol. 24, 416, 423–24.

22. Cited in Zorawar Daulet Singh, "Role Conceptions and Indian Statecraft During the Cold War" (PhD thesis, King's College London, 2017), 134, 139.

23. Allen to State Department, February 24, 1954, *FRUS 1952–1954*, vol. 11, pt. 1, doc. 1077.

24. Cited in McMahon, *Cold War on the Periphery*, 173.

25. Cited in Sarah Ellen Graham, "The Eisenhower Administration and Public Diplomacy in India: An Ambivalent Engagement, 1953–60," *Diplomacy and Statecraft* 25, no. 2 (2014): 270.

26. Cited in Sisir Gupta, *Kashmir: A Study in India-Pakistan Relations* (London: Asia Publishing House, 1966), 303.

27. Record of conversation, October 23, 1954, *SWJN SS*, vol. 26, 34.

28. Cited in Roby C. Barrett, *The Greater Middle East and the Cold War: US Foreign Policy Under Eisenhower and Kennedy* (London: I. B. Taurus, 2010), 28.

29. Note by foreign secretary, January 9, 1955, I(9)AAC/55, MEA, National Archives of India (hereafter NAI).

30. Matthew Jones, "A 'Segregated' Asia? Race, the Bandung Conference, and Pan-Asianist Fears in American Thought and Policy, 1954–55," *Diplomatic History* 29, no. 5 (2005): 855–56, 859.

31. Cited in Kux, *Estranged Democracies*, 119.

32. McGarr, *Cold War in South Asia*, 63.

33. Memorandum of conversation by Thatcher, October 8, 1954, *FRUS 1952–1954*, vol. 11, pt. 1, doc. 862.

34. Memorandum of conversation by Thatcher, December 28, 1954, *FRUS 1952–1954*, vol. 11, pt. 1, doc. 880.

35. Timothy Nunan, *Humanitarian Invasion: Global Development in Cold War Afghanistan* (Cambridge: Cambridge University Press, 2016), 60–64.

36. Hildreth to State Department, July 10, 1954, *FRUS 1952–1954*, vol. 11, pt. 2, doc. 1154.

37. McMahon, *Cold War on the Periphery*, 203–4.

38. Memorandum of NSC discussion, January 3, 1957, *FRUS 1955–1957*, vol. 8, doc. 4.

39. Cited in Merrill, *Bread and the Ballot*, 119.

40. G. L. Mehta to foreign secretary, February 11, 1956, 68(9) AMS/56, MEA, NAI.

41. Norman Thomas to G. L. Mehta, January 31, 1955, 70–2/55 AMS, MEA, NAI.

42. Cited in Merrill, *Bread and the Ballot*, 115.

43. Eisenhower to Dulles, *FRUS 1955–1957*, vol. 8, doc. 144; G. L. Mehta to foreign secretary, February 11, 1956, 68(9) AMS/56, MEA, NAI.

44. Memorandum of conversations between Dulles and Nehru, March 9–10, 1956; Dulles to Eisenhower, March 11, 1956, *FRUS 1955–1957*, vol. 8, docs. 156, 157.

45. Cited in Merrill, *Bread and the Ballot*, 131.

46. Note from Mehta to Dutt, April 28, 1956, 68(9) AMS/56, MEA, NAI.

47. NSC 5701, January 10, 1957, *FRUS 1955–1957*, vol. 8, doc. 5.

48. Raghavan, *War and Peace in Modern India*, 249.

49. Gyalo Thondup, *The Noodle Maker of Kalimpong: The Untold Story of My Struggle for Tibet* (Gurgaon: Penguin Random House India, 2015), 167–89; Lezlee Brown Halper and Stefan Halper, *Tibet: An Unfinished Story* (London: Hurst, 2014), 195–201. Also see Sulmaan Wasif Khan, *Muslim Trader, Nomad, Spy:*

China's Cold War and the People of the Tibetan Borderlands (Chapel Hill: University of North Carolina Press, 2015).

50. Chen Jian, "The Tibetan Rebellion of 1959 and China's Changing Relations with India and the Soviet Union," *Journal of Cold War Studies* 8, no. 3 (2006): 54–101.

51. Kenneth Conboy and James Morrison, *The CIA's Secret War in Tibet* (Lawrence: University of Kansas Press, 2002), 97, 117.

52. Gopal, *Nehru*, 2:103–4.

53. Oral History of Douglas Ensminger, Ford Foundation Papers, Yale University.

54. Nixon cited in McMahon, *Cold War on the Periphery*, 228–29; Merrill, *Bread and the Ballot*, 125–130.

55. NSC 5701, January 10, 1957, *FRUS 1955–1957*, vol. 8, doc. 5.

56. Cited in McMahon, *Cold War on the Periphery*, 236, 239.

57. Merrill, *Bread and the Ballot*, 143–144.

58. Note by consul general in New York (Arthur Lall) and comments by prime minister, foreign secretary, and secretary general, August–September 1954, S/54/3391/70/54, MEA, NAI.

59. Boquerat, *No Strings Attached*, 210–11.

60. Memorandum of NSC discussion, January 3, 1957, *FRUS 1955–1957*, vol. 8, doc. 4.

61. Memorandum of NSC discussion.

62. Cited in Merrill, *Bread and the Ballot*, 112, 156.

63. Rosen, *Western Economists and Eastern Societies*, 29.

64. From a large literature on modernization theory in US foreign policy, see Michael Latham, *Modernization as Ideology: American Social Science and "Nation Building" in the Kennedy Era* (Chapel Hill: University of North Carolina Press, 2000); Nils Gilman, *Mandarins of the Future: Modernization Theory in Cold War America* (Baltimore: Johns Hopkins University Press, 2003); David Engerman et al. (eds.), *Staging Growth: Modernization, Development, and the Global Cold War* (Amherst: University of Massachusetts Press, 2003); David Ekbladh, *The Great American Mission: Modernization and the Construction of an American World Order* (Princeton, NJ: Princeton University Press, 2009).

65. Michael H. Hunt, *Ideology and U.S. Foreign Policy* (New Haven, CT: Yale University Press, 2009), 161.

66. Cited in Merrill, *Bread and the Ballot*, 154.

67. On Indian reception of these resolutions, see the documents in 49(1)-AMS/59, MEA, NAI.

68. P. T. Bauer, *United States Aid and Indian Economic Development* (Washington, DC: America Enterprise Institute, 1959).

69. Cited in Roberts, "Afghanistan and Western Policy," 335.

70. Peter Gamble Bacon, "Ambassadors with Bulldozers: American Development in Afghanistan 1945–59" (BA thesis, Harvard University, 2011), 70–71.

71. Cited in Nick Cullather, "From New Deal to New Frontier in Afghanistan: Modernization in a Buffer State" (Working Paper No. 6, International Center for Advanced Studies, New York University, New York, 2002).

72. Markus Daechsel, "Sovereignty, Governmentality and Development in Ayub's Pakistan," *Modern Asian Studies* 45, no. 1 (2011): 131–57.

73. Graham, "The Eisenhower Administration and Public Diplomacy in India," 268–69.

74. Jack Masey and Conway Lloyd Morgan, *Cold War Confrontations: US Exhibitions and Their Role in the Cultural Cold War* (New York: Lars Muller Publishers, 2008), 38–55.

75. Masey and Morgan, *Cold War Confrontations*, 61–85.

76. Eric Pullin, "Money Does Not Make Any Difference to the Opinions That We Hold: India, the CIA and the Congress for Cultural Freedom," *Intelligence & National Security* 26, no. 2 (2011): 385.

77. James Burnham, "Parakeets and Parcheesi: An Indian Manifesto," *Partisan Review* (September 1951): 557–68.

78. Margery Sabin, *Dissenters and Mavericks: Writings About India in English, 1765–2000* (New York: Oxford University Press, 2002), 139–56. Also see Laaeq Fatehully, Achal Prabala, and Arshia Sattar (eds.), *The Best of Quest* (Chennai, India: Tranquebar Books, 2011).

Chapter 6: New Frontier in South Asia

1. "Inaugural Address of President John F. Kennedy," John F. Kennedy Presidential Library and Museum, January 20, 1961. Accessed online at https://www.jfklibrary .org/Research/Research-Aids/Ready-Reference/JFK-Quotations/Inaugural -Address.aspx.

2. Frank Costigliola, "US Foreign Policy from Kennedy to Johnson," in Westad and Leffler, *The Cambridge History of the Cold War*, 112–133 (quote on 115).

3. Eric Hobsbawm, *The Age of Extremes: The Short Twentieth Century* (London: Abacus, 1995); Akira Iriye, *Global Community: The Role of International Organizations in the Making of the Contemporary World* (Berkeley: University of California Press, 2002); Arthur Marwick, *The Sixties: Cultural Revolution in Britain, France, Italy and the United States c.1958–c.1974* (New York: Oxford University Press, 1998); Jeremy Suri, *Power and Protest: Global Revolution and the Rise of Détente* (Cambridge, MA: Harvard University Press, 2003).

4. Cited in McMahon, *Cold War on the Periphery*, 272.

5. Cited in Robert B. Rakove, *Kennedy, Johnson, and the Nonaligned World* (Cambridge: Cambridge University Press, 2013), 65.

6. Record of NSC meeting, January 22, 1963, *FRUS* 1961–1963, vol. 8, doc. 125.

7. Cited in McGarr, *Cold War in South Asia*, 92–93.

8. John F. Kennedy, *The Strategy of Peace* (New York: Popular Library Publishers, 1961), 177–78; record of NSC meeting, January 22, 1963, *FRUS 1961–1963*, vol. 8, doc. 125.

9. Merrill, *Bread and the Ballot*, 170–75; Boquerat, *No Strings Attached*, 281–86.

10. Nehru to Kennedy, May 13, 1961, *FRUS 1961–1963*, doc. 19.

11. Embassy in India to State Department, March 24, 1961, *FRUS 1961–1963*, doc. 12.

12. Rakove, *Kennedy, Johnson, and the Nonaligned World*, 69–70, 77–79.

13. Embassy in Pakistan to State Department, February 16, 1961, *FRUS 1961–1963*, doc. 5.

14. Embassy in Pakistan to State Department, March 22, 1961; memorandum of conversation, May 20, 1961, *FRUS 1961–1963*, docs. 11, 22.

15. Memorandum of conversation, June 8, 1961, *FRUS 1961–1963*, doc. 26.

16. Memorandum of conversation, July 11, 1961, *FRUS 1961–1963*, doc. 30.

17. Memorandum of conversation, November 7, 1961, *FRUS 1961–1963*, doc. 60; McMahon, *Cold War on the Periphery*, 281 (Kennedy quotes).

18. Embassy in Afghanistan to State Department, February 21, 1961, *FRUS 1961–1963*, doc. 7.

19. State Department to embassy in Afghanistan, May 18, 1961; embassy in Afghanistan to State Department, May 22, 1961, *FRUS 1961–1963*, doc. 21, doc. 23.

20. Embassy in Afghanistan to State Department, March 14, 1961, *FRUS 1961–1963*, doc. 9.

21. Embassy in Pakistan to State Department, March 22, 1961, *FRUS 1961–1963*, doc. 11.

22. Memorandum of conversation, July 11, 1961, *FRUS 1961–1963*, doc. 30.

23. Komer to Kennedy, August 2, 1961, *FRUS 1961–1963*, doc. 37.

24. Talbot to Rusk, September 6, 1961; embassy in Afghanistan to State Department, September 6, 1961, *FRUS 1961–1963*, docs. 39, 41.

25. State Department to embassy in Afghanistan, September 17, 1961; embassy in Afghanistan to State Department, September 20, 1961; State Department to embassy in Afghanistan, October 4, 1961, *FRUS 1961–1963*, docs. 44, 47, 51.

26. NIE (National Intelligence Estimate) 37-62, March 7, 1962, *FRUS 1961–1963*, doc. 109.

27. Memorandum of conversation, September 5, 1963, *FRUS 1961–1963*, doc. 327.

28. Weil to Talbot, December 6, 1961; Rusk to Galbraith, December 8, 1961; embassy in India to State Department, December 10, 1961, *FRUS 1961–1963*, docs. 61, 66, 68.

29. Cited in McGarr, *Cold War in South Asia*, 135; McMahon, *Cold War on the Periphery*, 282.

30. B. K. Nehru, *Nice Guys Finish Second: Memoirs* (New Delhi: Penguin, 1997), 431.

31. Kennedy to Nehru, January 18, 1962, *FRUS 1961–1963*, doc. 95.

32. McMahon, *Cold War on the Periphery*, 285.
33. Komer to Bundy, May 9, 1962, *FRUS* 1961–1963, doc. 119.
34. McGarr, *Cold War in South Asia*, 219–26; embassy in India to State Department, June 20, 1962, *FRUS* 1961–1963, doc. 141.
35. Komer to Bundy, December 28; embassy in India to State Department, December 28; State Department to embassy in Pakistan, December 29, 1961; Ayub to Kennedy, January 2, 1962, *FRUS* 1961–1963, docs. 78–80, 83.
36. Komer to Bundy, January 9, 1962, *FRUS* 1961–1963, doc. 87.
37. Paper prepared by Bureau of Near East and South Asian Affairs, n.d., *FRUS* 1961–1963, doc. 87.
38. Komer to Bundy, January 12, 1962, *FRUS* 1961–1963, doc. 90.
39. John W. Garver, "China's Decision for War," in *New Directions in the Study of China's Foreign Policy* (Stanford, CA: Stanford University Press, 2006), 107–8; Niu Jun, "1962: The Eve of the Left Turn in China's Foreign Policy" (Cold War International History Project Working Paper No. 48, Wilson Center, Washington, DC, June 2011), 24–25, 27.
40. Garver, "China's Decision for War," 110.
41. Conversation of McCone with Chiang, June 5, 1962; McCone meeting with Kennedy, June 18, 1962, *FRUS* 1961–1963, 12:241–44, 247–48.
42. Roderick MacFarquhar, *The Origins of the Cultural Revolution* (New York: Oxford University Press and Columbia University Press, for the Royal Institute of International Affairs, 1997), 3:272; Garver, "China's Decision for War," 110.
43. Embassy in Poland to State Department, June 23, 1962, *FRUS* 1961–1963, 22: 273–75.
44. Lawrence Freedman, *Kennedy's Wars: Berlin, Cuba, Laos, and Vietnam* (New York: Oxford University Press, 2000), 254–55; MacFarquhar, *Origins* 3, 272–73; Garver, "China's Decision for War," 110.
45. Bowles to State Department, March 3, 1962; Brubeck to Bundy, October 15, 1962, *FRUS* 1961–1963, docs. 107, 174.
46. Raghavan, *War and Peace in Modern India*, 301–4.
47. Embassy in India to State Department, October 25, 1962; State Department to embassy in India, October 27, 1962, *FRUS* 1961–1963, docs. 180, 182.
48. Galbraith to Kennedy, November 13, 1962, *FRUS* 1961–1963, doc. 196.
49. Nehru to Kennedy, November 19, 1962, NSC Box 111, India Nehru Correspondence 11.11.1962–11.19.1962, John F Kennedy Presidential Library, Boston.
50. State Department to embassy in India, November 20, 1962, *FRUS* 1961–1963, doc. 206.
51. Memoranda of record, April 25 and 26, 1963, *FRUS* 1961–1963, docs. 283, 285.
52. Ayub to Kennedy, November 5; State Department to embassy in Pakistan, November 18, 1962, *FRUS* 1961–1963, docs. 195, 201.

53. State Department to embassy in India, November 25, 1962, *FRUS 1961–1963*, doc. 211.

54. Embassy in India to State Department, November 29, 1962, *FRUS 1961–1963*, doc. 214.

55. Cited in Chaudhuri, *Forged in Crisis*, 137.

56. Howard Schafer, *Limits of Influence: America's Role in Kashmir* (New Delhi: Penguin, 2009), 86.

57. Kennedy to Macmillan, January 21, 1963; Kennedy to Nehru, February 6, 1963, *FRUS 1961–1963*, docs. 243, 251.

58. Komer to Kennedy, March 2, 1963, *FRUS 1961–1963*, doc. 261.

59. Y. D. Gundevia, *Outside the Archives* (New Delhi: Sangam Books, 1987), 290; Gopal, *Nehru*, 3:259.

60. Rusk to Kennedy, May 5, 1963, *FRUS 1961–1963*, doc. 290.

61. Memorandum of record, August 12, 1963, *FRUS 1961–1963*, doc. 318.

62. For excellent analyses of the global dimensions of Johnson's policy, see Francis J. Gavin and Mark Atwood Lawrence (eds.), *Beyond the Cold War: Lyndon Johnson and the New Global Challenges of the 1960s* (New York: Oxford University Press, 2014).

63. McMahon, *Cold War on the Periphery*, 305–6; McGarr, *Cold War in South Asia*, 279–80.

64. Bundy and Komer to Johnson, December 11, 1963, *FRUS 1961–1963*, doc. 342.

65. State Department to embassy in Pakistan, December 2, 1963, *FRUS 1961–1963*, doc. 341.

66. National Security Action Memorandum no. 279, February 8, 1964, *FRUS 1964–1968*, doc. 13.

67. Embassy in Pakistan to State Department, March 11–12, 1964, *FRUS 1964–1968*, docs. 27–28.

68. Komer to Johnson, February 26, 1964, *FRUS 1964–1968*, doc. 20.

69. Cited in McGarr, *Cold War in South Asia*, 293.

70. Memoranda of conversations, July 7 and 15, 1964, *FRUS 1964–1968*, docs. 63, 65.

71. McMahon, *Cold War on the Periphery*, 320–21; embassy in Pakistan to State Department, January 14, 1965, *FRUS 1964–1968*, doc. 84.

72. Embassy in India to State Department, April 21, 1965, *FRUS 1964–1968*, doc. 106.

73. Cited in MacMahon, *Cold War on the Periphery*, 323–24.

74. Read to Bundy, April 24, 1965, *FRUS 1964–1968*, doc. 107.

75. Memorandum by Bundy, June 9, 1965, *FRUS 1964–1968*, doc. 129.

76. McGarr, *Cold War in South Asia*, 297–98.

77. Embassy in Pakistan to State Department, July 4, 1965, *FRUS 1964–1968*, doc. 141.

78. Embassy in Pakistan to State; State Department to embassy in India and Pakistan, September 6, 1965, *FRUS 1964–1968*, doc. 187–89.

79. Komer to Johnson, September 7, 1965; memorandum of record, September 9, 1965, *FRUS 1964–1968*, docs. 191, 195.

80. MacMahon, *Cold War on the Periphery*, 330–31.

81. Rusk to Johnson; memorandum of record, September 9, 1965, *FRUS 1964–1968*, doc. 195–96.

82. Jagat S. Mehta, *Tryst Betrayed: Reflections on Diplomacy and Development* (New Delhi: Penguin, 2010), 155–56.

83. State Department to embassy in India; record of meeting, September 17, 1965, *FRUS 1964–1968*, doc. 208–9.

84. Record of meeting, December 15, 1965, *FRUS 1964–1968*, doc. 267.

85. Daniel Sargent, "Lyndon Johnson and the Challenges of Economic Globalization," in Gavin and Lawrence, *Beyond the Cold War*, 17–43.

86. Memorandum for the record, September 9, 1965, *FRUS 1964–1968*, doc. 195.

87. Nick Cullather, "LBJ's Third War: The War on Hunger," in Gavin and Atwood, *Beyond the Cold War*, 120; Kristin Ahlberg, "Machiavelli with a Heart: The Johnson Administration's Food for Peace Program in India," *Diplomatic History* 31, no. 4 (2007), 674–75.

88. Embassy in New Delhi to State Department, September 9, 1965; Komer to Bundy, September 12, 1965, *FRUS 1964–1968*, docs. 197, 203.

89. Cited in Ahlberg, "Machiavelli with a Heart," 683.

90. Nehru, *Nice Guys Finish Second*, 525.

91. Indira Gandhi to Haksar, n.d. (c. late February 1966), Correspondence with Indira Gandhi, Haksar Papers (I and II Installments), NMML.

92. Summary record of conversation, March 28, 1966, *FRUS 1964–1968*, doc. 307.

93. Bernard R. Bell, "Report to the President of the International Bank for Reconstruction and Development and the International Development Association on India's Economic Development Effort," October 1, 1965, World Bank Group Archives.

94. I. G. Patel, *Glimpses of Indian Economic Policy: An Insider's View* (New Delhi: Oxford University Press, 2002), 112–15.

95. John P. Lewis, *India's Political Economy: Governance and Reform* (Delhi: Oxford University Press, 1995), 146–47.

96. Rostow to Johnson, July 28, 1967; embassy in Pakistan to State Department, November 26, 1967; memorandum of conversation, December 23, 1967, *FRUS 1964–1968*, docs. 449, 470, 475.

97. Oehlert to Johnson, August 5, 1968, *FRUS 1964–1968*, doc. 508.

98. Walter P. Falcon and Gustav F. Papanek (eds.), *Development Policy II: The Pakistan Experience* (Cambridge, MA: Harvard University Press, 1971), 5.

99. Rehman Sobhan, *Basic Democracies Works Programme and Rural Development in East Pakistan* (Dhaka: University of Dhaka Press, 1968), 238.

100. Samuel P. Huntington, *Political Order in Changing Societies* (New Haven, CT: Yale University Press, 1968), 250–51.

101. Oehlert to Johnson, November 7, 1968, *FRUS 1964–1968*, doc. 523.

Chapter 7: The Dangerous Decade

1. Naresh Fernandes, *Taj Mahal Foxtrot: The Story of Bombay's Jazz Age* (New Delhi: Roli Books, 2012), 95.

2. Lisa Davenport, *Jazz Diplomacy: Promoting America in the Cold War Era* (Jackson: University Press of Mississippi, 2009).

3. Cited in Penny Von Eschen, *Satchmo Blows Up the World: Jazz Ambassadors Play the Cold War* (Cambridge, MA: Harvard University Press, 2004), 34–35.

4. Cited in Fernandes, *Taj Mahal Foxtrot*, 165.

5. Cited in Von Eschen, *Satchmo Blows Up the World*, 76 (emphasis in original).

6. Monica Whitlock, "When Duke Ellington Played Kabul," *BBC News Magazine*, September 20, 2013.

7. Cited in Von Eschen, *Satchmo Blows Up the World*, 130.

8. Fernandes, *Taj Mahal Foxtrot*, 166–68.

9. Peter Lavezzoli, *Bhairavi: The Global Impact of Indian Music* (New Delhi: HarperCollins, 2009).

10. Deborah Baker, *A Blue Hand: Allen Ginsberg and the Beats in India* (New Delhi: Penguin, 2008), 58–59.

11. Allen Ginsberg, *Indian Journals* (New York: Grove Press, 1970), 120.

12. Diana Eck, "'New Age' Hinduism," in Sulochana Raghavan Glazer and Nathan Glazer (eds.), *Conflicting Images: India and the United States* (Glenn Dale, MD: Riverdale, 1990), 111–41.

13. Slate, *Colored Cosmopolitanism*, 226–27.

14. Cited in Sarvepalli Gopal, "Gandhi: An Irrepressible Optimist," in *Imperialists, Nationalists, Democrats: Collected Essays* (Ranikhet, India: Permanent Black, 2013), 273.

15. David Hardiman, *Gandhi in His Time and Ours: The Global Legacy of His Ideas* (New Delhi: Permanent Black, 2003), 267–69.

16. Cited in Slate, *Colored Cosmopolitanism*, 236. Also see J. V. Pawar, *Dalit Panthers: An Authoritative History* (New Delhi: Forward Press, 2017).

17. For a brilliant account, see Daniel Sargent, *A Superpower Transformed: The Remaking of American Foreign Relations in the 1970s* (New York: Oxford University Press, 2015).

18. Moynihan to Nixon, March 21, 1973; entry of October 29, 1974, in Steven R. Wiesman (ed.), *Daniel Patrick Moynihan: A Portrait in Letters of an American Visionary* (New York: Public Affairs, 2010), 276, 357.

19. Srinath Raghavan, *1971: A Global History of the Creation of Bangladesh* (Cambridge, MA: Harvard University Press, 2013), 14–21.

20. Henry Kissinger, *The White House Years* (London: George Weidenfeld & Nicolson, 1979), 848.

21. Record of conversation between Indira Gandhi and Nixon, July 31, 1969, Subject File 19, T. N. Kaul Papers (I, II, and III Installments), NMML; record of meeting between Indian and American delegations, August 1, 1969, WII/121(31)/69, NAI. The American record of conversations is in *FRUS 1969–1976* E-7, doc. 29.

22. Haksar to Indira Gandhi, July 30, 1969, Subject File 42, Haksar Papers (I and II Instalments), NMML.

23. National Security Study Memorandum 26, February 21, 1969, *FRUS 1969–1976* E-7, doc. 10; Kissinger, *White House Years*, 846.

24. Memorandum of conversation in Lahore, August 1, 1969, *FRUS 1969–1976* E-7, doc. 32.

25. Meeting of Secretary Rogers with prime minister and foreign minister, New York, October 24, 1970, Subject File 19, T. N. Kaul (I, II, and III Installments), NMML; Kissinger, *White House Years*, 849.

26. Memorandum of conversation between Agha Hilaly and Harold Saunders, August 28, 1969, in F. S. Aijazuddin (ed), *The White House and Pakistan: Secret Declassified Documents, 1969–1974* (Karachi: Oxford University Press, 2002), 67–68 (hereafter *WHP*); Kissinger to Nixon, October 16, 1969, *WHP*, 73; Sher Ali Khan Pataudi to Yahya, October 10, 1969, in F. S. Aijazuddin, *From a Head, Through a Head, to a Head: The Secret Channel Between the US and China Through Pakistan* (Karachi: Oxford University Press, 2000), 27.

27. Memorandum of conversation between Nixon and Yahya, October 25, 1971, *FRUS 1969–1976* E-7, doc. 90.

28. Sultan Khan (Foreign Secretary) to Hilaly, November 23, 1971, in Aijazuddin, *Secret Channel*, 42–43; Sultan M. Khan, *Memoirs and Reflections of a Pakistani Diplomat* (London: Centre for Pakistan Studies, 1997), 246–47.

29. Kissinger to Nixon, December 16, 1970, enclosing text of *note verbale*, *WHP*, 115–16; Aijazuddin, *Secret Channel*, 50–53.

30. Minutes of Washington Special Actions Group (hereafter WSAG) meeting, March 26, 1971, *FRUS 1971*, 22–29.

31. US consul-general in Dhaka to State Department, April 6, 1971, *FRUS 1971*, 45–46. Also see US consul-general in Dhaka to State Department, April 10, 1971, *FRUS 1969–1976* E-7, doc. 130.

32. "Pakistan-American Relations: A Reassessment," n.d., *FRUS 1969–1976* E-7, doc. 132; Kissinger, *White House Years*, 854; Minutes of SRG meeting, April 19, 1971, *FRUS 1971*, 76–84.

33. Kissinger to Nixon, April 28, 1971, *FRUS 1971*, 95–97; note from Alexander Haig (Kissinger's deputy) to Nixon, April 28, 1971, and Nixon's handwritten note, *FRUS 1971*, 97n2 (emphases in original). Also see Kissinger, *White House Years*, 855–56.

34. Memorandum of conversation between Farland and Kissinger, May 7, 1971, *FRUS 1971*, 108.

35. Transcript of telephone conversation between Nixon and Kissinger, May 23, 1971, *FRUS 1971*, 140; conversation between Nixon and Kissinger, May 26, 1971, *FRUS 1969–1976* E-7, doc. 135.

36. Conversation among Nixon, Kissinger, and Swaran Singh, *FRUS 1969–1976* E-7, doc. 138.

37. Record of conversation with Kissinger, July 6, 1971, enclosed in Haksar to Jha, July 21, 1971, Subject File 169, P. N. Haksar Papers (III Installment), NMML.

38. Memorandum of conversation between Kissinger and Pakistani officials, July 8, 1971, *FRUS 1971*, 236–41; Kissinger to Haig, July 9, 1971, *FRUS 1971*, 242–43.

39. Memorandum of NSC meeting, July 16, 1971, *FRUS 1971*, 264–67.

40. Cited in Seymour Hersh, *The Price of Power: Kissinger in the Nixon White House* (New York: Summit Books, 1983), 452. Also see Helms to Nixon, July 29, 1971, *FRUS 1971*, 291; Saunders to Kissinger, September 7, 1971, *FRUS 1971*, 391–93; memorandum of conversation between Jha and Kissinger, September 11, 1971, *FRUS 1971*, 407–8.

41. Note for prime minister and foreign minister by T. N. Kaul, August 3, 1971, Subject File 49, P. N. Haksar Papers (II Installment), NMML.

42. This paragraph and the next two draw on Raghavan, *1971*, 142–47.

43. Memorandum of meeting between President Nixon and Prime Minister Indira Gandhi, *FRUS 1971*, 493–99.

44. Conversation among Nixon, Kissinger, and Haldeman, November 5, 1971, *FRUS 1969–1976* E-7, doc. 150.

45. Memorandum of meeting between Nixon and Indira Gandhi, November 5, 1971; conversation between Nixon and Kissinger, November 6, 1971, *FRUS 1969–1976* E-7, docs. 151, 162; Kissinger, *White House Years*, 848.

46. Telephone conversation between Nixon and Kissinger, December 3, 1971, *FRUS 1971*, 593–94.

47. Minutes of WSAG meeting, December 3, 1971, *FRUS 1971*, 597.

48. Telephone conversation between Nixon and Kissinger, December 5, 1971, *FRUS 1971*, 637–38.

49. Nixon to Brezhnev, December 6, 1971, *FRUS 1971*, 667–68.

50. CIA Intelligence Information Cable, December 7, 1971, *FRUS 1971*, 686–87.

51. Telephone conversation between Nixon and Kissinger, December 4, 1971, *FRUS 1971*, 612.

52. Conversation between Nixon and Kissinger, December 6, 1971, *FRUS 1969–1976* E-7, doc. 162.

53. Memorandum of conversation, December 10, 1971, *FRUS 1971*, 755–56.

54. Memorandum of conversation, December 10, 1971, 757–63.

55. Conversation between Nixon, Kissinger, and Attorney General Mitchell, December 8, 1971, *FRUS 1969–1976* E-7, doc. 165.

56. Telephone conversation between Nixon and Kissinger, December 11, 1971, *FRUS 1971*, 769.

57. Memorandum of conversation, December 12, 1971, *FRUS China*, doc. 177.

58. Transcript of telephone conversation between Nixon and Kissinger, December 16, 1971, *FRUS 1969–1976* E-7, doc. 191.

59. Embassy in India to State Department, July 24, 1972, *FRUS 1969–1976* E-7, doc. 293.

60. Memoranda of conversations, July 31 to August 1, 1969, *FRUS 1969–1976* E-7, doc. 29.

61. Paul McGarr, ". 'Quiet Americans in India': The CIA and the Politics of Intelligence in Cold War South Asia," *Diplomatic History* 38, no. 5 (2014): 1046–82.

62. Entry of August 6, 1974, in Wiesman, *Daniel Patrick Moynihan*, 346.

63. Moynihan to Kenneth Rush, May 25, 1973, in Wiesman, *Daniel Patrick Moynihan*, 290–92.

64. Speech to Indo-American Chamber of Commerce, May 3, 1973; record of conversation with Kissinger, June 15, 1973, T. N. Kaul Papers, Subject File 1, NMML.

65. Embassy in India to State Department, January 19, 1974, *FRUS 1969–1976* E-8, doc. 156.

66. Indira Gandhi, "India and the World," *Foreign Affairs* 50 (October 1972): 75.

67. State Department to US Mission in Geneva, May 18, 1974; Colby to Kissinger, June 22, 1974, *FRUS 1969–1976* E-8, docs. 162, 169.

68. Embassy in India to State Department, June 19, 1974, *FRUS 1969–1976* E-8, doc. 168.

69. Report on conversation with Kissinger, September 1974, T. N. Kaul Papers, NMML.

70. Scowcroft to President Ford, October 28, 1974, *FRUS 1969–1976* E-8, doc. 179.

71. Memorandum of August 19, 1975, cited in George Perkovich, *India's Nuclear Bomb: The Impact on Global Proliferation* (Berkeley: University of California Press, 1999), 193.

72. Perkovich, *India's Nuclear Bomb*, 191.

73. Vance to Carter, November 27, 1977, NLC-129-15-1-10-0, Jimmy Carter Presidential Library (hereafter JCPL), Atlanta, Georgia.

74. Entry of January 1, 1978, in Jimmy Carter, *White House Diary* (New York: Picador, 2010), 160.

75. Memorandum of conversation, April 24, 1979, NLC-24-102-1-1-9, JCPL. Also see entry of April 24, 1979, in Carter, *White House Diary*, 314.

76. Adrian Levy and Catherine Scott-Clark, *Deception: Pakistan, the United States and the Global Nuclear Weapons Conspiracy* (London: Atlantic, 2007), 19.

77. Ford to Bhutto, March 19, 1976, *FRUS* 1969–1976 E-8, doc. 225.

78. Levy and Scott-Clark, *Deception*, 21–46.

79. Douglas Frantz and Catherine Collins, *The Nuclear Jihadist: The True Story of the Man Who Sold the World's Most Dangerous Secrets…and How We Could Have Stopped Him* (New York: Twelve, 2007), 84.

80. Ayesha Jalal, *The Struggle for Pakistan: A Muslim Homeland and Global Politics* (Cambridge MA: Belknap Press, 2014), 209–15.

81. Kux, *Disenchanted Allies*, 239.

82. State Department to embassy in New Delhi, June 5, 1979, National Security Archives (hereafter NSA), George Washington University, Washington, DC.

83. Extract of memorandum of conversation, January 8, 1980, NSA.

Chapter 8: Sowing in the Wind

1. The next three paragraphs draw on Amin Saikal, "Islamism, Iranian Revolution and the Soviet Invasion of Afghanistan," in Melvyn Leffler and Odd Arne Westad (eds.), *The Cambridge History of the Cold War* (Cambridge: Cambridge University Press, 2010), 3:124–26.

2. Westad, *Global Cold War*, 301.

3. Memorandum of conversation, June 30, 1976, *FRUS* 1969–1976 E-8, doc. 24.

4. Antonio Guistozzi and Artemy Kalinovsky, *Missionaries of Modernity: Advisory Missions and the Struggle for Hegemony in Afghanistan and Beyond* (London: Hurst, 2016), 193–236; Nunan, *Humanitarian Intervention*, 150–80.

5. Westad, *Global Cold War*, 318–22.

6. Entry of February 14, 1979, in Carter, *White House Diary*, 291.

7. Robert M. Gates, *From the Shadows: The Ultimate Insider's Story of Five Presidents and How They Won the Cold War* (New York: Simon & Schuster, 1996), 144–46; entry of March 24, 1979, in Carter, *White House Diary*, 306.

8. Bruce Riedel, *What We Won: America's Secret War in Afghanistan, 1979–89* (Washington, DC: Brookings Institution, 2014), 99; "How Jimmy Carter and I Started the Mujahideen," *Le Nouvel Observateur*, January 15–21, 1998.

9. Brzezinski to Carter, December 26, 1979; Brzezinski to Vance, January 2, 1979, NSA.

10. Entry of December 27, 1979, in Carter, *White House Diary*, 382.

11. Entry of January 4, 1980, in Carter, *White House Diary*, 388; Kux, *Disenchanted Allies*, 246–49.

12. Riedel, *What We Won*, 104–6.

13. Gates, *From the Shadows*, 148–49.

14. Ethan Rosen, *The Bear, the Dragon, and the AK-47: How China, the United States, and Radical Islamists Conspired to Defeat the Soviet Union in Afghanistan*, Kindle loc. 391, 582.

15. Entry of October 3, 1980, in Carter, *White House Diary*, 471.

16. Cited in Levy and Scott-Clark, *Deception*, 81.
17. INR report, "Pakistan and US: Seeking Ways to Improve Relations," March 23, 1981, NSA.
18. Kux, *Disenchanted Allies*, 257–58.
19. Gates, *From the Shadows*, 251–52.
20. Embassy in Pakistan to State Department, July 5–6, 1982, NSA.
21. Embassy in Pakistan to State Department, October 17 and 25, 1982, NSA.
22. Shultz to Reagan, November 26, 1982, NSA.
23. Entry of December 7, 1982, in Douglas Brinkley (ed.), *The Reagan Diaries* (New York: HarperCollins, 2007), 117.
24. Embassy in Islamabad to State Department, June 1983, NSA.
25. Lawrence Wright, *The Looming Tower: Al-Qaeda's Road to 9/11* (London: Penguin Books, 2007), 94–100.
26. Cited in Westad, *Global Cold War*, 354.
27. Steve Coll, *Ghost Wars: The Secret History of the CIA, Afghanistan and Bin Laden from the Soviet Invasion to September 10, 2001* (London: Penguin, 2005), Kindle loc. 1716.
28. George Crile, *Charlie Wilson's War* (New York: Grove/Atlantic, 2002).
29. NSDD 166: "U.S. Policy, Programs and Strategy in Afghanistan," Federation of American Scientists, March 27, 1985. Accessed online at https://fas.org/irp/offdocs/nsdd.
30. Mohammad Yousaf and Mark Adkin, *Afghanistan: The Bear Trap* (Philadelphia: Casemate, 2001), 189–98.
31. Westad, *Global Cold War*, 368–69; Kalinovsky, *A Long Goodbye*, 74–84.
32. Gates, *From the Shadows*, 348–50.
33. Arif Jamal, *Shadow War: The Untold Story of the Jihad in Kashmir* (New York: Melville House, 2009), 109–15.
34. Gates, *From the Shadows*, 349.
35. Levy and Scott-Clark, *Deception*, 109–15.
36. Defense Intelligence Agency cable [recipient redacted], December 7, 1985; Briefing Book: "Visit of Pakistan Prime Minster Junejo, 15–21 July 1986," NSA.
37. Entry of July 16, 1986, in Brinkley, *Reagan Diaries*, 425.
38. Embassy in Islamabad to State Department, October 17, 1982, NSA.
39. Shultz to Reagan, November 26, 1982, NSA.
40. Entry of August 31, 1984, in Brinkley, *Reagan Diaries*, 262–63.
41. Levy and Scott-Clark, *Deception*, 111.
42. Shultz to Reagan, November 26, 1982, NSA; Perkovich, *India's Nuclear Bomb*, 242–43.
43. Embassy in India to State Department, May 2, 1987, NLC-131-5-7-5-8, John Gunther Dean Papers, JCPL.
44. Entry of March 6, 1987, in Brinkley, *Reagan Diaries*, 481.

45. National Security Decision Directive 270: "Afghanistan," May 1, 1987. Accessed online at https://fas.org/irp/offdocs/nsdd.

46. Westad, *Global Cold War*, 372–74.

47. Cited in Levy and Scott-Clark, *Deception*, 171.

48. Kalinovsky, *A Long Goodbye*, 93–176.

49. Entry of January 7, 1980, in Carter, *White House Diary*, 390.

50. Report of South Asia Chiefs of Mission Conference in embassy in India to State Department, March 7, 1980, NLC-6-22-5-11-4, JCPL.

51. Saunders to Christopher, NLC-6-22-5-11-4, JCPL.

52. Kux, *Estranged Democracies*, 382–83.

53. Embassy in India to State Department, May 30, 1986, NLC-131-5-5-13-1, John Gunther Dean Papers, JCPL.

54. J. N. Dixit, *An Afghan Diary: A New Beginning* (Delhi: Konark Publishers, 2002), 20–32.

55. Maharajakrishna Rasgotra, *A Life in Diplomacy* (New Delhi: Penguin Books, 2016), 336–37.

56. Entry of June 12, 1985, in Brinkley, *Reagan Diaries*, 334.

57. Embassy in India to State Department, February 4, 1988, NLC-131-5-10-1-8, John Gunther Dean Papers, JCPL.

58. Conversation between Gorbachev and Rajiv Gandhi, July 3, 1987; conversation between Gorbachev and Najibullah, July 20, 1987, Russian and Eastern European Database, NSA.

59. Embassy in India to State Department, April 25, 1988, NLC-131-5-10-31-8, John Gunther Dean Papers, JCPL.

60. Embassy in India to State Department, June 3, 1988, NLC-131-6-1-2-6, John Gunther Dean Papers, JCPL.

61. Ministry of External Affairs, Policy Planning Paper No. 31/75, on international negotiations on questions relating to oil, petrodollars, and raw materials, June 28, 1975, Subject File 84, Haskar Papers (I and II Installments), NMML.

62. Cited in Surjit Mansingh, *India's Search for Power: Indira Gandhi's Foreign Policy, 1966–1982* (New Delhi: Sage Publications, 1984), 326.

63. Dani Rodrik and Arvind Subramanian, "From 'Hindu Growth' to Productivity Surge: The Mystery of Indian Growth Transition" (IMF Working Paper, March 2004); Atul Kohli, *Poverty amid Plenty in the New India* (Cambridge: Cambridge University Press, 2012), 27–32, 97–106.

64. Dinesh C. Sharma, *The Long Revolution: The Birth and Growth of India's IT Industry* (New Delhi: HarperCollins, 2009).

65. Ian Little and Vijay Joshi, *India's Macroeconomics and Political Economy, 1964–1991* (Delhi: Oxford University Press, 1994), 59–60.

66. James M. Boughton, *Silent Revolution: The International Monetary Fund, 1979–89* (Washington, DC: International Monetary Fund, 2001), 709–16.

67. Perkovich, *India's Nuclear Bomb*, 232–35.

68. Broadcast to nation, November 12, 1984, in *Rajiv Gandhi Selected Speeches and Writings* (New Delhi: Publications Division, 1990), 9; Harish Kapur, *India's Foreign Policy, 1947–92: Shadows and Substance* (New Delhi: Sage, 1994), 70.

69. Senior Interagency Group meeting, June 20, 1985, NLC-131-5-5-11-3, John Gunther Dean Papers, JCPL.

70. Speech of June 12, 1985, in *Rajiv Gandhi Selected Speeches and Writings*, 328–29.

71. Richard Murphy to Armacost, May 24, 1986, NLC-131-5-5-11-3, John Gunther Dean Papers, JCPL.

72. Kux, *Estranged Democracies*, 410.

73. Meeting with Minister Tiwari, April 9, 1987, NLC-13-1-6-7-3-9, John Gunther Dean Papers, JCPL.

74. Dean to Weinberger, November 12, 1986, NLC-131-5-6-5-9, John Gunther Dean Papers, JCPL.

75. Bush to Gandhi, September 20, 1985, NLC-131-5-6-5-9, John Gunther Dean Papers, JCPL.

76. Murphy to Armacost, n.d., NLC-131-5-9-5-6, John Gunther Dean Papers, JCPL.

77. State Department to embassy in India, October 23, 1987, NLC-131-5-9-6-5, John Gunther Dean Papers, JCPL.

78. Embassy in India to State Department, June 3, 1988, NLC-131-6-1-2-6, John Gunther Dean Papers, JCPL.

79. "Indo-US Relations," File WII/104/82, 1989, MEA (Americas), NAI.

80. Embassy in India to State Department, December 7, 1987, NLC-131-5-8-15-6, John Gunther Dean Papers, JCPL.

Chapter 9: In the Unipolar World

1. Charles Krauthammer, "The Unipolar Moment," *Foreign Affairs* 70, no. 1 (1991); Francis Fukuyama, "The End of History?," *National Interest* (summer 1989).

2. First draft of DPG, National Security Archive, September 3, 1991. Accessed online at http://nsarchive.gwu.edu/nukevault/ebb245/doc02.pdf.

3. Hal Brands, *Making of the Unipolar Moment: US Foreign Policy and the Rise of the Post–Cold War Order* (Ithaca, NY: Cornell University Press, 2016), Kindle loc. 7314.

4. Excerpt from the draft Defense Planning Guidance, National Security Archive, February 18, 1992. Accessed online at http://nsarchive.gwu.edu/nukevault/ebb245/doc03_extract_nytedit.pdf.

5. J. N. Dixit, *My South Block Years: Memoirs of a Foreign Secretary* (New Delhi: UBSPD, 1996), 177.

6. On the latter, see George Lawson, Chris Armbruster, and Michael Cox (eds.), *The Global 1989: Continuity and Change in World Politics* (Cambridge: Cambridge University Press, 2010).

7. Jamal, *Shadow War*, 119–20.

8. K. Subrahmanyam, *From Surprise to Reckoning: The Kargil Review Committee Report* (New Delhi: Sage, 2000).

9. P. R. Chari, Pervaiz Iqbal Cheema, and Stephen Philip Cohen, *Perception, Politics and Security in South Asia: The Compound Crisis of 1990* (London: Routledge, 2003), 73–75.

10. Chari, Cheema, and Cohen, *Perception, Politics and Security in South Asia*, 98–100.

11. Chari, Cheema, and Cohen, *Perception, Politics and Security in South Asia*, 103–6.

12. Dixit, *My South Block Years*, 179.

13. Schaffer, *Limits of Influence*, Kindle loc. 1721–1754.

14. Kux, *Disenchanted Allies*, 302, 307–8.

15. Cited in Levy and Scott-Clark, *Deception*, 227–28.

16. Husain Haqqani, *Magnificent Delusions* (New York: PublicAffairs, 2013), 271–75.

17. Strobe Talbott, *Engaging India: Diplomacy, Democracy and the Bomb* (New Delhi: Penguin Books, 2004), 28.

18. Cited in Schaffer, *Limits of Influence*, Kindle loc. 1813–1839, 1882.

19. Dixit, *My South Block Years*, 200–2.

20. Talbott, *Engaging India*, 30–32 (emphasis in original).

21. Perkovich, *India's Nuclear Bomb*, 368; Talbott, *Engaging India*, 37.

22. CIA Report, "India: Problems and Prospects for the BJP Government," April 13, 1998, NSA.

23. George Tenet, *At the Center of the Storm: My Years at the CIA* (New York: HarperCollins, 2007), 69.

24. Talbott, *Engaging India*, 52.

25. Bill Clinton, *My Life* (London: Arrow Books, 2005), 786.

26. For the letter and the US-China joint statement, see "Nuclear Anxiety; Indian's Letter to Clinton on the Nuclear Testing," *New York Times*, May 13, 1998. Accessed online at http://www.nytimes.com/1998/05/13/world/nuclear-anxiety-indian-s-letter-to-clinton-on-the-nuclear-testing.html; "Sino-U.S. Joint Statement on South Asia," Embassy of the People's Republic of China in the United States of America, June 27, 1998. Accessed online at http://www.china-embassy.org/eng/zmgx/zysj/kldfh/t36228.htm.

27. Talbott, *Engaging India*, 24.

28. Dixit, *My South Block Years*, 200.

29. Raymond E. Vickery, *The Eagle and the Elephant: Strategic Aspects of US-India Economic Engagement* (New Delhi: Oxford University Press, 2011), 38–39, 111–13.

30. Dixit, *My South Block Years*, 183.

31. "Suo Motu Statement by Prime Minister Shri Atal Bihar Vajpayee in Parliament," NuclearFiles.org, May 27, 1998. Accessed online at http://www

.nuclearfiles.org/menu/key-issues/nuclear-weapons/issues/policy/indian-nuclear-policy/suo-motu-statement-pm.html.
32. Talbott, *Engaging India*, 86.
33. Talbott, *Engaging India*, 96–98.
34. Bruce Riedel, "The 1999 Blair House Summit," in Peter Lavoy (ed.), *Asymmetric Warfare in South Asia: The Causes and Consequences of the Kargil Conflict* (Cambridge: Cambridge University Press, 2009), 134.
35. Clinton, *My Life*, 865.
36. Talbott, *Engaging India*, 161.
37. Talbott, *Engaging India*, 164–68; Riedel, "Blair House Summit," 137–41.
38. Riaz Mohammed Khan, *Afghanistan and Pakistan: Conflict, Extremism, and Resistance to Modernity* (New Delhi: Oxford University Press, 2011), 83n47.
39. Vickery, *The Eagle and the Elephant*, 49.
40. Letter cited in Talbott, *Engaging India*, 181; "India, U.S. Natural Allies: Vajpayee," *The Hindu*, September 9, 2000.
41. Khan, *Afghanistan and Pakistan*, 29.
42. The best, if not always reliable, source on the origins of the Taliban is Abdul Salam Zaeef, *My Life with the Taliban* (London: Hurst, 2010).
43. Ahmed Rashid, *Taliban: The Story of the Afghan Warlords* (London: Pan Books, 2001), 26–29.
44. Gilles Kepel, *Jihad: The Trail of Political Islam* (Cambridge, MA: Harvard University Press, 2003); Olivier Roy, *The Failure of Political Islam* (Cambridge, MA: Harvard University Press, 1998).
45. Barbara Metcalf, *Islamic Revival in British India: Deoband, 1860–1900* (Princeton, NJ: Princeton University Press, 1982); Venkat Dhulipala, *Creating a New Medina: State Power, Islam, and the Quest for Pakistan in Late Colonial North India* (Cambridge: Cambridge University Press, 2015).
46. Cable to State Department (Afghan Desk), December 5, 1994; State Department to embassy in Pakistan, December 13, 1995, Electronic Briefing Book 227, NSA, docs. 1, 3.
47. State Department to embassy in Pakistan, December 22, 1995, Electronic Briefing Book 227, NSA, doc. 7.
48. Cited in Rashid, *Taliban*, 45.
49. Embassy in Pakistan to State Department, October 8, 1996, Electronic Briefing Book 295, NSA, doc. 2.
50. Wright, *Looming Tower*, 234–35.
51. Embassy in Pakistan to State Department, November 12, 1996, Electronic Briefing Book 227, NSA, doc. 18.
52. US Consulate in Peshawar to State Department, January 9, 1997, Electronic Briefing Book 295, NSA, doc. 6.

53. State Department to embassy in Pakistan, December 22, 1995; CIA note on HUA, August 1996, Electronic Briefing Book 227, NSA, docs. 7, 10.

54. US Consulate in Peshawar to State Department, January 9, 1997, Electronic Briefing Book 295, NSA, doc. 6.

55. Two cables from embassy in Pakistan to State Department, January 16 and March 10, 1997, Electronic Briefing Book 227, NSA, docs. 20–21.

56. Bill Richardson, *Between Worlds: The Making of an American Life* (New York: G. P. Putnam's Sons, 2005), 228.

57. Electronic Briefing Book 253, NSA, docs. 2, 8, 10.

58. Memorandum of conversation, December 2, 1998, William J. Clinton Presidential Library. Accessed online at https://clinton.presidentiallibraries.us/items/show/36612.

59. Embassy in Islamabad to State Department, December 18, 1998, Electronic Briefing Book 344, NSA, doc. 3.

60. Embassy in Pakistan to State Department, May 29, 1999, Electronic Briefing Book 344, NSA, doc. 5.

61. Talbott, *Engaging India*, 167; Riedel, "Blair House Summit," 140.

62. Bruce Riedel, *The Search for Al Qaeda: Its Leadership, Ideology and Future* (Washington, DC: Brookings Institution Press, 2008), 68–69.

Chapter 10: The New Century

1. For a thoughtful contemporary assessment, see Stephen Holmes, *The Matador's Cape: America's Reckless Response to Terror* (Cambridge: Cambridge University Press, 2007).

2. For a strong, if not entirely convincing, argument along these lines, see Frank. P. Harvey, *Explaining the Iraq War: Counterfactual Theory, Logic and Evidence* (Cambridge: Cambridge University Press, 2011).

3. Robert Jervis, *American Foreign Policy in a New Era* (New York: Routledge, 2005), 79–90.

4. Derek Chollet, *The Long Game: How Obama Defied Washington and Redefined America's Role in the World* (New York: Public Affairs, 2016), Kindle loc. 110.

5. Ashley Tellis, "Protecting American Hegemony," in Ashley Tellis and C. Raja Mohan (eds.), *The Strategic Rationale for Deeper US-Indian Economic Ties* (Washington, DC: Carnegie Endowment, 2015), 15–24.

6. For a pathbreaking analysis, see Chakravorty, Kapur, and Singh, *The Other One Percent*.

7. Cited in Pawan Dhingra, *Life Behind the Lobby: Indian American Motel Owners and the American Dream* (Stanford, CA: Stanford University Press, 2012).

8. Devesh Kapur, *Diaspora, Development and Democracy: The Domestic Impact of International Migration from India* (Princeton, NJ: Princeton University Press, 2010), 124–61.

9. Jocelyn Cullity, "The Global *Desi*: Cultural Nationalism on MTV India," *Journal of Communication Inquiry* 26, no. 4 (2002): 408–25.

10. Cited in Tej K. Bhatia and Mukesh Bhargava, "'America' in Indian Advertising: Change and Impact," *Comparative American Studies* 12, nos. 1–2 (2014): 74–75.

11. Kishore Dash, "McDonald's in India," *Harvard Business Review Case Study* (September 2005).

12. William M. O'Barr, "Advertising in India," *Advertising & Society Review* 9, no. 3 (2008). Accessed online at https://muse.jhu.edu/article/249785.

13. The term "market empire" is from Victoria de Grazia's brilliant *Irresistible Empire: America's Advance Through 20th-Century Europe* (Cambridge, MA: Harvard University Press, 2005). Also see David W. Ellwood, *The Shock of America: Europe and the Challenge of the Century* (Oxford: Oxford University Press, 2012).

14. Clarke to Rice, January 25, 2001, Electronic Briefing Book 147, NSA.

15. Richard Clarke, *Against All Enemies: Inside America's War on Terror* (New York: Free Press, 2004).

16. Armitage to ambassador in Pakistan, September 13, 2001, Electronic Briefing Book 358A, NSA, doc. 3.

17. Pervez Musharraf, *In the Line of Fire: A Memoir* (London: Simon & Schuster, 2008), 204–5; Bruce Riedel, *Deadly Embrace: Pakistan, America, and the Future of Global Jihad* (Washington, DC: Brookings Institution Press, 2011), 65–66.

18. Khan, *Afghanistan and Pakistan*, 89–90; Levy and Scott-Clark, *Deception*, 314.

19. Condoleezza Rice, *No Higher Honor: A Memoir of My Years in Washington* (London: Simon & Schuster, 2011), 91–92.

20. Rumsfeld's memorandum for the President, September 30, 2001; Rumsfeld's memorandum on "US Strategy in Afghanistan," October 30, 2001, doc. 13, 18, Electronic Briefing Book 358A, NSA.

21. Ahmed Rashid, *Descent into Chaos: How the War Against Islamic Extremism Is Being Lost in Pakistan, Afghanistan and Central Asia* (London: Allen Lane, 2008), 77–79, 240.

22. Carlotta Gall, *The Wrong Enemy: America in Afghanistan, 2001–2014* (New Delhi: Penguin Books, 2014), 65.

23. Rashid, *Descent into Chaos*, 234, 280.

24. Tenet, *At the Center of the Storm*, 433–35.

25. Condoleezza Rice, "Campaign 2000: Promoting the National Interest," *Foreign Affairs* (January/February 2000): 56; "The National Security Strategy of the United States of America," US Department of State, September 2002, 27. Accessed online at https://www.state.gov/documents/organization/63562.pdf.

26. Chaudhuri, *Forged in Crisis*, 228–32.

27. "Background Briefing by Administration Officials on U.S.–South Asia Relations," US Department of State Archive, March 25, 2005. Accessed online at https://2001-2009.state.gov/r/pa/prs/ps/2005/43853.htm.

28. Shivshankar Menon, *Choices: Inside the Making of India's Foreign Policy* (New Delhi: Allen Lane, 2016), 77.

29. Rice, *No Higher Honor*, 443.

30. Jason Burke, *The 9/11 Wars* (London: Allen Lane, 2011), 370.

31. Imtiaz Gul, *The Al Qaeda Connection: The Taliban and Terror in Pakistan's Tribal Areas* (New Delhi: Viking, 2009); Stephen Tankel, *Storming the World Stage: The Story of Lashkar-e-Taiba* (New Delhi: Hachette, 2011); Vahid Brown and Dan Rassler, *Fountainhead of Jihad: The Haqqani Nexus, 1973–2012* (New Delhi: Hachette, 2011).

32. Rice, *No Higher Honor*, 610–11.

33. "CIA Outlines Pakistan Links with Militants," *New York Times*, July 30, 2008.

34. Riedel, *Deadly Embrace*, 94.

35. Woodward, *Obama's Wars*.

36. Mark Landler, "The Afghan War and the Evolution of Obama," *New York Times*, January 1, 2017. Accessed online at https://www.nytimes.com/2017/01/01/world/asia/obama-afghanistan-war.html.

37. "Pakistan's Spy Agency Is Tied to Attack on U.S. Embassy," *New York Times*, September 22, 2011.

38. Jeffrey A. Bader, *Obama and China's Rise: An Insider's Account of America's Asia Strategy* (Washington, DC: Brookings Institution Press, 2012), 6.

39. "US-China Joint Statement," The White House: President Barack Obama, November 17, 2009. Accessed online at https://obamawhitehouse.archives.gov/realitycheck/the-press-office/us-china-joint-statement.

40. Hillary Clinton, "America's Pacific Century," *Foreign Policy*, October 11, 2011. Accessed online at http://foreignpolicy.com/2011/10/11/americas-pacific-century.

41. "Sustaining U.S. Global Leadership: Priorities for 21st Century Defense," Department of Defense, January 2012. Accessed online at http://archive.defense.gov/news/Defense_Strategic_Guidance.pdf; Leon Panetta, *Worthy Fights: A Memoir of Leadership in War and Peace* (New York: Penguin Books, 2015), 382–83.

42. Clinton, "America's Pacific Century."

43. Interview with Joshua T. White: "Pak Denied Strikes but India Can't Count on Similar Restraint in Future: Joshua T White, Obama Administration Official," *Indian Express*, June 8, 2017. Accessed online at http://indianexpress.com/article/india/pak-denied-strikes-but-india-cant-count-on-similar-restraint-in-future-joshua-t-white-obama-administration-official-4693883.

Conclusion

1. "Remarks by President Trump on Strategy in Afghanistan and South Asia," The White House, August 21, 2017. Accessed online at https://www.whitehouse.gov/briefings-statements/remarks-president-trump-strategy-afghanistan-south-asia.

INDEX

SRINATH RAGHAVAN is a senior fellow at the Centre for Policy Research in New Delhi and a visiting senior research fellow at King's College, London. He is the author of three books, including *India's War: The Making of Modern South Asia, 1939–1945*. He lives in Mumbai.

Photo credit: sc. sekhar